Governance of Automated Decision-Making and EU Law

Governance of Automated Decision-Making and EU Law

Edited by

HERWIG C.H. HOFMANN
Professor of European and Transnational Law, University of Luxembourg, Luxembourg

FELIX PFLÜCKE
Postdoctoral Researcher in Law, ADA Chair in Financial Law, University of Luxembourg, Luxembourg
Lecturer in Law, Somerville College, University of Oxford, UK

OXFORD
UNIVERSITY PRESS

OXFORD
UNIVERSITY PRESS

Great Clarendon Street, Oxford, OX2 6DP,
United Kingdom

Oxford University Press is a department of the University of Oxford.
It furthers the University's objective of excellence in research, scholarship,
and education by publishing worldwide. Oxford is a registered trade mark of
Oxford University Press in the UK and in certain other countries

Published in the United States of America by Oxford University Press
198 Madison Avenue, New York, NY 10016, United States of America

British Library Cataloguing in Publication Data
Data available

Library of Congress Control Number: 2024937029

ISBN 9780198919544

DOI: 10.1093/9780198919575.001.0001

Printed and bound by
CPI Group (UK) Ltd, Croydon, CR0 4YY

MIX
Paper | Supporting
responsible forestry
FSC® C013604

Acknowledgement

The authors are grateful for funding support by the NORFACE Joint Research programme on Democratic Governance in Turbulent Ages co-funded by the AEI, AKA, DFG, FNR, and the European Commission through the Horizon 2020 Grant Agreement No 822166.

Contents

Figures

Tables

Contributors

Sümeyye Elif Biber is Postdoctoral Researcher, Department of Law, University of Luxembourg, Luxembourg

Franziska Boehm is Professor of Law, Karlsruhe Institute of Technology and FIZ Karlsruhe, Karlsruhe, Germany

Franka Enderlein, Institute for Media and Information Law, Department of Public Law, University of Freiburg, Germany

Miikka Hiltunen, Erik Castrén Institute of International Law and Human Rights, University of Helsinki, Finland. https://orcid.org/0000-0002-6480-2665

Herwig C.H. Hofmann is Professor of European and Transnational Public Law, University of Luxembourg, Luxembourg. https://orcid.org/0000-0001-8608-2710

Päivi Leino-Sandberg is Professor of Transnational European Law, University of Helsinki, Finland. https://orcid.org/0000-0003-3691-785X

Davide Liga, Department of Computer Science (Faculty of Science, Technology and Medicine), University of Luxembourg, Luxembourg. https://orcid.org/0000-0003-1124-0299

Oriol Mir is Full Professor of Administrative Law, Pompeu Fabra University (UPF), Barcelona, Spain. https://orcid.org/0000-0001-5807-4748

Simon Oles, Institute for Media and Information Law, Department of Public Law, University of Freiburg, Germany

Paulina Jo Pesch is Assistant Professor for Civil Law and Law of Digitalisation, Institute of Law and Technology, Friedrich-Alexander-Universität Erlangen-Nürnberg, Germany

Felix Pflücke, University of Luxembourg, Luxembourg and Lecturer in Law, Somerville College, University of Oxford, UK. https://orcid.org/0000-0002-7988-2813

Jens-Peter Schneider is Professor of Public Law, University of Freiburg, Freiburg im Breisgau, Germany. https://orcid.org/0000-0002-5481-5470

Kester Siegrist is Research Assistant, Institute of Media and Information Law, Department of Public Law, University of Freiburg, Freiburg im Breisgau, Germany

Sam Wrigley, Postdoctoral Researcher, Faculty of Law, University of Helsinki, Finland

1

Automated Decision-Making (ADM) in EU Public Law

Herwig C.H. Hofmann

A. ADM technology and the legal system

Decision-making in EU public law for the implementation of policies is increasingly supported by automation. The understanding of the effects thereof on rights and procedures as well as on concepts of how to ensure accountability of such automated decision-making (ADM)[1] in EU public law is evolving. It is influenced by a developing legislative framework and case law by the Court of Justice of the European Union (CJEU) as well as by courts in the Member States.

ADM is based on software supporting, or replacing, elements of human decision-making in the implementation of EU law. ADM systems are deployed in an increasing number of policy areas. Improved availability of information, advanced computation power, and advanced forms of programming using fast evolving technologies to process such information produces benefits for decision-making. But integrating technological solutions into decision-making procedures also risks introducing potential dysfunctionalities, diminishing individual rights, and reducing accountability.

A key feature of the integration of ADM technologies in various phases of decision-making is that it has a profound effect on *procedures* leading to the delivery of public policies in the EU. This has the potential to improve the quality and efficiency of decision-making but equally it can influence the realization of key procedural values of public law in the EU. Influencing procedures on the basis of technical specifications without clear orientation towards values and rights in EU law risks a growing disconnection between real-life procedures and central values and principles of democratic societies operating under the rule of law, which in turn can result in increasing delegitimization of the exercise of public powers.

[1] I use the term with the background described here: an 'automated decision system' can be defined as a "software, a system, or a process that aims to aid or replace human decision-making". See Rashida Richardson, 'Confronting Black Boxes: A Shadow Report of the New York City Automated Decision System Task Force' (AI Now Institute 2019) 6 <https://ainowinstitute.org/publication/confronting-black-boxes-a-shadow-report-of-the-new-york-city-automated> accessed 1 February 2024.

Herwig C.H. Hofmann, *Automated Decision-Making (ADM) in EU Public Law* In: *Governance of Automated Decision-Making and EU Law.* Edited by: Herwig C.H. Hofmann and Felix Pflücke, Oxford University Press.
 DOI: 10.1093/9780198919575.003.0001

This chapter looks at central questions which the use of ADM in public decision-making procedures in the scope of EU law raises in terms of public law. It first analyses the role and the origin of information as a source of decision-making in EU public law and the automation of this decision-making. It then looks at the central values and fundamental rights affected by ADM. Third, the chapter asks which requirements of technical design of ADM systems and their relation to the databases which are used as sources of information searches and analysis are necessary.

Technology enabling ADM affects decision-making and rule-making procedures predominantly by its technological characteristics, the relation between ADM and databases, as well as the relation between ADM technology and human elements of decision-making.

I. ADM technology—algorithms, predictions, machine learning technology

ADM technologies are based on software[2] to automate, accelerate, and scale up the analysis of data.[3] Data extracted from one or several large-scale databases is used to calculate probabilities identifying a possible outcome. Both purpose-specific algorithms as well as general purpose artificial intelligence (AI) programming, such as in generative systems, may use elements of AI.[4] AI, according to the Commission's draft 'regulation on a European approach for artificial intelligence', is 'a fast-evolving family of technologies that can contribute to a wide array of economic and societal benefits'.[5] AI programming allows the inference of complex, non-linear relationships from the data which the software analyses. Hence various approaches to AI programming are currently evolving at a fast pace.[6] Technological solutions for best achieving goals are in competition with each other and at this point it is not clear which will be the most successful for which purpose. Most importantly, the time when software

[2] ADM systems are normally embedded in software which can also be a component of hardware devices (eg within robots used by emergency response teams, or in autonomous drones).

[3] Andrea Renda, 'Artificial Intelligence: Ethics, Governance and Policy Challenges' (CEPS Task Force 2019) 8 <https://www.ceps.eu/wp-content/uploads/2019/02/AI_TFR.pdf> accessed 1 February 2024.

[4] Annex 1 of the Commission's 'Proposal for a regulation of the European Parliament and of the Council laying down harmonised rules on artificial intelligence (Artificial Intelligence Act)' COM (2021) 206 finalizes a set of technologies to be covered, all of which include 'machine learning approaches, including supervised, unsupervised an reinforcement leaning, using a wide variety of methods including deep learning loci an knowledge-based approaches, including knowledge representation inductive (logic) programming, knowledge bases, inference/deductive engines (symbolic) reasoning and expert systems; statistical approaches, Bayesian estimation, search and optimization methods'.

[5] Artificial Intelligence Act Proposal of 21 April 2021.

[6] For a typology on the different ADM decision types, see eg Maja Brkan, 'Do Algorithms Rule the World? Algorithmic Decision-Making and Data Protection in the Framework of the GDPR and Beyond' (2019) 27 International Journal of Law and Information Technology 91, 94–95.

was based only on specific preprogrammed 'if–then' logical links is long past. Generative AI systems can be integrated into workflows calculating the next most probable outcome systematically initiated by various 'prompts' which can consist of language or other input to produce long and coherent language output. This form of AI calculates a possible outcome on the basis of previously unspecified input.[7] At the time of writing, such generative AI models are typically good at producing output which mimics human language and reasoning, but weak in pointing to the sources of its product or identifying sources for its results. To date, such systems do not show the inputs to the generative creation of texts and how the data taken into account was weighted as well as how such data processed by the system is relevant for the proposed output. Generative AI currently thus suffers from weaknesses in identifying relations between cause and effect,[8] but it cannot be ruled out that such weakness will be remedies in newer versions of software being released to the markets.

In terms of decision-making, various ADM systems may be used in several, sometimes subsequent, phases of decision-making procedures. Although to date ADM systems are rarely known to have been employed in all phases of a decision-making process, from agenda setting to implementation,[9] today's most frequent use of ADM is in agenda setting and investigation phases from which results can predefine certain types of decision-making. Growing technical capabilities of AI-based software used in ADM systems, however, contribute to their ability to reshape the procedural design of implementation of EU policies. Implicitly, such reshaping changes the conditions of accountability of administrative rule-making and decision-making procedures where ADM technology is used. It cannot be ruled out that in the very near future, beginning with financial regulation, regulatory tasks will be exercised in real-time with an integrated process of data collection, data computation, and the adoption of specific decision-making procedures.

From this it also becomes clear that understanding the output produced by advanced ADM systems using AI is not only opaque to non-experts but, because of the predictive mode of calculation of possible outcomes arising from a great pool of information used for the input, it will also not be predictable or necessarily explicable by technological experts. Therefore also, where it has been discussed whether the addressee of an act or the general public for transparency reasons should be given access to the source code or algorithms the automation is based on,[10] this

[7] Herbert Roitblat, *Algorithms Are Not Enough* (MIT Press 2020) 344.

[8] ibid.

[9] A rare example is a speed camera on the roadside analysing a violation of speed limitations and automatically mailing speeding tickets to the registered car owners. Even this is in reality an example of several separate ADM systems used in sequence.

[10] One of the early legislative approaches to transparency in ADM is the French code of administrative procedures, which is applicable to both individual decision-making as well as to the system rule-making level. Art L.311-3-1 of the 2016 *Code des relations entre le public et l'administration*. See also French Décret No 2017-330 du 14 mars 2017 relatif aux droits des personnes faisant l'objet de décisions individuelles prises sur le fondement d'un traitement algorithmique, JORF n°0064 du 16 mars 2017.

information might not be of value in terms of general purpose AI systems that are not specifically programmed for an administrative task. In the latter systems, the access to the source code will not contribute to understanding the individual decision-making output of an ADM system. Accessing the source code might give rise to understanding of the functioning of the system as such but not to how a specific decision was made.

II. The role of ADM programming in terms of public law

As much as the use of algorithmic decision-making by public institutions and bodies in Europe is evolving, it is, being increasingly addressed but not fully conceptualised.[11] ADM systems rely on the programming of software. In public law, the question arises as to the definition of the legal characteristic of such software, which becomes a tool integrated into a formal decision-making procedure. Identifying the necessities of the software, the programming of the software tool underlying a system, and the definition of its role within a decision-making procedure are thus decisive elements of the automation of individual decisions to be taken on that basis. The identification of the software system then needs to be distinguished from the actual process of decision-making with the help of an automated system.

Differences between a legal and an IT perspective arise not only from semantic and conceptual dimensions: ADM systems may be based on software designed by computer scientists' programming algorithms on a particular understanding of requirements under the law. Although legal requirements can—under certain circumstances—resemble a program, which can be portrayed in forms of an algorithm, the complex interaction of legal rules and principles does not necessarily open itself to current standards of programming. However, with advanced AI models, a program might not work in terms of subsuming factual situations under legal requirements at all but can model possible outcomes on information calculated from the data used to calculate predictions. The latter represents a different approach by comparison with a normative-driven system under which public action requires a legal basis and the facts of a case must be brought in relation to the normative requirements.

Here questions of normative programming of administrative rule-making and decision-making procedures arise which may contain specifics to be considered when thinking of a 'cascade' approach to normative programming. In the traditional model, public decision-making has a legal basis and a normative framework

[11] Marta Cantero Gamito and Martin Ebers, 'Algorithmic Governance and Governance of Algorithms: An Introduction' in Martin Ebers and Marta Cantero Gamito (eds), *Algorithmic Governance and Governance of Algorithms: Legal and Ethical Challenges* (Springer International Publishing 2021) 1–22 <https://doi.org/10.1007/978-3-030-50559-2_1> accessed 13 May 2023.

in constitutional norms and values. Programming of public activity within this framework takes place via legislative acts. Legislation may be further implemented by public bodies with the help of executive rule-making which defines conditions for single-case decision-making. The question that arises here is how such an ADM system must be conceived of and integrated into the structure of a constituted legal system. Such constituted system can be understood in terms of a cascade beginning with a generally enabling constitutional norm followed by a policy-defining legislative act to more precise administrative rule-making, identifying in an ever more detailed way the considerations to be taken into account and procedures to be followed in individual decision-making applied to a specific set of facts. In such model, ADM software is formulated in abstract general terms designed to be applicable to diverse individual cases.

This allows the use of the legal toolbox developed for such applications in new contexts. One central element of thinking about ADM software development in this way is to understand that any individual decision is generally predetermined by some kind of administrative abstract general rule-making. This can be either in the form of binding provisions such as administrative rule-making, which in the EU are generally undertaken in the forms of Articles 290 and 291 of the Treaty on the Functioning of the European Union (TFEU), or in the form of more 'soft' internal guidelines. ADM technology must comply with the normative framework and be employed in the context of legislative authorization. Software underlying ADM technology will therefore generally either replace or supplement executive rule-making in the identification of criteria and procedures involved in individual decision-making, which might be the direct or indirect result of the application of the computer program. Therefore, programming may define both rule-making and decision-making procedures. Accordingly, the CJEU has established that for ADM systems to be legally employed, legal rules must pre-establish 'models and criteria' for ADM systems.[12] ADM systems are thus based on a set of procedural rules designed to contribute to the translation of abstract legislative obligations to concrete individual decision-making.

However, the nature of the 'software element' of ADM systems, to date, appears rarely explicitly addressed in legislation—neither at the EU level nor at the Member State level. Case law will be more likely to address this matter, where it has been developed. An important question is whether approaches sought are predominantly technology neutral or whether they are designed specifically for certain specific use-cases. The question of policy-specific versus generally applicable solutions is particularly relevant in the fast-paced context of technology development of general purpose generative AI models.

[12] Case C-511-520/18 *La Quadrature du Net* [2020] ECLI:EU:C:2020:791, para 180 with references to Opinion 1/15 *EU-Canada PNR Agreement* [2017] EU:C:2017:592, para 172. These must, so the court be 'specific and reliable'.

The distinction between the general rules for the ADM element of a decision-making procedure and single case decision-making being based on that general rule also has an effect on the legality of individual decision-making. Rights and principles governing decision-making procedures and their protection will be assessed following individual decision-making and thus might implicitly address the general normative level. But here also the question arises whether legal systems develop specific approaches to decision-making by ADM in practice, or—normatively speaking—should do so. Alternatively, one might ask whether it would not be sufficient to review decisions - whether adopted with the help of an ADM system or without - by the same standards in order to hold public decision-making to account.

III. ADM technology and public law—first findings

ADM systems used in the context of the implementation of public policies and law must therefore be understood from two conceptual points of view. First is the notion of whether sufficiently abundant data and information can be taken into account by AI systems calculating probable best outcomes. A second question is the nature and the role of ADM technology within a system to empower public actors to engage in a certain policy area. Both are key factors of understanding the role of ADM in public law systems and are explored in the following sections.

B. Data and information in the context of the development of the EU as a regulatory Union

In EU public law, the development of ADM is often linked to the establishment of large-scale information systems. ADM requires large sets of data to be able to provide the quantity and quality of data processing. Large-scale datasets require ADM technology to process the data in order to make use of the advantages of data availability to turn the data into information used for decision-making.

I. Regulatory regimes and ADM

The challenges to understanding the effects of ADM in public decision-making are common to public law systems around the world but have specific relevance in the highly integrated European system of close cooperation within multiple levels of government and administration. In fact, the EU's model of governance is highly dependent on it being a regulatory Union, steering reality, very much like a 'regulatory state', by increasing the public role in setting standards for economic, social, environmental, and other matters as well as the growth and diversification of the executive branches of power.[13] The idea of regulation, broadly speaking, denotes diverse forms of governmental intervention to steer policy developments and private action.[14] Information gathering and compilation have been key to developing regulatory approaches as much as the use thereof in regulatory decision-making. In the EU's multilevel legal system, conceptualizing the flow of information between the participant bodies in the network at Union and Member State levels implies conceiving of information (including its generation, management, and distribution) as a legal *topos* apart, worthy of study in order to understand power relationships and modes of accountability, hence Schmidt-Aßmann's apt description of EU administrative law as largely consisting of information-related provisions, a description which in my view holds even more true today than it did when his article was published.[15]

In that sense, given that the broad notion of 'regulation' used in the context of the idea of the 'regulatory state' is a notion of regulation as a general term of 'steering' behaviour, the concept of a regulatory regime indicates that different policies require different mixes of tools and approaches to ensure that public policy-making is translated into real life effectively. The specific institutional design and institutional mix and the applicable forms of act used for such steering and creation of an internal market are the key elements of a particular regulatory regime.[16] The type and forms of use of ADM systems must now be understood as part of the specific regulatory regime applicable to a policy area.

II. Data collections and interoperability

Large-scale data collections are fed by multilevel systems and are used as the basis for ADM systems in the EU. Additionally, non-specific AI systems are based on large pools of available data. Some of the most well-known large-scale information systems in the EU are in the field of the area of freedom, security, and justice (AFSJ), such as the Schengen Information System (SIS II).[17] The link between the

[13] Herwig CH Hofmann, 'European Regulatory Union? The Role of Agencies and Standards' in Panos Koutrakos and Jukka Snell (eds), *Research Handbook in Internal Market Law* (Elgar Publishing 2016) 460–78.

[14] David Levi-Faur, 'Regulation and Regulatory Governance' in David Levi-Faur (ed), *Handbook on the Politics of Regulation* (Elgar Publishing 2013) 3–22.

[15] Eberhard Schmidt-Aßmann, 'Verwaltungskooperation und Verwaltungskooperationsrecht in der Europäischen Gemeinschaft' (1996) 31 Europarecht 270.

[16] Burkard Eberlein and Edgar Grande, 'Beyond Delegation: Transnational Regulatory Regimes and the EU Regulatory State' (2005) 12 Journal of European Public Policy 89–112, 90.

[17] A large-scale information system for border management in operation in thirty European countries, including twenty-six EU Member States (with the exception of Ireland and Cyprus) and four associated countries (Switzerland, Norway, Liechtenstein, and Iceland). Regulation (EU) 2018/1860 on the use of the Schengen Information System for the return of illegally staying third-country nationals [2018] OJ 2018 L 312/1; Regulation (EU) 2018/1861 on the establishment, operation and use of the

development of large-scale databases and ADM technology is explicit in the creation of a single agency (eu-LISA)[18] in charge of the development of information collection and storage within its fields of competence[19] as well as following the reforms within eu-LISA's mandate[20] in planning and preparing systems for ADM capacities. Other large-scale information systems exist, for example, in the areas regulating risk in food, animal feed, plant health,[21] and human and veterinary medicine products.[22] These examples of data collections in risk regulation in food, feed, and medical products, as well as in the AFSJ, illustrate the links between data collections in EU administrative law and ADM in at least three respects.

First, in single market regulation, as well as in data collections pertaining to the AFSJ, interoperability is becoming the norm for connecting different databases initially established to address different issues. The European Commission has presented a legislative draft on general policies towards interoperability.[23] The principle of interoperability enables interconnectivity of data collections and thereby enlarges data pools available to processing by ADM technology.[24] For

Schengen Information System (SIS) in the field of border checks [2018] OJ 2018 L 312/14; Regulation (EU) 2018/1862 on the establishment, operation and use of the Schengen Information System (SIS) in the field of police cooperation and judicial cooperation in criminal matters[2018] OJ 2018 L 312/56. Other EU large-scale information systems include Eurodac used by Europol and associated bodies. See Regulation (EU) 2016/794 of the European Parliament and of the Council of 11 May 2016 on the European Union Agency for Law Enforcement Cooperation (Europol) adopting the implementing rules governing Europol's relations with partners, including the exchange of personal data and classified information [2016] OJ L 135/53 and arts 4–7 and 15 of Council Regulation (EC) 2725/2000 of 11 December 2000 (No longer in force—Date of end of validity: 19 July 2015) Repealed by Regulation (EU) No 603/2013 of the European Parliament and of the Council of 26 June 2013 concerning the establishment of Eurodac [2013] OJ L 180/1.

18 EU-LISA is an agency established under Regulation (EU) No 1077/2011 of the European Parliament and of the Council of 25 October 2011 establishing a European Agency for the operational management of large-scale IT systems in the [AFSJ], [2011] OJ 211 L 286/1–17 replaced by Regulation (EU) 2018/1726 of the European Parliament and of the Council of 14 November 2018 on the European Union Agency for the Operational Management of Large-Scale IT Systems in the Area of Freedom, Security and Justice (eu-LISA), [2018] OJ 2018 L 295/99–137.

19 The EU-LISA agency is not only a technical operator in this, but by establishing the software and protocols is actually active in norm-setting for decision-making procedures. See eg eu-LISA, 'Elaboration of a Future Architecture for Interoperable IT Systems at Eu-LISA—Summary of the Feasibility Study' (2019) 4 <https://www.eulisa.europa.eu/Publications/Reports/eu-LISA%20Feasibility%20Study%20-%20Interoperability.pdf> accessed 1 February 2024.

20 Regulation (EU) 2018/1726 of the European Parliament and of the Council of 14 November 2018 on the European Agency for the operational management of large-scale IT systems in the [AFSJ], and amending Regulation (EC) No 1987/2006 and Council Decision 2007/533/JHA and repealing Regulation (EU) No 1077/2011, [2018] OJ 2018 L 295/99–137.

21 Commission Implementing Regulation (EU) 2019/1715 of 30 September 2019 laying down rules for official controls and its system components ('the IMSOC Regulation'), [2019] OJ 2019 L 261/37–96.

22 See Simona Demková, 'The Decisional Value of Information in European Semi-Automated Decision Making' (2021) 14 Review of European Administrative Law 29–50.

23 Commission, 'Proposal for a regulation of the European Parliament and of the Council laying down measures for a high level of public sector interoperability across the Union (Interoperable Europe Act)' COM (2022) 720 final.

24 Teresa Quintel, 'Connecting Personal Data of Third Country Nationals: Interoperability of EU Databases in the Light of the CJEU's Case Law on Data Retention' (2018) 002-2018 University of Luxembourg Law Working Paper Series, <SSRN abstract=3132506> (dx.doi.org/10.2139/ssrn.3132506).

example, in the field of AFSJ, the Electronic Travel Information and Authorisation System (ETIAS)[25] and the Passenger Name Record (PNR)[26] system are being linked with interoperability functions, allowing for searches taking place within these databases to be enriched with data from other interconnected databases.[27] It also allows for further integration of ADM technologies into decision-making procedures by introducing novel technical capacities for matching of available data.[28] Moves to increase this approach and make it more accessible for ADM systems exist also in the context of developments of a 'public cloud' approach linking national and European public data collections and offering safe storage solutions.[29]

Second, following interoperability requirements, relying on the sharing of information across different systems applied in policy areas, sharing data across levels—the EU and Member State administrations—is an important approach in EU administrative law to enlarge data availability. The distribution of data collections in Member States is a central approach to decentralize administration in the EU.[30] Decentralized implementation of EU policies is increasingly undertaken by administrative networks linking Member States and EU bodies.[31] These approaches arose initially from mutual assistance requirements between European administrations,[32] which have, in many areas, evolved towards more integrated informational cooperation following requirements of a single legal space in the EU

[25] Regulation (EU) 2018/1240 of the European Parliament and of the Council of 12 September 2018 establishing a European Travel Information and Authorisation System and amending Regulations (EU) No 1077/2011, (EU) No 515/2014, (EU) 2016/399, (EU) 2016/1624, and (EU) 2017/2226, [2018] OJ 2018 L 236/1–71.

[26] Directive (EU) 2016/681 of the European Parliament and of the Council of 27 April 2016 on the use of passenger name record (PNR) data for the prevention, detection, investigation and prosecution of terrorist offences and serious crime, [2016] OJ 2016 L 119/132–149.

[27] Niovi Vavoula, 'Consultation of EU Immigration Databases for Law Enforcement Purposes: A Privacy and Data Protection Assessment' (2020) 22 European Journal of Migration and Law 139, 145–46.

[28] Such novel ADM capacities are especially embedded in the Shared Biometric Matching Service interoperability tool, see eu-LISA, 'Shared Biometric Matching Service (SBMS): Feasibility Study—Final Report' (eu-LISA 2018) <http://op.europa.eu/en/publication-detail/-/publication/10175794-3dff-11e8-b5fe-01aa75ed71a1/language-en>.

[29] European Securities and Markets Authority, *Annual Report 2018* (14 June 2019), ESMA20-95-1136, p 54. In view of heightened awareness of the necessity of 'strategic autonomy' on the basis of an initiative of some Member State governments initiated the creation of 'GaiaX' based on a non-profit industry consortium of European private and public actors. The Gaia-X Association aisbl ('association internationale sans but lucratif'—a non-profit organization under Belgian law) was created on the initiative of the French and the German governments by a set of private companies and public research institutions.

[30] See eg Deirdre Curtin, 'Second Order Secrecy and Europe's Legality Mosaicism' (2018) 41 West European Politics 271.

[31] Federica Cacciatore and Mariolina Eliantonio, 'Networked Enforcement in the Common Fisheries Policy through Data Sharing: Is There Room Left for Traditional Accountability Paradigms?' (2019) 10 European Journal of Risk Regulation 522; Diana-Urania Galetta, 'Public Administration in the Era of Database and Information Exchange Networks: Empowering Administrative Power or Just Better Serving the Citizens?' (2019) 25 European Public Law 171.

[32] See on the evolution of EU administration Herwig CH Hofmann, 'Mapping the European Administrative Space' (2008) 31 West European Politics 662–76.

without internal frontiers.[33] For example, food and non-food mutual warning systems (the Rapid Alert System for Food and Feed (RASFF) and RAPEX, the rapid alert system for dangerous non-food products)[34] also serve as large-scale stores of information. Such sharing works in two ways. Either information collection is undertaken in national databases and shared in a single shared database across the EU, or a single European database can be 'mirrored' at the national level.[35] An example of the latter is the technical architecture of the SIS, which relies on the national systems, the so-called N.SIS, being connected to the centralized EU-level database. The N.SIS 'might contain a complete or partial copy of the SIS database, which may be shared by two or more Member States'.[36] Another example is the European Competition Network, which contains links between initially independent databases, the cooperation between them having evolved from mere mutual assistance obligations. The current wave of EU data-related legislation addresses many of the matters relating to data availability for data-driven public administration. In this context, following its European Strategy for Data of February 2020, the European Commission introduced numerous data-related draft regulations, some of which have passed the legislative procedure and entered into force. The Commission's European Strategy for Data foresaw an approach to regulate the use of data and data services but also to foster data sharing across economic, government, cultural, and scientific sectors in areas such as health, mobility, and agriculture to create various European data spaces. A prime example for the push in this direction is the European Commission's draft regulation, the 'Interoperable Europe Act' of November 2022, seeking to link data sources across Europe for use by public decision-making bodies; however the draft regulation is simultaneously remarkably silent on discussing means to ensure data quality in such exchanges.[37] Another legislative initiative by the Commission is the Regulation on

[33] See eg such information exchange under the Internal Market Information System (IMI) ('About IMI-Net' <https://ec.europa.eu/internal_market/imi-net/about/index_en.htm> accessed 1 February 2024). Micaela Lottini, 'An Instrument of Intensified Informal Mutual Assistance: The Internal Market Information System (IMI) and the Protection of Personal Data' (2014) 20 European Public Law 107. Demková (n 22).

[34] European Commission, 'Safety Gate: The Rapid Alert System for Dangerous Non-Food Products' (2024) <https://ec.europa.eu/consumers/consumers_safety/safety_products/rapex/alerts/repository/content/pages/rapex/index_en.htm>; European Commission, 'RASFF—Food and Feed Safety Alerts' (2024) <https://ec.europa.eu/food/safety/rasff_en>.

[35] This is not without danger for the integrity of EU database. A notorious recent example of the gravity of concerns arising from the unlawful copying of SIS data is the UK's illegal copying of SIS data prior to Brexit, discovered through the evaluation visit conducted by the European Commission in 2017. See 'UK-EU: Schengen Data Fiasco' (Statewatch, 7 August 2018) <https://www.statewatch.org/news/2018/august/statewatch-news-online-uk-eu-schengen-data-fiasco/>.

[36] Preamble (8) and art 4(1)(b) and (c) of the SIS-recast. The conditions for any sharing of national copies shall be arranged among the Member States concerned and communicated to the Commission (art 4(1)(c) SIS-recast). The data stored in the copies must be 'identical to and consistent with the SIS database' so that 'a search in national copy produces a result equivalent to that of a search in the SIS database' (art 9(2) SIS-recast).

[37] See eg Interoperable Europe Act Proposal of 18 November 2022.

Data Governance[38] which intends to support data flows between countries and sectors, thus benefitting public actors next to increasing the availability of public sector data to private parties, including business. Finally, in the draft regulation on a European Data Act, the Commission seeks to align rules on data transfers to outside the EU (and European Economic Area (EEA)) of non-personal data with those rules applicable in the General Data Protection Regulation (GDPR), an aspect particularly important for cloud service offers, including those used by public administrations.

Third, many policy areas allow access by public bodies to privately held or collected data. Travel, communications, banking, and finance institutions face certain data retention obligations in order to allow for subsequent access of data by public authorities.[39] But increasingly, EU policies also impose reporting obligations on the possibilities of regulatory agencies to demand provision of relevant information falling within the regulatory ambit of the agencies.[40] These reporting obligations allow for agencies to access information regarding the possible necessity for regulatory action by an agency and enforcement.[41] Further, beyond such 'push' and 'pull' approaches to privately held or generated data, widespread reporting duties of private entities allow for integrating private information flows to public decision-making in the field of financial regulation. This is marked by an increasing integration of information provision by regulated entities and regulatory decision-making by agencies in real time on the basis of this information. The integration of information reporting by regulated entities and regulatory decision-making by regulators is also in line with the deployment of advanced information technology—both information technology used by businesses as well as regulatory technology used by agencies.

Questions of accountability of ADM are complicated by the fact that the databases on which ADM relies are fed into multilevel legal systems and in some cases, the data collection activities are subject to the law of various Member State as well as EU law.[42] The composite aspect of regulation by information in the EU

[38] See eg Regulation of the European Parliament and of the Council on European data governance (Data Governance Act) of 25 November 2020, [2020] COM(2020) 767 final.

[39] See Joined Cases C-203/15 and C-698/15 *Tele2 Sverige AB and Watson* [2016] ECLI:EU:C:2016:970; Joined Cases C-511, 512, and 520/18, *La Quadrature du Net and Others* [2020] ECLI:EU:C:2020:791.

[40] For example in the field of financial regulation see reporting duties established by ESMA and national financial regulators under provisions such as arts 26a and 99e of Directive 2014/91/EU of the European Parliament and of the Council of 23 July 2014 amending Directive 2009/65/EC on the coordination of laws, regulations and administrative provisions relating to undertakings for collective investment in transferable securities (UCITS) as regards depositary functions, remuneration policies and sanctions Text with EEA relevance, [2014] OJ 2014 L 257/186.

[41] For example in the field of data protection, art 49(1) third sentence GDPR requires that data controllers 'shall inform the supervisory authority of the transfer' of data to a third country when acting under the criteria of art 49 GDPR.

[42] See eg Lilla Farkas, 'Analysis and Comparative Review of Equality Data Collection Practices in the European Union: Data Collection in the Field of Ethnicity' (European Commission, DG Justice and

can influence the conditions of addressing regulatory standards in EU administrative law. Also, due to the principle of interoperability the cross-policy nature of databases can enhance these same problems, especially in the absence of a general administrative procedure law of the EU addressing, across policy areas, basic standards of administrative procedure. Embedding the ADM technology within EU large-scale databases aids multilevel, decentralized implementation of EU policies in the context of composite decision-making within administrative networks providing, for example, for information exchange, joint warning systems, and structures of coordinated remedies.

Book VI of the *Research Network of European Administrative Law (ReNEUAL)* considers the identification of responsibility for EU information networks.[43] It suggests that the issues of responsibility for the multi-jurisdictional nature of data collections should be clarified. This, it suggests, might be best addressed by offering a single European-level body that could be co-responsible, together with the national body which has entered the information (and thus is responsible as the author of that information), for the quality of information in a database. In EU law, there are some examples of certain management powers over an information network centralized in the hands of a European agency. In the European energy regulators network,[44] for example, an EU agency is in charge of establishing a cooperative network of national regulatory agencies and is also in charge of maintaining a joint database on the topic. The same approach could be suggested for addressing the accountability of ADM built around databases.

III. Data quality

The composite approach to data collections and the interoperability paradigm also raise challenges concerning the quality and accuracy of data input into decision-making, which has in turn effects on accountability in ADM procedures based on such data.[45] In view of this being possibly one of the most crucial aspects of the possibility of successful use of ADM and at the same time a topic of high concern for the exercise of individual rights, the use of ADM requires supervision of the quality of data input.[46] Quality control of the data is also of extraordinary relevance due

Consumers 2017) <http://op.europa.eu/en/publication-detail/-/publication/1dcc2e44-4370-11ea-b81b-01aa75ed71a1/language-nl> accessed 13 May 2023.

[43] Paul Craig and others, *ReNEUAL Model Rules on EU Administrative Procedure* (OUP 2017) Book VI.

[44] Regulation (EC) n. 713/2009 of the European Parliament and of the Council, of 13 July 2009, establishing an Agency for the cooperation of Energy Regulators [2009] OJ L 211/1.

[45] For example arts 17, 18 EDPR requires that data must be correct and up to date. This requires access to data and its possible rectification are key in this context.

[46] See eg European Agency for the Operational Management of Large Scale IT Systems in the Area of Freedom, Security and Justice, *Data Quality and Interoperability: Addressing the Capability Gaps*

to the links between public and private data collections used as the basis for ADM in some policy areas. Information quality is not just a matter of maintaining up-to-date and correct data in public databases but also a control of information imported or accessed from private actors. Raising some of these conditions, Article 10 of the Commission's draft AI Act directs data and data governance in what the draft refers to as 'high-risk AI systems'.[47] Datasets must meet certain quality criteria including under Article 10(3) of the AI Act that such data 'shall be relevant, representative, free of errors and complete' and shall have 'the appropriate statical properties'.

C. Definition of interfaces

Discussing ADM tools must therefore address the interface between human action and information technology in decision-making and rule-making procedures. The use of ADM systems in different phases of decision-making procedures underlines that there are interactions between various ADM systems or different admixtures of human input into decision-making procedures and elements of ADM. Boundaries between human and ADM are thus not always clear.[48]

ADM systems are generally but one tool among several to be relied on by a human decision-maker, who ultimately bring their judgment to make the final decision themselves.[49] The integration of ADM into decision-making procedures could in most cases be described as augmented decision-making or as 'quasi- or

through Standardisation: Eu LISA 12th Industry Roundtable, 3 5 November 2020, Tallinn (Online Event). (Publications Office of the EU 2020) <https://data.europa.eu/doi/10.2857/497949> accessed 1 February 2024; European Union Agency for Fundamental Rights, *Data Quality and Artificial Intelligence—Mitigating Bias and Error to Protect Fundamental Rights* (Publications Office of the EU 2019) <https://fra.europa.eu/en/publication/2019/data-quality-and-artificial-intelligence-mitigating-bias-and-error-protect> accessed 1 February 2024. See also the EU efforts in standardizing the data quality requirements; for instance, in the context of biometric data collection and storing in EU AFSJ systems. Commission Implementing Decision (EU) 2020/2165 of 9 December 2020 on laying down rules for the application of Regulation (EU) 2018/1861 of the European Parliament and of the Council as regards the minimum data quality standards and technical specifications for entering photographs and dactyloscopic data in the Schengen Information System (SIS) in the field of border checks and return [2020] OJ L 431/61 and Commission Implementing Decision (EU) 2021/31 of 13 January 2021 on laying down rules for the application of Regulation (EU) 2018/1862 as regards the minimum data quality standards and technical specifications for entering photographs and dactyloscopic data in the [SIS] in the field of police cooperation and judicial cooperation in criminal matters [2021] OJ L 15/1.

[47] Artificial Intelligence Act Proposal of 21 April 2021.

[48] Algorithm Watch, 'Automating Society: Taking Stock of Automated Decision Making in the EU' (Algorithm Watch, in cooperation with Bertelsmann Stiftung, supported by the Open Society Foundations 2019) 9 <https://www.ivir.nl/publicaties/download/Automating_Society_Report_2019.pdf> accessed 1 February 2024.

[49] Jennifer Cobbe, 'Administrative Law and the Machines of Government: Judicial Review of Automated Public-Sector Decision-Making' (2019) 39 Legal Studies 636–38; Jean-Bernard Auby, 'Le droit administratif face aux défis du numérique' (2018) 15 Actualité Juridique Droit Administratif 835.

semi-automated decision-making'.[50] This results in factual changes to conditions of decision-making, which in turn have to be understood from a normative point of view.

The earlier sections of this chapter show that interfaces between data collections and ADM systems must also be considered from a legal point of view. How to ensure that the right data will be taken into account in decision-making, that the quality of the data is sufficient to allow it to be taken into account, that all relevant data is taken into account for a decision to be made, and to ensure that the conclusions are based on data taken into account are all requirements arising under the duty of care in EU law.[51] Both the interaction between data sources and ADM systems as well as between the programming of ADM systems and their application within decision-making procedures therefore turns the focus on questions of interfaces. How does a legal system understand and regulate the use of data and the selection of data by ADM systems? How, on the other hand, does a legal system govern the interface between the automated part of a decision-making procedure and the human input into decision-making?

I. Quantity and quality of data processing and data biases

In assessing the human–machine interface in the context of semi-automated decision-making with ADM technology, it is worth understanding the effects of the integration of ADM technologies into the decision-making process. The actual effect of the use of ADM impacts the *quantity* of information and *speed* by which information can be processed (quantitative effects) as well as the quality and depth by which information can be analysed (qualitative effects).

The *quantitative* effects consist primarily in increasing the volume of information that can be incorporated into decision-making and rule-making procedures. This consists in extracting greater amounts of relevant information from EU-wide databases and combine various datasets across sources than a human could undertake alone. This approach is particularly useful in areas in where fast-paced decision-making is central—like monetary policy and banking and finance supervision, where real-time market data may be essential for the capability of reacting to and influencing of market conditions by regulatory means.

Qualitative effects arise from the use of ADM systems. This is, for example, by way of simple possibilities of comparing datasets, for example in the context of the analysis of biometric data and matching of information which would not have been

[50] Council of Europe, 'Algorithms and Human Rights: Study on the Human Rights Dimensions of Automated Data Processing Techniques and Possible Regulatory Implications' (The Committee of Experts on Internet Intermediaries (MSI-NET) 2018) 7. Demková (n 22).

[51] See Herwig CH Hofmann, 'The Duty of Care in EU Public Law—A Principle Between Discretion and Proportionality' (2020) 2 Review of European Administrative Law (REALaw) 87–112.

possible for human-only analysis. The qualitative change also becomes clear where algorithms are programmed to improve search results by drawing comparisons between current analytical results and prior analytical results, making decisions built on probabilities based on statistical comparisons. Algorithms, therefore, calculate outcomes based on factual correlations on the basis of data collected in the past and will not necessarily be programmed in a way to include normative orientations or justifications or programmatic reasons when taking a specific decision.[52]

These effects make decision-making procedures faster and more data-reliant than human-only analysis of databases. Under EU law there is a legal requirement to use facts where possible in decision-making. Under the EU's duty of care principle, where data is necessary and sufficient quality of data is available, decision-making must make use of such data,[53] and arguably, use available ADM technology to analyse it. This is linked to the principle of proportionality, which will require that decision-making, in order to take into account relevant facts, makes use of available data-driven possibilities in decision-making.[54]

II. ADM and phases of decision-making

To date, ADM systems are only very rarely established to undertake all phases of an administrative procedure – irrespective of whether a procedure is undertaken within one jurisdiction on the European or the national levels or whether the procedure is undertaken in composite multi-jurisdictional procedures. ADM might be used to link various actors through granting access and processing data from large-scale databases. In composite procedures, questions of accountability are often linked to the identification of responsibility,[55] which then may define the steps of decision-making procedures, including which actor takes a decision, whether individual steps in a composite procedure could be identified as changing the legal position of individuals, and who should be obliged to remedy a potential violation.

A first factor is that of guaranteeing normative steering of decision-making processes—of ensuring that the rights, principles, and values of EU public law are complied with in procedures using ADM systems. This is a question of ensuring the values of democracy and the allocation of powers to various institutional actors.

[52] Auby (n 49) with further references also to Dominique Cardon, *À quoi rêvent les algorithmes. Nos vies à l'heure des big data* (Le Seuil 2015) 39.

[53] Auby (n 49) with further references also to Cardon (n 52) 39.

[54] For example, where individuals have a right of access to documents (art 42 CFR and Regulation 1049/2001), restrictions of such right of access must be proportionate. Where document management software can be applied to reduce the burden of analysis of existing data, this might reduce the possibility of an administration's justification for restrictions of access since screening of documents for relevant information or for business secrets that need to be protected can be automated.

[55] Simona Demková and Teresa Quintel, 'Allocation of Responsibilities in Interoperable Information Exchanges: Effective Review Compromised?' (2020) 1 Cahiers Jean Monnet 589.

It is also a question of how the limitation of fundamental rights is conducted and what the share of 'law' is in the decision as to limitations of rights.

A second factor is inextricably linked to considerations of accountability in principal–agent models. It has been argued that informational asymmetries make accountability essentially impossible 'if the logic underpinning a machine-generated decision is based on dynamic learning processes employed by various forms of machine learning algorithms'.[56] The reason for the impediment of meaningful human oversight and intervention then results from the 'major informational advantages' the machine has over a human operator.[57] This is particularly relevant in the discussion of possibilities of human oversight and review below.

Often introduced as a means of processing of information within large-scale databases, the real-life effects and the possible biases of ADM technology's reliance on data collections are particularly relevant in case of discretionary decisions. The use of ADM technologies could therefore *de facto* or *de jure* limit discretion of a human decision-maker in a later phase of a decision-making procedure.[58] For example, when used for establishing predictions in risk assessment procedures such as food safety, ADM could lead to the conclusion that specific acts of control and possibly enforcement would be necessary. Such predictions might limit a discretion concerning the assessment whether or not to act. Such predictions might equally—in view of the duty of care—create an obligation to react to the automated risk assessment.[59] This example illustrates how the use of ADM in early phases of decision-making, such as the phase of agenda setting or investigation, might have effects in subsequent phases of decision-making.

These factors are independent from the various biases reported in the sociological and socio-legal literature on the use of ADM systems, which alerts us to the fact that the interaction between humans and ADM in decision-making may be subject to certain biases.[60] Literature on ADM–human interaction reports, for example, on the human side so-called automation bias.[61] This might have an effect

[56] Karen Yeung, 'Why Worry about Decision-Making by Machine?' in Karen Yeung and Martin Lodge (eds), *Algorithmic Regulation* (OUP 2019) 21–48, 41; Emre Bayamlioglu, 'Contesting Automated Decisions: A View of Transparency Implications' (2018) 4 European Data Protection Law Review 434.

[57] Yeung (n 56); Bayamlioglu (n 56).

[58] Brkan (n 6) 105. The author finds that 'at least theoretically, a legal possibility of fully automated decisions is still a matter of the future', yet reminds that in practice often decisions are increasingly fully automated. See in this respect the 'human in the loop' as a minimum safeguard under art 22 against decision-making based solely on automated processing of personal data in the GDPR context.

[59] This would affect the discretionary decision whether to act—be it for investigative purposes or the purpose of taking a final binding decision (in German this is referred to with the more specific term of *Entschliessungsermessen*). See Yoan Hermstrüwer, 'Artificial Intelligence and Administrative Decisions under Uncertainty' in Thomas Wischmeyer and Timo Rademacher (eds), *Regulating Artificial Intelligence* (Springer 2020) 200–21, 215.

[60] It is unclear whether the biases of humans are temporary findings, which can change over time with ever more ADM technologies being rolled out, or whether these findings as to human biases are long-term structural features. In any case, when designing systems which necessarily link humans to ADM technology such findings should be taken into account.

[61] Yeung (n 56) 25 with reference to LJ Sktika, K Moiser, and MD Burdick, 'Accountability and Automation Bias' (2000) 52 International Journal of Human-Computer Studies 701–17.

especially in the context of discretionary decision-making when the exercise of discretion is influenced by input based on an ADM system.[62] ADM technologies thereby not only inform human decision-making and improve it by allowing more date to be taken into account, it may also shape, constrain, or remove human discretion by structuring information intake. Automation bias may lead to rigidity in decision-making and 'unproductive shirking of responsibility'.[63]

D. Rights and principles in the use of ADM

This section looks at the EU-specific legal framework and the requirements arising from EU constitutional values and principles for ADM in EU public law. It does so in view of technology design, information collections, and the different interfaces between information, ADM systems, and humans discussed so far. Increasingly, the EU is legislating in the field of data and information. Data protection, the regulation of AI, as well as diverse acts concerning data management such as the notion of interoperability, are being added. Since much of this legislation is not specifically addressed towards public law or public actors, one of the basic questions is whether automation will lead to a growing disconnect between real-life decision-making and the legal principles underlying the EU as a Union under the rule of law. How can we avoid the fact that the technical features of automation and the information sought to feed ADM take on a real-life dynamic that will not comply with values and legislative objectives? This is not only a question of compliance with the principle of legality in the use of ADM but also a question as to the steering capacity of a legal system and its values. Will the legal basis for public action and its limitations be complied with by systems based on AI and the calculation of predictions based on unknown procedures and principles? The idea of steering reality by law, which lies at the heart of the regulatory dimension of public law, would be negated by allowing such a disassociation between legislative objectives and technical realization and influence on decision-making.

The existing body of written and unwritten law contains both substantive as well as procedural provisions and principles. Some of these are more relevant to address *systemic* questions of the design of the ADM procedures. Others address questions of *individual* decision-making procedures.[64] This reflects the role of ADM systems to predefine decision-making in a way not unlike administrative rule-making procedures.[65]

[62] Demková (n 22) 29–50.

[63] Matthew Smith, Merel Noorman, and Aaron Martin, 'Automating the Public Sector and Organizing Accountabilities' (2010) 26 Communications of the Association for Information Systems 7, 4 <https://aisel.aisnet.org/cais/vol26/iss1/1> accessed 1 February 2024.

[64] ibid 10.

[65] Yeung (n 56).

I. Procedural rights

1. Legality and reviewability

The central issue of possible disconnection between ADM and the EU's public law legal framework arises from the fact that computer software is not a 'legal act' and thus not 'law' in the sense of Article 52(1) of the EU Charter of Fundamental Rights (CFR). Hence, the question arises regarding whether software governs reality or whether legal systems can impose their value choices over the technical realities. To answer this, it must be clear what are the standards to which ADM systems must comply. In terms of upholding the rule of law, next to notions of legality, procedural principles of good administration and rights to an effective and independent judicial remedy are relevant.

The principle of legality, more specifically of the requirement of a legal basis for action, is not only a general principle of EU law which may lead to annulment of an act, it is also a concept which is highly relevant in the construction of and the protection of individual rights under EU law.[66] Accordingly, any regulatory limitation of individual freedoms is protected as a 'right' in the context of the right to an effective remedy (Article 47 CFR).

In terms of limitations of freedoms, these can arise in all three elements of ADM systems—the data and information collections, the interface of transfer of data to an administration undertaking the regulatory action, and the ADM system-based processing of information and taking decisions which might also entail further limitations of rights. The CJEU has developed a general defence right against public intrusions in the private sphere[67] in terms of a 'protection against arbitrary or disproportionate intervention by public authorities in the sphere of the private activities of any natural or legal person'[68] by regulatory activity. Requirements for the legal basis for ADM are accordingly high when ADM systems are used as elements of regulatory decision-making.

The legal basis will have to ensure that the overall procedure, including the ADM system as a possible component (including the human input into the decision-making procedure in various of its phases), complies with principles of good administration. These are protected as general principles of EU law, largely in terms of defence rights, but are also more generally enumerated in Article 41 of the Charter, including the right to fair and impartial decision-making, compliance

[66] Art 52(1) CFR spells this out explicitly. It requires that '[a]ny limitation on the exercise of the rights and freedoms recognised by this Charter must be provided for by law' thereby codifying long established in case law on the possibilities of limitations of fundamental rights. See eg Case C-44/79 *Hauer v Land Rheinland-Pfalz* [1979] ECLI:EU:C:1979:290, para 23.

[67] Case C-682/15 *Berlioz Investment Fund SA* [2017] ECLI:EU:C:2017:373, para 51; C-121/04 P *Minoan Lines v Commission* [2005] EU:C:2005:695, para 30; Case C-94/00, *Roquette Frères* [2002] ECLI:EU:C:2002:603, para 27; Joined Cases 46/87 and 227/88 *Hoechst v Commission* [1989] ECLI:U:C:1989:337, para 19.

[68] Case C-682/15 *Berlioz Investment Fund SA* [2017] ECLI:EU:C:2017:373, para 51.

with the duty of care (full and impartial assessment of all relevant facts), and they include the right to hearing, to access to one's file, and to a reasoned decision. This package makes for a comprehensive set of criteria for the legality of ADM systems. Generally they are essential procedural requirements, violations of which may lead to the annulment of acts. Vital for the rule of law is the possibility of submitting public acts to an effective judicial review.[69]

2. The duty of care, good administration, and defence rights

Requirements for ADM procedures arise from the EU's specific notions of the duty of care, generally understood to be a component of good administration. Under this notion, the reasoning of a measure[70] must provide for information about compliance with the elements summarized by the 'duty of care': reasons must demonstrate that the decision was taken on the basis of 'the most complete "factually accurate, reliable and consistent" information possible'.[71] Generally speaking, reasoning is a concept requiring the administration to document that it has reflected on all matters which may be subject to later judicial review.[72] Under the duty of care, a proper reasoning will require documentation and reporting of the information sourcing and processing activities.[73] For example, the more important proportionality considerations are to a specific decision, the more indications of the taking into account of these matters must be documented in decision-making. Showing compliance with the duty of care is information related in that a decision-maker must show how a specific decision was made and with what information, requiring, in terms of ADM systems, the traceability of information in the reasoning.

Such compliance is a particular mode of the requirement of transparency through reason giving in public decision-making,[74] of which a central element is the recording of operations within a system, and the source and the type of data used to general informational input into decision-making. Information technology

[69] Amongst many see Case C-64/16 *Associação Sindical dos Juízes Portugueses* [2018] ECLI:EU:C:2018:117, paras 31, 40, and 41; Case C-216/18 PPU *Minister for Justice and Equality (Deficiencies in the system of justice)* [2018] ECLI:EU:C:2018:586, paras 63–67.

[70] See eg Case C-166/13 *Mukarubega v Seine-Saint-Denis* [2014] ECLI:EU:C:2014:2336 paras 43–49; Case C-604/12 *H. N.* [2014] ECLI:EU:C:2014:302, para 49; Case C-521/15 *Spain v Council* [2017] ECLI:EU:C:2017:982, para 89.

[71] Hofmann (n 51) 100. Citing Case C-525/04 P *Spain v Lenzing* [2007] ECLI:EU:C:2007:698, para 57. In this judgment the Court reiterated that 'not only must the Community judicature establish whether the evidence relied on is factually accurate, reliable and consistent but also whether that evidence contains all the information which must be taken into account in order to assess a complex situation and whether it is capable of substantiating the conclusions drawn from it'.

[72] The right to a reasoned decision is a right guaranteed under the right to good administration, also explicitly recognized in art 41(1)b) CFR as well as under the right to an effective judicial remedy, as also recognized in art 47(1) CFR.

[73] European Union Agency for Fundamental Rights and Council of Europe, *Handbook on European Data Protection Law* (Publications Office of the European Union 2018) <http://fra.europa.eu/en/publication/2016/handbook-european-law-relating-access-justice> accessed 29 March 2017.

[74] Ida Koivisto, 'The Anatomy of Transparency: The Concept and its Multifarious Implications' (2016) EUI MWP Working Papers.

developments for securing information in the form of 'tamper-evident record that provides non-repudiable evidence of all nodes' actions'[75] are becoming increasingly relevant. This would enhance traceability of data across its sources within multilevel information systems. It would also allow the review of its processing within an ADM system in a concrete process.[76]

The 'right to an explanation' with respect to single-case ADM[77] is thus linked to the right to a reasoned decision and the degree of reasoning necessarily required by the case law of the CJEU under principles of good administration and the right to an effective judicial protection. In fact, in the case of ADM, arguably the reasoning must be more complete regarding the information taken into account and processed as well as how the information has influenced the outcome of a decision than in a 'traditional' decision-making process, since probability used by AI systems is not the same type of reasoning as a human causality-driven approach would entail. Also the obligation to show the reasoning behind a decision with regard to the detailed amounts of information taken into account further follows from the right to an effective remedy, a general principle of EU law also protected under Article 47 CFR. A decision must demonstrate compliance with essential procedural requirements. Obligations are frequently restated by the CJEU's requiring that a decision's reasoning must enable a concerned person 'to ascertain the reasons upon which the decision taken in relation to him or her is based . . . so as to make it possible for him or her to defend his or her rights in the best possible conditions'.[78]

This does not exclude the fact that in individual cases, providing the rationale behind decision-making might also require explanations concerning the system-level functioning and logic of programs used in ADM,[79] but it does not require it as such, since the system level might only indicate the outcome in programming which is purpose built and to a certain degree static with respect to the outcome. Accordingly, demands have been made that in order to 'enable third parties to

[75] Aziz Z Huq, 'Constitutional Rights in the Machine Learning State' (2020) 105 Cornell Law Review, <SSRN.Com/abstract=3613282> 49; Deven R Desai and Joshua A Kroll, 'Trust but Verify: A Guide to Algorithms and the Law' (2017) 31 Harvard Journal of Law and Technology 1, 10–11. One currently increasingly widespread approach is based on distributed ledger technology often known as 'blockchain'.

[76] Herwig CH Hofmann and Morgane Tidghi, 'Rights and Remedies in Implementation of EU Policies by Multi-Jurisdictional Networks' (2014) 20 European Public Law 147–64, discussing notions of tagging of information.

[77] Lilian Edwards and Michael Veale, 'Slave to the Algorithm? Why a "Right to an Explanation" Is Probably Not the Remedy You Are Looking For' (2017) 16 Duke Law & Technology Review 18; Bryan Casey, Ashkon Farhangi, and Roland Vogl, 'Rethinking Explainable Machines: The GDPR's "Right to Explanation" Debate and the Rise of Algorithmic Audits in Enterprise' (2019) 34 Berkeley Technology Law Journal 143.

[78] Joined Cases C-225/19 and C-226/19 *R.N.N.S., K.A. v Minister van Buitenlandse Zaken* [2020] ECLI:EU:C:2020:951, para 43.

[79] Garry Coglianese and David Lehr, 'Regulating by Robot :Administrative Decision Making in the Machine-Learning Era' (2017) 105 The Georgetown Law Journal 1147–223, 1207 state that reason giving will require to also 'disclose algorithmic specifications, including the objective function being optimised, the method used for that optimisation and the algorithm's input variables'.

probe and review the behaviour of the algorithm', ADM 'should be accompanied by a "datasheet" that records the choices and manipulations of training data and the composition, collection process, recommended uses and so on'.[80] Providing such a datasheet to non-expert humans will however face obstacles by way of providing meaningful explanation in view of potentially formidable technical obstacles (depending on the complexity of an algorithm) as well as some questions of intellectual property rights and state and business secrets.[81]

In this respect, one of the early legislative approaches to transparency in ADM is the French code of administrative procedures, which is applicable to both individual decision-making as well as to the system rule-making level. Article L.311-3-1 of the 2016 *Code des relations entre le public et l'administration*[82] establishes the individual's rights of information regarding the extent of algorithm-based rules used to make administrative decisions, together with the criteria used and their weighting by the computer program. It equally provides that the person or persons concerned must be informed whenever a relevant administrative decision has been made on the basis of algorithmic processing and these persons have the option of requesting information about certain elements in the relevant procedure.[83] As much as this provision was innovative when it was introduced, early experience with this provision has not been very promising. Today's move towards generative AI systems which are general purpose systems makes such access to the systemic level appear even less promising. Access to the general level AI system cannot replace knowledge about the specific information processing that has led to the making of an individual decision.

The Commission's draft AI Act is much less demanding concerning transparency requirements.[84] Only Article 11(1) of the Commission's draft AI Act foresees an obligation for high-risk AI systems to maintain technical documentation 'in such a way to demonstrate that the high-risk AI system complies with the requirements of the law and to allow supervisory authorities to verify such compliance'.[85]

[80] Huq (n 75) 48.

[81] Brkan (n 6) 120.

[82] As a disclaimer, the author of this chapter was member of the cercle d'experts appointed by the French Prime Minister's office's legislative service to advise on the 2016 *Code des relations entre le public et l'administration.*

[83] See French Décret No 2017-330 du 14 mars 2017 relatif aux droits des personnes faisant l'objet de décisions individuelles prises sur le fondement d'un traitement algorithmique, JORF n°0064 du 16 mars 2017.

[84] Art 52 of the Artificial Intelligence Act Proposal of 21 April 2021 requires no specific type of transparency for AI systems that are not deemed to be high risk other than notifications to natural persons that they are interacting with an AI system, unless this is obvious (art 52(1)), and that they might be exposed to their data 'being processed by an emotion recognition system' (art 52(2)) or that their images have been artificially recreated or manipulated (art 52(3)) unless this is done for public security or other prevailing public interests.

[85] Artificial Intelligence Act Proposal of 21 April 2021.

However, a demand of traceability of data movements and data processing by ADM, which had been made in legal literature,[86] has found its way into Article 12 of the Commission's draft AI Act, albeit only for high-risk AI systems. The latter requires AI systems to contain record-keeping facilities to logging and tracking operations conducted by AI systems. Such record-keeping facilities, according to Article 12 of the Commission's draft AI Act, would need to 'ensure a level of traceability of the AI system's functioning throughout its lifecycle' (Article 12(2)), and the logging capabilities must provide at least 'recording of the period of each use of the system . . . the reference database against which input data has been checked by the system; the input data for which the search has led to a match' as well as 'the identification of the natural persons involved in the verification of the results'. This formulation is technology neutral but some work is being undertaken to harness distributed ledger technology such as blockchain approaches to maintain such tagging and tracking.

3. Oversight and effective remedies

Procedural rights in this context concern many aspects of information. Where the specific violation of a right cannot be submitted to judicial review because it is merely preparatory for a final act, independent of a separate violation of a right, such as in the case of the transfer of data and information or its processing, such violation will have to be subject to review of a final act.

Such review in reality requires a working interface between ADM systems and human review. In this sense, the Commission's draft AI Act also foresees that 'high-risk' AI systems must provide for appropriate 'human–machine interface tools' so that they can be subject to human oversight.[87] Such oversight by natural persons must be ensured through appropriate technical installations.[88] The individuals to whom human oversight is assigned must be enabled to 'fully understand the capacities and limitations of the high-risk AI system and be able to duly monitor its operation so that signs of anomalies, dysfunctions and unexpected performance can be detected as soon as possible'[89] and they must be trained to resist potential 'automation bias'.[90] The latter reference to an automation bias appears slightly out of sync with the reality of discretionary decision-making. In the reality of administrative decision-making it will be difficult if not impossible to make independent data collections, time-consuming to analyse these outside the computer system designed to undertake this task, and risky for the individual to override an established system to undertake an individual assessment and reasoning of the situation.

[86] See eg Hofmann and Tidghi (n 76) discussing notions of tagging of information.
[87] Art 14(1) of the Artificial Intelligence Act Proposal of 21 April 2021.
[88] ibid.
[89] Art 14(4)(a) of the Artificial Intelligence Act Proposal of 21 April 2021.
[90] Art 14(4)(b) of the Artificial Intelligence Act Proposal of 21 April 2021.

Irrespective of this, the case law of the CJEU and the legislation on data protection have developed more far-reaching human oversight requirements, as discussed earlier. The reason for relatively limited regulatory content on this in the Commission's draft AI Act may be that such an act addresses private and public uses of AI at the same time. Mixing public and private obligations is problematic, since each have different legal obligations as to their procedures. Arguably the use of AI in public decision-making would be better integrated into a general EU administrative procedures act and would address specific effects of ADM on decision-making and rule-making procedures.

One of the central questions regarding accountability of ADM is the right to oppose its use where the use of personal data is involved. The GDPR and the European Data Protection Regulation (EDPR)[91] proclaim the individual data subject's right to oppose to be made subject to a decision based solely on automated processing when such a decision produces legal effects. Under Articles 22 GDPR and 24 EDPR, data subjects have the right to oppose automated individual decision-making concerning them unless such a form of decision-making is explicitly authorized by EU or Member State legislation and the possibility of human intervention is ensured.[92] The right to oppose full ADM is explicitly stated under Articles 22(1) GDPR and 24(1) EDPR.[93] which are identical and read: 'The data subject shall have the right not to be subject to a decision based solely on automated processing, including profiling, which produces legal effects concerning him or her or similarly significantly affects him or her.'

The prohibition enshrined in Articles 22 GDPR and Article 24 EDPR is, however, applicable only in narrowly defined circumstances. First, the right to oppose ADM concerning personal data only concerns automation 'which produces legal effects' or 'significantly affects' the data subject. The EU's data protection authorities argued[94] under Article 22(1) GDPR that a decision producing legal effects shall be only those which 'significantly affect the circumstances, behaviour or choices of the individuals concerned; have a prolonged or permanent impact on

[91] Regulation 2018/1725 of the European Parliament and the Council of 23 October 2018 on the protection of natural persons with regard to the processing of personal data by the Union institutions, bodies, offices and agencies and on the free movement of such data, and repealing Regulation (EC) No 45/2001 and Decision No 1247/2002/EC, [2018] OJ 2018 L 295/39.

[92] A similar provision is contained in art 11 of the Directive on Data Protection in Criminal Matters Directive (EU) 2016/680 of the European Parliament and of the Council of 27 April 2016 on the protection of natural persons with regard to the processing of personal data by competent authorities for the purposes of the prevention, investigation, detection or prosecution of criminal offences or the execution of criminal penalties, and on the free movement of such data, and repealing Council Framework Decision 2008/977/JHA, [2016] OJ 2016 L 119/1.

[93] Brkan (n 6) 102.

[94] Art 29 Data Protection Working Party, 'Guidelines on Automated individual decision-making and Profiling for the purposes of Regulation 2016/679', 17/EN WP251rev.01, adopted on 3 October 2017, as last revised and adopted on 6 February 2018, 20–21.56.

the data-subject; or at its most extreme, lead to the exclusion or discrimination of individuals'.[95]

Second, the right to oppose decisions based on automated processing of personal data may have only a limited reach in cases of semi-automatic or augmented decision-making, especially where the automated processing takes place in a phase prior to the final decision-making by a human. Accordingly, the Data Protection Working Party (WP) 29 guidelines on ADM find[96] that Articles 22(1) GDPR and 24(1) EDPR[97] are applicable only in the absence of any meaningful human input into decision-making which is not the case where the automated component to decision-making is merely auxiliary to the human-made decision.[98] The data protection authorities (in the Article 29 WP's guidelines) state that:

> [t]o qualify as human involvement the controller must ensure that any oversight of the decision is meaningful, rather than a token gesture. It should be carried out by someone who has the authority and the competence to change the decision. As part of the analysis, they should consider all the relevant data.[99]

Therefore, the WP 29's guidelines make an implicit link between the right to human oversight and the duty of care in that a human should be capable of assessing 'all relevant' data. This makes for an important clarification and, arguably, a high hurdle with which ADM systems must comply. The 'human in the loop' should thus have the capability of extracting the data from the ADM system and considering it independently. For example, informational cooperation under the AFSJ is mostly based on humanly pre-programmed algorithms translating data input into specifically predefined outputs, not, thus far, using machine learning systems.[100] Although there are some conceptual considerations regarding developing self-learning capabilities, these are yet to be rolled out. Hence, a human agent remains finally responsible for acts adopted, irrespective of whether such

[95] Art 29 Data Protection Working Party, 'Guidelines on Automated individual decision-making and Profiling for the purposes of Regulation 2016/679', 17/EN WP251rev.01, adopted on 3 October 2017, as last revised and adopted on 6 February 2018.

[96] Art 29 Data Protection Working Party, 'Guidelines on Automated individual decision-making and Profiling for the purposes of Regulation 2016/679', 17/EN WP251rev.01, adopted on 3 October 2017, as last revised and adopted on 6 February 2018, 20–21.56.

[97] The Article 29 Data Protection Working Party, 'Guidelines on Automated individual decision-making and Profiling for the purposes of Regulation 2016/679', 17/EN WP251rev.01, adopted on 3 October 2017, as last revised and adopted on 6 February 2018 had stated on the basis of the predecessors of art 22 GDPR (ex-art 15 Regulation 95/46) and the equivalent Article 24 Regulation 2018/1725 (ex-Article 19 Regulation (EC) 45/2001) applying to EU institutions and bodies, and Article 11 Directive (EU) 2016/680 (the 'Law Enforcement Directive').

[98] See also Brkan (n 6) 101, 102; Tal Zarsky, 'Incompatible: The GDPR in the Age of Big Data' (2017) 47 Seton Hall Law Review 1016, <SSRN ssrn.abstract=3022646>.

[99] Article 29 Working Party 'Guidelines on Automated individual decision making and Profiling for the purposes of Regulation 2016/679' 17/EN WP251 rev.01, 21.

[100] European Union Agency for Fundamental Rights (n 46).

an agent has full understanding of the processing applications generating the suggestions. However, in order to fulfil the requirements, in view of the Article 29 WP, the human will have to be able to obtain full knowledge of all relevant decision-making factors and review them autonomously.

It also appears safe to state that a human merely implementing a decision taken by a full ADM will not be sufficient to qualify as 'human involvement'. On the other hand, some form of real and informed decision-making input will ensure that Article 22 GDPR and Article 24 EDPR do not lead to the illegality of decision-making procedures. The right to object to ADM is thus a right most relevant with respect to cyber delegation in the form of full delegation of powers to ADM. In those circumstances, however, the right to an effective judicial review in general, as well as the right to compliance with the duty of care and of reasoning obligations, will also have the effect that an ADM system will need to give detailed explanations as to the input taken into account into coming to a decision and the decision-making process and outcome that results.

A third factor limiting the reach of the right to oppose ADM is provided for by the GDPR and the EDPR, which allow for explicit authorization of ADM by EU or national law (eg Article 23 GDPR) in cases where ADM is required for matters of national security and other legitimate public interests.

Following this, the question is what the data subject's right not to be subject to a decision based solely on automated processing under Articles 22 GDPR and 24 EDPR contains. What should human review of a decision based on automated processing look like? Should it be understood in the sense that the initial decision-making procedure itself needs to be conducted with human input? Arguably the wording also permits understanding that right as a right to a complaint and subsequent handling of the decision in the context of a human form of oversight which could be granted, for example, in the context of the exercise of administrative oversight, such as in the form of complaint boards of EU agencies or other administrative review procedures.

Next to the right to oppose ADM in matters concerning the processing of personal data there is also a more general discussion about a right to human review. Given that the analysis of complex data collections by computer systems necessarily involves 'some margin of error', [101] any positive result obtained following automated processing of information must be subject to the possibility of an individual re-examination by non-automated means 'before an individual measure adversely affecting the persons concerned' may be adopted.[102]

This requirement raises several points. First, human review must cover the informational input into the decision-making in order to review such 'margin of

[101] Case C-511-520/18 *La Quadrature du Net* [2020] ECLI:EU:C:2020:791, para 182 referring specifically to the analysis of traffic and location data.
[102] ibid.

error'. The human reviewer must therefore either have some form of profound conceptual understanding of the ADM system or must be able take a decision in the knowledge of the concrete circumstances of a specific factual situation independent of the ADM system. Such knowledge can be brought to the human reviewer through independent expertise.[103] It however remains to be seen whether the case law or future legislation will require the latter review mechanisms to have the power of a full *de novo* investigation, in which a human administrator begins with a 'manual' collection of relevant information and derives a decision from this or whether, seemingly in opposition to the Working Group 29 WP, a more summary review would be accepted by the courts. For high-risk AI systems this is also subject to draft codification in the AI Act. The Commission's proposal puts far-reaching demands on the programming process by foreseeing that an AI system capable of ADM must allow a person conducting human oversight to 'intervene in an operation or to disregard, override or reverse the output of a high risk AI system'.[104] Where AI systems are employed in less sensitive matters or with less sensitive technology, such standards may still be used as benchmarks for assessing compliance of ADM systems with general principles of EU law.

II. Substantive rights

Not surprisingly, two of the most important rights concerning ADM are data-related non-discrimination and information rights.

1. Non-discrimination and ADM

The use of ADM technology has raised questions of non-discrimination.[105] In analysing data, ADM technology may rely on programming which results in groups of individuals becoming divided 'into different categories based on common characteristics in order to base decisions on their belonging to a specific group'.[106] Article 21 CFR lists a set of criteria which cannot, in principle, be used for distinguishing one group from another. This includes criteria of 'sex, race, colour, ethnic or social origin, genetic features, language, religion or belief, political or any

[103] For example, art 41 of Regulation (EU) 2018/1862 on the establishment, operation and use of the Schengen Information System (SIS) in the field of police cooperation and judicial cooperation in criminal matters, [2018] OJ 2018 L 312/56, states that '[i]n the event of a hit with the data entered pursuant to art 40, the identity of the person shall be established in accordance with national law, together with expert verification that the dactyloscopic data in SIS belong to the person'.

[104] Art 14(1) of the Artificial Intelligence Act Proposal of 21 April 2021.

[105] European Union Agency for Fundamental Rights, '*#BigData: Discrimination in Data-Supported Decision Making*' (Publications Office of the EU 2018) <https://fra.europa.eu/sites/default/files/fra_uploads/fra-2018-focus-big-data_en.pdf>.

[106] Giovanni De Gregorio and Sofia Ranchordas, 'Breaking down Information Silos with Big Data: A Legal Analysis of Data Sharing' in Joe Cannataci, Valeria Falce, and Oresto Pollicino (eds), *Legal Challenges of Big Data* (Edward Elgar 2020) 226.

other opinion, membership of a national minority, property, birth, disability, age or sexual orientation' (Article 21(1) CFR) as well as criteria of nationality of an EU Member State (Article 21(2) CFR). ADM must be programmed not to use these criteria as distinguishing factors unless this is—as limitation of the right to non-discrimination—provided for by law, respects the essence of the right and the limitation is proportionate (Article 52(1) CFR).

In that case, ADM technology, by its very nature, introduces distinctions which are prone to discriminations[107] resulting from biased training data and the analysis of situations by unsupervised learning technologies. ADM technology might then focus on decision-making criteria using distinctions which might be unacceptable under legal anti-discrimination provisions. Such biases in the training data are sometimes referred to as '*sample bias*'.[108] These arise from data used by an ADM system to train software algorithms. If training data used has certain in-built biases then the outcome of computer-based calculations can reflect or even accentuate that same bias.[109]

One of the challenges in the programming of ADM is therefore that discrimination might occur from the databases on which the searches are based. Data-based decision-making cannot be understood to be an entirely neutral. Databases are generally collected with a certain purpose and organized according to certain criteria and such data sources can be unbalanced or inept in view of normative requirements of the law.[110] These databases, whether used as training data or as search data, may display biases which may translate to the decision-making undertaken with the help of ADM systems.[111] The risk here is that the use of AI might actually reinforce and accentuate pre-existing biases within the datasets.[112] Therefore, the CJEU has held that ADM must be programmed to ensure that certain categories of data will not be used to determine the outcome of decision-making.

> [A]ny automated analysis carried out on the basis of models and criteria founded on the premise that racial or ethnic origin, political opinions, religious or philosophical beliefs, trade-union membership, or information about a person's health

[107] Brkan (n 6) 118.

[108] Huq (n 75) 34.

[109] For example, if hiring data shows that in the past predominantly men had been employed, a ADM system trained on such data of a potentially successful candidate might exclude certain categories of women. The normative requirement of ensuring gender equality and the acceptance of different biographies might not be best left to a machine learning system.

[110] It is unclear whether the biases of humans are temporary findings, which can change over time with ever more ADM technologies being rolled out, or whether these findings as to human biases are long-term structural features. In any case, when designing systems which necessarily link humans to ADM technology such findings should be taken into account.

[111] See above on the discussion of biases within this chapter. Further, see Tal Zarsky, 'The Trouble with Algorithmic Decisions: An Analytic Road Map to Examine Efficiency and Fairness in Automated and Opaque Decision Making' (2016) 41 Science, Technology, & Human Values 126; Huq (n 75).

[112] Bryce Goodman, 'Discrimination, Data Sanitisation and Auditing in the European Union's General Data Protection Regulation' (2016) 2 European Data Protection Law Review 498.

> or sex life could, in themselves and regardless of the individual conduct of that person, be relevant ... would infringe the rights guaranteed in Articles 7 and 8 of the Charter, read in conjunction with Article 21 thereof.[113]

Accordingly, sensitive personal data should not be made 'input variables' relevant for decision-making.[114] For AI technology, which might not be entirely predictable, therefore the reporting of decision-making and the transparency as to the data taken into account and the use of such data as information input into the decision will be important features.[115] This is the reason for the CJEU requiring not just oversight of programming but also 'regular re-examination' of the output of such programming.[116]

2. Information rights

Information rights do not only cover the protection of privacy and data protection (Articles 7 and 8 CFR), although the latter will be amongst the most frequently affected individual rights in the context of the use of ADM technology in public decision-making.[117] ADM relies on the use of data, often collected and stored within large-scale databases. Any processing of personal data is a limitation of these rights and thus requires a clear legal basis (Article 52(1) CFR). Accordingly, Article 5(1) GDPR and Article 4(1)(a) EDPR[118] require that a public body have a legal basis for the processing of data involved in decision-making, in order to comply with the obligation to process data lawfully, fairly, and transparently. Data subjects have a right to object to processing in violation of such preconditions.[119] Access to data collections by ADM, which is one of many forms of processing, must

[113] Case C-511-520/18 *La Quadrature du Net* [2020] ECLI:EU:C:2020:791, para 181. This further states that 'pre-established models and criteria for the purposes of an automated analysis that has as its objective the prevention of terrorist activities that constitute a serious threat to national security cannot be based on that sensitive data in isolation' with reference to Opinion 1/15 *EU-Canada PNR Agreement* [2017] EU:C:2017:592, para 165.

[114] Indre Zliobaite and Bart Custers, 'Using Sensitive Personal Data may be Necessary for Avoiding Discrimination in Data-Driven Decision Models' (2016) 24 Artificial Intelligence and Law 183–201.

[115] ibid 183; Niklas Eder, 'Non-Discrimination and Equal Treatment: Developing a Fundamental Rights Response to Behavioural Profiling' in Ebers and Cantero Gamito (eds), *Algorithmic Governance and Governance of Algorithms* (n 11).

[116] Case C-511-520/18 *La Quadrature du Net* [2020] ECLI:EU:C:2020:791, para 182 with reference to Opinion 1/15 *EU-Canada PNR Agreement* [2017] EU:C:2017:592, paras 173, 174.

[117] See eg Lee A Bygrave, 'Minding the Machine v2.0: The EU General Data Protection Regulation and Automated Decision-Making' in Yeung and Lodge (eds), *Algorithmic Regulation* (n 56) <https://www-oxfordscholarship-com.eui.idm.oclc.org/view/10.1093/oso/9780198838494.001.0001/oso-9780198838494-chapter-11> accessed 1 February 2024.

[118] Art 4(1)(a) of Regulation 2018/1725 of the European Parliament and the Council of 23 October 2018 on the protection of natural persons with regard to the processing of personal data by the Union institutions, bodies, offices and agencies and on the free movement of such data, and repealing Regulation (EC) No 45/2001 and Decision No 1247/2002/EC, [2018] OJ 2018 L 295/39 states: 'Personal data shall be processed lawfully, fairly and in a transparent manner in relation to the data subject ("lawfulness, fairness and transparency")'.

[119] Cobbe (n 49) 645.

be designed to be compatible with fundamental rights, including rights to privacy and data protection (Articles 7 and 8 CFR) and the rules on their limitations. The CJEU has acknowledged that the use of ADM technology can *de facto* intensify limitations to the right to privacy and the protection of personal data.[120] For example, according to the CJEU, automated searching and processing of databases may lead to 'particularly serious interference constituted by the automated analysis' of data.[121] Further, in case of ADM involving personal data, the GDPR and the EDPR oblige the data controller to provide the data subject with 'meaningful information about the logic involved, as well as the significance and the envisaged consequences of' ADM—regardless of whether the data was provided by or collected from data subject or was brought to the decision-making process from a pre-existing data base.[122] These requirements are information which must be provided regarding the 'system' of data processing. Similarly to data protection, protection is also afforded to business secrets in EU law. They are to be protected unless overriding reasons of public interest so allow (Article 339 TFEU).

E. Automated decision-making systems in EU public law

ADM systems are increasingly transforming decision-making procedures under EU public law. This requires considering changes implied in such move to ADM, notably changes to decision-making procedures, and (re)considering constitutional concepts in view of the specificities of ADM.

The first observation is that it is necessary to distinguish between conditions governing the quasi rule-making character of ADM *systems* from *individual decisions* made with the help of ADM technology. The first, the systemic element, requires considerations akin to those applied to administrative rule-making, whereas the application of ADM technology in individual procedures requires analysis from the consideration of legality of individual acts.

Today, ADM is mainly used to support certain phases of a decision-making procedure, such as the initiation or the investigation phases. Each has specific requirements to ensure accountability of public action and the protection of individual substantive and procedural rights. Legal principles applicable to review accountability may differ according to the phase in which the ADM system is used. In future this may start to change and indeed the first signs of this arise from banking and finance regulation concerning what might be referred to as real-time regulation. It is however also possible to combine several ADM systems in one decision-making procedure. However, the more policy phases of a decision-making

[120] See also European Union Agency for Fundamental Rights (n 46).
[121] Case C-511-520/18 *La Quadrature du Net* [2020] ECLI:EU:C:2020:791, para 177.
[122] Arts 13(2)(f), 14(2)(g), and 15 GDPR.

procedure are subject to ADM, the stronger the move towards forms of 'cyber delegation', that is, forms of delegation of decision-making powers to an automated system.[123] Criteria of legality of delegation of powers would be applicable in that context. These can however also be helpful for assessing more limited deployment of ADM technology.

This arises from linking different decision-making logics, akin to integrating expert knowledge into legally structured decision-making procedures. ADM systems are based on computer science logic and need to comply with requirements developed in law, especially EU public law. The use of ADM systems, often impenetrable by human review, accentuates problems arising from information asymmetries. The accountability of ADM systems is then also highly influenced by the design of human–machine interfaces allowing general review of an ADM system as well as the review of a specific decision made with the help of ADM technology.

The second main finding is that ADM systems and questions of their legality and accountability are often programmed with access to specific databases or data sources in mind. Conditions of accountability of ADM are thus linked to the nature of the data supplied for decision-making. Other types of AI systems, especially generative AI, may have more or less openly available data sources, for example the Internet, as their database. In all situations, accountability mechanisms require that the final decision-making is reasoned, with details about the type of data collected, how these were used as informational input into the decision-making process, and which outcome was drawn from this. Such information transparency is a prerequisite for possible human review or correction of ADM.

ADM cannot be dissociated from the databases it uses and the legal and practical problems of data collections, data protection, data interoperability, and data quality. In this context, factors of accountability will also differ regarding whether the ADM technology is applied to data stemming from private or from public data bases. They will also be linked to the nature of databases in the EU arising from multi-jurisdictional cooperation. Decision-making based on these databases is composite since a single administrative procedure will have received input from actors applying rules from a number of jurisdictional levels. The use of databases in which data is supplied might thus lead to the inclusion of ADM into composite decision-making procedures governed by a mix of national and EU law.

Overall, the inclusion of decision-making with the help of ADM technology raises the level of complexities to be addressed in administrative law: the features of human–machine interfaces, access to and processing of data from multilevel databases, integration of ADM into composite procedures, and the underlying complexities of AI programming undertaking this level of digitalization

[123] Although public administration in the EU lags the level of adoption of ADM systems known in some private sectors, there is an increasing level of use in diverse EU policy areas such as border control and immigration, financial market regulation and reporting as well as transport regulation.

of decision-making all contribute to growing complexity. Design choices in law and technology need to be made to ensure that there is no disconnection between, on the one hand, legal principles designed to ensure accountability and, on the other hand, the possibilities and restrictions of ADM technology and the *real-life design* of the procedures employed in the digitalization of government functions in the EU. Normative steering must be possible and as such it is a requirement of the principles of democratic steering in a system under the rule of law. If this is the case, the use of ADM can harness the increase in the decision-making speed and quality of data analysis made possible by technological advances. But technical approaches must be designed in a way to ensure that accountability is ensured whilst the promises of using automation in decision-making can be enjoyed in the public sphere. Normative steering is a necessity to ensure accountability of ADM used in public policies.

In this context, the discussions of considerable advances in information technology have also raised serious questions regarding the protection of individuals in a system under the rule of law. Data protection as well as rights of access to and transparency of information are essential elements of defining the position of individuals in a democratic society. These elements help to define the individual and the possibilities of exercising essential participatory roles within the public sphere and to hold actors to account effectively.

2

Assessing Cyber Delegation in European Union Public Law

Herwig C.H. Hofmann

A. Cyber Delegation—Functions, Concept, and Accountability

Tools to support accountability in public law, and associated legal principles, can be distinguished according to their position within in the decision-making cycle. Anticipatory tools govern the conditions of legislative conferral of powers or delegation to implement EU law to the administration.[1] These *ex ante* mechanisms for identifying the possibilities of the use of ADM in the exercise of public powers under EU law allow the definition of tasks and the imposition of conditions for their exercise. Such anticipatory requirements can be created by the legislative body conferring administrative powers on the executive and setting out conditions for their exercise and subsequent administrative rule-making and guidelines. This act delegating powers can additionally specify their use. *Ongoing* control and supervision of actors concerns a period during a decision-making procedure.[2] Subsequent, *ex post* forms of review will be undertaken after a decision was taken and include accountability mechanisms such as judicial review[3] often relying on reasoning obligations and aspects of transparency.[4]

[1] In EU law, unlike in several Member State systems, under the limited attribution of powers (arts 5 and 13 of the Treaty on European Union (TEU)), the executive branch of powers has in principle only those implementing powers explicitly conferred on it by legislation. Generally, with few exceptions, the EU's administration has no genuine implementing powers of EU legislation. Hence, EU agencies require a legislative basis empowering them to act in specific fields..

[2] These include for example controls concerning data protection in ongoing procedures by the European Data Protection Supervisor (EDPS) under the European Data Protection Regulation (EDPR) (Regulation 2018/1725 of the European Parliament and the Council of 23 October 2018 on the protection of natural persons with regard to the processing of personal data by the Union institutions, bodies, offices and agencies and on the free movement of such data, [2018] OJ L295/39).

[3] For a background discussion see Mark Bovens, 'Analysing and Assessing Accountability: A conceptual framework' (2007) 13 European Law Journal 447–68 speaking of political and legal approaches to accountability, both of which can be achieved by *ex-ante* and *ex-post* approaches.

[4] See with further references Melanie Fink and Michèle Finck, 'Reasoned A(I)administration: Explanation Requirements in EU Law and the Automation of Public Administration' (2022) 47 European Law Review 376–92; Mike Ananny and Kate Crawford, 'Seeing Without Knowing: Limitations of the Transparency Ideal and Its Application to Algorithmic Accountability' (2020) 20 New Media & Society 973–89 (discussing the various facets of transparency on the backdrop of AI and algorithms); Deven R Desai and Joshua A Kroll, 'Trust but Verify: A Guide to Algorithms and the Law' (2017) 31 Harvard Journal of Law & Technology 1–65.

Herwig C.H. Hofmann, *Assessing Cyber Delegation in European Union Public Law* In: *Governance of Automated Decision-Making and EU Law.* Edited by: Herwig C.H. Hofmann and Felix Pflücke, Oxford University Press.
 DOI: 10.1093/9780198919575.003.0002

This chapter explores whether criteria for *ex post* accountability mechanisms can be derived from rules and principles on the delegation of powers in EU law to be exercised with the help of automated decision making (ADM) procedures? This chapter uses the notion of 'cyber delegation' as shorthand to discuss the possibilities of this approach to allow for enhancing accountability of the use of public decision-making.

I. Specifics of the exercise of public powers with the help of ADM

As discussed in Chapter 1, ADM systems are increasingly deployed in EU policy areas, often implemented by multilevel data-sharing structures and common EU databases. ADM systems can be simple support tools for human decision-making. With advances in technology they may also become increasingly powerful and cover more elements or more of the central elements of a decision-making process.[5] ADM technology, it should be recalled, is used for essentially three reasons. First, it can increase the speed of decision-making, allowing more decisions to be taken in a shorter period of time. Second, automation also allows for enhanced cooperation and collaboration of various decision-making levels through sharing data and access to data in jointly established databases such as, for example, in the field of customs, immigration, and visas. Third, automation increases the data volumes that can be studied and taken into account in decision-making, which is an important aspect of competition law enforcement in complex markets, for example.

ADM technology is making rapid progress in line with advances in both specifically designed and general-purpose programming of what is often referred to as artificial intelligence (AI).[6] These features result in certain specific challenges of ensuring accountability of decision-making procedures to concepts of public law. Challenges might arise from insufficient or poor software design which may result in introducing IT-based dysfunctionalities into decision-making procedures, but detecting such links is difficult due to ADM systems being necessarily defined in computer code. Such code is based on theories of representation not immediately comprehensible to human non-experts and not easily translated into human language.

Therefore, accountability of decision-making supported by forms of automation must contend with these characteristics of using ADM, *inter alia* by the high speed by which vast amounts of information can be taken into account, and the

[5] For example of various ongoing ADM systems being used in the context of EU law, see Chapter 3 and 4 in this volume.

[6] See eg the advent of the OpenAI Chat GPT system <https://openai.com/blog/chatgpt/> as an example of large generative AI models (LGAIMs) that are machine learning models trained to generate new data, such as text, images, or audio.

high frequency by which decisions can be adopted. These specifics also result from the technological features of ADM system programming, which by nature of integrating software-driven elements into a process differ from 'purely' human decision-making processes. The question thus arises whether employing ADM requires a new set of public law tools for accountability or whether certain elements of the existing legal toolset can be applied to ensure accountability of ADM-enhanced procedures.

There are certain other factors which can influence the accountability mechanisms designed around ADM systems. One is that those ADM systems used in public law are often programmed within the context of specific databases and usually address a certain phase of a procedure only. For example, ADM-based searches of datasets may be used to select cases which call for the initiation of an investigation.[7] Another factor to consider is that the conferral of duties and powers to be addressed with the help of ADM—as in human-based decision-making procedures—can be circumscribed. Such a conferral can provide for precise procedural steps demanding compliance, or it can delegate a degree of flexibility to develop the approach to decision-making. The definition of the source and the use of data input into decision-making can be also defined. Alternatively, leaving these points open and giving leeway about which data to use, where to source the data from, and how to process the input data in decision-making will increase discretion in the decision-making process.

A further detail regarding the integration of ADM systems into EU decision-making procedures concerns interfaces—both between human and automated elements of decision-making procedures and between the ADM systems and databases used by them. This results from the observation that ADM systems currently do not and possibly will not, in the foreseeable future, cover all phases of a decision-making procedure—from agenda setting and the initiation of a given procedure, to the investigation of the matter at hand, to an actual formal decision made and its eventual implementation. Instead, as various chapters in this book show, ADM generally covers single phases of a decision-making process and sometimes several systems are combined in this process. Therefore, at various points interfaces will need to be provided for, depending on specific procedural design in an area, human initiation of ADM procedures, linking datasets to ADM systems, and linking ADM system results to humans. Interfaces must be designed not only between computer and human elements of decision-making but also between an ADM system and the databases it relies upon. Interfaces linking human elements of decision-making by treating ADM results as input into further (human) decision-making may also involve review by oversight mechanisms either on an

[7] For further analysis of specific examples see eg L Tangi and others, *European Landscape on the Use of Artificial Intelligence by the Public Sector*, European Commission JCR Report R 31088 EN (Publications Office of the European Union 2022) doi:10.2760/39336, JRC129301.

administrative or judiciary level—the latter regularly conducted by humans. One ADM system might also be employed to control another.[8] These specifics will have effects on the 'steering' of administrative decision-making via legislative acts and administrative rule-making.

The question thus arises whether employing ADM requires a new set of public law tools for accountability or whether certain elements of the existing legal toolset can be applied to ensure accountability of ADM-enhanced procedures. Can legal tools developed in the context of the control of delegation of powers be applied to advanced ADM systems in EU public law? Is it possible to develop a concept of accountability around a notion of 'cyber delegation'?[9] The described factors of ADM are the background to the question of whether it will be necessary to design specific mechanisms for 'cyber delegation' more generally—the conferral of powers for decision-making by ADM—and to analyse which of the existing legal tools used in 'traditional' modes of empowering administrative decision-making can also be employed in cyber delegation contexts.

II. ADM and the limitation and balancing of fundamental rights

The Court of Justice of the European Union (CJEU) practice controlling allocation of powers to be exercised with the support of ADM to the executive branch (in this chapter simply referred to as 'cyber delegation') has to date relied heavily on requirements of Article 52(1) of the Charter of Fundamental Rights and Freedoms of the EU (CFR) under which any limitation for public purpose reasons or to balance different CFR rights and freedoms must be 'provided for by law'.[10]

An illustrative example of the use of this provision in limitations of what has amounted to a de facto delegation of powers to balance fundamental rights in the pursuit of a public policy objective was decided by the CJEU in the 2022 case on

[8] It is reported, for example, that the developers of OpenAI's 'ChatGPT' system have used AI-based content moderation to block requests and output which could become problematic along the lines of racist, sexist, or violent results. See Philipp Hacker, Andreas Engel, and Theresa List: 'Understanding and Regulating ChatGPT, and Other Large Generative AI Models: With input from ChatGPT' (*VerfassungsBlog*, 20 January 2023) <https://verfassungsblog.de/chatgpt/> (accessed 8 June 2024).Similarly, such requirements are implicit in some legislation. For example, AI-driven content moderation on online platforms will be monitored by AI systems for violation of intellectual property (IP) rights under art 17(4) of the IP Directive as referred to and discussed in Case C-401/19 *Republic of Poland v European Parliament and Council of the European Union* [2022] ECLI:EU:C:2022:297.

[9] Concepts of delegation would thus be relevant irrespective of whether ADM gains in autonomy, especially in cases with reduced human input into decision-making or in cases where ADM takes over several decision-making phases—the moment where ADM evolves from a mere 'tool' supporting agency or institution in decision-making to becoming more of an 'actor'. See also Simona Demková, 'The Decisional Value of Information in European Semi-Automated Decision Making' (2021) 14 Review of European Administrative Law 29–50.

[10] Art 52(1) of the Charter of Fundamental Rights and Freedoms of the EU.

the interpretation of Article 17(4) of the Intellectual Property (IP) Directive.[11] This directive conferred on private Internet service providers liability for IP violations assuming that these private parties would need to undertake a balancing decision between rights protecting private property and freedom of expression by means of ADM systems.[12] On the basis of Article 52(1) CFR, the CJEU found that if basic elements of the balancing between freedom of speech and protection of property rights were to be undertaken by private parties, the power to do so must be laid down in legislation which 'must lay down clear and precise rules governing the scope and application of the measure in question and imposing minimum safeguards'.[13] In these situations, legislation must, in particular, 'indicate in which circumstances and under which conditions such measures may be adopted'[14] in order to ensure only strictly necessary limitation of rights. The CJEU in the *Poland IP* case states that the requirements of legislatively predefined criteria for limiting or balancing fundamental rights are 'all the greater where the interference stems from an automated process'.[15]

Article 52(1) CFR therefore contains certain limits to delegation by the legislature to the administration or, in other words, an in-built non-delegation doctrine. Any limitations of fundamental rights which might result from the application of computer code-based ADM systems must be predetermined by what is recognizable as law under Article 52(1) CFR.[16] Therefore, in the context of the conferral of powers to the administration to conduct its business using ADM, the requirement that the clear and precise rules must be contained in 'law' under Article 52(1) CFR obtains a new relevance. The notion of 'law' is conceptually linked to a rule of law-based requirement of accessibility. Individuals must be able to discern from freely available and officially published sources which limitations to their rights and

[11] Case C-401/19 *Republic of Poland v European Parliament and Council of the European Union* [2022] ECLI:EU:C:2022:297.

[12] For example, see art 17(4) of Directive (EU) 2019/790 of the European Parliament and of the Council of 17 April 2019 on copyright and related rights in the Digital Single Market and amending Directives 96/9/EC and 2001/29/EC, [2019] OJ L130/92 under which 'online content-sharing service providers shall be liable for unauthorised acts of communication to the public, including making available to the public, of copyright-protected works'. Internet service providers facing such potential liability undertake searches for IP-protected content by ADM systems, thereby potentially affecting artistic freedoms, freedom of expression, freedom to conduct a business, and other individual rights.

[13] Case C-401/19 *Republic of Poland v European Parliament and Council of the European Union* [2022] ECLI:EU:C:2022:297, para 67 with reference to Case C-311/18 *Facebook Ireland and Schrems (Schrems II)* [2020] EU:C:2020:559, para 176. The reason for this is 'that the persons whose exercise of those rights is limited have sufficient guarantees to protect them effectively against the risk of abuse'.

[14] Case C-401/19 *Republic of Poland v European Parliament and Council of the European Union* [2022] ECLI:EU:C:2022:297, para 67 with reference to Case C-311/18 *Facebook Ireland and Schrems (Schrems II)* [2020] EU:C:2020:559, para 176.

[15] Case C-401/19 *Republic of Poland v European Parliament and Council of the European Union* [2022] ECLI:EU:C:2022:297, para 67; Case C-311/18 *Facebook Ireland and Schrems* [2020] EU:C:2020:559, para 176.

[16] This raises a specific fundamental rights-related version of the old question of whether code is law. For the background discussion and the origin of the terminology see eg Lawrence Lessing, *Code and other Laws of Cyberspace* (Basic Books 1999) <https://lessig.org/images/resources/1999-Code.pdf>.

freedoms they might be asked to endure.[17] This requirement raises fundamental questions as to the nature of law in relation to software codes in a computer program. Pre-programming of decision-making procedures and considerations are features of computer programming,[18] relevant in cases of ADM, where computer programming *de facto* may play the role of administrative rule-making in translating legislative normative requirements towards individual decisions.

In these conditions, the CJEU understood requirements of pre-programming, in line with notions of transparency, in the sense of ensuring explicability of the basic functioning and functionalities of a computer program used for ADM. This is a key demand in much of the discussion on accountability of ADM,[19] but it is a demand which is hampered both by the complexity of computer code, which is often well-hidden in sometimes proprietary software, and the fact that it may also only be interpreted by experts trained in specific specialist areas of computer science. Where the code underlying ADM systems contains machine learning technology, even experts will find it difficult to predict the possible range of outcomes of decision-making procedures. The reason is that machine learning technology is made to refine its own decision-making approach by experimentally changing the weight of certain factors and parameters in view of optimizing the calculations towards achieving certain results. Where machine learning technology may amend the criteria of decision-making in a dynamic fashion by adjusting future output to the results of past calculations, it may become impossible to tell whether the system has complied with the essential elements of predefined requirements. There is no linear deduction which leads from comprehension of the computer code used to assist decision-making to the actual content of the decision itself, thus programmers of the code may not fully understand how the system will achieve its output. Also, the more general purpose the AI supporting software is, the less that access to the source code will allow specific insights into the pathways of decision-making in individual cases.

This raises fundamental questions for a system developed with the help of machine learning tools, the logic of which goes against predefined criteria for the limitation or balancing of rights. Ensuring that the approach developed by a 'self-improving' algorithm will not be regarded as arbitrary or disproportionately limiting rights in violation of standards under Article 52(1) of the Charter is difficult. For example, the protection against discrimination contains criteria which may

[17] Case C-345/06 *Heinrich* [2009] EU:C:2009:140, paras 41–47 and 64–66; Opinion of Advocate General Sharpston in Case C-345/06 *Heinrich* [2008] EU:C:2008:212, paras 70–77.

[18] Bruno Lepri and others, 'Fair, Transparent, and Accountable Algorithmic Decision-Making Processes' (2018) 31 Philosophy & Technology 611–27; Daniel Innerarity, 'Making the Black Box Society Transparent' (2021) 36 AI & Society 975–81.

[19] For an overview of the diverse approaches to the requirement of transparency in ADM see eg Desai and Kroll (n 4); Ananny and Crawford (n 4); Tobias D Krafft, Katharina A Zweig, and Pascal D König, 'How to Regulate Algorithmic Decision-Making: A Framework of Regulatory Requirements for Different Applications' (2020) 16 Regulation & Governance 1–18, 18.

not be used for differentiation purposes. Article 21(1) of the CFR prohibits 'any' discrimination based on grounds 'such as sex, race, colour, ethnic or social origin, genetic features, language, religion or belief, political or any other opinion, membership of a national minority, property, birth, disability, age or sexual orientation'. The CJEU states that the 'pre-determined criteria must be defined in such a way that, while worded in a neutral fashion, their application does not place persons having the protected characteristics at a particular disadvantage'.[20] ADM used for decision-making, irrespective of whether it uses predetermined algorithms or machine learning approaches, must not distinguish outcome on the basis of any such criteria, and this must be both guaranteed and documented.

More generally, where it comes to limiting or balancing fundamental rights, programming software will have to show how in each case a proportionate solution has been found. Such justification relies, by definition, on counterfactual considerations to be developed by a decision-maker who must demonstrate that the measure chosen is limits the right in the least possible way. This balancing and justification can be programmed and would require extensive documentation of the calculation and comparison of alternative outcome scenarios documenting various counterfactual considerations in a specific decision-making path. It appears that today's AI systems generally do not provide for information about the details of which elements were taken into account, the balancing of the information and counterfactual considerations on less limiting interventions. The same appears to be true for large generative AI models such as ChatGPT.

An additional blow to today's forms of programming using machine learning tools comes from requirements on the degree of precision of the pre-established or predefined models and criteria required which, according to the CJEU case law in the field, must contain criteria for limitations or balancing of rights which 'should be specific and reliable'.[21] In other words, the normative legal programming of limitations of rights must not only be predefined in the delegating legal act but this programming must be reliably representable in the computer programming code underlying ADM systems.[22]

Computer programming may thus play *de facto* functions of administrative rule-making, notably by the transposition of legislative normative requirements to individual decisions. Where predefined criteria are contained in legislation, the CJEU has held, for example in the *Belgian PNR* (Passenger Name Record) case, that such requirement then 'precludes the use of artificial intelligence technology in self-learning systems ("machine learning"), capable of modifying without human intervention or review the assessment process and, in particular, the

[20] Case C-817/19 *Ligue des droits humains v Conseil des ministres (Belgian PNR)* [2022] ECLI:EU:C:2022:491, para 197.
[21] Opinion 1/15 *EU-Canada PNR Agreement* [2017] EU:C:2017:592, para 172.
[22] Lepri and others (n 18); Innerarity (n 18).

assessment criteria on which the result of the application of that process is based as well as the weighting of those criteria'.[23] This statement is possibly an *obiter dictum.* It refers to final decisions made by AI tools. As such, it should be understood not as a prohibition of the use of machine learning technology. Instead, it precludes technology which does not allow for human review or intervention in decision-making because of a lack of information about what information has been taken into account, how this information was processed, and under what criteria and to offer what result. These criteria are, not coincidentally, criteria for judicial review under the duty of care, a key principle of *ex post* judicial forms of supervision and accountability.

III. Limits on delegation of discretion

The basic approaches to delegation of powers to the executive branch have been established in EU law in a set of principles already outlined in early case law of the CJEU such as *Meroni*,[24] a case concerning sub-delegation of powers from the Commission (then the European Coal and Steel Community's High Authority) to a private company under Belgian law. Today, private companies are involved in public ADM, for instance in the programming of software. For example, eu-LISA,[25] the EU agency in charge of some of the Union's large-scale databases, confers on private contractors the design and maintenance of ADM systems used for the exercise of EU public policies.[26] ADM software used by public administration is either purchased 'ready-made' or ordered to be produced by a private company. In certain cases, a public–private partnership model will be sought to either provide or maintain the software for the databases. Alternatively, public and private cooperation will take place with respect to the provision of the data used to

[23] Case C-817/19 *Ligue des droits humains v Conseil des ministres (Belgian PNR)* [2022] ECLI:EU:C:2022:491, para 194.

[24] Case 9/56, *Meroni v ECSC High Authority* [1958] ECLI:EU:C:1958:7.

[25] eu-LISA is an agency established under Regulation (EU) No 1077/2011 [2011] OJ L286/1 replaced by Regulation (EU) 2018/1726, [2018] OJ L295/99. This European agency is responsible for the management of basic information systems for Member States' control of the Union's borders, such as the Schengen Information System (SIS II), the Visa Information System (VIS), and the asylum information system (Eurodac). It is also developing new information systems already regulated by EU law, such as the Entry/Exit System (EES), ETIAS, and the European Criminal Records Information System—Third-Country Nationals (ECRIS-TCN), for their forthcoming entry into operation.

[26] For example, in the area of AFSJ, eu-LISA's biometric matching systems are not developed in-house by eu-LISA but by private contractors on the basis of the technical specifications set by eu-LISA, which also tests their proper functioning. See eg the eu-LISA call for tender for a framework contract for implementation and maintenance in working order of the biometrics part of the EES and future Shared Biometrics Matching System (sBMA), LISA/2019/RP/05 EES BMS and sBMS, now awarded to a private consortium <https://ted.europa.eu/udl?uri=TED:NOTICE:200083-2020:TEXT:EN:HTML> (as of 29 July 2022). According to research conducted by Oriol Mir, eu-LISA will not have access to the training datasets on which the algorithms for this AI-based system will be trained, leaving eu-LISA unaware of the data used and unable to verify whether it suffers from any biases.

maintain decision-making. This means that the public body will not always have access to the data on which AI systems are based and developed.[27]

Next to contracting and sub-contracting models, EU legislation is also conferring the wholescale exercise of EU regulatory powers in situations where, as in *Poland IP*,[28] private parties are empowered to enforce property rights, balancing these with other freedoms such as that of expression and the exercise of professional freedoms.

One central notion of the *Meroni* doctrine-based limitations on delegation is the limitation on delegation of discretionary powers to parties not empowered to exercise them under Treaty provisions.[29] This is a concept also linked to the notion of institutional balance, equally protected within the principles enumerated in the *Meroni* doctrine as limits to delegation. In terms of ADM this enshrines the principle of lawfulness and the requirement of a legal basis for action. Linked to this notion of institutional balance in *Meroni* is the limitation to delegation of certain types of discretionary powers. *Meroni* originally limited delegation of those types of discretion which are so essential to a policy matter that they should be handled by the institutions authorized by the Treaty. Arguably, this would relate today to questions of legislative discretion, since the CJEU has rightly accepted that agencies may be delegated powers to exert discretion, sometimes qualified by the courts as 'broad discretion',[30] but always to be exercised in the context of relevant EU legislation.[31]

Under this approach, limits to the delegation of powers to be exercised with the support of ADM could be limited to the type of discretion which in today's understanding can also be delegated to EU agencies. This requires that a legislative act conferring the given power must circumscribe the essential decision-making

[27] It is exceptionally noteworthy when an EU agency like the European Intellectual Property Office (EUIPO) develops sophisticated and tailor-made AI tools in-house, without acquiring them from third parties. See <https://euipo.europa.eu/tunnel-web/secure/webdav/guest/document_library/contentPdfs/Strategic_Plan_2025/project_cards/SD3_Artificial_Intelligence_implementation_PC_en.pdf> accessed 29 July 2022.

[28] Case C-401/19 *Republic of Poland v European Parliament and Council of the European Union* [2022] ECLI:EU:C:2022:297.

[29] This includes that, for example, the delegator may not delegate powers it does not have. Only powers conferred on the Commission or, by extension to today's approach, to EU agencies by law may thus be further delegated to private parties or EU executive agencies. See Council Regulation (EC) No 58/2003 of 19 December 2002 laying down the statute for executive agencies to be entrusted with certain tasks in the management of Community programmes, [2002] OJ L011.

[30] See eg with regard to the European Plant Varieties Office, Case C-38/09 P *Schräder v CPVO* [2010]ECR I-3209, para 77 and Case C-534/10 P *Brookfield New Zealand v CPVO and* [2012] ECLI:EU:C:2012:813, para 50. For other policy areas see eg Case C-281/10 P *PepsiCo*[2011] ECR I-10153, para 67; Joined cases C-101 and 102/11 P *Neuman and Galdeano* [2012] ECLI:EU:C:2012:641, para 41; Case T-145/08 *Atlas Transport v OHIM* [2011] ECR II-2073, para 69, 70.

[31] This was eg in Case C-61/15 P *Heli-Flight v European Aviation Safety Agency (EASA)* [2016] ECLI:EU:C:2016:59, para 101; Case C-270/12 *UK v EP and Council (ESMA Short Selling)* [2014] ECLI:EU:C:2014:18, paras 45–47 and 54; Case T-187/06 *Schräder v Community Plant Variety Office (CPVO)* [2008] ECR II-3151, confirmed on appeal in Case C-38/09 P *Schräder v Community Plant Variety Office (CPVO)* [2010] ECR I-3209.

elements and may not leave them to other forms of decision making such as an AI tool embedded in an ADM system to (implicitly or explicitly) take balancing decisions concerning basic values.

The underlying reasons for such limitations of delegation of discretion are highly relevant in the context of delegation of powers to be conducted with the help of ADM systems. Principal–agent theories discussing delegation relations often point to the difficulties for a principal, the delegator, of holding the agent, the recipient of delegation, to account due to information asymmetries. This is especially true in the context of machine learning technology often underpinning AI systems. It has been argued that informational asymmetries make the control essentially impossible 'if the logic underpinning a machine-generated decision is based on dynamic learning processes employed by various forms of machine learning algorithms'.[32] The reason for the impediment of meaningful human oversight and intervention then results from the substantive informational advantages and ADM system may have over a human operator.[33] Such advantage arises from the amount of information which can be processed automatically and the speed by which this takes place as well as from the powerful possibilities of machines to calculate correlations, not immediately apparent to the human. Such information asymmetries are particularly relevant in the discussion of possibilities of human oversight and review from the point of a delegating body too.

These factors bring back the question of transparency requirements in an act delegating powers to be exercised by the administration. Transparency would be ensured both with respect to the access and use of data as well as its processing in the ADM system. Factors necessary for transparency therefore include information-related aspects of decision-making. This covers the sources of input of information for decision-making to be used by the ADM program. It then also extends to the criteria used for weighting and balancing of input sources taken into account in a decision-making procedure. The procedural steps and phases that the ADM program is designed to assist or replace must illustrate the chosen criteria for decision-making. Therefore transparency is necessary to both the informational input, the selection of information going into a specific decision-making process, as well as the further processing of this information, the weight which is given to specific information points, and the choices made as to their use.

Responsibility for information use and balancing must also extend to responsibility for the data sources and decision-making taking place using them basis. The reason is that ADM systems in EU administrative law are mostly built on complex

[32] Karen Yeung, 'Why Worry about Decision-Making by Machine?' in Karen Yeung and Martin Lodge (eds), *Algorithmic Regulation* (OUP 2019) 24, 41, <https://www-oxfordscholarship-com.eui.idm.oclc.org/view/10.1093/oso/9780198838494.001.0001/oso-9780198838494-chapter-2>; Emre Bayamlioglu, 'Contesting Automated Decisions: A View of Transparency Implications' (2018) 4 European Data Protection Law Review 433–36, 434.

[33] Yeung (n 32) 41; Bayamlioglu (n 32).

databases issuing from both Member State and EU bodies. ADM systems are used to link various actors via granting access and processing data from large-scale databases. EU policies, for example the Commission's draft interoperability act, intends to pursue this approach across policy areas.[34] Current examples for specific multi-layered data collections feeding into decision-making both by EU bodies and by national authorities can be found in the fields of food and feed safety, medicinal products, and general product safety as well as in the EU's area of freedom, security and justice (AFSJ). For example in the Schengen Information System (SIS II),[35] the principle of interoperability requires interconnectivity of data collections and thereby enlarges the 'data lake' available to processing by ADM technology.[36] The AFSJ's Electronic Travel Information and Authorisation System (ETIAS)[37] and the PNR[38] system is becoming linked with interoperability functions, allowing for searches taking place within these databases to be enriched with data from other interconnected databases.[39]

Linking various administrative levels therefore often takes place by creating joint databases on which automated administrative procedures are built. This requires careful design not just of the software used for the ADM but also identifying responsibilities for their use and maintenance. The reason is that holding actors to account in the multilevel reality of implementation of EU law is thus often linked to the identification of responsibility of different actors in joint

[34] Commission, 'Proposal for a Regulation of the EP and the Council laying down measures for a high level of public sector interoperability across the Union (Interoperable Europe Act)' COM(2022) 720 final.

[35] A large-scale information system for border management in operation in all EU Member States (with the exception of Ireland and Cyprus) and four associated countries (Switzerland, Norway, Liechtenstein, and Iceland) based on Regulations (EU) 2018/1860-1862, [2018]OJ 2018 L 312/1, 14, and 56. Other large-scale information systems exist for example in the areas regulating risk in food, animal feed, plant health (see Commission Implementing Regulation (EU) 2019/1715, [2019]OJ 2019 L 261/37, human and veterinary medicine products (see with further references Demková (n 9).

[36] Teresa Quintel, 'Connecting Personal Data of Third Country Nationals: Interoperability of EU Databases in the Light of the CJEU's Case Law on Data Retention' 002–2018 University of Luxembourg Law Working Paper Series (2018) <https://ssrn.com/abstract=3132506> or <http://dx.doi.org/10.2139/ssrn.3132506>.

[37] Regulation (EU) 2018/1240 of the European Parliament and of the Council of 12 September 2018 establishing a European Travel Information and Authorisation System (ETIAS) and amending Regulations (EU) No 1077/2011, (EU) No 515/2014, (EU) 2016/399, (EU) 2016/1624, and (EU) 2017/2226, [2018] OJ L236, 1–71, pursuant to which visa-free Third Country Nationals (TCNs) have to apply for an electronic authorization in order for the risk they pose to be assessed in advance.

[38] Directive (EU) 2016/681 of the European Parliament and of the Council of 27 April 2016 on the use of passenger name record (PNR) data for the prevention, detection, investigation and prosecution of terrorist offences and serious crime, [2016] OJ L119, 132–49.

[39] For example, travel, communications, and banking and finance institutions face certain data retention obligations in order to allow for subsequent access of data by public authorities. See Joined Cases C-203/15 and C-698/15 *Tele2 Sverige AB v Post-och telestyrelsen* [2016] ECLI:EU:C:2016:970; Case C-698/15 *Secretary of State for the Home Department v Tom Watson, Peter Brice, Geoffrey Lewis* [2016] ECLI:EU:C:2016:970; Case C-511-520/18 *La Quadrature du Net* [2020] ECLI:EU:C:2020:791. Niovi Vavoula, 'Consultation of EU Immigration Databases for Law Enforcement Purposes: A Privacy and Data Protection Assessment' (2022) 22(2) European Journal of Migration and Law 139–77, 145–46.

or composite multi-jurisdictional decision-making procedures.[40] This in turn requires identifying who is responsible for which element of a decision-making procedure, including the question of which ADM system is using which set of information in which way.

Such requirements of pre-establishing in an anticipatory manner procedural elements enhances not only procedural transparency but it also enhances the conditions of accountability. Conceptually this has been an underlying element of delegation theory, which has identified informational asymmetries as one of the central elements of a delegation structure, making control of delegated powers difficult. Obscurity in the use and the computation of information under the logic underpinning 'dynamic learning processes employed by various forms of machine learning algorithms'[41] thus complicates conditions for accountability of an agent in a principal–agent relation.

IV. Non-delegation principles in the TFEU

The discussion on delegation-related principles in EU law shows that tools capable of predetermining ADM must be in place. These tools are both legislative and administrative rule-making. However, software programming an ADM system may *de facto* serve the same purpose as administrative rule-making procedures in that it may specify, like administrative rule-making, legislative policy objectives and it will structure procedural steps undertaken in order to translate policy choices into specific decision-making. EU law, however, does define limits to the possibilities of delegation of administrative rule-making powers. The 'hard-core' of non-delegable content of 'essential' elements of formal EU legislation is established in in Article 290(1) TFEU, which requires that EU legislation contain all essential elements of a policy decision which will include the 'objectives, content, scope and duration' of a delegation of powers. This is an explicit limitation laid down for legislation empowering the Commission to adopt delegated acts but it is arguably a general standard in EU law for the identification of matters to be addressed in legislation as opposed to be capable of delegation to executive action. It is thus relevant also for delegation in the context of ADM-based decision-making.

Accordingly, the CJEU identified—in line with the values expressed in Article 290 TFEU—that 'legislation must, in particular, indicate in what circumstances and under which conditions'[42] certain measures interfering with or limiting

[40] Simona Demková and Teresa Quintel, 'Allocation of Responsibilities in Interoperable Information Exchanges: Effective Review Compromised?' (2020) 1 Cahiers Jean Monnet 589.

[41] Yeung (n 32) 24; Bayamlioglu (n 32).

[42] Case C-401/19 *Republic of Poland v European Parliament and Council of the European Union* [2022] ECLI:EU:C:2022:297, para 67. Therein, the CJEU did not mention the formulation of art 290 TFEU but arguably the conceptual similarities in thought are clear.

general principles of EU law will be possible. In other words, essential proportionality criteria must be contained in the enabling legislation to be implemented by the recipient of the delegation of rule-making powers—also when the exercise of such powers is going to be conducted with ADM systems.

This approach is linked to *Opinion 1/15* on the transfer for automated processing of air passenger data to Canada in which the CJEU established the minimum safeguards approach according to which 'the legislation in question which entails the interference must lay down clear and precise rules governing the scope and application of the measure in question and imposing minimum safeguards'.[43] Accordingly, in *Poland IP* the CJEU reiterated that 'the act which permits the interference with those rights must itself define the scope of the limitation on the exercise of the right concerned'.[44] Not surprisingly, requirements identified as legislative in nature under the criteria listed in Article 290 TFEU merge with those discussed above arising from Article 52(1) of the CFR. The legality of the possible interference with rights by automated analyses of data, 'essentially depends on the pre-established models and criteria and on the databases on which that type of data processing is based'.[45]

Various early use cases of complex ADM systems might require review under these criteria. For example, where the Commission has regulated satellite-based monitoring of EU agriculture subsidies by a Commission Implementing Regulation of 2018,[46] it will be expected that the details of the balancing of substantive and procedural rights of individuals will be detailed in the implementing regulation and not only in software tools driving the AI systems used for the analysis of the satellite pictures and the assessment of possible subsidy fraud.[47] Similarly, with regard to the EU's Entry and Exit System (EES), a biometric system being developed in the AFSJ field enabling simultaneous search and comparison of biometric data in various information systems[48] and ensuring interoperability of the shared biometric matching service (sBMS), these functions are foreseen and regulated within the enabling regulations.[49] However, the type of analysis of these data and

[43] Opinion 1/15 *EU-Canada PNR Agreement* [2017] EU:C:2017:592, paras 139–141.

[44] Case C-401/19 *Republic of Poland v European Parliament and Council of the European Union* [2022] ECLI:EU:C:2022:297, para 64; Case C-311/18 *Facebook Ireland and Schrems* [2020] EU:C:2020:559, para 175.

[45] Opinion 1/15 *EU-Canada PNR Agreement* [2017] EU:C:2017:592, para 172.

[46] Commission Implementing Regulation (EU) 2018/746 of 18 May 2018 amending Implementing Regulation (EU) No 809/2014 as regards modification of single applications and payment claims and checks. See especially the new art 40a on checks by monitoring.

[47] For information on this first use case, see the project's website <http://esa-sen4cap.org>, as well as the Special Report 04/2020 <https://op.europa.eu/webpub/eca/special-reports/new-tech-in-agri-monitoring-4-2020/en/> of the European Court of Auditors, which evaluates it positively and recommends its promotion.

[48] Eu-LISA, Call for Tender—Framework contract for implementation and maintenance in working order of the biometrics part of the Entry Exit System and future Shared Biometrics Matching System, LISA/2019/RP/05 EES BMS and sBMS, Executive Summary, 7–8.

[49] For example, art 12(1) of Regulation (EU) 2019/817 of the European Parliament and of the Council of 20 May 2019 on establishing a framework for interoperability between EU information

the criteria for their processing would need to be addressed in a legal act delegating such powers to the Commission or an EU agency.

The requirements concerning the administrative rule-making and, specifically, the review thereof was further developed in *La Quadrature du Net* where the CJEU, without mentioning criteria of delegation, held that 'it is essential that the *decision authorising automated analysis* be subject to effective review, either by a court or by an independent administrative body whose decision is binding'.[50] This indicates a requirement that there be not only a possibility of submitting the actual individual decision-making based on ADM to judicial review but also to submit the criteria involved in the decision making and the procedure to judicial review.

V. Obligations of anticipatory assessments and ongoing supervision

Under the *Meroni* doctrine, a public body sub-delegating its powers to another body such as a private company must be obliged to supervise the exercise of powers by the recipient of the delegation.

This necessity of continuous control and review is well anchored in public law. For example, generally applicable administrative law decisions, which have an effect similar to rule-making, must be subject to continuous and regular review and to periodic checks as a precondition for their continuous validity.[51] The CJEU has found ongoing supervision to be a legal requirement for certain types of data-related decisions, for example in *Schrems I*.[52] There the Commission was requested to regularly review the preconditions of its decision to conferral on a non-EU country the status of having an adequate level of protection of data to take corrective actions where necessary. Such checks are required regularly and whenever evidence gives rise to a doubt in that regard.[53]

This same approach has been developed by the CJEU in the *Belgian PNR* case[54] to become a particular requirement where ADM systems with a potential impact

systems in the field of borders and visa [2019] OJ L135/27, and Regulation (EU) 2019/818 of the European Parliament and of the Council of 20 May 2019 on establishing a framework for interoperability between EU information systems in the field of police and judicial cooperation, asylum and migration [2019] OJ L135/85.

[50] Case C-511-520/18 *La Quadrature du Net* [2020] ECLI:EU:C:2020:791, para 179 (emphasis added). The paragraph continues to state that 'the aim of that review being to verify that a situation justifying that measure exists and that the conditions and safeguards that must be laid down are observed'.

[51] As to this obligation periodic review as a precondition of validity and whether a decision once taken in the past is 'still factually and legally justified' see Case C-362/14 *Schrems v DPC (Schrems I)* [2015] ECLI:EU:C:2015:650, para 76.

[52] ibid.

[53] ibid.

[54] Case C-817/19 *Ligue des droits humains v Conseil des ministres (Belgian PNR)* [2022] ECLI:EU:C:2022:491.

on fundamental rights are deployed. In those cases, 'review must take into account the experience acquired in the context of the application of pre-determined criteria, in order to reduce, as much as possible, the number of "false positives"' and, thereby, contribute to the strictly necessary nature of the application of those criteria.'[55]

Accordingly, in *La Quadrature du Net* the CJEU stated that in order to ensure that in practice ADM technology and the 'databases used' comply with the conditions under EU law, 'a regular re-examination should be undertaken to ensure that those pre-established models and criteria and the databases used are reliable and up to date'.[56] It thus falls to the Union legislator to frame the relationship between the Union interest in using databases, and regulate their quality, the participation of private actors in establishing and maintaining databases, and public bodies' supervision of such activities.

The requirement of regular review and supervision of a system has become part of Article 21 of the Commission's draft AI Act concerning the ongoing supervision of working with high-risk AI systems.[57] This is also the practice in certain policy fields. For example, the EU's EES contains biometric information about individuals and will be supported by an ADM system based on machine learning algorithms.[58] An external contractor running this system will be submitted to regular (at least monthly) monitoring of the performance of the system to be carried out by eu-LISA.[59] Arguably, this obligation to monitor must not only take place against certain performance indicators but also to ensure that rights and principles of EU law more generally are complied with in terms of the production of results of the AI system.

Importantly, in my view, is that the CJEU has acknowledged the necessity that the legal basis for an ADM system would thus also have to address supervision requirements concerning data quality. In EU law, most large-scale data collections result from composite structures feeding into the approach to collecting data, and

[55] See eg Case C-817/19 *Ligue des droits humains v Conseil des ministres (Belgian PNR)* [2022] ECLI:EU:C:2022:491, para 201 with reference by analogy also to Case C-140/20, *Commissioner of An Garda Síochána and Others* [2022] EU:C:2022:258, para 82.

[56] Case C-511-520/18 *La Quadrature du Net* [2020] ECLI:EU:C:2020:791, para 182 with reference to Opinion 1/15 *EU-Canada PNR Agreement* [2017] EU:C:2017:592, paras 173, 174.

[57] Art 21 of the Commission's 'Proposal for a Regulation of the EP and the Council laying down harmonised rules on Artificial Intelligence (Artificial Intelligence Act)' COM (2021) 206 final states that '[p]roviders of high-risk AI systems which consider or have reason to consider that a high-risk AI system which they have placed on the market or put into service is not in conformity with this Regulation shall immediately take the necessary corrective actions to bring that system into conformity, to withdraw it or to recall it, as appropriate'.

[58] Eu-LISA, Call for Tender—Framework contract for implementation and maintenance in working order of the biometrics part of the Entry Exit System and future Shared Biometrics Matching System, LISA/2019/RP/05 EES BMS and sBMS, Executive Summary, 7–8.

[59] For the EES see the Annex of the Commission Implementing Decision (EU) 2019/329 of 25 February 2019 laying down the specifications for the quality, resolution and use of fingerprints and facial image for biometric verification and identification in the Entry/Exit System (EES) [2019] OJ L57/18.

the interoperability paradigm also raises challenges concerning the quality and accuracy of data input into decision-making—which has in turn effects on accountability in ADM procedures based on such data.[60] Data stemming from various levels and sources (EU and Member State, public and private) is collected and processed. In view of this being one of the most crucial aspects of the successful use of ADM and a topic of high concern for the exercise of individual rights, the use of ADM requires supervision of the quality of data that is used.[61]

The concern of quality control is also of relevance due to the links between public and private data collections that form the basis for ADM in specific policy areas. Information quality is not just a matter of maintaining up-to-date and correct data in public databases but also the control of information imported/accessed from private actors. This consideration is reflected in Article 10(3) of the Commission's draft AI Act (concerning what the draft refers to as 'high-risk AI systems')[62] under which datasets must meet certain quality criteria in that they 'shall be relevant, representative, free of errors and complete' and shall have 'the appropriate statistical properties'. In this context, it is important to note that the sensitivity surrounding data quality—although long a matter of concern in data protection—is under-represented in current draft legislative proposals concerning data. The Commission's draft regulation, the so-called Interoperable Europe Act, for example, does not concern itself with criteria on data quality.[63]

Ongoing supervision, by now established as a requirement in various contexts and forms, could be made a general requirement of the use of ADM systems. Similarly, suggestions exist to introduce anticipatory impact assessments prior to the deployment of ADM systems. Practically speaking, such impact assessment would need to be undertaken on the level of administrative rule-making deciding the conditions of use and deployment of the ADM system. A general impact

[60] For example, arts 17, 18 EDPR requires that data must be correct and up to date. This requires access to data, and its possible rectification is key in this context. For case law see also Opinion 1/15 *EU-Canada PNR Agreement* [2017] EU:C:2017:592, para 172: 'Similarly, it should be stated that the databases with which the PNR data is cross-checked must be reliable, up to date and limited to databases used by Canada in relation to the fight against terrorism and serious transnational crime.' Although this CJEU statement in Opinion 1/15 relates predominantly to Canadian data cross-referenced to EU PNR data, this is a clear statement regarding the necessity of upholding data quality; see generally on data quality concepts Lena-Sophie Deißler, *Gewährleistung von Informationsqualität in europäischen Informationssystemen* (Nomos 2018).

[61] See eg the EU efforts in standardizing the data quality requirements in the context of biometric data collection and storing in EU AFSJ systems: Commission Implementing Decision (EU) 2020/2165 of 9 December 2020 on laying down rules for the application of Regulation (EU) 2018/1861 of the European Parliament and of the Council as regards the minimum data quality standards and technical specifications for entering photographs and dactyloscopic data in the Schengen Information System (SIS) in the field of border checks and return [2020] OJ L431/61 and Commission Implementing Decision (EU) 2021/31 of 13 January 2021 on laying down rules for the application of Regulation (EU) 2018/1862 as regards the minimum data quality standards and technical specifications for entering photographs and dactyloscopic data in the [SIS] in the field of police cooperation and judicial cooperation in criminal matters [2021] OJ L15/1.

[62] Artificial Intelligence Act Proposal of 21 April 2021.

[63] See eg Interoperable Europe Act Proposal of 18 November 2022.

assessment requirement for administrative rule-making is not so far accepted by EU law.[64] By contrast, calls for a general obligation of impact assessment for administrative rule-making have been made by the Research Network for European Administrative Law (ReNEUAL) model rules on administrative procedure.[65] In line with this, a detailed suggestion for an ADM-related impact assessment was developed by a group of scholars under the direction of the European Law Institute for algorithmic decision-making systems used by public administration.[66] In terms of AI regulation, the draft AI act takes up this concept by requiring systemic quality checks for certain forms of high-risk AI through 'conformity assessment procedures'.[67] According to this draft, the conformity of the AI system either with pre-established standards or with the rules of the AI Act will be reviewed prior to the implementation of the AI system. Review of the system could also be undertaken by showing that the system is compliant with standards accepted in the Union[68] which should make the impact assessment less burdensome by introducing a presumption of conformity of an AI system with provisions of the AI Act.

Whether, additionally, compliance with common technical specifications—to be adopted by the Commission under Article 41 of the AI Act—will be regarded to be sufficient remains to be seen.[69] One concern is that there are no compliance mechanisms or real control possibilities to assess the real-life performance of AI systems foreseen in the Commission's draft. Additionally, standard setting shows the type of issues that might give cause for concern also in terms of the creation of ADM code by private actors or by public–private partnerships: where Union institutions retreat and leave it to private and semi-private standardization bodies to fill a legal void, the procedural legitimacy of such standard setting becomes an issue of public interest. This might be all the more relevant in the case of standards created not within the EU, under known but imperfect procedures, but in international bodies or organizations as well as ad hoc regulatory bodies.[70]

[64] See point 13 of the Inter-institutional Agreement between the European Parliament, the Council of the European Union and the European Commission on Better Law-Making of 13 April 2016 [2016] OJ L123/1 defining the scope of impact assessments as follows: 'The Commission will carry out impact assessments of its legislative and non-legislative initiatives, delegated acts and implementing measures which are expected to have significant economic, environmental or social impacts. The initiatives included in the Commission Work Programme or in the joint declaration will, as a general rule, be accompanied by an impact assessment.' The approach to conduct ADM impact assessment would thus differ and require a much more granular approach.

[65] See art II-3(1)(b) of the model rules.

[66] European Law Institute (ELI), Model Rules on Impact Assessment of Algorithmic Decision-Making Systems Used by Public Administration, Report of the European Law Institute <https://www.europeanlawinstitute.eu/projects-publications/completed-projects-old/ai-and-public-administration/> accessed 12 April 2022.

[67] Arts 19 and 43 of the Artificial Intelligence Act Proposal of 21 April 2021.

[68] See art 40 of the Artificial Intelligence Act Proposal of 21 April 2021.

[69] For a first discussion see eg Mark McFadden and others, 'Harmonising Artificial Intelligence' (2021) Oxford Information Labs Working Paper 5 <https://www.oii.ox.ac.uk/news-events/reports/harmonising-artificial-intelligence/>.

[70] See further discussion eg Herwig CH Hofmann, 'Dealing with Trans-Territorial Executive Rule-Making' (2013) 78 Missouri Law Review 423–42.

Additionally, similar to ADM computer code, standards are generally not accessible to the public. In line with the argument that the notion of 'law' is conceptually linked to its accessibility,[71] already discussed in the context of Article 52(1) of the CFR, in order for a norm to be applicable to the obligations imposed upon or to be held against an individual, those individuals must be able to discern from freely available and officially published texts which limitations to their rights and freedoms they might be asked to endure. Therefore, it appears doubtful whether certification of inaccessible computer code with possibly inaccessible standards will be sufficient to provide for the necessary predetermination of limitations to rights.

B. An outlook on cyber-delegation in the EU regulatory reality

Anticipatory tools to ensure accountability are highly relevant in terms of the use of cyber delegation and the use of ADM in administrative law. The case law of the CJEU in this matter is in its early days but so far the Court has adopted an approach requiring predefinition of criteria of ADM procedures and ongoing control of results, especially when the latter are relevant in terms of decisions concerning the limitation of fundamental rights. The latter are based on general requirements for the delegation of powers in the context of limits to legislative delegation to the executive branch of powers and limitations of fundamental rights (Article 52(1) CFR) adapted for the reality of ADM. Further, the case law has begun to apply notions of limitations to the delegation of powers developed since the seminal *Meroni* case. These principles contain many guidelines on criteria for the delegation of powers in the context of ADM. Therefore central elements of decision-making need to be contained in law either in legislative acts or in forms of regulatory rule-making. These will regulate interfaces between technology and the human elements of decision-making as well as addressing the underlying issue of the quality of databases on which ADM systems rely. The basic norms will also have to identify documentation requirements in order to make subsequent accountability tools possible. This chapter argues that to ensure accountability in the context of cyber delegation, conditions of delegation need to be clearly defined, more so than in purely terms of human decision-making. In *La Quadrature du Net* the CJEU defines the aim of an act authorizing ADM to ensure that review mechanisms may 'verify that a situation justifying that measure exists and that the conditions and safeguards that must be laid down are observed'.[72]

This includes the requirement that an act allowing for cyber delegation contains conditions and safeguards for the compliance with higher-ranking EU law including general principles of EU law. The reason why a legal act, empowering

[71] Case C-345/06 *Heinrich* [2009] ECR I-1659, paras 41–47 and 64–66.
[72] Case C-511-520/18 *La Quadrature du Net* [2020] ECLI:EU:C:2020:791, para 179.

ADM systems, needs to be more detailed also arises from the fact that ADM programming software is, under the current system of judicial review, not in itself a regulatory act subject to an action for annulment, nor can it be subject for that purpose to indirect review under Article 277 TFEU since computer code in and of itself is not an act of EU institutions, bodies, or agencies. Therefore, accountability requires that individual decisions taken with the help of ADM systems are reviewed for their compliance with predefined norms, established on the basis of predefined procedural requirements such as impact assessments, and they must comply with obligations of supervision. These requirements must be added to the review of whether the right consequences have been drawn from the informational input which was taken into account in a decision-making under principles of the duty of care. Documentation of the processing operations including the information taken into account and its balancing in the individual decision are thus key to the possibilities of holding decision making using ADM to account against predefined criteria.

3

Algorithms, Automation, and Administrative Procedure at EU Level

*Oriol Mir**

A. Introduction

The automation of administrative action is not a new phenomenon. In his 1966 doctoral thesis Luhmann already predicted the great impact it would have on administrative organization,[1] and the German Federal Administrative Procedure Act devoted some relevant provisions to it in its initial version of 1976.[2]

The great interest in its legal regulation today is due to two main factors. The first, of course, is the significant technological development that has taken place in recent years in the field of computing, which has greatly boosted automation capacities in both the public and private sectors, and has made possible the qualitative leap that machine learning algorithms represent.

The second factor, linked to the previous one, is the risks associated with this quantitative and qualitative change, which have already materialized in numerous episodes of administrative malfunctioning. Such episodes have occurred both in Europe[3] and, above all, in the United States,[4] whose agencies have relied heavily

* I sincerely thank the participants of the INDIGO project workshop held at the University of Freiburg on 29–30 September 2022 for their valuable contributions to an earlier version of this chapter which was prepared in the framework of the research project PCI2020-112207/AEI/10.13039/501100011033. Subsequent to the drafting of this chapter, the European Parliament has adopted important amendments to the proposed AI Act (see n 6) which incorporate some of the suggestions made in section D, such as the obligation to carry out an impact assessment prior to the use of high-risk systems or to inform persons who may be affected by such use. For more details, see my paper 'The Impact of the AI Act on Public Authorities and on Administrative Procedures' (2023) 4 *CERIDAP* 238, 243ff. These amendments have been included in the finally adopted version of the AI act, albeit with considerable changes.

[1] Niklas Luhmann, *Recht und Automation in der öffentlichen Verwaltung* (Duncker & Humblot 1966).

[2] Verwaltungsverfahrensgesetz (VwVfG) 1976, §§ 28(2)4, 37(4), and 39(2)3.

[3] Particularly well known is the case of the Dutch SyRI system for the detection of benefit fraud, which was declared illegal by the District Court of The Hague by judgment of 5 May 2020 (*Federation of Dutch Trade Unions v The State of the Netherlands* ECLI:NL:RBDHA:2020:1878 <https://uitspraken.rechtspraak.nl/inziendocument?id=ECLI:NL:RBDHA:2020:1878> accessed 31 August 2022). See 'How Dutch Activists Got an Invasive Fraud Detection Algorithm Banned' (Algorithm Watch, 6 April 2020) <https://algorithmwatch.org/en/story/syri-netherlands-algorithm/> accessed 31 August 2022.

[4] See the many cases documented by Danielle Keats Citron, 'Technological Due Process' (2008) 85 Washington Law Review 1249, 1256ff, 1267ff; Ryan Calo and Danielle Keats Citron, 'The Automated Administrative State: A Crisis of Legitimacy' (2021) 70 Emory Law Journal 797, 799ff, 818ff, mainly involving state agencies.

Oriol Mir, *Algorithms, Automation, and Administrative Procedure at EU Level* In: *Governance of Automated Decision-Making and EU Law*. Edited by: Herwig C.H. Hofmann and Felix Pflücke, Oxford University Press.
 DOI: 10.1093/9780198919575.003.0003

on automation, often to reduce personnel costs. They have often led to massive and hard-to-detect errors in the reduction of social benefits for disadvantaged groups. The proliferation of these episodes has even called into question the very legitimacy of the administrative state.[5]

This chapter aims to underline the important contribution of the classical institution of administrative procedure to the current debate on algorithmic accountability in the public sector. It will argue that the administrative procedure constitutes an important instrument to achieve an adequate development of automation and artificial intelligence (AI) in administrative decision-making, extracting its great potential without undermining the rights of the citizens concerned.

Special attention will be paid to the EU's own administration (consisting mainly of the Commission and the European agencies), in line with the case study that have been carried out in recent months and which are summarized in the annex. The chapter will explore the possibilities for improving the Proposal for a Regulation on Artificial Intelligence (AI Act) currently under discussion by the EU legislator,[6] with some suggestions that could be incorporated into a new specific Chapter on the use of advanced algorithms by the EU administration.

B. The central role of administrative procedure in the analogue and in the digital administration

Administrative procedure has been a basic guarantee of the rule of law in the context of analogue administration and should continue to be so in the context of digital administration, both in the adoption of single-case decisions and administrative rules.

I. Single-case decisions

As is well known, administrative authorities on both sides of the Atlantic have been required for decades to observe a series of procedural formalities and guarantees before adopting decisions that may have relevant legal effects on private citizens and legal persons, such as the imposition of penalties and prohibitions, the granting and withdrawal of authorizations and subsidies, the expropriation of property for reasons of public interest, etc. (single-case decisions). In the United

[5] Calo and Citron (n 4) passim.

[6] European Commission, Proposal for a Regulation of the European Parliament and the Council laying down harmonised rules on Artificial Intelligence (Artificial Intelligence Act) of 21.4.2021, COM(2021) 206 final, 2021/0106 (COD).

States, as in most EU countries, there are even general Administrative Procedure Acts that codify its guiding principles.

EU law has reinforced the importance of administrative procedure for the adoption of single-case decisions in two main ways: on the one hand, through the adoption of a large number of sectoral secondary legislation imposing detailed procedures on both the EU administration and the Member States' administrations (procedures which often have a national and a EU phase—composite procedures); and on the other hand, through the general principles of EU law elaborated over the years by the Court of Justice, which must also be observed by both the EU administration and the Member States' administrations when they implement EU law.[7] Some of these principles have been enshrined at the highest normative level as part of the fundamental right to good administration in Article 41 of the Charter of Fundamental Rights of the EU (CFR). Due to their weight and tradition, the guarantees contained in paragraph 2 of this provision stand out in particular: the *right of the interested parties to be heard*, their *right of access to the file*, and the duty of the administration to *give reasons* for its decisions. Of particular importance in the case law of the Court of Justice is also the *duty of care*, which requires a thorough and impartial investigation and examination of all the relevant elements of the case, including those that are favourable to the interested parties. This duty has been established by the Court as a general principle of EU law as it is inherent in the principle of good administration.[8]

The special normative status of the general principles of EU law and Article 41 CFR means that these procedural safeguards must be observed by any EU or national administrative authority that intends to automate the adoption of decisions with legal effects on specific persons in the implementation of EU law. Moreover, given their constitutional status, even the legislators of the EU and the Member States must respect them when they authorize such automation.

These safeguards are essential to avoid the risks of malfunctioning of the automated systems referred to above. This has also been understood by the US literature, which has underlined the importance of scrupulously observing the *due process* guarantees derived from Amendments V and XIV of the US Constitution, as well as the more specific procedural rules contained in the Federal Administrative Procedure Act of 1946 (US APA) and its state counterparts.[9]

[7] Diana-Urania Galetta and others, 'The General Principles of EU Administrative Procedural Law. An In-Depth Analysis' (2015) 5 Rivista italiana di diritto pubblico comunitario 1421.

[8] Case C-337/15 P *European Ombudsman v Claire Staelen* [2017] ECLI:EU:C:2017:256, paras 34ff.

[9] Citron (n 4) 1278ff; Deirdre K Mulligan and Kenneth A Bamberger, 'Procurement as Policy: Administrative Process for Machine Learning' (2019) 34 Berkeley Technology Law Journal 773, 801ff, both formulating proposals to ensure compliance with due process requirements in the case of automated or semi-automated decisions.

The use cases of machine learning algorithms by the EU administration that have been identified in the framework of the case study carried out confirm this statement.

In the case of the use of satellite monitoring tools for European crops,[10] the duty of care obliges the administration to check *ex officio*—through a human review of the images or, where appropriate, a field inspection—the alerts on possible non-compliance with subsidy regulations issued by the system, and the farmers' right to be heard enables them to point out and refute any errors that may occur before a previously granted subsidy is revoked.

In the case of the registration of trademarks by the European Union Intellectual Property Office (EUIPO),[11] the aforementioned duty of care obliges the official or officials deciding on the registration to review the proposal formulated by the AI system in the light of the arguments invoked by the applicant and the party opposing the registration applied for. In turn, the duty to state reasons obliges those officials to give reasons for their decision and makes it possible for the applicant or the opponent to challenge the decision before the Boards of Appeal of EUIPO and, where appropriate, before the General Court of the European Union.

Finally, the examination of the information systems operated by eu-LISA[12] illustrates how the European Travel Information and Authorisation System (ETIAS) Regulation takes into account these procedural safeguards, for example by obliging Frontex to verify that no error has occurred when the system produces a hit that prevents the automatic granting of authorization to travel to a territory of the Union by obliging the competent national authority to give reasons for the refusal of such authorization and by requiring that all operations carried out by the automated system be recorded in the application file.

II. Administrative rule-making

Administrative procedure and its guarantees are not only required with respect to the adoption of single-case decisions endowed with legal effects. In many legal systems there is also a more or less detailed regulation of the procedure that an administration must follow in order to pass general-abstract rules that develop statutory provisions.

The paradigmatic case is that of the US APA, which establishes a notice-and-comment procedure that has been very influential and which allows for the participation of citizens and affected sectors during the drafting of rules by federal

[10] See Annex, case 1.
[11] See Annex, case 3.
[12] See Annex, case 4.

agencies. A provision equivalent to Article 41 CFR, that imposes general procedural obligations on national administrations when they adopt rules implementing EU law, does not exist. Nor are there any provisions of primary or secondary legislation that impose such requirements on the Commission, beyond the obligations to consult the European Parliament, the Council, and the Member States that arise from Articles 290 and 291 of the Treaty on the Functioning of the European Union (TFEU) and the comitology regulation.[13] However, for years now the Commission has observed remarkable procedural rules when drafting its legislative proposals and (only) some delegated and implementing acts. These include extensive *consultation* of the public and the sectors concerned, and *ex-ante* and *ex-post assessment* of the various economic, social, and environmental impacts of the proposed and adopted rules.[14] It has formally committed to this in the 2016 Interinstitutional Agreement on Better Law-Making.[15]

Such procedural steps may also help to detect errors that occur as a consequence of the use of algorithmic systems at some point in the process of gestation of new administrative rules. The case study of the partial automation of the Systematic Review process of the existing scientific literature undertaken by the European Food Safety Authority (EFSA) when issuing a scientific opinion assessing a given risk can be mentioned here.[16] When such a systematic review is carried out in the framework of a rule-making procedure (eg to decide whether or not to ban the food use of a certain substance), the fact that the scientific opinion is integrated into the documentation submitted for public consultation makes it easier to detect any omissions it may contain (such as previous relevant scientific papers that have not been considered in its risk assessment due to an error in the screening of the literature carried out by the algorithm).

C. Relevant distinctions regarding the use of algorithms within administrative procedures

When it comes to assessing the legal requirements of the use of algorithms within procedures governed by EU law, it is useful to make further distinctions beyond the differentiation between single-case decision-making and administrative rule-making.

[13] European Parliament and Council Regulation (EU) 182/2011 of 16 February 2011 laying down the rules and general principles concerning mechanisms for control by Member States of the Commission's exercise of implementing powers [2011] OJ L55/13.

[14] 'Better Regulation: Why and how' <https://ec.europa.eu/info/law/law-making-process/planning-and-proposing-law/better-regulation-why-and-how_en> accessed 31 August 2022.

[15] Interinstitutional Agreement of 13 April 2016 between the European Parliament, the Council of the European Union and the European Commission on Better Law-Making [2016] OJ L123/1.

[16] See Annex, case 2.

I. Distinction according to the stage of the procedure where the algorithm is used and its influence on the final decision

The legal impact of the use of algorithms varies depending on the stage of the procedure at which it takes place and its influence on the content of the final decision. Automating the acknowledgement of receipt sent to the applicant is obviously not the same as automating the adoption of the final decision on the application. Nor is automating the imposition of penalties or the revocation of social benefits the same as using algorithms—as is often done—to identify possible infringements and frauds on which to launch investigations and proceedings. In general, automated actions should not be subject to requirements that the same actions should not be subject to when carried out by humans.[17]

This is related to the different degrees of automation that can occur in a given procedure and its influence on the final decision. Thus, a distinction can be made between algorithmic systems that merely provide an additional input to the human who must decide (input), those that propose a default decision that the human can correct (default), and those that adopt the decision without any human intervention (decision).[18] In the latter case, we are dealing with a fully automated procedure, while the first two are partially automated or semi-automated procedures.

As noted above and will be emphasized later, human intervention in the procedure is important and can serve to correct errors that algorithmic systems may make. But it should not be overestimated. As jurists, marked by the judicial model in which one or several people definitively resolve legal controversies, we tend to incur a certain *human bias* and to trust that the fact that it is a human who finally decides the matter will solve the problems that an algorithmic system may present. The legislator himself often incurs in this bias and provides safeguards only when the procedure is fully automated.[19] Reality shows time and again, however, that the well-known risk of *automation bias* is very real, and that it is very common for officials who resolve procedures to accept, without questioning or examining them, the proposals made by automated systems. In many of the documented cases of malfunctioning in the United States, the final decision was made by humans, who did not notice the errors of the system.[20] Therefore, as will also be discussed later,

[17] Alejandro Huergo Lora, 'Administraciones Públicas e inteligencia artificial: ¿más o menos discrecionalidad?' (2021) 96–97 El Cronista del Estado Social y Democrático de Derecho 78 (7 and 12 of the online version), giving the example of administrative actions that are not subject to the duty to state reasons and that cannot be challenged, such as, in Spain, the decision to carry out an inspection.

[18] Cary Coglianese, 'A Framework for Governmental Use of Machine Learning' [2020] Report for the Administrative Conference of the United States 1, 72–73.

[19] This is the case of the Spanish regulation (Act 40/2015 [Ley 40/2015, de 1 de octubre, de Régimen Jurídico del Sector Público], Article 41), widely criticized for this, and which provokes an administrative escape ('*huida*', '*Flucht*') towards semi-automated systems (Lorenzo Cotino Hueso, 'El nuevo reglamento de Administración electrónica, que no innova en tiempos de transformación digital' (2021) 63 Revista Catalana de Dret Públic 117, 131).

[20] Citron (n 4) 1271.

it is particularly important to take appropriate (procedural) measures to ensure the proper functioning of algorithmic systems, whether they are used in fully automated or only semi-automated procedures.

Algorithmic systems must be subject to legal control (and, in particular, as far as this is relevant here, to the guarantees inherent in the administrative procedure, such as transparency and giving reasons) whenever they contribute to determine the content of the administrative decision[21] and not only when they dictate it in an automated way. The reasoning of the decision must duly explain the use of the algorithm and the influence it has had on the decision, and both the interested parties and, where appropriate, the judge, must be able to verify that its operation has been correct and in accordance with the law.

II. Distinction according to the type of algorithm used

From the point of view of procedural requirements, it is also important to take into account the type of algorithm used by the automated system. In addition to the traditional conditional algorithms of expert systems, machine learning algorithms—and within them, deep learning algorithms based on neural networks inspired by the human brain—have developed enormously in recent years. The former operate on the basis of rules predetermined by programmers ('if–then'), while machine learning systems establish their own rules based on the correlations they infer from large amounts of data (big data) with which they have been trained.[22] In the case of deep learning, the process takes place through multiple successive layers and is particularly complex and opaque, with the programmers themselves often unable to explain why the system has suggested a particular outcome. This is why such systems are described as black boxes, and why they can be very problematic from the point of view of meeting the requirements of duly stating the reasons of administrative decisions.[23]

Giving adequate reasons is simpler when traditional conditional algorithms are used since, when well designed, they codify the legal and regulatory rules that govern the administration's actions at any given time, and which will be applied to the specific case.[24]

[21] Huergo Lora (n 17) 12.
[22] Mulligan and Bamberger (n 9) 814ff.
[23] Eduardo Gamero Casado, 'Compliance (o Cumplimiento Normativo) de desarrollos de Inteligencia Artificial para la toma de decisiones administrativas' (2021) 50 Diario La Ley 8. Coglianese (n 18) 53 downplays the giving reasons problem of machine learning algorithms.
[24] Of course, it may happen that the algorithm is poorly designed and includes rules that are contrary to existing laws. Moreover, the verification of their correct design may be technically complex and hampered by confidentiality clauses of the companies developing them. This is illustrated by the cases studied by Citron (n 4), most of which were not yet machine learning cases.

A simpler automated system based on such traditional conditional algorithms will often be preferable to an opaque machine learning system. This is the case with the ETIAS automated travel authorization system for non-EU citizens,[25] which adequately combines administrative efficiency with procedural safeguards for applicants and the necessary regulatory predetermination (by the legislator itself) of the grounds on which a negative decision may be based.[26]

Recently, in the important *Ligue des droits humains* judgment of 21 June 2022, the Court of Justice has ruled against the use of machine learning systems in the automated assessment of risks to public security that may be posed by air passengers, considering that these systems are incompatible with the requirement that such assessment be based on predetermined criteria (insofar as these systems can modify such criteria or their weighting without human intervention or review), with the necessary human review of the positive matches that the system may give and with the fundamental right to an effective judicial remedy (due to the opacity that characterizes such systems and which prevents knowledge of the reason for a positive match).[27]

III. Distinction according to the favourable or unfavourable nature of the automated decision

Automated decisions or proposals for decisions should also be distinguished according to whether they are favourable or unfavourable to the interested parties in the procedure. Automating the granting of aid or authorization is obviously not the same as automating the refusal or revocation of aid or authorization. Nor is the imposition of a penalty or prohibition the same as its revocation. Procedural guarantees are particularly necessary in the case of decisions unfavourable to individuals, as evidenced by Article 41(2)(a) CFR in limiting the right to a hearing to administrative decisions which 'adversely affect' the persons to whom they are addressed.

The ETIAS case[28] again provides an interesting example by automating only the granting of authorization but not the refusal of authorization, which can only be done manually, by a human. The official is only bound by the outcome of automated processing in a number of clear cases (in which the authorization must be

[25] See Annex, case 4.

[26] Notwithstanding the risks of errors and discrimination noted by Niovi Vavoula, 'Artificial Intelligence (AI) at Schengen Borders: Automated Processing, Algorithmic Profiling and Facial Recognition in the Era of Techno-Solutionism' (2021) 1 European Journal of Migration and Law 457, <https://ssrn.com/abstract=3950389> accessed 31 August 2022; Charly Derave, Nathan Genicot, and Nina Hetmanska, 'The Risks of Trustworthy Artificial Intelligence: The Case of the European Travel Information and Authorisation System' (2022) 3 European Journal of Risk Regulation 1. Such risks make it advisable to carefully monitor the implementation of ETIAS.

[27] Case C-817/19 *Ligue des droits humans v Conseil des ministres* [2022] ECLI:EU:C:2022:491, paras 194 and 195.

[28] See Annex, case 4.

refused), and in the most doubtful (when a hit occurs with the specific risk indicators of Article 33 of the ETIAS Regulation) it is expressly stated that he or she cannot automatically assume such an outcome, and that he or she must make an individual assessment of the security, illegal immigration, or epidemic risks that the applicant may pose.[29] This individual assessment derives from the procedural duty of care referred to above.

Of course, there are a large number of multipolar administrative procedures, where there are different parties with conflicting interests, and where the administrative decision may be favourable to one or more stakeholders and unfavourable to others. Nor should it be forgotten that the administrative procedure aims not only to protect the rights of persons affected by administrative decisions but also the due satisfaction of public interests. This means that mechanisms must be articulated to ensure the correctness of the automated decision, even if it is favourable to the interested party.

IV. Distinction according to the discretionary or non-discretionary nature of the automated decision

Finally, it is important to distinguish whether or not the automated decision has discretionary elements. Automated discretionary decision-making is much more controversial than decisions that are fully predetermined by the applicable law. Many authors consider that only non-discretionary administrative decision-making can or should be fully automated,[30] as expressly provided for in German law following the addition of § 35a to the German Federal Administrative Procedure Act.[31]

This is a substantive issue related to the legal nature of the algorithms used by the administration and the competence of the administration to design them.[32] However, it also has a procedural dimension because discretionary decisions of the administration are always associated with reinforced requirements of giving reasons, in order to rule out arbitrariness. If a discretionary decision can be automated, it must be reasoned in at least as much detail as would be required of a human being.

[29] European Parliament and Council Regulation (EU) 2018/1240 of 12 September 2018 establishing a European Travel Information and Authorisation System (ETIAS) and amending Regulations (EU) No 1077/2011, (EU) No 515/2014, (EU) 2016/399, (EU) 2016/1624, and (EU) 2017/2226 [2018] OJ L236/1, art 26.

[30] Citron (n 4) 1304; Huergo Lora (n 17) 15; Juli Ponce Solé, 'Inteligencia artificial, Derecho administrativo y reserva de humanidad: algoritmos y procedimiento administrativo debido tecnológico' (2019) 50 Revista General de Derecho Administrativo 14, basing it on the lack of empathy of machines.

[31] See on this provision, in English, Elena Buoso, 'Fully Automated Administrative Acts in the German legal System' (2020) 1 European Review of Digital Administration & Law 113.

[32] See section D.III.

D. Some necessary procedural adaptations when using algorithms

In addition to complying with the traditional requirements discussed above, which are still fully in force and which technology cannot turn into a dead letter,[33] some adaptations seem necessary in order to ensure full respect for the aims pursued by the institution of the administrative procedure.

I. The need to adequately inform the parties and the public about the automated systems deployed

The first adaptation is to specifically inform affected parties and the public about decisions taken in an automated way.

For the avoidance of doubt, it could be expressly required that such information be provided to the affected parties in the statement of reasons for the decision. At the very least, it should indicate that the decision has been produced in an automated way and give the affected parties the possibility, if they so wish, to request access to the details of the automated processing.

This individualized communication to persons affected by single-case decisions could be combined with generic information to the public on the main types of automated decisions taken by each administrative authority, which would be available on their respective websites.

This is the line taken by the current French legislation. It provides that the administration must inform the affected person when it adopts a decision based on algorithmic processing, and that he or she may be informed, on request, of the rules governing such processing and the main characteristics of its application to the specific case.[34] The regulation implementing this legal provision states that this implies obtaining intelligible information on the degree and manner of contribution of the algorithmic processing to the decision-making; the data processed and their sources; the parameters of the processing and, where appropriate, their weighting, as applied to the person's situation; and the operations performed by the processing.[35]

The same French Act also obliges administrations to publish online the rules governing the main algorithmic treatments used by them in making individual

[33] In fact, technology greatly facilitates the fulfilment of many of these requirements, eg by making it cheaper and easier to hear interested parties or to provide them with access to the file (where automated processes can be fully recorded). Algorithms can also help to motivate administrative decisions in much greater depth by providing data and analytical tools that were previously unavailable or very difficult to obtain.

[34] Loi n° 2016-1321 du 7 octobre 2016 pour une République numérique (1), art 4, which introduced this provision as French APA (Code des relations entre le public et l'administration), art L311-3-1.

[35] French APA, added by Décret n° 2017-330 du 14 mars 2017, art R311-3-1-2.

decisions.[36] A similar, somewhat more detailed obligation is provided for in Spanish law.[37]

This specific information on automated decision-making (ADM) is an important measure of algorithmic transparency for several reasons. It enables administrative decisions to be properly reasoned and to fulfil the two main functions of the statement of reasons (guaranteeing the defence of affected parties and allowing judicial review). It alerts the parties to the possibility of any of the absurd errors that only machines can make and prevents them from checking those aspects in which machines are infallible. It allows public scrutiny of the automation undertaken by the administration. It facilitates the consolidation and acceptance of automation by the public, once it is found to work well. It is not unreasonable to imagine that, in a few years' time, the indication that a certain decision has been adopted in an automated way will be positively valued by the interested parties, as it will be perceived as a guarantee of correctness and objectivity.

This detailed information should not lead to a weakening of the control measures for the proper functioning of the automated system by the administration and a transfer of this burden to the interested parties and the public.

Such information must also be in accordance with the existing exceptions to the right of access to the file and the general right of access to official documents, in particular with the exceptions aimed at ensuring the effectiveness of the investigations carried out by the administration.[38] The commercial interests of the developers of algorithmic systems must yield to the rights of defence of the affected parties, and this must be indicated in the contract specifications, in order to prevent confidentiality clauses from being invoked at a later stage.[39]

II. The establishment of a principle of human oversight

A second important adaptation would be to expressly establish the principle of human oversight of automated administrative decisions. This principle is clearly derived from Article 47 CFR in relation to judicial review of administrative action, which necessarily has to be exercised by humans according to the current regulatory framework in Europe. There is no doubt that administrative decisions must be subject to judicial review by humans, without it being necessary to specify that

[36] Loi n° 2016-1321 (n 34), art 6, which introduced this provision as French APA, art L312-1-3.

[37] Royal Decree 203/2021 (Real Decreto 203/2021, de 30 de marzo, por el que se aprueba el Reglamento de actuación y funcionamiento del sector público por medios electrónicos), art 11(1)(i).

[38] CFR, art 41(2)(b), and, in relation to the Union's administration, Council Regulation (EC) 1049/2001 of 30 May 2001 regarding public access to European Parliament [2001] OJ L145/43, art 4.

[39] This is recommended by the Administrative Conference of the United States (ACUS, the federal agency in charge of formulating proposals to improve the performance of the US Administration) to the different federal agencies (ACUS, 'Administrative Conference Statement #20, Agency Use of Artificial Intelligence' (2021) 86 Federal Register 6616, section 1).

this also includes administrative automated decisions. In the case of decisions of the EU administration, such judges are the members of the General Court and the Court of Justice (Article 253 et seq TFEU).

It is less clear, however, that this principle extends to the administrative phase prior to judicial review. It can be argued that it is implicit in the aforementioned duty of care, when it obliges the administrative authority to investigate and examine thoroughly and impartially all the relevant elements of the case. At least if, in the course of the procedure, the interested party provides factual elements that have not been taken into account by the automated system, as provided for in § 24(1)3 of the German Federal Administrative Procedure Act since 2016. Nevertheless, an express affirmation of this principle by the European legislature or the Court of Justice would avoid any doubt.

This would be consistent with the purpose pursued by Article 22 of the General Data Protection Regulation[40] and the equivalent provision applicable to the EU Administration,[41] when they provide that 'the data subject shall have the right not to be subject to a decision based solely on automated processing . . . which produces legal effects concerning him or her or similarly significantly affects him or her' (paragraph 1), and expressly recognize the right to obtain human intervention (in addition to being able to express his or her opinion and contest the decision) in two of the three cases in which ADM is allowed (paragraph 3). The third exception requires in any case authorization by EU or Member State law and 'suitable measures to safeguard the data subject's rights and freedoms and legitimate interests' (paragraph 2(b)). Human oversight is one such possible measure, as is clear from paragraph 3.

The principle of human oversight can also be inferred from the case law of the Court of Justice on automated processing of personal data for reasons of public security. In its judgment *La Quadrature du Net* of 6 October 2020, it has stated that the errors that automated systems can make imply that 'any positive result obtained following automated processing must be subject to an individual re-examination by non-automated means before an individual measure adversely affecting the persons concerned is adopted'.[42] This guideline of the Court of Justice, which is a kind of 'Grundrechtsschutz durch Verfahren' of the fundamental right to the protection of personal data, seems perfectly capable of being extended to

[40] European Parliament and Council Regulation (EU) 2016/679 of 27 April 2016 on the protection of natural persons with regard to the processing of personal data and on the free movement of such data, and repealing Directive 95/46/EC (General Data Protection Regulation) [2016] OJ L119/1.

[41] European Parliament and Council Regulation (EU) 2018/1725 of 23 October 2018 on the protection of natural persons with regard to the processing of personal data by the Union institutions, bodies, offices and agencies and on the free movement of such data, and repealing Regulation (EC) No 45/2001 and Decision No 1247/2002/EC [2018] OJ L295/39, art 24.

[42] Joined Cases 511/18, C-512/18, and C-520/18, *La Quadrature du Net and others v Conseil des ministres* [2020], ECLI:EU:C:2020:791, para 182. Earlier in its Opinion 1/15 (EU-Canada PNR Agreement) [2017], ECLI:EU:C:2017:592, para 173. More recently, again and in more detail, in the aforementioned *Ligue des droits humains* (n 27) paras 179 and 202ff. The latter states that the number of false positives in the automatic detection of suspicious air passengers affects as many as five out of six persons identified (para 106).

any unfavourable administrative decision, even if it concerns legal persons and not natural persons. It has been taken over by the ETIAS Regulation, as seen above.

Human oversight not only allows for the correction of errors in automated systems. It also brings citizens closer to administrative authorities and makes it easier for them to accept (and comply with) decisions taken by the latter, which is another important function of the administrative procedure. A measure introduced in Italy many years ago and proposed to be extended to the EU administration is precisely the designation of an official responsible for managing the procedure,[43] a specific public employee who is responsible for processing and communicating with the interested parties, in order to avoid administrative depersonalization, which has increased enormously with digitalization and automation. This human intervention is particularly necessary in the case of the EU administration, which is so distant for many Europeans. It is also simpler because it does not handle such massive procedures as the Member States' administrations.

Ultimately, it does not seem that a 'human-centric AI', as the Commission intends,[44] can be developed if humans are completely taken out of the administrative equation.

This human oversight may have different shapes and intensities depending on the type of procedure and administrative action in question. It seems that, at the very least, it should involve the right to an appeal to one or more humans in the administrative authority concerned before going to court.[45]

When human intervention takes place, on the one hand the automation bias referred to above[46] must be avoided. On the other hand, the human limitations that the specific algorithm seeks to overcome, and which justify its use, must be taken into account:[47] the human cannot spoil, by his or her intervention, the added value provided by the algorithmic system.

III. The need to conduct impact assessments before and after automating administrative decision-making

Humans do not only have to be involved in the automated procedure. They also intervene in a decisive way in a previous, crucial moment: the design of the automated system and of the algorithm on which it is based.

[43] Paul Craig and others (eds), *ReNEUAL Model Rules on EU Administrative Procedure* (OUP 2017), art III-7 and the corresponding explanations (paras 33 and 34).

[44] Communication from the Commission to the European Parliament, the Council, the European Economic and Social Committee and the Committee of the Regions—Building Trust in Human-Centric Artificial Intelligence (COM(2019)168), expressly including 'human oversight' among the key requirements for trustworthy AI (p 4).

[45] As can be inferred, in Spain, from Act 40/2015, art 41(2) (Gamero (n 23) 3).

[46] See section C.I.

[47] On these limitations, extensively, to justify a wide use of machine learning algorithms by administrative agencies, Coglianese (n 18) 8ff.

This raises numerous issues of interest, such as the legal nature of algorithms, the type of rules they may contain, the scope of administrative competence to configure them, or the involvement of private contractors who are very often commissioned to design them.

The fact that the algorithms used by administrative authorities predetermine the content of the automated decisions to be taken in future concrete cases has led many authors to argue that they have a normative nature and that they can be equated to administrative rule-making.[48] Others, on the other hand, deny this, considering algorithms to be mere technical instruments used by the administration.[49]

In my view, the computer algorithm[50] must be distinguished from the rules that it encodes in each case, in traditional conditional algorithms, or that it infers during its learning, in machine learning algorithms. The factual and the legal level must be differentiated as well. Such algorithmic rules can certainly predetermine the content of future administrative decisions, being the 'norms' (legitimate or not) that the automated system will apply to the specific cases it is presented with. They thus fulfil, *de facto*, a function similar to the rules governing *de jure* administrative action. However, they should not be confused with them, since the legal system attributes this status, and validity, only to the rules approved by a series of specific subjects (the legislator and the administrative authority in each case competent), following a pre-established procedure (the corresponding legislative or administrative rule-making procedure) and their publication in an official gazette. In other words, the rules that govern or should govern administrative action are not those that encode or determine its algorithms but those that meet the aforementioned organizational and procedural requirements, which have been progressively decanted over the long history of public law.

Algorithmic rules cannot therefore contradict rules formally adopted as such by the legislator and the administration itself—usually an administration other than the one designing and using the algorithm, as will often be the case at EU level.[51] If

[48] For example, in Spanish literature, Andrés Boix Palop, 'Los algoritmos son reglamentos: la necesidad de extender las garantías propias de las normas reglamentarias a los programas empleados por la administración para la adopción de decisiones' (2020) 1 Revista de Derecho Público: Teoría y Método 223, passim; Marcos Vaquer Caballería, '¿Para qué sirve el procedimiento administrativo?' in Luciano Parejo Alfonso and Marcos Vaquer Caballería (eds), *Estudios sobre el procedimiento administrativo. III. Instituciones* (Tirant lo Blanch 2020) 53, 67.

[49] Again, in Spanish literature, Ponce (n 30) 16; Julián Valero Torrijos, 'Las garantías jurídicas de la inteligencia artificial en la actividad administrativa desde la perspectiva de la buena administración' (2019) 58 Revista Catalana de Dret Públic 82, 87–88; Alejandro Huergo Lora, 'Una aproximación a los algoritmos desde el Derecho administrativo' in Alejandro Huergo Lora (ed), *La regulación de los algoritmos* (Aranzadi Thomson Reuters 2020) 23, 64ff; Luis Arroyo Jiménez, 'Algoritmos y reglamentos' (*Almacén de Derecho* 25 February 2020) <https://almacendederecho.org/algoritmos-y-reglamentos> accessed 31 August 2022; Agustí Cerrillo i Martínez, 'Robots, asistentes virtuales y automatización de las administraciones públicas' (2021) 61 Revista Galega de Administración Pública 271, 292.

[50] It is clear that the algorithm of a word processor or a spreadsheet used by the administration does not constitute a legal norm, as does neither a biometric recognition algorithm, a risk prediction algorithm, nor a personnel selection algorithm used by a private company.

[51] As is well known, only the Commission, and not the agencies, can adopt major non-legislative acts of general application (delegated and implementing acts).

these rules are not observed, and if, for example, illegal requirements for obtaining social benefits are introduced, or penalties are provided for conduct that is not defined as an infringement in a legislative act, this will be grounds for annulling the subsequent automated decision.

It happens, however, that the (formal) rules applicable to the administration do not completely predetermine its actions and entrust it with broad areas of discretion.[52] The question then arises whether it is possible for each administrative authority to exercise this discretion 'in advance' by defining the algorithms it will use in ADM (by specifying the discretionary criteria that the system will apply automatically), or whether it can only do so by means of individual human decisions taken in the single cases it must resolve, in view of their particularities.[53] This is the substantive question concerning the admissibility of discretionary algorithmic decisions referred to above,[54] and which it is not possible to elaborate on in these pages.

What is important to underline here is that, despite these theoretical divergences on the nature of the algorithms used by administrative authorities, there is a broad consensus in the academic literature on the convenience of extending some of the guarantees inherent in the administrative procedure to the design phase of algorithms.[55] Although they are not considered to be regulations (administrative rule-making), there are good arguments for subjecting them, in particular, to the usual procedural formalities of administrative rule-making and of single-case decisions of special transcendence, such as the authorization of industrial activities with a high environmental impact. In particular, it is broadly advocated to subject the drafting of algorithms to *impact assessments* and *public consultations*, two typical instruments in the preparation of Commission rules, as we are already aware. The most detailed proposal in this vein is the one recently put forward by the European Law Institute,[56] building on previous experience such as that of the Canadian government.[57]

This 'proceduralization' of the development of the most potentially dangerous administrative algorithms seems fully justified. As we have seen, algorithms not

[52] Although EU law, in line with continental systems, attaches greater importance than US law to non-delegation and to legislative predetermination of administrative action (see CFR, art 52(1)), it also recognizes broad areas of discretion for the Commission and the agencies.

[53] It is, of course, also possible for the administration to adopt a formal regulation, where it is competent to do so. This option does not pose any problems: the algorithm should reflect the rules contained in this regulation.

[54] See section C.IV.

[55] See Boix Palop (n 48); Vaquer Caballería (n 48); Valero Torrijos (n 49); Huergo Lora (n 49); Arroyo Jiménez (n 49); Cerrillo i Martínez (n 49); Citron (n 4) 1308ff; Dillon Reisman and others, 'Algorithmic Impact Assessments: A Practical Framework for Public Agency Accountability' (AI Now Report 2018); Mulligan and Bamberger (n 9) 835ff; Gamero (n 23) 9–10.

[56] European Law Institute, Model Rules on Impact Assessment of Algorithmic Decision-Making Systems Used by Public Administration (ELI Model Rules) (2022).

[57] Directive on Automated Decision-Making (Government of Canada). Although in a laxer manner, the ACUS has also recommended federal agencies to adequately evaluate the various risks of artificial intelligence systems before they are deployed (ACUS (n 39) passim).

only determine fully automated administrative decisions but also significantly condition many of the decisions taken by administrative officials, in the wide range of semi-automated actions.[58] Algorithms are also increasingly important in administrative actions that do not result in single-case decisions covered by administrative procedures, such as the provision of public services or the issuing of warnings.[59]

Subjecting algorithms to this careful *ex-ante* assessment reduces the risk of errors and malfunctioning mentioned above. From the outset, it requires the respective administrative authority to have sufficiently qualified staff to carry out the assessment and to properly evaluate the impact that the use of the algorithm will have.[60] It obliges the administrative authority to consider the risks the use of algorithms may entail and to weigh them against the benefits the use of these algorithms presents. Submission to public consultation and/or audits by external experts[61] strengthens the control of the design of the algorithm and allows for public discussion of potentially controversial uses.

In economic terms, this careful assessment is justified by the massive use that the algorithm will have afterwards and the high social costs that a defective design may have. Such assessment is necessary because not all the addressees of the decisions that will then be taken on the basis of the algorithm—in particular the most vulnerable groups—will be in a position to defend themselves adequately in the administrative procedure.

In any case, the fact that the algorithm is carefully evaluated does not exempt the procedure required for subsequent individual decision-making, discussed in the preceding sections of this chapter, from being followed. This is because it must be possible to verify that the use of the algorithm in the specific case has been correct and adequate. If following administrative procedure for the approval of a formal regulation does not exempt following appropriate administrative procedure for its application to single cases, even less should such exemption occur when what is applied is an algorithm.

As in the case of regulatory impact assessment, the assessment of algorithms should not only take place *ex ante*, but also *ex post*, once the algorithm has been put into operation. This is advocated by the academic literature and established in

[58] According to art 2(1) of the ELI Model Rules, these rightly apply not only to fully automated systems but also to those that 'support . . . human decision-making'.

[59] Art 2(3) of the ELI Model Rules also rightly uses a broad concept of decision, defined as 'any determination by a public authority to take or not to take action'. See the justification given at 41–42, with some examples.

[60] On the difficulties of administrative authorities to have sufficiently specialized staff in artificial intelligence, Coglianese (n 18) 40. On the need for algorithmic systems to be developed by multidisciplinary teams that also include lawyers, Gamero (n 23) 4, 9.

[61] Which are also covered by arts 10 and 11 of the ELI Model Rules for systems that merit a high-risk rating. On algorithmic audits see Sasha Costanza-Chock, Inioluwa Deborah Raji, and Joy Buolamwini, 'Who Audits the Auditors? Recommendations from a Field Scan of the Algorithmic Auditing Ecosystem' (FAccT'22, 2022) proposing that they should be mandatory.

the various initiatives mentioned above.[62] This periodic assessment should check that the system is working properly, as intended. In the event that dysfunctions are detected, this will not only make it possible to correct the algorithm[63] but also to review *ex officio* any erroneous decisions that may have been taken under it. Of course, the algorithm will also have to be modified whenever circumstances arise that make this necessary, for example a change in the rules governing the administrative action in question.

In view of the above, consideration could be given to the possibility that this *ex-ante* and *ex-post* impact assessment of new algorithms used by the administration be, at least in certain cases, legally required.[64] This would help to increase the confidence of European citizens in their use, which can bring great social benefits, and to avoid algorithms being perceived as a transgenic version of traditional decision-making processes.

E. Annex. The use of AI by the EU Administration: A mapping exercise

I. Scope and case studies

We in the Indigo project felt it was important to devote the first few months of its development to studying in some detail the use of advanced algorithms by the EU Administration itself (mainly the European Commission and the various EU agencies). In particular, the use of such algorithms to fully or partially automate the taking of administrative decisions with legal effects on citizens and businesses, be they rules of general scope (non-legislative acts of general application adopted by the Commission, often on the proposal of the agencies) or single-case decisions. Although the administrative implementation of EU law is primarily the responsibility of the Member States, the Treaties and secondary legislation also give the Commission and the European agencies significant powers to adopt this type of decisions. In the ReNEUAL Model Rules[65] we proposed a set of minimum procedural rules applicable to the adoption of such decisions by the EU Administration, drawn from existing sectoral rules and national procedural laws to be observed by Member States' administrations.

This task of studying the use of AI tools by the EU Administration has been undertaken mainly by the group from the Pompeu Fabra University in Barcelona.[66]

[62] ELI Model Rules (art 14); Directive on Automated Decision-Making (Government of Canada), section 6.3.2; ACUS (n 39), section 9.

[63] As Coglianese (n 18) 24, 49 points out, it is easier to correct flawed or biased algorithms than to retrain public employees who incur in those same biases or flaws.

[64] As proposed for the EU Administration on p 12 of the ELI Model Rules.

[65] See Craig and others (n 43).

[66] Integrated by Migle Laukyte, Clara Velasco, and Oriol Mir.

Methodologically, it has had two distinct phases. First, the existing literature and the websites of the Commission and the different agencies were carefully reviewed in search of adequate information on the use of such tools. Particular attention has been paid to the Official Journal of the European Union (OJEU) supplement on public procurement (TED), taking into account that experience at national level shows that many of the AI tools used by public administrations are not developed by them but are purchased on the market from external suppliers. This first phase has shed very little light on the matter. The information available online or in previous publications is very scarce and fragmentary. There are detailed and interesting reports on national experiences coordinated by EU institutions[67] but none on their use of AI systems. This contrasts sharply with the situation in the United States where there is a wealth of information on federal agencies. In fact, the most detailed report on the use of AI tools at the federal level has been commissioned and provided by one of its agencies, the ACUS.[68] There is nothing similar at the EU Administration level.

Given the limited information available, a second phase of semi-structured interviews was carried out with various officials from the Commission and some European agencies. After contacting DG-Connect, the Directorate General of the European Commission responsible for drafting the important AI Act Proposal, and after multiple requests to successive potential interlocutors in the Commission and different agencies, interviews were held between July and December 2021 with representatives of DG Agriculture (DG-Agri) and the agencies EFSA, EUIPO, and eu-LISA (European Union Agency for the Operational Management of Large-Scale IT Systems in the Area of Freedom, Security and Justice).[69] These interviews were very informative and should be briefly summarized.

1. Case 1 (DG-Agri/ESA): The use of AI for satellite monitoring of European crops and compliance with CAP agricultural subsidy rules

The first use case concerns a pilot experiment in the field of the Common Agricultural Policy (CAP) aimed at satellite monitoring of European crops and compliance with agricultural subsidy rules. Currently, Member States are obliged to inspect 5 per cent of subsidised crops on the ground in order to check

[67] Of particular interest are those produced by the Commission's Joint Research Centre (JRC), which form part of the AI Watch series. Especially the reports by Gianluca Misuraca and Colin van Noordt, *Overview of the use and impact of AI in public services in the EU*, EUR 30255 EN (Publications Office of the European Union 2020), Luxembourg, doi:10.2760/039619, JRC120399; and Luca Tangi and others, *AI Watch. European Landscape on the Use of Artificial Intelligence by the Public Sector*, EUR 31088 EN (Publications Office of the European Union 2022), Luxembourg, doi:10.2760/39336, JRC129301.

[68] David Freeman Engstrom and others, 'Government by Algorithm: Artificial Intelligence in Federal Administrative Agencies' [2020] Administrative Conference of the United States.

[69] They are Doris Marquardt (DG-Agri, 30.07.2021), Ermanno Cavalli (EFSA, 14.10.2021), Rahul Bhartiya (EUIPO, 30.11.2021), and Aleksandrs Cepilovs (eu-LISA, 22.07.2021 and 14.12.2021), to whom we are very grateful for their excellent cooperation.

compliance and prevent fraud. The new system uses machine learning algorithms to improve the recognition accuracy of satellite images.[70] It aims, among other things, to monitor all European fields, including those that are more difficult to access, and to reduce and optimize the number of field inspections, to the benefit of national administrations and farmers themselves, for whom the system can also make it easier to obtain subsidies.

The system, driven by the European Space Agency (ESA) and guided by a steering committee composed of the three Commission Directorates-General involved in the CAP (DG-Agri, DG-Grow, and DG-JRC), is being technologically developed by a public–private consortium led by a Belgian university, in the framework of a research project of the European Horizon 2020 programme. It is being implemented on a pilot basis in six Member States: Czech Republic, Italy, Lithuania, the Netherlands, Romania, and Spain.

The system does not take automated decisions but merely issues alerts in cases of possible non-compliance. Such alerts are verified by humans through the review or zoom of images or, where appropriate, an on-site inspection, before a legal decision is taken to deny the requested subsidy or to reimburse the previously granted subsidy. Satellite monitoring can therefore form part of the complex procedures for the granting, control, and revocation of CAP subsidies. It constitutes an additional means of proof of compliance or non-compliance with the rules and, as such, would form part of the information-gathering phase of the decision-making procedure provided for in Book III of the ReNEUAL Model Rules (Chapter 3, Article III-10 et seq). Such satellite monitoring has been admitted and regulated by a Commission Implementing Regulation of 2018,[71] which does not address the technology used and, in particular, the use of AI tools for the analysis of the images taken.[72]

2. Case 2 (EFSA): The use of AI for the analysis of relevant scientific literature in food risk assessments

The second use case concerns the automation, using machine learning algorithms, of part of the process of analysis of relevant scientific publications carried out by EFSA when performing risk assessments of certain substances or products. This comprehensive review of the scientific literature, known as a Systematic Review, is a fundamental part of the risk assessment performance that characterizes EFSA and similar agencies such as the European Medicines Agency (EMA), the

[70] Mainly ESA's Sentinel-1 and Sentinel-2 satellites.

[71] Commission Implementing Regulation (EU) 2018/746 of 18 May 2018 amending Implementing Regulation (EU) No 809/2014 as regards modification of single applications and payment claims and checks [2018] OJ L125/1. See especially the new art 40a on checks by monitoring.

[72] For more information on this first use case, see the project's website (http://esa-sen4cap.org), as well as the Special Report 04/2020 of the European Court of Auditors, which evaluates it positively and recommends its promotion.

European Centre for Disease Prevention and Control (ECDC), and the European Chemicals Agency (ECHA). It consumes a large part of their resources, forcing the experts conducting them to sift through a huge and exponentially growing volume of publications. The process is slow, tedious, and often obsolete by the time it is completed.

EFSA has been working on the partial automation of this process for several years now.[73] It already routinely uses automation of the initial phase of selection of relevant publications, which operates on the basis of an analysis of their title and abstract. This selection excludes papers considered irrelevant and normally reduces the number of papers to be studied from several thousands to a few hundred. This is done using the DistillerSR software marketed by Evidence Partners, and allows one of the two experts usually required for the review to be replaced. In their final report, the experts indicate that they have used the tool.

EFSA would like to automate further stages of the review process, such as the extraction of relevant data from previously selected papers and even the critical appraisal of these papers to determine their quality. Concerning the data extraction, it is collaborating with the US Environmental Protection Agency (EPA) to provide food safety data to train a machine learning program (Fiddle) developed by Sciome with a grant from the EPA.[74]

The final scientific opinion on the risk assessment is always elaborated by a human expert, although an error in the automated screening of relevant publications may, of course, leave out important scientific papers and evidence that could not be considered in the preparation of that opinion.

3. Case 3 (EUIPO): The use of AI in the trade mark and design registration procedure

EUIPO annually registers around 135,000 trade marks and 100,000 designs, processing applications filed in twenty-three different languages, so it is not surprising that it has made a significant commitment to the introduction of AI tools aimed at facilitating the work of its employees and applicants.[75] Between July 2020 and June 2025, it is developing a project to implement AI solutions in different areas of its activity with a budget of 2.86 million euros and 24.5 full-time employees.[76]

[73] Stijn See Jaspers; Ewoud De Troyer; Marc Aerts, 'Machine learning techniques for the automation of literature reviews and systematic reviews in EFSA' (EFSA supporting publication 2018:EN-1427 2018), doi:10.2903/sp.efsa.2018.EN-1427.

[74] See the EFSA Call for Proposals GP/EFSA/AMU/2020/03—Support for Automating some specific steps of Systematic Review process using Artificial Intelligence (no longer available on the EFSA website), calling for a grant for the development of such training datasets.

[75] On the use cases developed by its US counterpart, the US Patent and Trademark Office, see Engstrom and others (n 68) 46ff.

[76] European Union Intellectual Property Office EUIPO, 'Artificial Intelligence Implementation' (EUIPO) <https://euipo.europa.eu/tunnel-web/secure/webdav/guest/document_library/contentPdfs/Strategic_Plan_2025/project_cards/SD3_Artificial_Intelligence_implementation_PC_en.pdf> accessed 31 August 2022.

Among the various tools being introduced, two can be highlighted in relation to the registration procedure. The first is the possibility to search for similar images through the eSearchPlus database, which is available on the EUIPO website for anyone who is considering registering a particular trade mark or design and wants to check whether the one they have in mind is already registered.

The second tool enables an AI-based comparison of goods and services that allows EUIPO officials to assess opposition cases (those in which a third party opposes the trade mark sought to be registered) more easily and with better quality. Applicants for a particular trade mark must indicate the goods and services it is intended to cover, and there are trade marks that can cover up to 2,000 different goods and services. In case of opposition, officials must undertake a comparison of the goods and services covered by the respective trade marks, which is time-consuming and tedious, as well as complex in the many cases where there is no clear distinction between two goods or services. The implemented AI tool facilitates this comparison by suggesting to the official an answer to the pair of conflicting goods and services on the basis of the thousands of previous decisions issued by the EUIPO. The system even provides the reasons given in the previous decisions, in order to facilitate the drafting of the decision, which is in any case the responsibility of the official(s) of the respective Opposition Division.[77] Such decisions can be challenged by the interested parties before the EUIPO Boards of Appeal, which are also composed of one or three natural persons.[78]

It is remarkable that, contrary to the usual practice, EUIPO is developing these AI tools in-house, without acquiring them from third parties.

4. Case 4 (eu-LISA): The use of AI for biometric recognition of persons at the EU's borders

The fourth and final use case refers to eu-LISA, the European agency responsible for the management of basic information systems for Member States' border and law enforcement authorities, such as the Schengen Information System (SIS II), the Visa Information System (VIS), and the asylum information system (Eurodac). It is also developing new information systems already regulated by EU law, such as the Entry/Exit System (EES), the ETIAS, and the European Criminal Records Information System—Third-Country Nationals (ECRIS-TCN), for their forthcoming entry into operation.

AI is used in the first three systems and in the forthcoming EES and ECRIS-TCN for biometric identification and verification of persons at EU borders and

[77] See EUIPO, New AI-based comparison of goods and services (EUIPO 2022) < https://euipo.europa.eu/ohimportal/en/-/news/new-ai-based-comparison-of-goods-and-services> accessed 31 August 2022.

[78] Arts 66ff and 159ff of European Parliament and Council Regulation (EU) 2017/1001 of 14 June 2017 on the European Union trade mark [2017] OJ L154/1.

within Member States.[79] All of them employ biometric matching systems, which use advanced machine learning algorithms to match facial images and fingerprints taken at the borders with those stored in these information systems. Each system has its own biometric matching service,[80] but the companies developing the EES biometric system are also working on implementing a tool to enable simultaneous search and comparison of biometric data in all these information systems at the same time.[81] This is the shared biometric matching service (sBMS), foreseen and regulated in Articles 12 et seq of the Regulations that allow interoperability between all these information systems.[82]

These biometric matching systems are not developed by eu-LISA but by private contractors on the basis of the technical specifications set by eu-LISA, which also tests their proper functioning. The contract for the development of the EES and the sBMS was awarded for 302 million euros to a consortium of European companies.[83] As is well known, an essential aspect of any machine learning system is its training, which must be done with a large amount of quality data for the system's performance to be adequate. The establishment of this training dataset is very costly and is covered by the commercial confidentiality of the contractors, which do not allow eu-LISA to access them. Eu-LISA is therefore unaware of the data used by its contractors to train the systems, and whether it suffers from the (mainly racial and gender) biases that have been frequently observed in the training of biometric recognition systems.[84] To mitigate this, eu-LISA will carry out independent assessment and testing of the performance of the sBMS, where, among other parameters, it will test on possible gender and racial biases.

In any case, the systems that eu-LISA makes available to Member States would be among the most advanced in the world and would have a very high performance, superior to that of the most experienced border official. Their accuracy

[79] On the use cases of facial recognition by the US federal border control agency, Customs and Border Protection (CBS), see Engstrom and others (n 68) 30ff.

[80] Eu-LISA, *Shared Biometric Matching Service (sBMS) Feasibility Study—final report*, [2018] doi:10.2857/84504, p 5 <https://op.europa.eu/en/publication-detail/-/publication/10175794-3dff-11e8-b5fe-01aa75ed71a1/language-en> accessed 31 August 2022.

[81] Eu-LISA, Call for Tender—Framework contract for implementation and maintenance in working order of the biometrics part of the Entry Exit System and future Shared Biometrics Matching System, LISA/2019/RP/05 EES BMS and sBMS, Executive Summary, pp 7–8.

[82] European Parliament and of the Council Regulation (EU) 2019/817 of 20 May 2019 on establishing a framework for interoperability between EU information systems in the field of borders and visa [2019] OJ L135/27, and European Parliament and of the Council Regulation (EU) 2019/818 of 20 May 2019 on establishing a framework for interoperability between EU information systems in the field of police and judicial cooperation, asylum and migration [2019] OJ L135/85.

[83] <https://ted.europa.eu/udl?uri=TED:NOTICE:200083-2020:TEXT:EN:HTML> accessed 31 August 2022.

[84] See eg the famous paper by Joy Buolamwini and Timnit Gebru, 'Gender Shades: Intersectional Accuracy Disparities in Commercial Gender Classification' (Conference on fairness, accountability and transparency 2018), Proceedings on Machine Learning Research 77–91, which led the first of the authors to testify before the US Congress on the impact of facial recognition technology on citizens' rights.

would have increased tenfold since such systems began to be used by eu-LISA in 2014, and would be facilitated by the controlled environments in which they operate (airports with good cameras, where images are taken without movement, with adequate lighting, etc, as opposed to video surveillance cameras).

The existing EU law governing these biometric matching systems used at EU borders does not address the particularities arising from the fact that they are based on machine learning algorithms, or that they are developed by external contractors. It does establish, *inter alia*, the quality requirements to be met by the fingerprints and facial images used, the rate of false positives and negatives allowed, and the regular (at least monthly) monitoring of the performance of the system to be carried out by eu-LISA.[85]

It is important to note that the other major information system currently being implemented by eu-LISA, ETIAS,[86] does not rely on machine learning algorithms. The Regulation governing it predefines in detail the aspects to be checked by the system when a third-country national applies for authorization to travel to the territory of the Union.[87] The computerized system will automatically grant the authorization to travel when these predefined checks produce a negative result. When the result is positive and a hit occurs (eg because the applicant uses a passport that is in the Interpol database of lost or stolen passports, or is on the ETIAS watchlist as a terrorist suspect, or fits into one of the specific risk indicators to be developed in accordance with Article 33 of the Regulation), the system will inform Frontex to carry out the relevant verification and, if a positive result is confirmed, transmit the application to the competent Member State to decide the application manually (ie via a human) and in a reasoned manner. It is therefore a traditional algorithmic system, perfectly traceable, which is limited to checking that the conditions previously established by the legislator-programmer are met ('if–then' system), without establishing new rules based on correlations that can be extracted from large amounts of data, as is the case with machine learning algorithms.[88]

It is objectionable that AI systems that are integrated into these eu-LISA-operated information systems before thirty-six months after the entry into force

[85] See, for the EES, the Annex of the Commission Implementing Decision (EU) 2019/329 of 25 February 2019 laying down the specifications for the quality, resolution and use of fingerprints and facial image for biometric verification and identification in the Entry/Exit System (EES) [2019] OJ L57/18.

[86] The European equivalent of the US Electronic System for Travel Authorization (ESTA). ETIAS will require non-EU citizens from visa-free countries to obtain authorization to travel to the territory of the Union for a maximum period of 90 days. It is expected to come into operation in the first half of 2025.

[87] See arts 20ff of European Parliament and of the Council Regulation (EU) 2018/1240 of 12 September 2018 establishing a European Travel Information and Authorisation System (ETIAS) and amending Regulations (EU) No 1077/2011, (EU) No 515/2014, (EU) 2016/399, (EU) 2016/1624, and (EU) 2017/2226 [2018] OJ L236/1.

[88] A detailed and critical analysis of the facial recognition and risk assessment algorithms employed by these eu-LISA-operated information systems can be found in Vavoula (n 26) and Derave, Genicot, and Hetmanska (n 26).

of the proposed AI Act are excluded from the Act,[89] despite being considered high-risk under its Annex III.[90]

II. Some conclusions that can be drawn from the mapping exercise

Some conclusions can be drawn from the mapping exercise.

The first is the limited information available on existing AI use cases within the EU Administration. It is striking that not only is this information not available on the Internet but it is not even available to any centralized EU service. There is an informal network among certain European agencies ('AI Virtual Community') that exchanges experiences on AI use cases, but neither the Commission nor all agencies participate in it. It is questionable that the DG behind the important AI Act Proposal is unaware of the existing use cases at EU level and the problems they may raise. Having such information is essential to adequately assess the impact of the new Proposal on the EU Administration itself, as well as to consider possible specific rules applicable to the use of AI systems by public authorities.

It is not surprising, therefore, that the Proposal practically ignores the specificities of the use of AI by the public sector and focuses mainly on the private sector. The establishment by Article 60 of the Proposal of a centralized database within the Commission with the existing use cases in both the public and private sector is a positive step to overcome the current lack of information, but in the case of public authorities it could be extended to all AI systems and not be limited only to those that deserve the (elusive) high-risk qualification. The possible objections of competence that could oppose a regulation by the European legislator of the use of AI by national administrations would not be applicable to the administration of the Union itself: the European legislator can regulate its own administration as it wishes (Article 298 TFEU).

The mapping exercise also revealed that there is considerable interest and growing use of AI tools by the EU Administration itself. However, its use is still sporadic and does not respond to a centralized and conscious policy of the Commission but is the result of the individual initiatives of the different Directorates-General and agencies, sometimes in collaboration with their counterparts in other regions (as witnessed in the case of EFSA and its collaboration with the US EPA). AI is used both by the authorities that have their own decision-making powers (EUIPO, EFSA—as regards the issuing of scientific opinions) and those that provide information systems to the Member States for the corresponding decisions to be taken (DG-Agri/ESA, eu-LISA).

[89] Art 83 of the Proposal, in relation to its art 85(2) and Annex IX.

[90] Paras 1 and 7 of Annex III of the Proposal.

The mapping exercise also confirms the importance of outsourcing in this area and the limited capacities of the EU Administration to develop its own AI systems. With the notable exception of EUIPO, the other authorities have to rely on public procurement (eu-LISA, for very significant amounts) or non-commercial external partners (DG-Agri/ESA, EFSA) to develop them.[91] As we have seen, this sometimes raises the problem of not being able to access the training data of machine learning systems, which are protected by commercial confidentiality.

The use cases examined also show the great potential that AI can have for improving certain administrative functions, increasing their quality and effectiveness and not only reducing their cost. For some tasks it is already unimaginable, even reprehensible, *not* to use AI. This is the case for machine translation of texts, in which the Commission is investing large amounts of resources, as confirmed by several interviewees. In the cases studied, AI makes it possible to significantly strengthen the control of agricultural subsidies and EU borders, as well as to speed up the food risk assessment process and to facilitate the consistency of decisions on the registration of trade marks.

The mapping exercise reveals that the use of AI also poses risks, risks that go beyond the breach of the right to personal data protection and of which the interviewees were well aware. The cases analysed are limited in scope and no instances of malfunction have surfaced. Nor is there a complete replacement of humans, who end up making the final decisions. However, it has been observed that there is no specific regulatory framework or even internal guidelines within each authority aimed at avoiding the occurrence of such risks, establishing, for example, the obligation to carry out an impact assessment before introducing a new AI system, the conditions to be imposed on contractors commissioned to develop it, the tests to be carried out before it is put into operation, or the measures to avoid excessive reliance by staff on the automated systems (automation bias).

The mapping exercise in turn confirms the importance of administrative procedural rules to avoid the risks mentioned above, further discussed in the main part of this chapter. Procedural guarantees, far from being seen as a hindrance of an analogue administration that has already been superseded, are fundamental requirements of the new digital administration, and must be maintained and adapted where necessary.

[91] On the situation in US federal agencies see Engstrom and others (n 68) 88ff: more than half of the identified 157 AI use cases (53 per cent) were developed in-house by agency technologists, and nearly as many came from external sources, with 33 per cent coming from private commercial sources via the procurement process and 14 per cent resulting from non-commercial collaborations, including agency-hosted competitions and government–academic partnerships.

4

Collaborative Governance of the EU Digital Single Market Established by the Digital Services Act

Jens-Peter Schneider, Kester Siegrist, and Simon Oles

A. Introduction

This chapter contributes to the INDIGO project by focusing on decision-making procedures implementing EU policies for the Digital Single Market. A key infrastructure of the EU Digital Single Market consists of online platforms and other intermediary services provided by private operators—mainly from the United States.[1] These platforms have gained considerable economic power according to the economics of networks. Thereby, very large online platforms (VLOPs) as well as very large online search engines (VLOSEs) perform a gatekeeper function concerning access to the EU Digital Single Market including ever more increasing communication on social media. Central instruments of VLOPs and VLOSEs for performing their gatekeeper function are fully or partially automated recommender, content moderation, or advertising systems using algorithms including artificial intelligence (AI) technologies.

While legislators in the United States and in Europe have been very reluctant in the past to interfere into this private governance of major parts of our digital economy, times have changed. This chapter will show that recent EU legislation builds upon the gatekeeper function of VLOPS and VLOSEs, including their automated decision-making (ADM) systems, in order to implement effectively EU policies 'for a safe, predictable and trusted online environment'[2] on the one side, and the legislation establishes, on the other, a regulatory framework for the exercise of this private gatekeeper function and for the respective ADM systems which shall 'facilitate . . . innovation, [and effectively protects] fundamental rights enshrined in [the EU Charter of Fundamental Rights], including the principle of consumer

[1] As established in the field of data protection these US providers will fall into the DSA's scope of application as far as they offer their intermediary services to recipients that have their place of establishment or are located in the Union (art 2(1) DSA).

[2] Art 1(1) Digital Services Act (in the following DSA, for details see n 12).

Jens-Peter Schneider, Kester Siegrist, and Simon Oles, *Collaborative Governance of the EU Digital Single Market Established by the Digital Services Act* In: *Governance of Automated Decision-Making and EU Law.* Edited by: Herwig C.H. Hofmann and Felix Pflücke, Oxford University Press.
DOI: 10.1093/9780198919575.003.0004

protection'.[3] This combination of outsourcing certain public policing functions concerning the Digital Single Market with due diligence obligations or accountability structures for VLOPS, VLOSEs, and other intermediary services enforced by various administrative supervisory authorities qualifies as a complex arrangement of collaborative governance.[4] Another focus of this chapter concerns various knowledge gaps concerning the concrete impact of intermediary service providers in general and especially of VLOPs and VLOSEs on public values such as democracy and free speech as well as legislative options to cope with these gaps.

In 2015 the European Commission published its communication 'A Digital Single Market Strategy for Europe'.[5] The strategy describes the relevant policy context of this chapter and consists of three pillars:

- Better access for consumers and businesses to online goods and services across Europe...
- Creating the right conditions for digital networks and services to flourish...
- Maximising the growth potential of our European Digital Economy....

The Commission identified cross-border e-commerce rules that consumers and business can trust and a modern European copyright framework providing better access to digital content as important elements of the first pillar.[6] These rules are an interesting background for this chapter. However, they raise primarily problems of private law and only to a rather limited extend challenges for administrative law. Thus, the first pillar is of no further interest for this chapter. The same applies to the third pillar which requires investment in ICT infrastructures and technologies such as Cloud computing and Big Data, and research and innovation to boost industrial competitiveness.[7]

Especially relevant for this study are the measures within the second pillar. The Commission highlighted in this regard reforms of EU telecom regulation[8] and of the Audiovisual Media Services Directive (AVMS-Directive),[9] both of which were

[3] Art 1(1) DSA.

[4] For an explanation of the understanding of the term see section B.

[5] Commission, 'A Digital Single Market Strategy for Europe' (Communication) COM(2015) 192 final.

[6] COM(2015) 192 final 4–5, 6–8.

[7] COM(2015) 192 final 4.

[8] COM(2015) 192 final 9–10; see the respective Directive (EU) 2018/1972 of the European Parliament and of the Council of 11 December 2018 establishing the European Electronic Communications Code (EECC-Directive) (2018) OJ L321/36; for a comprehensive analysis Jens-Peter Schneider, 'Telekommunikation' in Michael Fehling and Jens-Peter Schneider (eds), *Regulierungsrecht* (2nd edn, Mohr Siebeck forthcoming).

[9] COM(2015) 192 final 10–11; Directive 2010/13/EU of the European Parliament and of the Council of 10 March 2010 on the coordination of certain provisions laid down by law, regulation or administrative action in Member States concerning the provision of audiovisual media services (AVMS-Directive) (2010) OJ L95/1 as amended by Directive 2018/1808, OJ L 303/69.

realized in 2018. These two legislative components of single market governance are important. However, telecom regulation concerns mainly the technical infrastructure and less the cross-border intermediary services, whose collaborative, as well as increasingly automated, governance is the focus of this study. In contrast, the AVMS-Directive obviously regards cross-border intermediary services. Thus, this directive will be investigated as an important example of (media) sector-specific regulation raising problems of coordination with the general DSA-framework mentioned below (section C.II).

Recently the EU legislative organs agreed on another cornerstone of the Digital Single Market Strategy's second pillar:[10] a new 'digital rulebook' consisting of the Digital Markets Act (DMA)[11] and the Digital Services Act (DSA).[12] The European Commission described its respective proposals as an 'ambitious reform of the digital space, a comprehensive set of new rules for all digital services, including social media, online market places, and other online platforms that operate in the European Union'[13] and the European Parliament qualifies the 'new EU digital rulebook [as] unprecedented standards on the accountability of online companies, within an open and competitive digital market'.[14] The rulebook addresses growing political and societal concerns about the market power of platforms and other online intermediaries as well as societal risks arising from the spread of illegal content and online disinformation on the internet. The DMA introduces harmonized rules defining and prohibiting unfair practices by online platforms acting as digital 'gatekeepers' to the single market and provides an enforcement mechanism based on market investigations. Even more important in the context of this chapter is that the DSA introduces (i) a framework with various positive obligations for online platforms graduated according to their size and impact[15] as well as (ii) an innovative oversight structure and cooperation process among public authorities to ensure effective private and public enforcement across the digital single market.

This new framework for online platforms is fundamental for the future governance of the digital single market. Online platforms provide cross-border digital

[10] COM(2015) 192 final 11–12.

[11] Regulation (EU) 2022/1925 of 14 September 2022 on contestable and fair markets in the digital sector and amending Directives (EU) 2019/1937 and (EU) 2020/1828 (Digital Markets Act) L265/1 (DMA).

[12] Regulation (EU) 2022/2065 of 19 October 2022 on a Single Market for Digital Services and amending Directive 2000/31/EC (Digital Services Act) L 277/1 (DSA).

[13] Commission, 'Europe fit for the Digital Age: Commission proposes new rules for digital platforms' (Press release) IP/20/2347.

[14] European Parliament, 'Digital Services: Landmark rules adopted for a safer, open online environment' (Press release) 20220701IPR34364.

[15] For details about this so-called asymmetric regulation see Jens-Peter Schneider, 'Digitale Online-Dienste' in Fehling and Schneider (eds) (n 8) paras 16–17; for an example see section B.II.3.b with n 102.

services or digitally support offline cross-border transactions concerning goods, information, and other services. Therefore, they are essential digital infrastructures of the EU digital single market. From the perspective of European administrative law the new framework presents distinct new features and poses some important challenges, as follows:

1. The new rulebook assigns—and thereby outsources—to platforms comprehensive public policy functions concerning the combat against disinformation and illegal or otherwise harmful content on the Internet and combines in this regard extensive industry self-regulation with procedural accountability safeguards and public supervisory mechanisms. We describe this collaborative governance (section B) and analyse its impact on values, principles, and rights enshrined in EU public law (sections B.I.3, B.II.3, B.III).
2. As autonomous or as legally assigned governors of parts of theInternet, online platforms and search engines intensively and increasingly rely on algorithmic or even artificial intelligence technologies in order to cope with the sheer mass of online content distributed by them and falling into the scope of their assigned public policy functions; the DSA addresses this specific form of digital governance of the Internet by an innovative legal framework for information technology (IT) as being both a policy tool or medium as well as an object of collaborative governance (sections B.II.2, B.II.3).
3. The rulebook introduces extensive powers for centralized regulation by the EU Commission supported by new EU agencies but also new forms of multilevel oversight by national authorities and EU authorities often using composite procedures of adaptive decision-making (section C.I).
4. As mentioned, the rulebook provides a general framework concerning 'for all digital services, including social media, online market places, and other online platforms';[16] this poses challenges to a balanced, effective as well as efficient coordination of various sector-specific legal requirements and of the respective competent authorities (section C.II).
5. A general challenge combined with the other challenges mentioned earlier arises from knowledge gaps and other epistemic uncertainties concerning economic and societal impacts of the expanding digital economy in general and more specifically concerning 'systemic risks' connected with VLOPs or VLOSEs and especially with their widespread use of algorithmic technologies for governing the Internet. We will tackle these societal and democratic challenges throughout the study (sections B.IV, C.III, D).

[16] Commission, 'Europe fit for the Digital Age: Commission proposes new rules for digital platforms' (Press release) IP/20/2347.

B. Outsourcing of public functions to online platforms and search engines in a collaborative governance framework

As mentioned in the Introduction, the new EU digital rulebook outsources comprehensive public policy functions to platforms. These functions have an individual as well as a systemic dimension. In the individual dimension, platforms are made responsible to combat disinformation and illegal or otherwise harmful content in individual cases according to a formalized and digitalized notice-and-action procedure (sections B.II.1, B.II.2). Concerning the second dimension, the DSA explicitly addresses systemic risks potentially caused by VLOPs and VLOSEs and assigns the assessment and mitigation of these risks to those actors themselves (section B.III).

Before we develop the 'collaborative governance' concept in the field of digital services some remarks about our terminology and its theoretical background are necessary. While the upcoming legal framework certainly departs from concepts of pure self-regulation,[17] it equally does not implement a classic command-and-control regulation of digital communication and transactions by public agencies, mainly due to the sheer volume of uploaded content.[18] Rather, the new EU digital rulebook provides incentives for self-regulatory measures in order to use the resources and expertise of the regulated entities but at the same time implements duties as well as powers for regulatory monitoring of intermediaries' measures by public authorities.[19] Such forms of governance are placed in the middle between self-regulation and classic command-and-control regulation and encompass a broad range of nuanced variations.[20]

Particularly in situations where the private sector has technical expertise, which regulating bodies cannot access or build up by themselves, or the dynamics of the regulatory environment are particularly high, such 'mixed forms of governance' are regarded as suitable.[21] Exemplary instruments for effective regulatory

[17] For a critical account of such strategies see Commission, 'Impact Assessment DSA Part 1/2' SWD(2020) 348 final 30 para 105; Mark D Cole, Christina Etteldorf, and Carsten Ullrich, *Updating the Rules for Online Content Dissemination: Legislative Options of the European Union and the Digital Services Act Proposal* (1st edn, Nomos 2021) 51, 122; Judit Bayer, Lorna Woods, and Bernd Holznagel, 'Introduction' in Judit Bayer and others (eds), *Perspectives on Platform Regulation: Concepts and Models of Social Media Governance across the Globe* (1st edn, Nomos 2021) 17; Lorna Woods, 'Introducing the Systems Approach and the Statutory Duty of Care' in Bayer and others (eds), *Perspectives on Platform Regulation* ibid; Ethan Shattock, 'Self-regulation 2.0? A Critical Reflection of the European Fight Against Disinformation' (2021) 2 Harvard Kennedy School Misinformation Review 1, 2.

[18] See section B.II.2.

[19] See sections B.II, B.III.

[20] The term 'hybrid' is used frequently. See Margot E Kaminski, 'Binary Governance: Lessons from the GDPR's Approach to Algorithmic Accountability' (2019) 92 Southern California Law Review 1529, 1560; Andrew Selbst, 'An Institutional View of Algorithmic Impact Assessments' (2021) 35 Harvard Journal of Law & Technology 117, 153; from a German perspective see Martin Eifert, '§ 19 Regulierungsstrategien' in Andreas Voßkuhle, Martin Eifert, and Christoph Möllers (eds), *Grundlagen des Verwaltungsrechts* (3rd edn, C.H. Beck 2022) s 19 para 52ff.

[21] Kaminski (n 20) 1560; Selbst (n 20) 153ff; for the German discussion Eifert (n 20) s 19 para 59.

backstops can be '*ex-ante*' accountability structures forcing the regulated private actors to explain, justify and verify their actions.[22] In general, public authorities must qualify as an effective 'background threat' to force the private sector into compliance.[23]

Governance models which deploy such mechanisms are described by a plethora of terms. Amongst these are 'new governance',[24] 'monitored or regulated self-regulation',[25] 'multi-stakeholder governance',[26] 'coregulation',[27] and 'collaborative governance',[28] all of which are partially used interchangeably.[29] While these concepts may differ in detail, their common denominator is that the regulator relies on the capabilities of the regulated entities and monitors their compliance.

In our context, the term 'collaborative governance' is optimal to capture first the partially cooperative but also regulated collaboration of various private and state actors with conflicting interests—existing by nature in multipolar constellations like digital platforms—as well as secondly, the complementary use of automatic and human content moderation.[30] In addition, the term conveys more of

[22] Evelyn Douek, 'Content Moderation as Systems Thinking' (2022) 136 Harvard Law Review 526, 602ff; Rory van Loo, 'The Missing Regulatory State: Monitoring Businesses in an Age of Surveillance' (2019) 72 Vanderbilt Law Review 1563, 160ff.

[23] Kaminski (n 20) 1561; the famous 'shadow of hierarchy' developed by Fritz W Scharpf, 'Die Handlungsfähigkeit des Staates am Ende des zwanzigsten Jahrhunderts' (1991) 32(4) Politische Vierteljahresschrift 621, 629.

[24] Orly Lobel, 'New Governance as Regulatory Governance' in David Levi--Faur (ed), *The Oxford Handbook of Governance* (OUP 2012) 65ff; Orly Lobel, 'The Renew Deal: The Fall of Regulation and the Rise of Governance in Contemporary Legal Thought' (2004) 89 Minnesota Law Review 371–76.

[25] Douek (n 22) 604; for the German discussion see Wolfgang Hoffmann-Riem, 'Öffentliches Recht und Privatrecht als wechselseitige Auffangordnungen—Systematisierung und Entwicklungsperspektiven' in Wolfgang Hoffmann-Riem and Eberhard Schmidt-Aßmann (eds), *Öffentliches Recht und Privatrecht als wechselseitige Auffangordnungen* (Schriften zur Reform des Verwaltungsrechts vol 3, 1st edn Nomos 1996) 301ff; Eberhard Schmidt-Aßmann, 'Regulierte Selbstregulierung als Element Verwaltungsrechtlicher Systembildung' in Wilfried Berg and others (eds), *Regulierte Selbstregulierung als Steuerungskonzept des Gewährleistungsstaates: Ergebnisse des Symposiums aus Anlaß des 60. Geburtstages von Wolfgang Hoffmann-Riem* (Die Verwaltung Beiheft vol 4, Duncker & Humblot 2001) 253ff; Eifert (n 20) s 19 para 52ff.

[26] Hannah Bloch-Wehba, 'Automation in Moderation' (2020) 53 Cornell International Law Journal 41, 45.

[27] See Rec 14 AVMS Directive (2018).

[28] Kaminski (n 20) 1559ff; Selbst (n 20) 153ff; see also Jody Freeman, 'Collaborative Governance in the Administrative State' (1997) UCLA Law Review 1ff; Giovanni de Gregorio and Pietro Dunn, 'The European Risk-Based Approaches: Connecting Constitutional Dots in the Digital Age' (2022) 59 Common Market Law Review 473, 486; Bloch-Wehba (n 26) 45.

[29] Bloch-Wehba (n 26) 45; Matthias Cornils, *Designing Platform Governance: A Normative Perspective on Needs, Strategies, and Tools to Regulate Intermediaries* (Algorithm Watch 2020) 38; Kaminski (n 20) 1559; the list is non-exhaustive, see Cary Coglianese and David Lazer, 'Management-Based Regulation: Prescribing Private Management to Achieve Public Goals' (2003) 37(4) Law & Society Review 691, 692 refer to 'management-based regulation', 'enforced self-regulation', 'mandated self-regulation', 'reflexive' regulation, or 'process-based' and 'systems-based' standards, which all somewhat resemble the concept of 'collaborative governance'.

[30] See on conflicting interest of actors in platform governance Bloch-Wehba (n 26) 48ff, 74ff; Urs Saxer, *Von den Medien zu den Plattformen: Die Regulierung öffentlicher Kommunikation im Zeichen der digitalen Revolution* (Mohr Siebeck 2023) 159f.

a substantive concept than 'new governance' or 'multi-stakeholder governance'. Hence, it is for good reason that 'collaborative governance' seems to be the most established term, especially in US literature on platform regulation.[31]

According to the collaborative governance framework for both functional dimensions—the individual as well as the systemic—the DSA establishes accountability safeguards on several levels starting with formal mechanisms for self-control by VLOPs and VLOSEs complemented by audits or out-of-court dispute settlement performed by independent private bodies and finally supervised by either national or European authorities (sections B.II.3, B.III). This collaborative governance framework and the design of some of its components reflect the knowledge problems connected with the regulation of digital services (section B.IV). For a deeper understanding and contextualization of the new European framework, we will start our analysis with a short account of the evolution of digital governance, the governance of digital services, and will refer in this regard, in accordance with its paradigmatic relevance, to the legal and political development in the United States. Jonathan Zittrain described this development in 2019 by differentiating between 'Three Eras of Digital Governance'[32] (section B.I).

I. Three eras of digital governance

1. The Rights Era: putting individual freedom to generate content first

In the early 'Rights Era' the legal discourse focused on rights, 'particularly those of end-users, and the ways in which abstention by intermediaries is important to facilitate citizen flourishing'. This—partly cyber-libertarian[33]—discourse emphasized positive effects of social networking via online platforms and other web

[31] Kaminski (n 20) 1559ff; Selbst (n 20) 153ff; Gregorio and Dunn (n 28) 486; Bloch-Wehba (n 26) 45; van Loo (n 22) 1565ff; Douek (n 22) 560; Evelyn Douek, 'Governing Online Speech: From "Posts-as-Trumps" to Proportionality and Probability' (2021) 121 Columbia Law Review 759, 827; Dennis Hirsch, 'Going Dutch? Collaborative Dutch Privacy Regulation and the Lessons It Holds for U.S. Privacy Law' (2013) Michigan State Law Review 83ff; Amelie Heldt and Stephan Dreyer, 'Competent Third Parties and Content Moderation on Platforms: Potentials of Independent Decision-Making Bodies From A Governance Structure Perspective' (2021) 11 Journal of Information Policy 266, 281ff; Gregorio and Dunn (n 28); emphasizing the importance of industry collaboration and subsequent 'sensible governmental involvement' see Martha Minow and Newton Minow, 'Social Media Companies Should Pursue Serious Self-Supervision: Soon: Response to Professors Douek and Kadri' (2023) 136 Harvard Law Review F 431, 438ff.

[32] Jonathan Zittrain, 'Three Eras of Digital Governance' (SSRN, 2 October 2019) <https://ssrn.com/abstract=3458435> accessed 4 August 2023. Other US legal scholars refer to Zittran's framing: Douek (n 22) 552; Douek (n 31) 764; alternatively—but to some extent correspondingly—Nirit Weiss-Blatt as a scholar of journalism organizes the evolution of the media coverage about social media in a pre-Techlash era, a Techlash era and a post-Techlash era, referring increasingly negative perception of the influence of tech companies, Nirit Weiss-Blatt, *The Techlash and Tech Crisis Communication* (1st edn, Emerald Publishing Limited 2020) 3ff, 37ff, 121ff.

[33] See the account of Bloch-Wehba (n 26) 49–50.

services.[34] These effects included connectivity, innovation, and empowering everyone with the rights free speech and participation in the market place of ideas or in market places for e-commerce.[35] US courts supported the rights-based individualistic approach by striking down, on First Amendment grounds, core provisions of the US Communications Decency Act of 1996 (CDA), which sought to protect minors from indecent content by penalizing not only the originators of this material but also online intermediaries for 'knowing' transmission as long as intermediaries do not take good faith effective action to restrict access by minors. The Court referred in its ruling to chilling effects of such good faith actions on protected speech.[36]

In extending this reasoning based on free speech arguments, US courts construed another provision of the CDA, the famous liability shield provided in Article 230 CDA, extensively. This judicial approach minimized legal incentives for online platforms to establish effective moderation measures against harmful content uploaded by their users.[37] However, the rights-based approach resulted in a remarkable dialectic with a *laissez-faire* approach concerning offensive or even harassing speech while copyright holders had been more successful in protecting their individual property rights against infringements in form of unlicensed uploads and the like.[38]

2. The Public Health Era: Realizing systemic risks and developing automated content moderation

That individualistic approach has been modified or at least complemented during a second phase of digital governance called by Zittrain the 'Public Health Era'[39] aiming at a 'healthier online discourse'[40]—a term corresponding to the DSA's objective of effectively implementing EU policies 'for a safe, predictable and trusted online environment'.[41] Starting roughly around 2010, an increasing number of political and societal actors became aware not only of the Internet's benefits but also of—individual or systemic—harms and risks connected with social networks. Turning points have been real-time transmissions on social media platforms of brutal violence by various kinds of terrorists or other criminals, the suspected Russian interventions into the Brexit referendum, and the 2016 US presidential election, disinformation during the COVID-19 pandemic, and finally the

[34] For an account of the corresponding positive media coverage in the pre-Techlash era see Weiss-Blatt (n 32) ch 1.

[35] Zittrain (n 32) 1.

[36] *Reno v ACLU* 521 US 844, 870–874 (1997).

[37] Danielle K Citron and Mary A Franks, 'The Internet as a Speech Machine and Other Myths Confounding Section 230 Reform' (2020) University of Chicago Legal Forum 45, 46, 50ff.

[38] See Bloch-Wehba (n 26) 62–64, 66–69; Douek (n 31) 794.

[39] Zittrain (n 32) after note 9.

[40] Bloch-Wehba (n 26) 43.

[41] Art 1(1) DSA.

6 January 2021 US Capitol attack.[42] As a consequence, politicians as well as scholars asked for 'systemic interventions' curtailing such risks without unduly trimming the Internet's benefits.[43] The importance of informal political pressure on platforms to strengthen their content moderation efforts is significant, while formal legislation played only a limited role until the EU Digital Services Act.[44] If legislators imposed—sometimes rather demanding—obligations of content moderation, they preferred to leave it to the private platform providers to determine how to comply,[45] for instance by using unpopular automated upload filters or not.[46]

In addition to the already mentioned specific case of protecting copyrights, two of the prominent amongst these systemic risks are especially instructive from this perspective. The first concerns cyber-mobbing and individual harassment. Most of the victims of these systemic harms in the cyberspace are women, especially women of colour, or sexual minorities. Online abuse of social media and other digital infrastructures for public discourse silences these social groups and, consequently, deforms the market place of ideas by exaggerating the right to free speech of other—privileged and powerful—social groups or even individuals.[47] Danielle Keats Citron and Mary Anne Franks draw the conclusion that '[e]ven as the internet has multiplied the possibilities of expression, it has multiplied the possibilities of repression'.[48] In line with the public health approach identified by Zittrain, they argue for systemic interventions by incentivizing platforms to establish reasonable content moderation practices in accordance with the types and scale of risks caused by the respective platform as well as the respective platform´s resources for content moderation including algorithmic moderation technologies.[49]

The second example regarding the systemic public health approach concerns combating mis- and disinformation. Empirical studies show the relevance of this problem, although it still is a matter of debate whether observed correlations also indicate causal responsibilities of online intermediaries.[50] After the Congressional

[42] Compare Bloch-Wehba (n 26) 42, 60–61; Douek (n 31) 767, 778–81, 796; Evelyn Douek, 'Facebook's Role in the Genocide in Myanmar: New Reporting Complicates the Narrative' (*Lawfare*, 22 October 2018) <https://perma.cc/UB39-UM35> accessed 4 August 2023; Evelyn Douek, 'Two Calls for Tech Regulation: The French Government Report and the Christchurch Call' (*Lawfare*, 18 May 2019) <https://perma.cc/8QFX-AY4T> accessed 4 August 2023; See also the account of big tech´s scandals starting in 2016: Weiss-Blatt (n 32) ch 2.

[43] Zittrain (n 32) 1 and after note 9.

[44] Bloch-Wehba (n 26) 59, 61, 78, 95. The German NetzDG as well as—according to the Conseil Constitutionnel unconstitutional—the French 'Loi Avia' are interesting exceptions and probably important incentives, and models, for EU legislation.

[45] Bloch-Wehba (n 26) 45.

[46] Especially inconsistent in this regard is art 17 DSM-Directive in the field of copyright protection, causing obvious interpretative struggles for the ECJ: C-401/19 *Republic of Poland v European Parliament and Council of the European Union* (2022) ECLI:EU:C:2022:297 paras 39ff.

[47] Citron and Franks (n 37) 54–56, 67–68.

[48] ibid 68.

[49] ibid 71–74.

[50] See Jonathan Haidt, 'Why the Past 10 Years of American Life Have Been Uniquely Stupid' (*The Atlantic*, 11 April 2022) <https://www.theatlantic.com/magazine/archive/2022/05/social-media-democracy-trust-babel/629369/> accessed 4 August 2023; Jonathan Haidt, 'Yes, Social Media Really

hearings concerning the impact of Russian interference in the 2016 US Presidential election and reacting to the global public debate about misinformation during the COVID-19 pandemic, platforms have introduced policies against misinformation,[51] regularly implemented through algorithmic or even AI technologies.[52]

Evelyn Douek characterizes this new automated form of proactive content moderation as the systemic balancing of impacts on society with individual rights of uploading users of online systems by the relevant online platforms.[53] However, solving a fundamental social and political problem by technology is not without challenges and risks of 'unwarranted optimism'.[54] This is even more true as there is still an ongoing debate about the causal responsibility of social media for recent democratic challenges.[55]

3. The Legitimacy Era: A case for regulating private content moderation?

Against this complexity of balancing conflicting social interests through fully or semi-automated content moderation, online platforms are no longer perceived by many scholars as neutral intermediaries simply facilitating communication between people. Instead, they are the 'new governors' of online speech, as Kate Klonick and others have classified them.[56] Platforms evolved to become actors that implement algorithmic technologies, shaping opportunities in the market place of ideas according to their non-neutral business interests and their contested understanding and management of systemic risks.[57] In addition, the public

Is Undermining Democracy' (*The Atlantic*, 28 July 2022) <https://www.theatlantic.com/ideas/archive/2022/07/social-media-harm-facebook-meta-response/670975/> accessed 4 August 2023 who caused a scholarly debate about the empirical basis for his interpretation; Gideon Lewis-Kraus, 'How Harmful Is Social Media?' (*The New Yorker*, 3 June 2022) <https://www.newyorker.com/culture/annals-of-inquiry/we-know-less-about-social-media-than-we-think> accessed 28 September 2023; see also the collection abstracts of empirical studies Jonathan Haidt and Chris Bail, 'Social Media and Political Dysfunction: A Collaborative Review' <https://docs.google.com/document/d/1vVAtMCQnz8WVxtSNQev_e1cGmY9rnY96ecYuAj6C548/edit> accessed 28 September 2023 and the study review Philipp Lorenz-Spreen and others, 'A Systematic Review of Worldwide Causal and Correlational Evidence on Digital Media and Democracy' (2022) *Nature Human Behaviour* 1ff <https://www.nature.com/articles/s41562-022-01460-1> accessed 4 August 2023.

[51] Douek (n 31) 761–63, 766, 800–04, 830.

[52] ibid 792–96.

[53] ibid 763, 764.

[54] Bloch-Wehba (n 26) 43, 82, citing Felten's third law: 'lawyers put too much faith in technical solutions, while technologists put too much faith in legal solutions'; see also Douek (n 31) 797–98, 802, 813; Lewis-Kraus (n 50).

[55] See n 50.

[56] Kate Klonick, 'The New Governors: The People, Rules and Processes Governing Online Speech' (2018) 131 Harvard Law Review 1598ff; see also Jack Balkin, 'Free Speech is a Triangle' (2018) 118 Columbia Law Review 2011, 2021–32; Hannah Bloch-Wehba, 'Global Platform Governance: Private Power in the Shadow of the State' (2019) 72 Southern Methodist University Law Review 27, 33–40; Bloch-Wehba (n 26) 44, 51; Douek (n 31) 768; Giancarlo Frosio, 'Platform Responsibility in the Digital Services Act: Constitutionalising, Regulating and Governing Private Ordering' in Andrej Savin and Jan Trzaskowski (eds), *Research Handbook on EU Internet Law* (Edward Elgar Publishing 2023) 253, 255–262 <https://ssrn.com/abstract=4236510> accessed 4 August 2023.

[57] Zittrain (n 32) by note 14ff.

health approach supports—potentially anti-competitive—horizontal cooperation between platforms, for instance by establishing shared industry databases with fingerprints or hashes of illegal content,[58] by providing advanced moderation technologies to smaller competitors[59] or by cross-platform collaboration with certain—often self-interested—trusted flaggers.[60] Finally, the instrumental role of platforms for public interest content moderation provides opportunities of regulatory capture, particularly because public regulators may be less critical ofa centralized private governance of the Internet by dominant platform providers.[61] New regulatory concepts are starting to reflect this analysis. Zittrain calls this third phase of digital governance the 'Process or Legitimacy Era'.

More generally, platforms with dominant market power may perform a gatekeeper function to online market places of ideas or products. As private enterprises, platforms follow incentives of the digital economy which might conflict with public interests or fundamental rights of platform users. Platform providers might even abuse their gatekeeper function, especially if the platform serves as an infrastructure in vertically integrated markets. Consequently, an increasing number of commentators demand procedural and organizational safeguards for a fair balancing of competing legal and economic interests and against abuse of platform power. These safeguards for private platforms mirror, at least in some features, accountability and legitimacy mechanisms usually applied to administrative bodies.

The current debate in the United States concerns first the question of whether this governing role of private platforms is protected free speech under the First Amendment in accordance with the traditional state/private action distinction or whether social media platforms of a certain size should be treated as common carriers obliged to respect the free speech rights of their users.[62] According to traditional US constitutional law this is a binary test. In contrast, both German and European constitutional law allow for a more nuanced approach of combining and balancing both perspectives. Consequently, content moderation by private platforms can be regarded as an activity protected by their own fundamental communicative or business rights while they can also be obliged to respect fundamental

[58] Bloch-Wehba (n 26) 58–59.

[59] ibid 85–86.

[60] ibid 61, also 94–95; Naomi Appelman and Paddy Leerssen, 'On "Trusted" Flaggers' 15ff <https://law.yale.edu/sites/default/files/area/center/isp/documents/trustedflaggers_ispessayseries_2022.pdf> accessed 4 August 2023; Sebastian F Schwemer, 'Trusted Notifiers and the Privatization of Online Enforcement' (2019) 35(6) Computer Law & Security Review 105339 6ff.

[61] Jack Balkin, 'Old-School/New-School Speech Regulation' (2014) 127 Harvard Law Review 2296, 2325–26; Bloch-Wehba (n 26) 46–47, 61, and 94–95 on informal state interventions.

[62] *Netchoice v Ken Paxton* US 596 US ___ No 21A720 (2022); Evelyn Douek and Genevieve Lakier, 'First Amendment Politics Gets Weird: Public and Private Platform Reform and the Breakdown of the Laissez-Faire Free Speech Consensus' (2022) The University of Chicago Law Review Online <https://lawreviewblog.uchicago.edu/2022/06/06/douek-lakier-first-amendment/> accessed 4 August 2023.

rights of their users (horizontal effects of fundamental rights or '*mittelbare Drittwirkung*').

A second aspect of scholarly debate in the United States and around the world concerns the appropriate types of specific safeguards for broad-scale content moderation increasingly performed or supported by algorithmic or even AI systems. We will focus on this aspect in the following.

A first, widely shared approach to regulating (automated) content moderation follows traditional models of *ex-post* individual review of contested moderation measures combined with individual process rights to be heard, complaint mechanisms, and duties of platform operators to give reasons for their actions of content moderation.[63] Some scholars criticize this adjudicatory model as insufficient if not as a mere 'accountability theatre' inappropriate for automated mass speech administration.[64]

These scholars argue that such individual *ex-post* review or complaint mechanisms should be substituted or complemented by structural and procedural mechanisms in accordance with new or collaborative governance models targeting the key *ex-ante* and systemic decision-making or even rule-making by platforms that occurs before any individual case.[65] Complaint-handling mechanisms are again part of the proposed frameworks but these are complemented by proposals ranging from the separation of platform functions, duties to disclose the nature and extent of contacts with third-party decision-makers, retention and access to (moderation) data, annual content moderation plans and compliance reports[66] including algorithmic impact assessments, and auditing schemes, to frameworks for aggregated court proceedings.[67]

Such a systemic procedural approach needs to be accompanied by adequate substantial principles. For example, US scholars are starting to discuss the balancing of multiple interests and rights in the framework of proportionality which is well-known to European lawyers but intensively disputed in the United States.[68] The second less developed principle concerns probability or more concretely the acceptance of error rates of algorithmic decision-making in platform governance.[69] This chapter will show that automated content moderation of large-scale

[63] Douek (n 22) 564ff; for a critical analysis of Facebook's Oversight Board and describing alternative instruments in form of multi-stakeholder Social Media Councils see Bloch-Wehba (n 26) 90–94; Bloch-Wehba (n 56) 76–78; David Wong and Luciano Floridi, 'Meta's Oversight Board: A Review and Critical Assessment' (2023) 33 Minds & Machines 261ff.

[64] Douek (n 22) 528, 533, 572ff.

[65] ibid 528, 533, 584ff; Kaminski (n 20) 1552ff: 'two-pronged approach'; Jack Balkin, 'Free Speech Versus the First Amendment' (2023) 70 UCLA Law Review1206, 1245ff <https://ssrn.com/abstract=4413721> accessed 26 September 2023.

[66] For an account of important deficits of early transparency obligations see also Bloch-Wehba (n 26) 87–90.

[67] Douek, (n 22) 584ff.

[68] Douek (n 31) 763, 765, 776–89; 805–08, 814–26.

[69] ibid 763–68, 789–99, 808–13, 824–25, 828–29; see also Bloch-Wehba (n 26) 78.

user-generated content (mass communication 2.0) will in a number of cases cause over-blocking of legal content or under-blocking of illegal or harmful content (section B.II.2). The proposed probability principle would be an instrument to take this unavoidable reality into account as well as to set boundaries for the acceptance of error rates. In comparison to the principle of proportionality, the dogmatic details of such a probability principle are even less developed and accepted.

II. A collaborative governance framework for (automated) content moderation

As mentioned earlier, the new EU digital rulebook, consisting of the DMA and mainly the DSA, outsources comprehensive public policy functions, particularly to so-called VLOPs and VLOSEs. These functions have either an individual rights dimension (section B.II.1) or concern systemic risks potentially caused by these digital service providers (section B.III).

1. Outsourcing of content moderation combatting illegal content and protecting individual rights holders

A central objective of the DSA is to combat illegal content while also enhancing the protection of individual rights in the context of content moderation. According to Article 3(h) DSA, illegal content means any information which, in itself or in relation to an activity, including the sale of products or the provision of services, does not comply with Union law or the law of any Member State. Obviously, enforcement of Union or national law has a public policy dimension and we will develop this argument at the end of this section.

The DSA provides a framework for private law enforcement through content moderation. Article 3(t) DSA defines content moderation very broadly as:

> activities, automated or not, undertaken by providers of intermediary services aimed, in particular, at detecting, identifying and addressing illegal content or information incompatible with their terms and conditions, provided by recipients of the service, including measures taken that affect the availability, visibility, and accessibility of that illegal content or that information, such as demotion, demonetization, disabling of access to, or removal thereof, or the recipients' ability to provide that information, such as the termination or suspension of a recipient's account.[70]

[70] Please note also art 17(1) DSA requiring a statement of reasons in case of restrictions imposed by host providers as a result of their content moderation and defining various types of restrictions which are notwithstanding a divergent terminology functional equivalents to moderation measures listed in art 3(t) DSA. This functional equivalence is highlighted in art 14(1) DSA referring in sentence 1 to restrictions and in sentence 2 to content moderation measures.

The definition covers moderation of illegal content as well as moderation of content incompatible with the platform´s community standards, the latter qualifying as contractual self-regulation through terms and conditions. Interestingly, the DSA acknowledges the relevance of this self-interested variant of content management and includes it in the accountability safeguards analysed below (section B.II.3.a). This comprehensive approach is also relevant with regard to the analysis of outsourcing public functions, as the 'self-interested' enforcement of community standards overlaps to quite an extent with combatting illegal content, and platforms tend to prefer enforcing their community standards in their content moderation. In addition, community standards sometimes address legal but individually or socially harmful content. In this case they complement legal standards which is especially important in the US constitutional order with its extensive—or even excessive—protection of free speech, probably to the systemic detriment of certain marginalized groups in society (so-called silencing).[71]

The traditional approach concerning illegal content distributed by intermediaries under the E-Commerce-Directive—following the model of Section 230 CDA—has been to conceptualize platforms as neutral digital intermediaries and to protect them against liability for user-generated content as long as they do not have actual knowledge of the illegality of that content. Articles 4–8 DSA maintain this approach as a starting point but transforms it by introducing new due diligence obligations.[72]

A central due diligence obligation to combat illegal content is a clearly structured notice-and-action mechanism. According to Article 16(1)1 DSA, '[p]roviders of hosting services[73] shall put mechanisms in place to allow any individual or entity to notify them of the presence on their service of specific items of information that the individual or entity considers to be illegal content'. Those mechanisms shall be 'easy to access, user-friendly' and shall also 'facilitate the submission of sufficiently precise and adequately substantiated notices' (Article 16(1)2, (2)1 DSA). In contrast to the German NetzDG, Article 16(6) DSA does not provide for defined response times but requires a timely—although also diligent, non-arbitrary, and objective—decision in respect of the notified content by the respective platform or host provider.

A strong incentive to engage in content moderation concerning notified content follows from Article 16(3) DSA according to which such notices 'shall be considered to give rise to actual knowledge or awareness . . . where they allow a diligent provider of hosting services to identify the illegality of the relevant activity

[71] See n 48.

[72] See also arts 1(1), 2(a) and (b) DSA stating that the DSA 'establishes: (a) a framework for the conditional exemption from liability of providers of intermediary services; (b) rules on specific due diligence obligations tailored to certain specific categories of providers of intermediary services'.

[73] Art 3(g)(iii) DSA defines hosting services as consisting of the storage of information provided by, and at the request of, a recipient of the service.

or information without a detailed legal examination'. Consequently, the respective platform would no longer be protected against liability.

These incentives are amplified by duties to inform the notifying person about the provider´s decision in respect of the notified content and the notifying person's option to lodge a complaint (Article 20 DSA), to initiate an out of-court dispute settlement (Article 21 DSA), or to file a suit against the platform or hosting provider in court (Article 21(1) sub-paragraph 3 DSA) (section B.II.3.a). Finally, national or European authorities have powers under the DSA to enforce compliance with these obligations (section B.II.3.a).

Another component of the new 'public health' framework is provided in Article 22 DSA. This provision establishes so-called trusted flaggers, whose notices are to be processed with priority by the platform and other host providers. The status of trusted flaggers is linked to certain requirements and granted by the national Digital Services Coordinators (DSCs)[74] (Article 22(2) DSA). As these trusted flaggers are often private persons such as instance holders of copyrights, they present another layer of private law enforcement.

Previous experience (see section B.II.2) indicates that this structured private notice-and-action mechanism will be much more important, at least in a quantitative dimension, than 'accessory' actions of intermediaries against illegal content upon the receipt of a court or administrative order according to Article 9 DSA. However, Article 9 DSA sheds light on the public policy dimension of the private notice-and-action mechanism.[75] Thus, the DSA obliges platforms to engage in private enforcement of legal compliance duties of content providers as a third party. In contrast to other examples of private enforcement, Article 16 DSA does not only cover digital content moderation in the self-interest of the platform or host provider—as in the case of enforcing a platform´s own community standards—but also includes 'altruistic' moderation of content infringing either legal provisions purely in the public interest or individual rights of third parties. This obligation to 'altruistic' content moderation qualifies as a form of outsourcing of a public function to platforms and host providers. In another words, these gatekeeping intermediaries become instruments for implementing public policies concerning the digital space. Even the 'self-interested' moderation of content incompatible with a platform's community standards might implement digital public policies. This is for instance the case if community standards reflect legal standards or complement them in policing socially harmful but legal content such as some forms of hate speech. The EU legislator acknowledges the social function of voluntary content moderation in the new Good Samaritan Clause provided in Article 7 DSA.[76]

[74] For more details about the Digital Services Coordinators see section C.I.1 this chapter.

[75] See also art 18 DSA.

[76] However, art 7 DSA will probably have only limited impact as the provision only aims at not discouraging voluntarily effective content moderation but it does not provide a proactive incentive to become a good Samaritan; for similar questions in art 230 CDA see Citron and Franks (n 37) 66–67, 71–74.

Our analysis that the DSA is outsourcing important functions to platforms and other digital intermediaries can be further developed with regard to the quasi-judicial functions these private actors perform by moderating digital content. Conflicts about moderation of presumably illegal content or content infringing community standards are often multipolar in nature. This is the case if such a conflict involves not only rights of the content provider like free speech or business rights but also affects individual rights holders as third parties, for instance in their copyrights or rights to privacy and non-discrimination. The determination of such multipolar conflicts raises often complex legal questions involving fundamental rights and the like. Even if these disputes might in some cases finally be investigated and decided by an administrative authority or even a court, the vast number of cases will not only be temporarily but finally settled by platforms in their self-regulated content moderation and complaint-handling procedures.

2. Content moderation by ADM of online platforms and search engines

Especially relevant for the INDIGO project is the fact that online platforms and search engines intensively and increasingly rely for their content moderation on algorithmic or even AI technologies in order to cope with the sheer volume of online content processed and distributed by them.[77]

To take YouTube as an example: according to business observers, 500 hours of video material was uploaded every minute during the year 2019.[78] According to YouTube's latest Transparency Report, in 2021 the platform removed over 15 million channels worldwide with nearly 280 million videos based on violations against the company's community guidelines. In addition, in the same year the platform removed nearly 26 million individual videos in this period. The overwhelming majority of these removed videos (94 per cent) had been detected by automated flagging while only about 1 million videos has been notified by humans, mainly users but also trusted flaggers.[79] Fewer than 300 videos were notified by government agencies. Automated flagging plays an even more important role in the moderation of comments. Of the roughly 4.6 billion comments removed, 99.5 per cent were detected automatically. The majority—63 per cent—were removed because the comment qualified as spam.[80] Even more relevant, nearly 20 per cent or over 850 million removed comments had been classified as child abuse, 14 per cent (or

[77] For an instructive account about the technologies—especially fingerprinting and hashing—and practical relevance of automated content moderation see Bloch-Wehba (n 26) 56–58, 61, 62, 64–66, 70, 72, 79; Douek (n 31) 792–98.

[78] <https://www.statista.com/statistics/259477/hours-of-video-uploaded-to-YouTube-every-minute/> accessed 28 September 2023; in 2015 400 hours of content had been uploaded per minute: <https://www.tubefilter.com/2015/07/26/YouTube-400-hours-content-every-minute/> accessed 4 August 2023.

[79] YouTube already recognized certain 'trusted flaggers' before the DSA established a duty in this regard. See Appelman and Leerssen (n 60) 2ff.

[80] Concerning the legal abate about spam filters see Bloch-Wehba (n 26) 52–55.

617 million) as harassment or cybermobbing, and 4 per cent—over 190 million comments—as hate speech. Of course, these enormous annual numbers are aggregated worldwide, but only for YouTube. They do not include the similarly massive number of removals based on copyright infringements.

This highlights the massive scale of content moderation on online platforms. It is without doubt that these case numbers need to be processed by or at least with substantial support of automated systems. Equally obvious is the assumption that this case load exceeds the resources of any court system in the world. Consequently, automated private content moderation is unavoidable if we do not want to shut down the popular and commercial Internet of today nor wish to take a *laissez-faire* approach by accepting an Internet within a legal vacuum.

The DSA proves that the European legislative bodies accept automated forms of digital governance of the Internet, at least implicitly, although not without limits, as we will elaborate in the following sections (sections B.II.3, B.III). Article 16(1)2 DSA facilitates ADM indirectly by stating that the obligatory notice mechanisms shall 'allow for the submission of notices exclusively by electronic means'. Explicitly mentioned are ADM systems in Article 16(6)2 DSA obliging the platform concerned to inform notifying persons about the use of automated content moderation systems, as well as in Article 17(3)I DSA obliging platforms to inform users affected by a restriction about automated content moderation systems either used for content detection or content evaluation. None of these provisions explicitly legitimize automated content moderation but they do indicate legislative acceptance.

However, automated content moderation systems are far from being perfect. Unfortunately, there no really comprehensive and balanced independent evaluation of automated moderation systems for online platforms seems to exist.[81] Ideally, such studies would provide clear evidence about over-blocking of legal content or content falsely qualified as illegal (false positives) as well as evidence concerning false negatives or under-blocking of illegal or unacceptable harmful content.

Nevertheless, at least some indicators exist to support the hypothesis that recent automated content moderation systems produce false positives as well as false negatives at relevant rates. Concerning false positives, the important field of automated

[81] Nevertheless, some smaller studies seem to support the assumption that over- as well as under-blocking exist: Robert Gorwa, Reuben Binns, and Christian Katzenbach, 'Algorithmic Content Moderation: Technical and Political Challenges in the Automation of Platform Governance' (2020) 7 Big Data & Society 1, 7–10; Bloch-Wehba (n 26) 45, 65; Douek (n 22) 548ff; for the US context Global Witness, *TikTok and Facebook Fail to Detect Election Disinformation in the US, while YouTube Succeeds* (2022) <https://www.globalwitness.org/documents/20434/TikTok_and_Facebook_fail_to_detect_election_disinformation_in_the_US_-_October_2022.pdf> accessed 28 September 2023; Thomas Davidson, Debasmita Bhattacharya, and Ingmar Weber, 'Racial Bias in Hate Speech and Abusive Language Detection Datasets' in Sarah T Roberts and others (eds), *Proceedings of the Third Workshop on Abusive Language Online* (1 August 2019, Florence, Italy) 25ff.

copyright enforcement provides, notwithstanding its specifics, some useful insights. According to YouTube's first copyright transparency report covering the first six months of 2021, in this period the platform's Content ID system generated at least 2.2 million unjustified claims of right holders against YouTube users generating and uploading content. YouTube's Content ID system is based on fingerprinting technology and scans uploaded videos against a database of audio and visual content that has been submitted to YouTube by copyright owners. When Content ID finds a match, it applies a Content ID claim to the matching video. In most cases a Content ID claim results in a form monetizing in favour of the right holder or in access of the right holder to the video's viewership statistics, but may also, depending on the copyright owner's Content ID settings, lead to blocking of the respective video.[82] Although only 0.5 per cent of all claims processed through Content ID have been disputed by concerned users[83] and only 60 per cent of these disputes have been resolved in favour of the uploader,[84] the total number of these cases of false positives and at least potential over-blocking is significant.[85] In addition, independent research suggests that only a fraction of potential over-blocking cases are referred to YouTube's complaint procedure.[86]

With regard to under-blocking, the Facebook Files suggest that this a similarly important problem of automated content management. According to leaked internal benchmarking tests comparing automated detection of hate speech and similar problematic content with human detection, the accuracy of the automated systems varies between 3 and 5 per cent and, in case of violent content, below 1 per cent.[87] Consequently, the number of false negatives might be massive compared to the already huge volume of content that is taken down.

[82] See <https://support.google.com/YouTube/answer/2797370?hl=en>; see also <https://en.wikipedia.org/w/index.php?title=Content_ID_(system)&oldid=1106919199> both accessed 4 August 2023.

[83] Users can dispute a Content ID claim.. The claimant has within a specified deadline to respond to the claim by either releasing the claim, letting the claim expire, or submit a formal takedown request based on the applicable copyright law and subject to a counter-notification option for the uploading user. The user can appeal if the claim is reinstated by the claimant. In the case of a blocked video the affected user can directly appeal the decision, thus shorten the procedure.

[84] <https://blog.YouTube/news-and-events/access-all-balanced-ecosystem-and-powerful-tools/>, accessed 4 August 2023. In the most recent YouTube Copyright Transparency Report for the second half of 2021 the numbers differ only slightly see <https://storage.googleapis.com/transparencyreport/report-downloads/pdf-report-22_2021-7-1_2021-12-31_en_v1.pdf> accessed 4 August 2023.

[85] <copyrightblog.kluweriplaw.com/2021/12/09/YouTube-copyright-transparency-report-overblocking-is-real/> accessed 4 August 2023.

[86] Jennifer M Urban, Joe Karaganis, and Brianna Schofield, 'Notice and Takedown in Everyday Practice' (2017) Notice and Takedown in Everyday Practice UC Berkeley Public Law Research Paper No 2755628 44–46, 116.

[87] Deepa Seetharaman, Jeff Horwitz, and Justin Scheck, 'Facebook Says AI Will Clean Up the Platform. Its Own Engineers Have Doubts' *The Wall Street Journal* (New York, 17 October 2021) <https://www.wsj.com/articles/facebook-ai-enforce-rules-engineers-doubtful-artificial-intelligence-11634338184?mod=article_inline>, accessed 4 August 2023, citing internal estimations of a detection rate of 2 per cent of all views of hate speech on Facebook in 2019 and 3–5 per cent in 2021. The detection accuracy rate for content against Facebook's policies against violence and incitement is estimated to be 0.6 per cent.

To sum up, it seems to be a fair assumption that both problems—over- and under-blocking—exist. Of course, automated content moderation systems do not have a monopoly in this regard. Human moderators will also fail to detect a certain percentage of harmful content, and this holds true for moderators hired by platforms as well as for judicial decision-making concerning moderation cases. And it is obvious, that human content moderation would not even remotely be able to check the same amount of content detected by automated systems. Thus human content moderation alone, if not complemented by automated systems, would result in a huge amount of under-blocking and produce the often cited 'legal vacuum'. However, if automated or hybrid content moderation is unavoidable and if we have to assume that these automated tools fail in a significant number of cases, we need to explore safeguards to encourage learning and to optimize the performance of these systems, as well as to support effective legal remedies for uploading users falsely blocked or for persons affected by harmful content that was not detected. To use administrative law terminology, we need to analyse accountability safeguards provided by the DSA for automated content management.

3. Accountability safeguards concerning (automated) content management

As mentioned earlier (section B.I.3), legal scholars differentiate in the debate about accountability safeguards for broad-scale content moderation between traditional models of *ex-post* individual review of contested moderation measures combined with individual *ex-ante* process rights (section B.II.3.a) and collaborative governance mechanisms targeting the systemic dimension of automated content moderation by platforms (section B.II.3.b).

a) Legal safeguards for individuals affected by (automated) content management measures

A first dimension of accountability safeguards established by the DSA provides legal protection for individuals affected by decisions about concrete content moderation measures or restrictions of digital services.[88]

The starting point is a transparency obligation of providers of intermediary services in Article 14 DSA.[89] Platforms and other providers have to set out in 'user friendly and unambiguous language' in their terms and conditions (eg community standards) 'any policies, procedures, measures and tools used for the purpose of content moderation, including algorithmic decision-making, and human review as well as rules of procedure of their internal complaint handling system'. Of course, such *ex-ante* transparency is no equivalent to an *ex-ante* hearing before

[88] As mentioned above the terminology varies in arts 3(t), 14(1), 17 DSA, section B.II.1 with n 70.

[89] In line with its concept of asymmetric regulation (section A with note 15) the DSA provides for specific groups of intermediaries additional transparency and especially reporting obligations about content moderation (arts 15, 24, 42 DSA, see also regarding trusted flaggers art 22(3) DSA), recommender systems (art 27 DSA), and online advertising systems (arts 26, 39 DSA).

imposing any restriction, but it at least allows the fact that users can 'calculate' the risk of moderation measures concerning content they intend to upload.[90] The position of users against unjustified moderation measures is considerably strengthened by the obligation of private providers of intermediaries services, explicitly anchored in Article 14(4) DSA, to take into account the rights and legitimate interests of all parties involved, including the fundamental rights of the recipients of the service, such as freedom of expression, freedom and pluralism of the media, and other fundamental rights and freedoms as enshrined in the Charter.[91]

An especially important procedural safeguard according to Article 17 DSA is the duty of host providers, including platforms, to state the reasons to any affected user for restrictions of the visibility of specific content, of monetary payments, or of the provision of services including the suspension or termination of the user's accounts. In addition to the general duty the provision stipulates certain minimum information requirements including information about redress possibilities as well as the objective that the statement shall 'reasonably allow the recipient of the service concerned to effectively exercise the redress possibilities'.

In addition to these *ex-ante* obligations, the DSA establishes new or referrals to existing redress possibilities concerning content moderation measures. Under this framework, recipients of digital services and especially platform users as well as notifying persons in the meaning of Article 16 DSA are able to choose between an internal complaint mechanism (Article 20 DSA), a non-binding out-of-court dispute settlement (Article 21 DSA), and the possibility to initiate, at any stage, judicial proceedings according to the applicable national law (see Article 21(1) sub-paragraph 3 DSA).[92] Consequently, these persons may use any of these possibilities either alternatively or successively.

According to Article 20 DSA, platforms have to provide internal complaint-handling systems that are 'easy to access, user-friendly and enable and facilitate the submission of sufficiently precise and adequately substantiated complaints' against

[90] Note that with regard to potential copyright valuations, some platforms like YouTube provide for their users automated self-control systems.

[91] For an account of the debate about this legislative extension of the EU Charter of Fundamental Rights to private service providers see João P Quintais, Naomi Appelman, and Ronan Ó Fathaigh, 'Using Terms and Conditions to Apply Fundamental Rights to Content Moderation' (2023) German Law Journal 1, 11ff; Michael Denga, 'Plattformregulierung durch europäische Werte: Zur Bindung von Meinungsplattformen an EU-Grundrechte' (2021) 56(5) Europarecht 569, 584ff; Martin Eifert and others, 'Taming the Giants: The DMA/DSA Package' (2021) Common Market Law Review 987, 1013. The EP did not adopt proposals for *an ex-ante* counter-notification as a specific safeguard for media enterprises see Lina Rusch, 'Grünes Licht für DSA im Europaparlament' *Tagesspiegel Background* (21 January 2022) Tagesspiegel Background <https://background.tagesspiegel.de/digitalisierung-und-ki/briefing/gruenes-licht-fuer-dsa-im-europaparlament> accessed 2 July 2024; Torben Klausa, 'Erhebliche Änderungswünsche im EU-Parlament' *Tagesspiegel Background* (18 January 2022) <https://background.tagesspiegel.de/digitalisierung-und-ki/briefing/erhebliche-aenderungswuensche-im-eu-parlament> accessed 2 July 2024; EP, 'Report of the Committee on the Internal Market and Consumer Protection' (Report) A9-0356/2021 Amendment 511.

[92] Recital 59 DSA highlights this option to choose among various redress possibilities.

listed content moderation decisions. Potential complainants are not only users affected by a service restriction concerning their uploaded content when it has been qualified as illegal or incompatible with community standards. In addition, persons that have submitted a notice under Article 16 DSA are entitled to lodge a complaint. Providers of online platforms shall handle complaints submitted through their internal complaint-handling system in a timely, non-discriminatory, diligent, and non-arbitrary manner and they shall reverse their original decision if necessary (Article 20(4) DSA). In contrast to Article 4(3)2 P2B Regulation 2019/1150,[93] the DSA does not provide a 'put-back'-obligation.[94] The complaint decision must be taken under the control of appropriately qualified staff and not solely on the basis of automated means (Article 20(6) DSA). This safeguard of human oversight in case of ADM is especially relevant for the INDIGO project. Finally, the complaint decision has to include a statement of reasons as well as information about available redress possibilities including out-of-court dispute settlements according to Article 21 DSA.

Article 21 DSA provides a framework for non-binding out-of-court dispute settlements.[95] While the complaint-handling mechanism according to Article 20 DSA regulates internal procedures of platforms this framework qualifies clearly as a collaborative structure. According to Article 21(3)(a) DSA, settlement bodies must be independent of platforms, platform users, and notifying persons in the meaning of Article 16 DSA in order to be certified by a competent public authority, in other words the national DSC of their—and not the platform's—origin.[96] This national DSC is also competent to monitor settlement bodies based on information originating from reporting duties of these bodies or other sources and to revoke any certification if a settlement body no longer meets the legislative requirements (Article 21(7), (3), (3b) DSA). Member States may support activities of certified settlement bodies or even establish additional 'public' settlement bodies (Article 21(6) DSA). Article 21(5) DSA provides a framework for a fair distribution of cost-efficient fees charged by settlement bodies from platforms and users.[97]

As mentioned Article 21(1) sub-paragraph 3 DSA explicitly acknowledges the right of any affected user or notifying person to initiate, at any stage, proceedings

[93] For details see Daniel Holznagel, *Notice and Take-Down-Verfahren als Teil der Providerhaftung* (Mohr Siebeck 2013) 252ff.

[94] Philipp Adelberg, 'Hassrede in sozialen Netzwerken: Reichweite und Grenzen der Pflichten und Rechte der Netzwerkbetreiber' (2022) Kommunikation und Recht 19, 22; 'put-back obligation' means an explicit civil claim by the user to reinstate the content/accounts etc.

[95] For a positive evaluation see Cole, Etteldorf, and Ullrich (n 17) 197; for a critical evaluation see Daniel Holznagel, 'Zu starke Nutzerrechte in Art. 17 und 18 DSA' (2022) Computer und Recht 594, 602ff; Daniel Holznagel, 'Nutzerrechte bei Facebook: Klärung durch den BGH und bevorstehende Irrwege des EU-Gesetzgebers' (2021) Computer und Recht 733, 736; Jörg Wimmers, 'The Out-of-Court Dispute Settlement Mechanism in the Digital Services Act: A Disservice to its Own Goals' (2021) Journal of Intellectual Property, Technology and Electronic Commerce Law 381ff.

[96] For details about Digital Service Coordinators see section C.I.1.

[97] See also Recital 59 DSA.

to contest moderation decisions of online platforms before a court in accordance with the applicable law. As settlement bodies, according to Article 21(2) subparagraph 3 DSA, only issue non-binding proposals, the parties are not prevented from initiating judicial proceedings in relation to the same dispute.[98] In contrast to Article 14 P2B Regulation 2019/1150, the DSA does not provide an explicit rule fostering judicial proceedings by representative organizations or associations. However, according to Article 86 DSA, users may mandate a legal person or public body to exercise their rights conferred by the DSA for instance to notify illegal content or lodge a complaint.[99] In addition, Article 86 DSA leaves explicitly untouched the full application of Directive (EU) 2020/1828 on representative actions for the protection of the collective interests of consumers or any other type of consumer representation under national law.

Finally, according to Article 53 DSA, recipients of digital services[100] shall have the right to lodge a complaint against providers of intermediary services alleging an infringement of this Regulation with the Digital Services Coordinator of the Member State where the recipient is located or established.[101] Thus individuals have the possibility to initiate a public enforcement procedure against either unjustified or omitted content moderation measures. In order to respect the DSA's general competence framework (section C.I.1), the DSC, addressed by the complainant, shall assess the complaint but must, if the complaint is founded, transmit it to the DSC of establishment of the platform, accompanied, where considered appropriate, by an opinion (Article 53 sentence 2 DSA). The DSC of establishment of the platform will take the final decision about the justification of the contested moderation measure or its omission and consequently about the adoption of an enforcement order under Article 51 DSA. If a contested moderation measure was issued by a VLOP or VLOSE, the DSC addressed by the complainant may send through the EU information sharing system referred to in Article 85 DSA a reasoned request to the Commission to assess the matter (Article 65(2), (3) DSA).

b) Systemic accountability safeguards concerning (automated) content management

As discussed (section B.I.3), it is important that the DSA does not only provide legal safeguards in individual content moderation cases. Instead, the DSA establishes complementing accountability safeguards addressing systemic challenges or problems of (automated) content moderation.

[98] Recital 59 DSA.

[99] See also Recital 149 DSA.

[100] As well as any body, organization, or association mandated by them to exercise on their behalf the rights conferred by this Regulation.

[101] For a detailed analysis of this innovative regulatory mechanism see Jens-Peter Schneider, 'Das verwaltungsrechtliche Beschwerderecht für Plattformnutzer gem. Art. 53 DSA—Erster Überblick zum zentralen Baustein des neuen Aufsichtsregimes für digitale Dienste' (2023) 39(1) Computer und Recht 45ff.

The most important systemic accountability safeguard consists in obligations of VLOPs and VLOSEs to independently assess and mitigate systemic risks *inter alia* caused by their content moderation systems (Article 34(2)(a), (b), Article 35(1)(c), (d) DSA). These self-assessment duties are themselves subject to a complex collaborative accountability framework (section B.III).

Another element of the DSA's systemic accountability framework concerning automated content moderation consists of asymmetric transparency and public reporting obligations.[102] According to Article 15(1) DSA all intermediaries—or, with regard to some topics, all host providers—except those qualifying as micro or small enterprises have to publish an annual content moderation report including *inter alia* specified information about

- the use and practice of their notice-and-action mechanism under Article 16 DSA including information about the use of automated tools and the various types of illegal content or violations of their community standards;
- the use and practice of their internal complaint-handling systems according to Article 20 DSA;
- 'any use made of automated means for the purpose of content moderation, including a qualitative description, a specification of the precise purposes, indicators of the accuracy and the possible rate of error of the automated means used in fulfilling those purposes, and any safeguards applied'.

Additional transparency obligations apply to online platforms first about their reasoned service restrictions as regulated in Article 17(1) DSA[103] and second concerning the use and practice of out-of-court dispute settlement procedures under Article 21 DSA (Article 24(1)(a), (5) DSA). The most demanding reporting duties apply to VLOPs and VLOSEs (Article 42(2) DSA). These duties comprise—next to reporting duties concerning the VLOPs' and VLOSEs' risk assessments (section B.III)—information *inter alia* about human resources dedicated to content moderation, the expertise and training of moderating staff, and the accuracy of automated moderation systems per official language of the Union and not only aggregated as under Article 15 DSA.

An important element of expanding systemic regulatory knowledge about automated content management consist in rights for national authorities or the Commission to gain access themselves to data and algorithms of VLOPs and VLOSEs or to request such data access for so-called vetted researchers (Article 40,

[102] See also reporting duties concerning recommender systems (art 27 DSA) and online advertising systems (art 26, 39 DSA). Finally, reporting obligations of 'trusted flaggers' and the Commission's public database based on their submitted information should be taken into account (art 22(3), (4), (5) DSA); see also section A with note 15.

[103] The decisions and statements of reasons submitted by the platform providers shall not contain personal data and will be included into a publicly accessible machine-readable database managed by the Commission, art 24(5) DSA.

Article 69(2)(d), Article 72(1)2 DSA; see section B.III). Remarkably, Article 65(2), (3)(b) DSA providing powers for national authorities to send a request to the Commission to assess activities of VLOPs and VLOSEs (section C.I.3) refers explicitly to suspected infringements of a systemic nature.

Finally, we would like to draw attention to Article 23 DSA which provides duties of online platforms to restrict misuse either by users that 'frequently provide manifestly illegal content', or by persons 'that frequently submit notices or complaints that are manifestly unfounded'. Such frequent misuse has at least some systemic relevance, although the provisions concerns misuse by individual users, notifying persons, or claimants.

III. A collaborative governance framework for systemic risk management

Probably the most innovative building block of the new rulebook for digital services are Articles 34–37, 40, 42 DSA. These provisions offer a framework for VLOPs and VLOSEs to examine, assess, and mitigate systemic risks emanating in particular from their algorithmic systems under independent and regulatory control. In this way, the legislator is responding to the increasing—while not yet settled—debate about societal impacts of today's platform economy (section B.I.2). The framework is—in accordance with the DSA's general collaborative governance concept—characterized by its reflexive, knowledge-generating, and learning-oriented approach, which on the one hand specifically encourages and pre-structures self-regulation by VLOPs and VLOSEs,[104] and on the other hand provides regulatory monitoring powers supported by independent research. Noteworthy in this respect are:

- obligations of VLOPs and VLOSEs to carry out a risk assessment on their own responsibility and to take effective risk reduction measures (Article 34, 35(1) DSA);[105]

[104] Alexander Peukert, 'Five Reasons to be Skeptical About the DSA' in Heiko Richter, Marlene Straub, and Heiko Tuchfeld (eds), *To Break Up or Regulate Big Tech? Avenues to Constrain Private Power in the DSA/DMA Package* (Max Planck Institute for Innovation and Competition, 2021) 22f; Herbert Zech in Richter, Straub, and Tuchfeld (eds), *To Break Up or Regulate Big Tech?* ibid 37, 40; Nicolo Zingales, 'The DSA as a Paradigm Shift for Online Intermediaries' Due Diligence: Hail to Meta-Regulation' (*Verfassungsblog*, 2022) <https://verfassungsblog.de/dsa-meta-regulation/> accessed 26 September 2023.

[105] Quintais, Appelman, and Ó Fathaigh (n 91) 14, 25–27; Gregorio and Dunn (n 28) 487ff; Alessandro Mantelero, 'Fundamental Rights Impact Assessments in the DSA' (2022) Verfassungsblog <https://verfassungsblog.de/dsa-impact-assessment/> accessed 28 September 2023; Johannes Buchheim, 'Der Kommissionsentwurf eines Digital Services Act—Regelungsinhalte, Regelungsansatz, Leerstellen und Konfliktpotential' in Indra Spiecker Döhmann, Michael Westland, and Ricardo Campos (eds), *Demokratie und Öffentlichkeit im 21. Jahrhundert—zur Macht des Digitalen* (1st edn, Nomos 2022) 249,

- the verification of these measures by independent and competent—while not certified by public authorities like settlement bodies—audit bodies on behalf and at the expense of the respective VLOPs and VLOSEs (Article 37 DSA)[106] as well as by in-house compliance officers (Article 41(3) DSA);[107]
- the mandatory and to be documented implementation of operational change recommendations from the independent audit reports by the respective VLOPs and VLOSEs (Article 37(6) DSA);
- the preparation and—while respecting confidentiality concerns—the publication of a company-related annual report by VLOPs and VLOSEs on identified systemic risks, risk mitigation measures taken, results of the independent audit, and implementation of the audit recommendations (Article 42(4), (5) DSA);
- obligations of VLOPs and VLOSEs to submit an annual report to the competent national DSC and the Commission, as well as, upon request, the original audit documents, which are to be kept (Article 42(5) and Article 34(3) DSA);
- access rights for the national DSCs or the Commission to the data of the VLOPs and VLOSEs relevant for enforcement monitoring (Article 40(1), (2), (7), Article 72(1) DSA), while respecting the security concerns and trade secrets of the companies (Article 40(2) DSA); the Commission has additional access rights to algorithms of VLOPs and VLOSEs (Article 69(2)(d), (3), Article 72(1) DSA), but must respect confidentiality claims (Article 80(2) DSA);[108]
- the possible access to data of VLOPs and VLOSEs for vetted independent researchers according to Article 40(4), (7) DSA for research contributing to the

259ff; Paolo Cesarini, 'Regulating Big Tech to Counter Online Disinformation: Avoiding Pitfalls while Moving Forward' (2021) Media Laws 11 <https://www.medialaws.eu/wp-content/uploads/2021/02/Cesarini.pdf> accessed 28 September 2023; Henrike Weiden, *Mehr Freiheit und Sicherheit im Netz: Gutachten zum Entwurf des DSA* (Friedrich-Naumann-Stiftung Für die Freiheit 2021) 22 <https://shop.freiheit.org/download/P2@1201/553388/FNF%20DSA-Gutachten_150222_web%20final.pdf> accessed 4 August 2023; Joan Barata, 'The Digital Services Act and Its Impact on the Right to Freedom of Expression: Special Focus on Risk Mitigation Obligations' 20 <https://libertadinformacion.cc/wp-content/uploads/2021/06/DSA-AND-ITS-IMPACT-ON-FREEDOM-OF-EXPRESSION-JOAN-BARATA-PDLI.pdf> accessed 4 August 2023.

[106] For a critical account of the DSA's auditing framework see Caroline Cauffman and Catalina Goanta, 'A New Order: The Digital Services Act and Consumer Protection' (2021) European Journal of Risk Regulation 758, 771; Cole, Etteldorf, and Ullrich (n 17) 201 with reference to (failed) examples in which such audits have been relied on rather than regulatory oversight; Deirdre Mulligan and Kenneth A Bamberger, 'Saving Governance-By-Design' (2018) 106 California Law Review 697, 718–19 <https://escholarship.org/content/qt9pk2h7m9/qt9pk2h7m9_noSplash_7cb98b172fe4879fa374960fb0436186.pdf> accessed 4 August 2023; Julie E Cohen, 'The Regulatory State in the Information Age' (2016) Theoretical Inquiries in Law 369, 403ff; Carsten Ullrich, *Unlawful Content Online, Towards a New Regulatory Framework for Online Platforms* (Nomos 2021) 538ff.

[107] Art 28 DMA requires such a gatekeeper/internal compliance function independent of a review of systemic risks.

[108] The extent to which additional powers concerning the compulsory submission of data on grounds of exceptional necessity at the request of national or Union authorities will result from art 14 et seq. of the Data Act proposal, Commission, 'Proposal on harmonised rules on fair access to and use of data (Data Act)' (Proposal) COM(2022) 68 final cannot yet be assessed.

detection, identification, understanding, and mitigation of systemic risks;[109] access has to be granted by VLOPs and VLOSEs only upon request of the national DSC responsible according to Article 55 DSA, who also decides on the approval of the researchers and the respective research projects upon application by researchers (Article 40(4), (8) et seq DSA);[110] in this context, the security concerns and business secrets of VLOPs and VLOSEs must be safeguarded, if necessary, by modifying access requests (Article 40(4), (5), (13) DSA);
- the preparation and publication of a pan-European and cross-platform annual report about the most prominent recurring systemic risks and about best-practice risk mitigation measures by the European Board for Digital Services (EBDS) in cooperation with the Commission (Article 35(2), DSA);
- the initiation, facilitation, and monitoring by the Commission and the EBDS of pan-European—including, where appropriate, binding—codes of conduct developed with the participation of VLOPs and VLOSEs and civil society organizations to address significant systemic risks affecting multiple VLOPs or VLOSEs (Article 45(2) DSA);[111]
- the possible issuance of guidelines presenting best practices or recommending certain risk management measures by the Commission in cooperation with national DSC and after conducting a public consultation (Article 35(3) DSA);[112]
- the enforcement of these obligations of VLOPs and VLOSEs by the Commission pursuant to Article 73 in conjunction with Article 75 DSA.[113]

Subject of assessment are systemic risks presumably arising from platform operation or platform use, in particular the content moderation, recommender, and

[109] A mechanism which grants researchers access to internal data of platforms was one of the most requested obligations prior to the legislative process. See Paddy Leerssen, 'The Soap Box as a Black Box: Regulating Transparency in Social Media Recommender Systems' (2020) European Journal of Law and Technology 1ff; Jef Ausloos, Paddy Leerssen, and Pim ten Thije, 'Operationalizing Research Access in Platform Governance: What to Learn from Other Industries?' (Algorithm Watch 2020) 3ff <https://algorithmwatch.org/de/wp-content/uploads/2020/06/GoverningPlatforms_IViR_study_June2020-AlgorithmWatch-2020-06-24.pdf> accessed 4 August 2023; Irene Pasquetto, Briony Swire-Thompson, and Michelle A Amazeen, 'Tackling Misinformation: What Researchers Could Do with Social Media Data' (2020) Harvard Kennedy School Misinformation Review 1ff <https://misinforeview.hks.harvard.edu/article/tackling-misinformation-what-researchers-could-do-with-social-media-data/> accessed 4 August 2023; for an assessment of the data access rules in the DSA see Mathias Vermeulen, 'Researcher Access to Platform Data' (2022) 1(4) Journal of Online Trust and Safety 2ff; Lena I Löber, 'Der Forschungsdatenzugang nach dem neuen Art. 40 DSA' (2022) ZD-Aktuell 01420.

[110] Löber (n 109) 01420ff; missing more specific criteria for the official evaluation of research applications, see Gerald Spindler, 'Der Vorschlag für ein neues Haftungsregime für Internetprovider—der EU-Digital Services Act Teil 2: Große und besonders große Plattformen' (2021) Gewerblicher Rechtsschutz und Urheberrecht 653, 660.

[111] Judit Bayer, 'Procedural Rights as Safeguard for Human Rights in Platform Regulation' (2022) Policy & Internet 1, 6.

[112] For a critical comparison with art 17(10) DSM Directive see Weiden (n 105) 22.

[113] According to some commentators these powers do not—at least not explicitly—address non-compliance with recommendations proposed by the independent auditors Judit Bayer and others, 'Conclusions: Regulatory Responses to Communication Platforms: Models and Limits' in Bayer and others (eds) (n 17) 580; Weiden (n 105) 28; Spindler (n 110) 659.

online advertising systems (Article 34(1)1, (2) DSA). Article 34(1)1 DSA requires VLOPs and VLOSEs to investigate 'all systemic risks'. Hence, the catalogue in Article 34(1)2 only highlights currently suspected risk categories that the legislator considers to be in particular need of investigation, but is not to be understood as conclusive.[114] Where significant systemic risks within the meaning of Article 34(1) emerge and concern several VLOPs or VLOSEs, according to Article 45(2) DSA the Commission may invite their operators or other providers of intermediary services, as appropriate, as well as relevant competent authorities, civil society organizations, and other relevant stakeholders to participate in the collaborative drawing up of codes of conduct.[115] These codes of conduct will be monitored by the Commission and the EBDS (Article 45(3), (4) DSA). Another strong incentive to participate in the drawing up of codes of conduct follows from Recital 104 DSA.[116] This framework leaves some flexibility and provides a remarkable

[114] An additional 'in particular', as introduced in some other provisions of the DSA during the legislative debates, would have explicitly clarified this point. However, the recent wording allows for a non-conclusive interpretation which certainly best fits the general objectives of the DSA. In addition, art 45(2) DSA indicates the potential emergence of additional new systemic risks. See finally DSA Recital 79 ('providers should consider the severity of the potential impact and the probability of all such systemic risks') and Recital 80 ('Four categories of systemic risks should be assessed in-depth'). See for a similar position Ruth Janal, 'Der Entwurf eines Digital Services Acts' (2021) Kommunikation und Recht Beilage 1, 6, 10; Cole, Etteldorf, and Ullrich (n 17) 193; Asha Allen and Ophélie Stockhem, 'A Series on the EU Digital Services Act: Due Diligence in Content Moderation' (18 August 2022) <https://cdt.org/insights/a-series-on-the-eu-digital-services-act-due-diligence-in-content-moderation/> accessed 4 August 2023; for a similar teleological argument concerning the proposed AI Act Jan C Kalbhenn, 'Designvorgaben für Chatbots, Deepfakes und Emotionserkennungssysteme: Der Vorschlag der Europäischen Kommission zu einer KI-VO als Erweiterung der medienrechtlichen Plattformregulierung' (2021) Zeitschrift für Urheber- und Medienrecht 663, 667; probably dissenting Markus Rössel, 'Digital Services Act Vorschlag zur Harmonisierung der Verantwortlichkeit von Onlineplattformen' (2021) ITRB 35, 41; at least sceptical Weiden (n 105) 22.

[115] See Recital 88 DSA: 'In particular, where risks are shared across different online platforms or online search engines, they should cooperate with other service providers, including by initiating or joining existing codes of conduct or other self-regulatory measures.' Emphasizing the importance of involving multiple stakeholders, not only limited to the drawing up of Codes of Conduct, see Neil Netanel, 'Applying Militant Democracy to Defend Against Social Media Harms' (2023) 45 Cardozo Law Review 489, 556 ff; Niklas Eder, 'Making Systemic Risk Assessments Work: How the DSA Creates a Virtuous Loop to Address the Societal Harms of Content Moderation' (2023 forthcoming) 3ff <https://ssrn.com/abstract=4491365> accessed 26 September 2023; Brenda Dvoskin, 'Representation without Elections: Civil Society Participation as a Remedy for the Democratic Deficits of Online Speech Governance' (2022) 67 Villanova Law Review 447, 457; P Leerssen, *Seeing What Others Are Seeing: Studies in the Regulation of Transparency for Social Media Recommender Systems* (University of Amsterdam 2023) 210ff.

[116] According to Recital 104 DSA the refusal to participate in codes of conduct 'could be taken into account . . . when determining, whether the online platform . . . or the online search engine has infringed the obligations laid down by this regulation'; however, the recital also highlights that the 'mere fact of participating in and implementing a given Code of Conduct should not in itself presume compliance with this Regulation'. On the voluntary nature of the Codes of Conduct see Rachel Griffin and Carl Vander Maelen, 'Codes of Conduct in the Digital Services Act: Exploring the Opportunities and Challenges' (2023) Draft paper—Law, AI & Regulation Conference, Erasmus University, Rotterdam 9 June 2023 (forthcoming) 1, 6ff <https://ssrn.com/abstract=4463874> accessed 26 September 2023; Eva E Wagner, 'Verhaltenskodizes und Branchennormen im Ordnungskonzept des Digital Services Act' (2023) Zeitschrift für das Recht der digitalen Wirtschaft 96, 100ff; Katharina Kaesling, 'Art. 45 DSA' in Franz Hofmann and Benjamin Raue (eds), *Digital Services Act: DSA: Gesetz über digitale Dienste* (1st edn, Nomos 2023) art 45, paras 27–40.

collaborative governance structure. However, it also raises questions with regard to legal certainty and clear allocation of responsibilities.[117]

Pursuant to Article 34(1)3 DSA, the risk assessment focuses on certain systemic risks, albeit broadly defined, with regard to (i) the dissemination of illegal content; (ii) any negative effects on Charter fundamental rights such as, in particular, rights to human dignity, the protection of personal data, freedom of expression including the pluralism of the media, and prohibition of discrimination; (iii) foreseeable negative effects on civic discourse, electoral processes, or public security; and (iv) foreseeable adverse effects on gender-based violence, the protection of public health, or minors, among others. This list addresses the most important areas of at least suspected societal impacts of the platform economy at present.[118] In addition, the list shows the extent to which VLOPs and VLOSEs are assigned to protect public interests. Due to suspected causal contributions and at least the factual proximity of these platforms to these risks,[119] and taking into account legislative margins of appreciation, these obligations appear to be justified and to be at least in principle proportionate.[120] In any case, it is a step forward that the regulatory framework no longer focuses solely on individual violations of rights by means of platform moderation but also takes into account the more fundamental and systemic changes connected to digital capitalism.[121] However, the precise contribution of online platforms to the societal risks mentioned is still a matter of ongoing debate in the social sciences.[122] The collaborative and primarily procedural concept of the DSA, designed for cooperative knowledge generation, reflects this situation appropriately.[123]

[117] Compare Bayer and others (n 113) 580; European Parliamentary Research Service, *Online platforms: Economic and societal effects* (2021) 83ff; Weiden (n 105) 28; BEUC, 'The Digital Services Act Proposal' (2021) 30 <https://www.beuc.eu/sites/default/files/publications/beuc-x-2021-032_the_digital_services_act_proposal.pdf> accessed 4 August 2023; referring to similar problems arising from art 40 GDPR Cesarini (n 105) 10; Mathias Vermeulen, 'The Keys to the Kingdom' (27 July 2021) 26ff <https://knightcolumbia.org/content/the-keys-to-the-kingdom> accessed 4 August 2023.

[118] See European Parliamentary Research Service (n 117) 53ff; Spindler (n 110) 653, 658f; proposals of the EP to include rules against 'deep fakes' were not successful, compare art 30a as proposed after the first reading in EP, 'Digital Services Act Amendments' (Resolution) P9_TA(2022)0014.

[119] See n 50.

[120] On constitutional conditions for legislative instrumentalization of economic actors see BVerfGE 30, 292 = NJW 1971, 1255 (compulsory oil stockpiling by energy suppliers); BVerfGE 125, 260, 362 = NJW 2010, 833, 851 (compulsory retention of telecom traffic data by grid operators for criminal prosecution); on the instrumentalization of social networks by the German NetzDG Martin Burgi and Christoph Krönke, 'Die ausgleichspflichtige Indienstnahme' (2018) 109 VerwArch 423, 445; concerning the DSA see Cauffman and Goanta (n 106) 770ff.

[121] Folkert Wilman, 'The Digital Services Act (DSA)—An Overview' (2022) SSRN Journal 13 <https://ssrn.com/abstract=4304586> accessed 28 September 2023.

[122] See n 50.

[123] Similar Wolfgang Beck, 'Der Entwurf des Digital Services Act—Hintergrund, Ziele und Grundsätze künftiger Regulierung des virtuellen Raumes in der EU' (2021) Deutsches Verwaltungsblatt 1000, 1003; Cauffman and Goanta (n 106) 770–71; Douek (n 22) 597; Ruth Janal, 'Haftung und Verantwortung im Entwurf des Digital Services Acts' (2021) Zeitschrift für Europäisches Privatrecht 227, 269; with regard to Algorithmic Impact Assessments see Selbst (n 20) 126, 147ff; Joan Barata is more sceptical, 'The Digital Services Act and Social Media Power to Regulate Speech: Obligations, Liabilities and Safeguards' in Maja Cappello (ed), *Unravelling the Digital Services Act Package IRIS*

As shown, the risk management obligations of the DSA apply primarily to the algorithmic systems of VLOPs and VLOSEs and thus regulate their widespread use of AI technologies. In this respect, the DSA would supersede the proposed EU AI Act.[124] Counterintuitively, the AI systems of VLOPs and VLOSEs covered by the DSA are not listed as high-risk AI systems in the Draft AI Act 2021.[125] In comparison with Article 9 of the Draft AI Act, Articles 34, 35 DSA as sector-specific rules describe the systemic risks to be particularly assessed as well as possible risk mitigation measures rather precisely. In addition, Article 37 DSA requires an independent audit by competent, although not necessarily officially certified, third parties. In contrast, a pure self-assessment is generally sufficient according to the Draft AI Act. Article 43(1) of the Draft AI Act 2021 only provides for an external conformity assessment with regard to biometric AI systems and only if no harmonized standards have been applied. This external assessment audit would involve an officially notified body pursuant to Articles 30–39 Draft AI Act 2021. The public may, in accordance with Article 60 and Annex VIII Draft AI Act 2021, obtain information about all stand-alone high-risk AI systems offered on the market in the EU via a central European database. In addition to primarily formal basic information, the database contains content-related information in form of a description of the intended purpose of the respective system, the certificate of conformity as defined in Article 48 and Annex V Draft AI Act 2021, and, above all, the respective

Special (European Audiovisual Observatory 2021) 15ff; see also Lennart Laude, *Automatisierte Meinungsbeeinflussung* (Mohr Siebeck 2021) 306–07, arguing against legislative 'overreactions' concerning only suspected manipulation risks by 'social bots'.

[124] Compare art 2(5) Draft AI Act 2021 and recital 12, COM(2021) 206 final as well as p 5 of the Commission's Explanatory Memorandum; Sebastian Schwemer, 'Recommender Systems in the EU: from Responsibility to Regulation?' (2021) 3 <https://ssrn.com/abstract=3923003> accessed 4 August 2023; generally about the Draft AI Act 2021 David Bomhard and Marieke Merkle, 'Europäische KI-Verordnung' (2022) Recht Digital 276ff; Andreas Ebert and Indra Spiecker gen. Döhmann, 'Der Kommissionsentwurf für eine KI-Verordnung der EU: Die EU als Trendsetter weltweiter KI-Regulierung' (2021) Neue Zeitschrift für Verwaltungsrecht 1188ff; Hanna Hoffmann, 'Regulierung der Künstlichen Intelligenz: Fundamentalkritik am Verordnungsentwurf zur Regulierung der Künstlichen Intelligenz der EU-Kommission vom 21.4.2021' (2021) Kommunikation und Recht 369ff; Irina Orssich, 'Das europäische Konzept für vertrauenswürdige Künstliche Intelligenz' (2022) Europäische Zeitschrift für Wirtschaftsrecht 254ff; Gerald Spindler, 'Der Vorschlag der EU-Kommission für eine Verordnung zur Regulierung der Künstlichen Intelligenz (KI-VO-E): Ansatz, Instrumente, Qualität und Kontext' (2021) Computer und Recht 361ff; Matthias Valta and Johann J Valta, 'Kommissionsvorschlag für eine Verordnung über Künstliche Intelligenz: Mit viel Bürokratie und wenig Risiko zum KI-Standort?' (2021) Zeitschrift für Rechtspolitik 142ff; Martin Ebers and others, 'The European Commission's Proposal for an Artificial Intelligence Act—A Critical Assessment by Members of the Robotics and AI Law Society (RAILS)' (2021) 4(4) Multidisciplinary Scientific Journal 589ff; Michael Veale and Frederik Zuiderveen Borgesius, 'Demystifying the Draft EU Artificial Intelligence Act' (2021) Computer Law Review International 97ff.

[125] Winston Maxwell, 'Applying Net Neutrality Rules to Social Media Content Moderation Systems' (2022) Annales des Mines—Enjeux Numériques 90, 97. In its resolution of 14 June 2023, the European Parliament partially pursues a different concept in this respect and includes the recommendation systems of very large 'social media platforms', but not their algorithmic moderation systems, as high-risk AI systems within the scope of the AI Act, see Parliamentary Draft (P9_TA(2023)0236 Amendment 740) Annex III No 8 a b. It remains to be seen which position will prevail.

instructions for use. Pursuant to Article 13(3) Draft AI Act 2021, the instructions for use contain, among other things, information on the accuracy and robustness of the system and on the risks to health and safety or fundamental rights associated with it. Significantly, more extensive information is contained in the technical documentation pursuant to Article 11(1) and Annex IV Draft AI Act 2021. This documentation must provide the competent national authorities and the notified bodies with all information required to assess whether the AI system meets all legal requirements. According to Article 64 Draft AI Act 2021, the national market surveillance authorities have access not only to the technical documentation but also, among other things, to training data or the source code of the high-risk AI system. These transparency obligations are structured differently from the DSA. However, a final evaluation needs to be based on the future final version of the AI Act.

A specific public interest framework has been integrated into the DSA concerning the handling of extraordinary crisis situations for public safety or health. According to Article 48 DSA, the Commission shall promote and monitor the cooperative drafting of so-called crisis protocols by VLOPs and VLOSEs and, where appropriate, other platforms or search engines. Crisis protocols may include a highlighted presentation of official crisis information on platforms in order to combat misinformation. In the legislative process, Article 36 DSA was added establishing crisis response mechanisms as an option. The provision grants the Commission, upon the recommendation of the EBDS, powers in the event of the occurrence of extraordinary circumstances leading to serious threats to public safety or health, to oblige the VLOPs and VLOSEs to examine their contribution to the crisis situation and, if necessary, to implement autonomous countermeasures within a dialogical framework.

IV. Collaborative knowledge management concerning automated content moderation and systemic risks

Targeting the information asymmetry between digital services providers, such as VLOPs and VLOSEs, and their regulators is a major component of the new European digital rulebook. The DSA introduces a structure of regulatory learning, as well as procedures, for the exchange of the newly generated information. While causal impact relationships between the operation of VLOPS or VLOSEs and systemic impairments on, for example, civic discourses and democratic processes cannot yet be conclusively identified in a scientific sense, the DSA aims at information generation and an evolving scientific and societal engagement and discussion about such presumed impacts.

Significant in this regard are for instance cross-case transparency obligations of all intermediary service providers regarding their private autonomous platform moderation, expanding regulatory knowledge and enabling public discussion

(Article 15(1)2(c) DSA), and even more demanding obligations for online platforms (Article 24(1)(a), (b) DSA). Similarly important is the framework for risk assessments in Article 34 et seq DSA. That collaborative framework is characterized by its reflexive, knowledge-generating, and learning-oriented approach, which on the one hand specifically encourages and pre-structures self-reflection by the VLOPs and VLOSEs, and on the other encourages regulatory learning supported by independent vetted researchers.

C. Administrative coordination

The DSA does not only introduce a collaborative governance framework for automated content moderation and for coping with knowledge gaps concerning suspected systemic risks connected with digital services. Another important building block of the DSA highly relevant for future EU administrative law concerns the allocation and coordination of administrative competences for enforcing the DSA in the multilevel system of the EU (section C.I) as well as the coordination of sectoral regulatory powers addressing the multi-dimensionality of digital services (section C.II).[126]

I. Cross-border coordination

Cross-border coordination is essential to the functioning of digital services regulation under the DSA. Coordination mechanisms shall enable the implementation of European or cross-border interests in national procedures, the inter-administrative sharing of information, and the development of 'best practices' as well as of European expertise concerning the regulation of digital services. Finally, cross-border coordination can encourage a more uniform and coherent application of the DSA throughout the EU. For these purposes, the DSA establishes a typical administrative network.[127] We start our analysis with demonstrating the

[126] Bengi Zeybek and Joris van Hoboken, 'The Enforcement Aspects of the DSA, and its Relation to Existing Regulatory Oversight in the EU' (2022) <https://dsa-observatory.eu/2022/02/04/the-enforcement-aspects-of-the-dsa-and-its-relation-to-existing-regulatory-oversight-in-the-eu/> accessed 4 August 2023; Cauffman and Goanta (n 106) 771ff; ERGA, 'Proposals Aimed at Strengthening the Digital Services Act (DSA): With Respect to Online Content Regulation' (2021) sections 2–4 <https://erga-online.eu/wp-content/uploads/2021/06/2021.06.25-ERGA-DSA-Paper-final.pdf> accessed 4 August 2023; EDPS, 'Opinion 1/21 on the Proposal for a Digital Services Act' (2021) 19ff <https://edps.europa.eu/system/files/2021-02/21-02-10-opinion_on_digital_services_act_en.pdf> accessed 4 August 2023; BEUC (n 117) 30 ff. See also more generally Giorgio Monti and Alexandre de Streel, 'Improving EU Institutional Design to Better Supervise Digital Platforms' (2022) 13ff <https://cerre.eu/wp-content/uploads/2022/01/20220117_CERRE_Report_Improving-EU-Institutional-Design_Final.pdf> accessed 4 August 2023.

[127] See, for instances, the similar structures in ch 7 of the GDPR, and of the CPC-Network, Jay Modrall and Julien Haverals, 'The CPC Network—Consumer Protection, EU Style' (2021) <http://

vertical and horizontal centralization of regulatory powers by the DSA (section C.I.1), before we assess the horizontal (section C.I.2) as well as vertical (section C.I.3) coordination mechanisms.

1. Vertical and horizontal centralization of regulatory powers concerning digital services

Article 56 DSA distributes powers and responsibilities for enforcing the DSA in an innovative concept.[128] For a start, the DSA differentiates between the vertically centralized regulation of VLOPs and VLOSEs on the one hand and the horizontally centralized regulation of the other platforms or intermediary services on the other.[129] For the regulation of VLOPs and VLOSEs, the Commission has exclusive competence pursuant to Article 56(2) DSA with regard to the implementation of their specific (asymmetric) obligations from Articles 33–48 DSA. In contrast, the Commission only has concurrent competence with regard to (symmetric) obligations that affect VLOPs and VLOSEs as well as all other intermediary services or platforms, so that Member State authorities can intervene at least subsidiarily (Article 56(4), Article 66(2) sub-paragraph 3 DSA). For all other platforms, search engines, and other intermediary services, the enforcement competence according to Article 56(1) DSA lies with the Member State of establishment and in this respect corresponds to other supervisory structures relevant for digital services, such as in data protection or media law,[130] with a horizontally centralized distribution of competences according to the country of origin principle typical for the EU administrative space in the digital field.[131] According to Article 49 DSA, Member States shall designate one or more competent authorities as responsible for the supervision of providers of intermediary services and enforcement of this Regulation, and shall designate one of them as their DSC. This partial opening clause for national legislators takes into account the DSA's multidimensionality, as well as the need for cross-sectoral coordination (section C.II). In this context, it is worth noting that the EU legislative bodies and in particular the Council, due to negative experiences in

competitionlawblog.kluwercompetitionlaw.com/2021/12/02/the-cpc-network-consumer-protection-eu-style/> accessed 4 August 2023.

[128] In contrast, the enforcement of the DMA is completely centralized at the Commission.

[129] Regarding providers of digital services from third countries, such as the United States in particular, the market location principle laid down in art 2(1) DSA applies.

[130] cf on the lead data protection supervisory authority see art 56 GDPR; on the regulatory competence for audiovisual media services see art 2 AVMSD.

[131] The country-of-origin principle in the digital sector can be traced back in particular to art 3(1, 2) of the E-Commerce Directive. It is often regarded as the only solution suitable for the digital single market, as online intermediary systems are generally provided across borders, see Commission (n 17) paras 65, 171; Luca Bertuzzi, 'Ireland Draws a Red Line on Country of Origin Principle in DSA' (2021) <https://www.euractiv.com/section/digital-single-market/news/ireland-draws-a-red-line-on-country-of-origin-principle-in-dsa/> accessed 4 August 2023; Monti and Streel (n 126) 18ff; critical, particularly regarding the cross-border effectiveness of user complaints, BEUC (n 126) 32.

data protection law, have strengthened the vertical and horizontal coordination by establishing a cooperative EU agency and various composite procedures.

2. Horizontal coordination and composite administration

Horizontal coordination measures are a reaction to tensions between the centralization of competences at the Member State where the main establishment of the provider of intermediary services is located (Article 56(1) DSA, section C.I.1) and the typically strong cross-border effects of enforcement measures concerning digital services.[132] Horizontal coordination has an organizational as well as a procedural dimension.

A new organizational mechanism for horizontal coordination is the EBDS established in Article 62 DSA, composed of the national DSCs, who shall be represented by high-level officials and chaired by the Commission. While each Member State has one vote, the Commission does not have voting rights. The EBDS adopts its acts by simple majority.

In its horizontal function the EBDS issues opinions, recommendations, or advice to DSCs and supports the coordination of joint investigations (Article 63(1)(a), (c) DSA). DSCs and, where applicable, other competent authorities of Member States that do not follow the opinions, requests, or recommendations addressed to them adopted by the EBDS shall provide the reasons for their dissent, including an explanation about the investigations, actions, and the measures that they have implemented (Article 63(2) DSA). In the event of continuing differences of opinion, the EBDS may consider a referral to the Commission in the constellations covered by Article 59(1) and Article 60(3) DSA.

The horizontal coordination provided by the EBDS is complemented by coordination among DSCs from different Member States through composite procedures. First, Article 58(1) DSA creates the possibility for a country of destination coordinator to request the country of origin coordinator to investigate alleged violations of the law and, if necessary, to enforce remedial measures. The country of destination coordinator must give sufficient reasons for the request and may submit proposals for regulatory measures. According to Article 58(4) and (5) DSA, the country of origin coordinator must take utmost account of a proper request and notify the country of destination coordinator and the EBDS without delay, but at the latest within two months, of its assessment of the alleged infringement and the regulatory measures it has already taken or plans to take. Such a request by the country of destination coordinator may be triggered by complaints from affected users or associations mandated by them, which are admissible under Article 53 DSA (section B.II.3.a).[133]

[132] See also art 40(9) DSA, which is a similar reaction to the horizontal centralization of the regulatory review of access applications of designated researchers.

[133] For details see Schneider (n 101) 45ff.

Second, Article 58(2) DSA provides an additional coordination procedure. While the request procedure according to Article 58(1) DSA is purely horizontal between two Member State coordinators, Article 58(2) DSA combines horizontal and vertical elements as at least three national destination coordinators can request the EBDS to in turn request the country of origin coordinator to intervene against suspected DSA violations according to the principles just outlined. The horizontal or combined composite procedures under Article 58 DSA can continue in a vertical composite procedure provided in Article 59 DSA if the EBDS does not agree with the measures taken by the requested country of origin coordinator or if the latter misses his deadline for reply. The EBDS may then refer the matter to the Commission. After consulting the country of origin coordinator, the Commission assesses the matter and, if necessary, requests the coordinator to reconsider in the light of its assessment. The country of origin coordinator must take the utmost account of the Commission's position in its review and inform the Commission and the EBDS[134] of the outcome of the review and the enforcement action ultimately taken. If there is still disagreement about the sufficient effectiveness of the measures envisaged by the country of origin coordinator, there is no final dispute resolution mechanism on the European level similar to Article 65 of the General Data Protection Regulation (GDPR): neither the Commission nor the EBDS can pronounce a final verdict on matters not regarding VLOPs or VLOSEs. Consequently only the option of infringement proceedings remains. Also, no emergency powers similar to those in Article 60(11), Article 66 GDPR, or Article 3(2)–(7), Article 4(3)–(5) AVMSD are provided by the DSA. It remains to be seen if the adopted DSA framework will effectively prevent the problems observed with regard to the GDPR concerning insufficient enforcement by Ireland[135] and enforcement divergences between Member States.[136]

One mechanism that could be useful for cross-border control is the right to complain to the DSC where the recipient of the service is located or established (Article 53 DSA).[137] According to Recital 118, the purpose of this right is, among other things, to provide an overview of concerns regarding compliance with the regulation and, possibly, to point out overarching problems. According to Article 53

[134] Or the country of destination coordinator originally initiating the procedure under art 58(1) DSA.

[135] The debate over the enforcement of the GDPR by the Irish Data Protection Authority began notably after a report by the non-profit organization Irish Council for Civil Liberties. See Johnny Ryan and Alan Toner, 'Europe's Enforcement Paralysis: ICCL's 2021 Report on the Enforcement Capacity of Data Protection Authorities' (2021) <https://www.iccl.ie/wp-content/uploads/2021/09/Europes-enforcement-paralysis-2021-ICCL-report-on-GDPR-enforcement.pdf> accessed 4 August 2023. See also Ilaria Buri and Joris van Hoboken, 'The General Approach of the Council on the DSA' (2021) <https://dsa-observatory.eu/2021/12/07/the-general-approach-of-the-council-on-the-digital-services-act/> accessed 4 August 2023; Sarah Harford, 'EU Official Warns Data Rules May Need to Change Putting Irish DPC in the Spotlight' (2021) <https://www.siliconrepublic.com/enterprise/dpc-ireland-eu-change-gdpr> accessed 4 August 2023.

[136] Cauffman and Goanta (n 106) 773.

[137] For a more detailed discussion see Schneider (n 101) 45ff.

sentence 2 DSA, the DSC handling the complaint also has the power to investigate those.

DSCs at the destination can thus receive information about violations of the DSA by providers under the jurisdiction of other DSCs and, if necessary, initiate the above-mentioned cross-border procedures. However, the right to complain does not help if the DSC at the place of establishment assesses the matter differently.[138] In this respect, Article 53 DSA cannot make up for possible shortcomings in the design of the cross-border procedures. At best, the information obtained through the right of appeal can help increase political pressure on the authorities at the place of establishment.

Additional mechanisms for horizontal coordination include mutual assistance (Article 57 DSA) and joint investigations (Article 60 DSA), where investigatory and enforcement powers are shared among Member States. These provisions serve primarily to support the country of origin coordinator with its enforcement tasks, and thus to support the effectiveness and efficiency of the DSA enforcement.

3. Vertical coordination and composite administration

Vertically, the DSA relies primarily on the Commission's centralized enforcement competences vis-à-vis VLOPs and VLOSEs (section C.I.1).

Again, we can start our analysis with the EBDS as it shall support the Commission and provide, due to its composition, knowledge from national DSCs. In relation to the Commission, the EBDS also has an advisory support function (Article 61(2), Article 63(1)(d), (e) DSA). This applies in particular to the Commission's supervision of VLOPs and VLOSEs, where the Commission must take utmost account of the opinions of the EBDS (Article 66(4) 3, Article 75(1) 2 DSA). In addition, the EBDS can in many cases provoke the initiation of Commission procedures (Article 36(1), (8), Article 48(1), Article 59(1), Article 66(1) DSA) as well as prepare annual reports on systemic risks in cooperation with the Commission (Article 35(2) DSA) and, alongside the Commission, promote self-regulation through codes of conduct (Article 45 DSA).

Additional procedural coordination mechanisms include requests of Member States DSCs to the Commission to assess suspected infringements of VLOPs or VLOSEs (Article 65(2), (3) DSA) and the Commission's power to request from national regulators restrictions of access to services of VLOPs or VLOSEs (Article 75(4), or Article 82(1) sub-paragraph 1 in connection with Article 51(3) sub-paragraph 1(b) DSA). Especially remarkable from the perspective of EU administrative law is the concentration of the hearing of parties in composite proceedings at the Commission's stage according to Article 51(3) sub-paragraph 2 with Article 82(1) sub-paragraph 2 DSA.

[138] See BEUC (n 117) 32.

Finally, the possibility of the Commission to set up guidelines for the application of Article 35(1), (3) DSA, the generally stated duty to close cooperation of the Commission and Member States' authorities in Article 56(5) DSA, the possibility to request general support of any DSC (Article 66(3) DSA), and a variety of specific supporting services (Article 68(2), Article 69(3), (7)–(9), Article 72(2) DSA) in enforcement procedures against VLOPs or VLOSEs are noteworthy.

II. Cross-sectoral coordination

While cross-border coordination is essential for the enforcement of the DSA across territorial borders, cross-sectoral coordination serves to overcome borders of classical regulatory sectors.[139] Through its broad scope (broad definition of illegal content, definition of regulated intermediary services, and transparency and due diligence provisions), the DSA overlaps with several classical regulatory sectors of platform regulation (media law, consumer protection law, competition law, data law, etc)[140] and, thus, with several existing EU directives and regulations (Audiovisual and Media Services Directive (AVMSD), Digital Single Market Directive (DSM-D), GDPR, Regulation on addressing the dissemination of terrorist content online (TERREG), P2B Regulation, etc). This may lead to administrative decisions of DSA authorities touching different regulatory sectors already governed by other national regulators. This constellation calls for coordination mechanisms between those different regulators.

1. Goals of cross-sectoral coordination

Cross-sectoral coordination shall increase the knowledge of regulatory bodies competent for implementing the DSA, for instance concerning the enforcement of rules on systemic risk-management, through sharing of sector-specific expertise.[141] It is even more important to ensure efficiency and coherence of the application of different sector-specific regulations where these overlap with the DSA.[142] The DSA only states that it is applicable without prejudice to the existing sectoral acts of EU law.[143] Because of the general design of the DSA as a 'comprehensive rulebook' of the digital domain, it will most likely be applicable complementary where

[139] Thorsten Siegel, *Entscheidungsfindung im Verwaltungsverbund: Horizontale Entscheidungsvernetzung und vertikale Entscheidungsstufung im nationalen und europäischen Verwaltungsverbund* (Mohr Siebeck 2009) 330ff.

[140] Zeybek and van Hoboken (n 126).

[141] See eg art 64(4) DSA: the Member States shall make available the expertise and capabilities of their DSC and other competent authorities to help the commission enforce the rules against VLOPs/VLOSE.

[142] Zeybek and van Hoboken (n 126).

[143] Art 2(4) DSA.

special rules do not apply.[144] However, because the DSA does not specifically state the relation of its partially rather specific rules with similar, potentially overlapping rules of other regulations, the competent authorities and courts ultimately need to clarify the relationship between specific legal provisions, for example the relationship of the out-of-court dispute settlement mechanisms in Article 21 DSA and in the DSM-D, AVMSD, and P2B Regulation,[145] of the DSA with the GDPR, where personal data is processed (especially in the context of Articles 34, 35 DSA),[146] or of the notice-and-action mechanisms in Article 16 DSA and Article 17 DSM-D[147] or Article 28b(3)(d) AVMSD. In these closely related legal fields, regulators could profit from each other's expertise and experience. They should coordinate enforcement measures or at least share opinions on proper enforcement measures in order to ensure coherence, to use scarce regulatory resource efficiently, and to avoid excessive strain on regulated digital providers.

From a more abstract perspective, coordination between regulators with overlapping competences would ideally enable a more holistic view on the regulation of digital services, balance different sectoral public interests,[148] and reach more overall coherence, efficiency, and efficacy of the digital regulatory framework.[149]

2. Cross-sectoral coordination measures in the DSA

The DSA reacts to these challenges of regulatory overlaps by introducing few but significant rules on cross-sectoral cooperation.

Especially significant are provisions for cross-sectoral coordination at Member State level. Next to the DSC, Member States may assign DSA enforcement competences to multiple sector-specific authorities (Article 49(1); Recital 109 DSA; see also section C.I.1). In this case, the DSC must internally coordinate the enforcement activities of those national authorities to ensure the efficacy and effectiveness of enforcement (Article 49(2) sub-paragraph 1 DSA). DSCs shall also ensure

144 Joao Quintais and Sebastian Schwemer, 'The Interplay between the Digital Services Act and Sector Regulation: How Special is Copyright?' (2022) European Journal of Risk Regulation 191, 215ff; Cauffman and Goanta (n 106) 760.

145 Wimmers (n 95) 390ff.

146 Zeybek and van Hoboken (n 126); EDPB, 'Statement on the Digital Services Package and Data Strategy' (2021) 3 <https://edpb.europa.eu/system/files/2021-11/edpb_statement_on_the_digital_services_package_and_data_strategy_en.pdf> accessed 4 August 2023.

147 Quintais and Schwemer (n 144) 23–26; Eleonora Rosati, 'The Digital Services Act and Copyright Enforcement: The Case of Article 17 of the DSM Directive' inCapello (ed) (n 123) 71ff; Ruth Janal, 'Friendly Fire? Das Urheberrechts-Diensteanbieter-Gesetz und sein Verhältnis zum künftigen Digital Services Act' (2022) Gewerblicher Rechtsschutz und Urheberrecht 211, 212ff.

148 See Julian Jaursch, 'Wie die deutsche Plattformaufsicht aufgebaut sein sollte: Empfehlungen für einen starken "Digital Services Coordinator"' (2022) 37 <https://www.stiftung-nv.de/sites/default/files/snv_empfehlungen_fur_einen_starken_dsc_0.pdf> accessed 4 August 2023.

149 Which is why some people suggest the centralization of the different sectoral enforcement competences at one national authority (similar to the centralization at the Commission at the EU level), see regarding Germany, Julian Jaursch, 'New EU Rules for Digital Services: Why Germany Needs Strong Platform Oversight Structures' section 4 <https://www.stiftung-nv.de/sites/default/files/snv_why_germany_needs_strong_platform_oversight_structures.pdf> accessed 4 August 2023.

the 'diagonal' cooperation of the Commission and the EBDS with sector-specific national regulators (Article 49(2) sub-paragraph 2 DSA). Such coordination will require the emergence of national administrative networks: in alignment with the principal procedural autonomy of the Member States, these will have to organize the internal distribution of decision-making powers, the procedural coordination of different actors, and perhaps the formation of pan-sectoral organizations similar to the Article 40 DMA 'high-level-group'[150] in search of increasing the efficacy, efficiency, and coherence of the EU's digital rulebook.

While forming such national administrative networks, Member States will have to take into account few but important exceptions to their procedural autonomy laid down in the DSA: as already stated, Member States must appoint a DSC and—if applicable—give him powers to coordinate additional national DSA regulators or sector-specific regulators. Competent authorities implementing the DSA have to be independent and adequately resourced (Article 50(1), 49(4) DSA). These provisions primarily require complete legal and technical independence from national governments. They are an element of the cross-border administrative framework but they also have implications for the cross-sectoral coordination: coordination might raise questions of hierarchy in between the DSC and other relevant authorities.[151] A connected issue is raised by sector-specific independence requirements for different sectoral regulators, especially in the field of media law and data protection. At least, Article 50(3) DSA generally states that cooperation between different national regulators regarding the application of the DSA does not affect their independence. Finally, constitutional questions of democratic legitimacy of independent administrative bodies arise in case of highly political decisions, for instance about trade-offs in between sectoral public interests.[152]

At EU level, Recital 134 and Article 62(5) DSA clarify the option and obligation of the EBDS to invite sectoral regulators to its hearings. Interestingly though, despite the overlapping of the DSA with several regulatory sectors and the need for coordination, the EBDS will not be part of the cross-sectoral 'high-level-group' established by Article 40 DMA. The DSA seems to rely on the Commission's centralized and overlapping enforcement powers in the DSA and the DMA and its position in the EBDS as well as in the 'high-level group'. In addition, the national procedures for cross-sectoral coordination of the DSA enforcement might reduce the need for coordination at EU level.

[150] See Jaursch (n 148) 27ff, which calls for a 'DSC-Forum' to enable permanent, case-independent, cooperation between various sectoral authorities and the DSC.

[151] Zeybek and van Hoboken (n 126).

[152] See Jens-Peter Schneider, 'Art. 51 GDPR' in Heinrich A Wolff and Stefan Brink (eds), *BeckOK Datenschutzrecht* (C. H. Beck 41st edn, 2022) art 51 DSGVO para 4; Jens-Peter Schneider, 'Art. 52 GDPR' in ibid, art 52 DSGVO para 20, raising this question regarding the enforcement of the GDPR.

III. Inter-administrative knowledge management by cross-border and cross-sectoral coordination

As stated earlier, the DSA relies on many private and public actors to gain expertise and information about online platforms and their regulation.[153] Among authorities, such generated knowledge must be transferred to the competent regulating authority in order to facilitate well-informed regulatory decisions and thus enhance the effectiveness of the DSA and its standards. Knowledge transfer is, on one hand, a cross-border problem because information is usually more efficiently and effectively gathered in a decentralized manner, due to (eg linguistic) the proximity to the object of regulation.[154] However, on the other hand it is also a cross-sectoral challenge: sectoral authorities should have the best expertise and information about their regulating field. Due to the broad perspective of the DSA rules, specialized expertise, for example on systemic risks in the meaning of Article 34 DSA arising in specific regulated sectors like the media industry, might be highly beneficial for a coherent and comprehensive digital regulation.[155]

The cross-border exchange of information and expertise is managed in the DSA through typical structures of vertical and horizontal cooperation mechanisms, most significantly the EBDS and the information sharing system established by Article 85 DSA.[156] At EU-level, cross-sectoral exchange seems to depend on the central enforcement competences of the Commission in the DSA and other relevant legal acts (eg the DMA), and on the position of the Commission on the DMA's 'high-level group' (Article 40 DMA) and in the EBDS.[157] At national level, cross-sectoral cooperation is left to the Member States' autonomy, and therefore dependant on the distribution of competences and coordination mechanisms introduced in national legislation.

However, a widespread criticism is that the DSA does not provide for a clear legal basis for the exchange of information among various sectoral authorities at the EU level.[158] An appropriate regulatory framework would, on the one hand, exploit the potential of cross-sectoral mutual exchange of information and, on the other, respect limits to such exchange, especially in terms of data protection. Therefore, for example, procedural involvement of data protection authorities in procedures relevant to them should be legally provided.[159]

[153] See section B.IV.

[154] See Monti and Streel (n 126) 60.

[155] For example, media regulators' expertise on disinformation campaigns. See Rec 83, 84, 88 DSA, that all include these in the systemic risks.

[156] See section C.I.

[157] In which, interestingly, the EBDS is not a part of (see section C.II.2).

[158] Zeybek and van Hoboken (n 126); ERGA (n 126) 2, 19ff.

[159] EDPB (n 146) 4, 5.

D. Knowledge management in regulating digital services revisited

As mentioned throughout this chapter, a significant challenge for regulating digital services arises from knowledge gaps and other epistemic uncertainties concerning economic and societal impacts of the expanding digital economy in general and more specifically concerning 'systemic risks' connected with VLOPs and VLOSEs and especially with their widespread use of algorithmic technologies for governing the Internet.[160]

In view of the dynamic developments of the platform economy, pre-DSA legislation already provided various instruments for societal and administrative knowledge generation. In addition to the multiple transparency requirements of the P2B Regulation, the requirements for an exchange of experience by means of a joint register of the Member States on legally established illegal practices of online intermediary services (Article 14(2) P2B Regulation) are particularly noteworthy.

The new legal framework contains a large number of additional and partially innovative instruments for knowledge generation, most of which have already been mentioned, such as the required transparency of general terms and conditions (section B.II.3.a), the reporting systems for the discovery of illegal content (section B.II.1), the obligation of host providers to state reasons in the case of access restrictions and to submit such reasoned decisions in order to establish a publicly accessible, but nevertheless collection that is compatible with data protection principles in a Commission database[161] (section B.II.3.b) and various other transparency obligations of the platform operators. Particularly noteworthy is the independently verified assessment of systemic risks by the VLOPs and VLOSEs under public scrutiny (sections B.II.3.b, B.III) as well as the administrative and scientific access to data of VLOPs and VLOSEs, *inter alia* for independent scientific algorithm control (sections B.III, B.IV). The information exchange system provided for in Article 85 DSA to strengthen the European administrative information network should also be taken into account (section C.III). The protection of commercial users who inform the authorities of problematic practices of gatekeeper platforms also serves to generate knowledge (Article 5(6) DMA). Finally, Article 19 DMA should be mentioned, which empowers the Commission to conduct market investigations into new services and new practices.

In this chapter we cannot discuss in detail but only note the challenges connected with the balancing of subjective rights to protection of business secrets with public interests in effective regulatory supervision and democratic control.

[160] Lorenz-Spreen and others (n 50); Löber (n 109); van Loo (n 22) 1565, 1595ff.
[161] See n 103.

E. Outlook: Perspectives for legal frameworks for digital public administration

In this final section we will present some initial ideas about potential lessons for the future governance framework for digitalized public administrations which can be drawn from the DSA and its collaborative framework for the governance of digital communication on private platforms. In this regard we will refer to some insights presented in the chapters of Herwig Hofmann and Oriol Mir in this book. More precisely, we will show that their conceptual approach is at least partially reflected in the DSA. Moreover, the DSA might add some material concerning innovative instruments for governing ADM in fields relevant for public policy. In addition, we will refer at least to some aspects of the CJEU ruling concerning platform duties enshrined in the DSM directive to protect IP rights by using automated upload filters.

Herwig Hofmann discussed requirements for legislative cyber-delegation. He referred in this regard to the *Meroni* principles. However, in the field of digital services the EU did not delegate powers previously assigned by law to public bodies. Rather, the DSA mobilizes private actors like platforms for implementing public objectives concerning effective governance of digital communication by establishing totally new obligations. Thus, we might need to differentiate between various forms of outsourcing.

Nevertheless, the rulebooks for platform regulation provide inspiration also for future frameworks for AI systems used by public authorities. Oriol Mir highlighted four procedural safeguards relevant to administrative AI systems, namely hearing rights, algorithm transparency, various forms of human oversight, and impact assessments. There are no *ex-ante* hearing rights established in the DSA but there are other procedural safeguards. Concerning algorithm transparency, the DSA provides various obligations: Article 14 DSA obliges intermediaries to inform about their automated content moderation in their terms and conditions. Article 17 DSA requires a statement of reasons for content moderation measures, including information on whether the decision was taken using automated means. Additional asymmetric transparency obligations comprise reporting about automated content moderation practice (Article 15 DSA), a database with reasons for content moderation (Article 24 DSA), and information about the accuracy of content moderation systems (Article 42 DSA). The DSA also provides safeguards for human oversight. Internal complaint decisions must be 'taken under the supervision of appropriately qualified staff, and not solely on the basis of automated means' (Article 20(6) DSA). However, in contrast to case law concerning decision-making of public authorities,[162] the CJEU in the recent DSM upload

[162] Opinion 1/15 *EU-Canada Passenger Name Record (PNR) Agreement* ECLI:EU:C:2017:592 paras 172–173; C-817/19 *Ligue des droits humains v Conseil des ministres*, paras 124, 178 with paras 106, 194ff in these cases the ECJ highlighted legislative provisions requiring ex-ante human oversight before

filter case initiated by Poland did not require *ex-ante* human oversight before restrictions by private platform providers are imposed.[163] Finally, Oriol Mir argued for *ex-ante* and post-implementation impact assessments as proposed in the ELI Model Rules.[164] The DSA does not require such an *ex-ante* impact assessment nor an *ex-ante* conformity assessment like the Draft AI Act, b we highlighted the importance of the obligation of VLOPs and VLOSEs to conduct a periodic systemic risk assessment, especially focusing on their ADM systems (sections B.III, B.IV). This assessment serves as a partial functional equivalent at least to repeated impact assessments after the deployment of algorithmic decision-making systems which are part of the proposed ELI Model Rules.

A specific and innovative safeguard for reliable algorithmic systems of VLOPs and VLOSEs is provided by data and algorithm access rules empowering authorities to demand such access for either themselves or for so-called vetted researchers. The latter variant of data access for independent researchers might also be an option for democratic control of AI systems used by public authorities, of course with certain limits in order to safeguard state secrets and avoiding the gaming of such systems.

Finally, a point for discussion might be that the Advocate General in the Polish upload filter case argued that procedural safeguards like complaint mechanisms are important and even a 'necessary component of any [automated] filtering system, given the resulting risk of "over-blocking"'. But he also stated that such procedural safeguards 'are not *sufficient* on their own to ensure a "fair balance" between copyright and users' freedom of expression'.[165] Consequently, the Advocate General highlights the obligation of legislators to ensure 'that the collateral effect of a filtering and blocking measure is minimised' *ex ante*. Minimization of overblocking would accept at least some over-blocking raising the important question of the needed threshold for minimization—further developed in another study.[166] Here we can only draw attention to the fact that the DSA seems to accept some over-blocking by automated content moderation as long as platforms provide complaint-handling mechanisms, conduct systemic risk assessments and comply

any adverse actions are taken by public authorities as a—presumably needed—compensation for margins of errors connected with ADM.

[163] C-401/19 *Republic of Poland v European Parliament and Council of the European Union* (2022) ECLI:EU:C:2022:297; for a more detailed analysis of this case law Jens-Peter Schneider, 'Plattformregulierung als Baustein der europäischen KI-Governance' in Matthias Ruffert (ed), *Die Regulierung digitaler Plattformen* (Nomos 2023).

[164] See Chapter 3 of this book 14–18; see also the comparative study by Jonathan Dollinger, *Folgenabschätzungen für Verwaltungs-Algorithmen* (Mohr Siebeck 2023).

[165] C-401/19 *Republic of Poland v European Parliament and Council of the European Union* (2022) ECLI:EU:C:2022:297 Opinion of GA Saugmandsgaard Øe paras 178, 180.

[166] Jens-Peter Schneider, 'Plattformregulierung als Baustein der europäischen KI-Governance' in Ruffert (ed) (n 163).

with their duty laid down in Article 14(4) DSA to give 'due regard to the rights and legitimate interests of all parties involved'.[167]

Acknowledgement

Many thanks to all the participants of the INDIGO-workshop in Freiburg on 28–30 September 2022, and especially to Professor Joris van Hoboken for the helpful comments and criticism. All remaining errors are entirely our own.

[167] Wilman (n 121) 17 highlights that the success of the framework will depend on how the supervisory system will work in practice regarding the cooperation between the Commission and the DSCs, as well as the exercising of the powers by the Commission.

5

A Digital Health Infrastructure for Cross-Border Governance of Communicable Diseases

A Case Study on the COVID-19 Pandemic

Franka Enderlein

A. Introduction

The functioning of the Digital Single Market is fundamental for the economic development of the European Union.[1] The 'EU eGovernment Action Plan 2016–2020' outlines important steps to implement the Digital Single Market. According to the Action Plan, administrations should be 'digital', 'cross-border', and 'interoperable' by default.[2] A case study which illustrates the importance of the three principles 'digital', 'interoperable', and 'cross-border' by default is fighting the COVID-19 pandemic in the European Union. Since it is also one of the greatest challenges the European Union faced recently, it constitutes a suitable topic for this chapter.[3]

Regarding the first principle 'digital' by default, we have learned that digital technology is necessary to combat the COVID-19 pandemic. As Thierry Breton, Commissioner for the Internal Market, stated: 'Digital technologies, mobile applications and mobility data have enormous potential to help understand how the virus spreads and to respond effectively.'[4] Indeed, digital technologies are essential

[1] Commission, 'A Digital Single Market Strategy for Europe' (Communication from the Commission to the European Parliament, the Council, the European Economic and Social Committee and the Committee of the Regions) COM(2015) 192 final 3.

[2] Commission, 'EU eGovernment Action Plan 2016–2020, Accelerating the digital transformation of government' (Communication from the Commission to the European Parliament, the Council, the European Economic and Social Committee and the Committee of the Regions) COM(2016) 179 final 4.

[3] Although a pandemic occurs worldwide, this chapter does not focus on international law, specifically not on International Health Regulations. The cross-border spread of COVID-19 is particularly relevant in the European Union due to its internal market. In contrast, the international border controls between the EU and third countries were maintained for a longer period than those within the EU, and did generally not violate international law.

[4] European Commission, 'Coronavirus: Commission adopts Recommendation to support' (8 April 2020) </ec.europa.eu/commission/presscorner/detail/en/ip_20_626> accessed 1 August 2023.

Franka Enderlein, *A Digital Health Infrastructure for Cross-Border Governance of Communicable Diseases* In: *Governance of Automated Decision-Making and EU Law*. Edited by: Herwig C.H. Hofmann and Felix Pflücke, Oxford University Press.
 DOI: 10.1093/9780198919575.003.0005

for the gathering, exchange, and evaluation of information, which is the basis for the governance of communicable diseases.

Concerning the second principle, 'cross-border' by default, only a cross-border fight against a pandemic is efficient.[5] The definition of a pandemic is '[a]n epidemic that occurs in a very large area, crosses international borders and usually affects a large number of people'.[6] It already shows that COVID-19 is a cross-border problem, the solution to which is a common European interest.[7] Nevertheless, it was mostly the Member States and not the European Union that took the decisive measures to combat the pandemic.[8] This did not only reduce the effectiveness of the measures but also posed a problem for the European internal market.[9] When Member States introduced uncoordinated border controls at the beginning of the pandemic, which were accompanied by entry restrictions and quarantine requirements,[10] this led to economic losses of approximately 774 billion Euros and 14.1 million jobs for the tourism industry in 2020 according to the World Travel & Tourism Council.[11] Moreover, border controls with entry restrictions legally restrict the general right to freedom of movement (Article 21 TFEU,[12] Article 45 CFR[13]), the free movement of goods (Articles 28–37 TFEU), the freedom of workers (Articles 45–48 TFEU), the right of establishment (Articles 49–55 TFEU), and the freedom to provide services (Articles 56–62 TFEU).[14] This is especially

[5] Patrick Stockebrandt, 'Impuls für eine Europäische Gesundheitsunion' in Indra Spiecker gen. Döhmann (ed), *Mehrebenensystem im Gesundheitswesen* (Peter Lang Verlag 2022) 51; Karin Henke, 'Der Aufbau der Europäischen Gesundheitsunion—Lernen aus der Corona-Krise' (2021) 39 Medizinrecht 890, 891.

[6] Miquel Porta, *A Dictionary of Epidemiology* (6th edn, OUP 2014) keyword: 'pandemic'.

[7] Constanze Janda, 'Digitalisation of Health Data and Their Interoperability in the European Union' [2022] Fascicolo Speciale n 1 CERIDAP Rivista Interdisciplinare Sul Diritto Delle Amministrazioni Pubbliche 50, 59; Hans-Heinrich Trute, 'How to Deal with Pandemics' in Thomas Eger, Stefan Oeter, and Stefan Voigt (eds), *International Law and the Rule of Law Under Extreme Conditions: An Economic Perspective: Contributions to the XIVth Travemünde Symposium on the Economic Analysis of Law (27–29 March 2014)* (Mohr Siebeck 2017); Andreas T Müller, 'Europa und die Pandemie. Zuständigkeitsdefizite und Kooperationszwänge' (2021) 80 Veröffentlichungen der Vereinigung der Deutschen Staatsrechtslehrer 105, 106.

[8] Alberto Alemanno, 'The European Response to COVID-19: From Regulatory Emulation to Regulatory Coordination?' (2020) 11 European Journal of Risk Regulation 307; Alessio M Pacces and Maria Weimer, 'From Diversity to Coordination: A European Approach to COVID-19' (2020) 11 European Journal of Risk Regulation 283; Müller (n 7) 106.

[9] Commission, 'Building a European Health Union: Reinforcing the EU's resilience for cross-border health threats' (Communication from the Commission to the European Parliament, the Council, the European Economic and Social Committee and the Committee of the Regions) COM(2020) 724 final 1; Constanze Janda, 'Die Europäische Gesundheitsunion—Vorschläge der EU-Kommission' in Spiecker gen. Döhmann (ed) (n 5) 22.

[10] Council Recommendation (EU) 2020/1475 of 13 October 2020 on a coordinated approach to the restriction of free movement in response to the COVID-19 pandemic [2020] OJ L337/3, recital 5.

[11] World Travel & Tourism Council, 'EU Economic Impact from COVID-19' <http://wttc.org/Portals/0/Documents/Reports/2020/EU%20Recovery%20Scenarios%20Nov%202020.pdf?ver=2021-02-25-183016-500> accessed 1 August 2023.

[12] Consolidated version of the Treaty on the Functioning of the European Union [2012] OJ C326/47 (TFEU).

[13] Charter of Fundamental Rights of the European Union [2012] OJ C326/391 (CFR).

[14] Daniel Thym, 'Travel Bans in Europe: A Legal Appraisal' (*Verfassungsblog*, 19 March 2020) <doi.org/10.17176/20200319-123125-0> accessed 1 August 2023.

problematic as border controls do not help to prevent infections in every pandemic situation.[15] More precisely, the timing of border controls determines their effectiveness.[16] Border controls can delay the progression of the disease by a few weeks at the beginning of a pandemic, when there are still only a few cases in the Member State.[17] However, their effectiveness is limited if the rate of infections across the border does not differ markedly from the situation inside the Member State.[18]

Lastly, an efficient fight against a pandemic needs information systems which are 'interoperable' by default. Medical, especially epidemiological, information is very important as a basis for decisions about communicable diseases.[19] For the fight against COVID-19 information on infection rates is particularly relevant for assessing the spread of the disease. Furthermore—as vaccination prevents severe courses of COVID-19—information on the effectiveness and safety of vaccines is fundamental. Communicable disease control is characterised by a large number of different actors—for example patients, doctors, administrations, or insurance companies—who gather information on infection rates and vaccines.[20] Hence, for the exchange of information via various information systems the interoperability of the systems is essential.[21] In addition, new techniques such as artificial intelligence (AI) that validate data rely on growing volumes of digital medical data.[22] Thus they depend on interoperable information systems as well.[23]

Having understood the importance of the three principles in the fight against COVID-19, this chapter asks how a digital, cross-border, and interoperable fight against communicable diseases might look like. Section B describes the structure of the legal framework in the public health sector. This also includes the distribution of competences between the European Union and the Member

[15] Neil M Ferguson and others, 'Strategies for Mitigating an Influenza Pandemic' (2006) 442 Nature 448; Moritz UG Kraemer and others, 'The Effect of Human Mobility and Control Measures on the COVID-19 Epidemic in China' (2020) 368 Science 493; Matteo Chinazzi and others, 'The Effect of Travel Restrictions on the Spread of the 2019 Novel Coronavirus (COVID-19) Outbreak' (2020) 368 Science 395.

[16] Ferguson and others (n 15) 449.

[17] ibid.

[18] Thym (n 14) 5.

[19] Trute (n 7) 118–19. On the connection between information and decisions generally, cf Jens-Peter Schneider, 'Basic Structures of Information Management in the European Administrative Union' (2014) 20 European Public Law 89.

[20] Markus Frischhut and Scott L Greer, 'EU Public Health Law and Policy—Communicable Diseases' in Tamara K Hervey, Calum A Young, and Louise E Bishop (eds), *Research Handbook on EU Health Law and Policy* (Edward Elgar Publishing 2017) 326; Sebastian Bretthauer, 'Perspektiven für das Gesundheitssystem: Lehren aus der Pandemie' (2021) 54 Die Verwaltung 411; Jürgen Kühling and Christian Seidel, 'Teil 1: Grundlagen—Allgemeiner Teil' in Thorsten Kingreen and Jürgen Kühling (eds), *Gesundheitsdatenschutzrecht* (Nomos 2015) 50–54.

[21] Janda (n 7) 51.

[22] Moritz Lehne and others, 'Why Digital Medicine Depends on Interoperability' (2019) 2 Nature Portfolio Journal Digital Medicine 79.

[23] ibid. On the (planned) use of AI to analyse the data, see eg Regulation (EU) 2022/2371 of the European Parliament and of the Council of 23 November 2022 on serious cross-border threats to health and repealing Decision No 1082/2013/EU [2022] OJ L314/26, art 14(2)(a).

States in the area of public health and how it may impede interoperability. Section C analyses which functions the information systems have and how they protect public health. Section D then examines how the information systems promote the four levels of interoperability (legal, organizational, semantic, and technical). Finally, Section E draws conclusions and addresses the remaining challenges.

B. Structure of the legal framework in the public health sector

To evaluate the structure of the legal framework in the public health sector, this section analyses the limited competences of the European Union according to Article 168 of the Treaty on the Functioning of the European Union (TFEU) in a first step. It also asks whether the competences impede interoperability (section B.I). In a second step, the contribution explains which legal acts the European Union has already adopted based on Article 168 TFEU (section B.II).

I. Limited competences of the European Union

According to Article 168(1) TFEU health protection is a cross-sectorial task in the European Union. The Union has a shared competence (Article 4(2)(a, k) TFEU) in some areas of public health and a supplementary competence (Article 6(2)(a) TFEU) in others.

Shared competence refers to the areas that concern public health safety, which includes health aspects related to product safety (Article 168(4) TFEU).[24] The European Union may adopt harmonization measures in these areas, especially to set high standards of quality and safety for medicinal products including vaccines.[25] Harmonization measures may also be adopted for information systems that record the side effects of medicinal products and thus contribute to their safety. Alternatively, shared competence can derive from Article 114 TFEU if the regulation does not focus on safety concerns but on the free internal movement of medicinal products and devices for medical use.[26]

[24] Janda (n 7) 52; Markus Kotzur, 'Art. 168 TFEU' in Rudolf Geiger, Daniel-Erasmus Khan, and Markus Kotzur (eds), *European Union Treaties: Treaty on European Union, Treaty on the Functioning of the European Union, Charter of Fundamental Rights of the European Union* (C.H. Beck; Hart Publishing 2015) art 168 TFEU para 7; Ulrich M Gassner, 'Versorgung mit kritischen Gesundheitsprodukten' in Spiecker gen. Döhmann (ed) (n 5) 120.

[25] Daniel Thym and Jonas Bornemann, 'Kapitel 2: Binnenmarktrechtliche Grundlagen des Infektions- und Gesundheitsschutzrechts' in Stefan Huster and Thorsten Kingreen (eds), *Handbuch Infektionsschutzrecht* (C.H. Beck 2021) para 48.

[26] Thorsten Kingreen, 'Art. 168 AEUV' in Christian Calliess and Matthias Ruffert (eds), *EUV/AEUV* (6th edn, C.H. Beck 2022) art 168 AEUV para 23; Thym and Bornemann (n 25) paras 57–58.

In all other areas of public health, the European Union only has a supplementary competence (Article 168(2)(1), (3) TFEU), which entitles it to support, coordinate, or supplement the actions of the Member States to ensure public health. According to Article 168(5) TFEU, the supplementary competence 'exclud[es] any harmonisation of the laws and regulations of the Member States'. However, the European Union may adopt incentive measures 'in particular to combat the major cross-border health scourges'. Incentive measures in this sense are, for example, action programmes or the establishment of agencies of the European Union, as long as their tasks are limited to coordination activities and knowledge management.[27] The development of European information systems is also included.[28]

Some authors argue that Article 168(5) TFEU includes the harmonization of terminologies and standards because otherwise the European Union could not fulfil its mandate from Article 168(1) TFEU to ensure a high level of health protection.[29] Others claim that the European Union already has a broad competence base *de lege lata*, derived from a 'network' of competences in the treaties.[30] According to these treaty interpretations, interoperability of national and European information systems could be established without an amendment of European treaties. However, they ignore the fact that it is the very difference between shared competence and supplementary competence that only the shared competence includes the harmonization of Member State's legislation.[31] In addition, Article 168(7) TFEU strongly emphasizes that Union actions shall respect the responsibilities of the Member States for the definition of their health policy and for the organization and delivery of health services and medical care.[32] Therefore, the primary responsibility for pandemic responses remains at the level of the Member States.[33] The deployment of information systems in the national health systems is entirely a national competence, too.[34]

[27] Birgit Schmidt am Busch, 'Art. 168 AEUV' in Eberhard Grabitz, Meinhard Hilf, and Martin Nettesheim (eds), *Das Recht der Europäischen Union* (78th supp. C.H. Beck 2023) part 168 AEUV para 70.

[28] ibid.

[29] Henrique Martins, *EU Health Data Centre and a Common Data Strategy for Public Health: Study for the Panel for the Future of Science and Technology* (Mihalis Kritikos, Scientific Foresight Unit, Panel for the Future of Science and Technology (STOA) 2021) 9–10.

[30] Kai P Purnhagen and others, 'More Competences than You Knew? The Web of Health Competence for European Union Action in Response to the COVID-19 Outbreak' (2020) 11 European Journal of Risk Regulation 297, 302.

[31] Christian Calliess, 'Braucht die Europäische Union eine Kompetenz zur (Corona-) Pandemiebekämpfung?' [2021] Neue Zeitschrift für Verwaltungsrecht 505, 508.

[32] Janda (n 7) 52.

[33] Alemanno (n 8) 313; Pacces and Weimer (n 8) 286; Kotzur (n 24) art 168 TFEU para 9; Simone Kuhlmann, 'Wissensgenerierung zur Pandemievorsorge und -steuerung durch (digitale) Public Health Surveillance' (2022) 40 Medizinrecht 730, 733; Müller (n 7) 110–11.

[34] Directive 2011/24/EU of the European Parliament and of the Council of 9 March 2011 on the application of patients' rights in cross-border healthcare [2011] OJ L88/45, recital 56; Janda (n 7) 59; Stockebrandt (n 5) 53–54.

The European Union is not authorized to establish the interoperability of information systems on the basis of other provisions of the TFEU either, specifically not on the basis of Article 196 TFEU, Article 222 TFEU, or Article 122 TFEU. Even if Article 196 TFEU and Article 222 TFEU are applicable to natural disasters such as the COVID-19 pandemic they only grant a supplementary competence as Article 168 TFEU does. Therefore, they neither allow for harmonization of information systems.[35]

Likewise, the European Union cannot rely on Article 122 TFEU as a basis of competence. Article 122 TFEU is only applicable in cases of serious difficulties of the Member States. While the COVID-19 pandemic constitutes such a difficulty,[36] the information systems transmit data not only during the pandemic but also during periods of low infection rates. Additionally Title VIII of the TFEU (in which Article 122 is found) regulates the economic and monetary policy of the Union. As the information systems primarily serve a purpose other than economic or monetary policy—namely public health—the European Union's competence cannot derive from Title VIII.

Hence, the European Union can only establish 'soft law' to achieve the interoperability of information systems *de lege lata*. It must rely on the cooperation of the Member States.[37] In the past, however, cooperation has often been weak, resulting in regulatory fragmentation.[38] The measures taken by the Member States have remained heterogeneous.[39]

II. Legal acts adopted on the basis of Article 168 TFEU

Public health information systems existed in part since 1998. However, due to various health crises, the European Union has adapted them several times. The following sections outline the development of the information systems for data on communicable diseases (section B.II.1) and for data on vaccine safety (section B.II.2). Furthermore, section B.II.3 explains how the European Commission adapted information systems on the basis of three regulations from 2022 in response to the COVID-19 pandemic.

[35] Janda (n 9) 29.

[36] Päivi Leino-Sandberg and Matthias Ruffert, 'Next Generation EU and Its Constitutional Ramifications: A Critical Assessment' (2022) 59 Common Market Law Review 433, 444.

[37] Directive 2011/24/EU of the European Parliament and of the Council of 9 March 2011 on the application of patients' rights in cross-border healthcare [2011] OJ L88/45, recital 56; Janda (n 7) 63; Stockebrandt (n 5) 48; Calliess (n 31) 508.

[38] Andrea Renda and Rosa Castro, 'Towards Stronger EU Governance of Health Threats after the COVID-19 Pandemic' (2020) 11 European Journal of Risk Regulation 273, 277.

[39] Müller (n 7) 111.

1. Data on communicable diseases

For the transmission of data on communicable diseases, the European Union established a so-called Community Network in 1998. The network should ensure the epidemiological surveillance of communicable diseases and promote the prevention and control of communicable diseases through an early warning and response system.[40] The Commission and public health agencies of the Member States coordinated the Community Network.[41] However, during the SARS crisis in 2003, it became apparent that there was a need for a coordinating agency to manage the network.[42] Therefore, the European Parliament and the Council adopted Regulation (EC) No 851/2004 on the basis of Article 168(5) TFEU.[43] The Regulation set up the European Centre for Disease Prevention and Control (ECDC) as a coordinating and advisory body.[44] It also transferred the coordination of the Community Network from public health agencies of the Member States to the ECDC.[45]

In 2013, in response to the H1N1 swine flu pandemic, Decision No 1082/2013/EU[46] reorganized the Community Network and split it into two networks: The decision established in Article 6 a network for the epidemiological surveillance of communicable diseases and, in Article 8, an Early Warning and Response System (now called EWRS). The information systems have retained their structure until today. Yet the Commission adopted some legislative acts that regulate the procedure of the information systems and thus can improve their interoperability. It established case definitions for communicable diseases in Implementing Decision (EU) 2018/945[47] for the network for the epidemiological surveillance of communicable diseases. For the EWRS, Commission Recommendation 2012/73/EU provides data protection guidelines. In addition, Commission Implementing Decision (EU) 2017/253 specifies the procedures for the notification of alerts in the EWRS.

[40] Decision No 2119/98/EC of the European Parliament and of the Council of 24 September 1998 setting up a network for the epidemiological surveillance and control of communicable diseases in the Community [1998] OJ L268/1, art 1; Paolo Guglielmetti and others, 'The Early Warning and Response System for Communicable Diseases in the EU: An Overview from 1999 to 2005' (2006) 11(12) Eurosurveillance 215; Frischhut and Greer (n 20) 321–22.

[41] Decision No 2119/98/EC of the European Parliament and of the Council of 24 September 1998 setting up a network for the epidemiological surveillance and control of communicable diseases in the Community [1998] OJ L268/1, art 1.

[42] Frischhut and Greer (n 20) 322; Andrea Ammon and Daniel Faensen, 'Surveillance von Infektionskrankheiten auf europäischer Ebene' (2009) 52 Bundesgesundheitsblatt 176, 176–77.

[43] Consolidated Version of the Treaty establishing the European Community [1997] OJ C340/173, ex art 152(5).

[44] Regulation (EC) No 851/2004 of the European Parliament and of the Council of 21 April 2004 establishing a European centre for disease prevention and control [2004] OJ L142/1, art 1.

[45] ibid art 5(1), art 8(1).

[46] Decision No 1082/2013/EU of the European Parliament and of the Council of 22 October 2013 on serious cross-border threats to health and repealing Decision No 2119/98/EC [2013] OJ L293/1.

[47] Commission Implementing Decision (EU) 2018/945 of 22 June 2018 on the communicable diseases and related special health issues to be covered by epidemiological surveillance as well as relevant case definitions [2018] OJ L170/1.

2. Data on vaccine safety

For a better understanding of the functioning of the information systems for the transmission of data on vaccine safety, we need to distinguish the marketing authorization procedures for medicinal products in the European Union: the national,[48] decentralized,[49] and centralized[50] procedure and the procedure of mutual recognition.[51] Almost all new vaccines are authorized via the centralized procedure on the basis of Regulation (EC) No 726/2004, which is based on shared competence of today's Article 114 TFEU and Article 168(4)(b) TFEU.[52]

Before vaccines are approved, experts conduct extensive clinical trials on their efficacy and safety and evaluate them.[53] Authorization of vaccines requires evidence of a positive benefit–risk balance.[54] Nevertheless, continuous surveillance and collection of further data after the authorization and in the context of widespread use is essential to identify further potential risks as soon as possible.[55] For this purpose, Article 24(1) of Regulation (EC) No 726/2004 states that the European Medicines Agency (EMA) shall set up and maintain a database called EudraVigilance.[56] Commission Implementing Regulation (EU) No 520/2012 governs procedural rules for the performance of pharmacovigilance activities, especially via EudraVigilance.

3. Regulations for building a European Health Union

Due to the problems that became apparent during the COVID-19 pandemic, the European Union issued three regulations in November 2022 intended to build a European Health Union.[57] In a communication issued with the proposals for the

[48] See eg in Germany Gesetz über den Verkehr mit Arzneimitteln (Arzneimittelgesetz – AMG) vom 16.5.1962 in the version of the announcement of 12 December 2005 [2005] BGBl I/3394, s 21(1).

[49] Directive 2001/83/EC of the European Parliament and of the Council of 6 November 2001 on the Community code relating to medicinal products for human use [2001] OJ L311/67, art 28(3).

[50] Regulation (EC) No 726/2004 of the European Parliament and of the Council of 31 March 2004 laying down Community procedures for the authorisation and supervision of medicinal products for human and veterinary use and establishing a European Medicines Agency [2004] OJ L136/1, art 3(1), 10(1–2).

[51] Directive 2001/83/EC of the European Parliament and of the Council of 6 November 2001 on the Community code relating to medicinal products for human use [2001] OJ L311/67, art 28(2).

[52] Elke Roos, 'Der Impfschadensprozess—Risiken und Nebenwirkungen' [2020] Zeitschrift für die sozialgerichtliche Praxis 210, 211; Nils Schaks, '§ 14 Verhütung übertragbarer Krankheiten: Schutzimpfungen' in Sebastian Kluckert (ed), *Das neue Infektionsschutzrecht* (2nd edn, Nomos 2021) § 14 para 9.

[53] BGM and others, *Nationale Impfstrategie COVID-19—Strategie zur weiteren Durchführung und Evaluierung der Impfung gegen SARS-CoV-2 in Deutschland* (2nd edn, 2021) 21.

[54] ibid.

[55] ibid.

[56] For databases as a category of information exchange, see Jens-Peter Schneider, 'Information Exchange and Its Problems' in Carol Harlow, Päivi Leino, and Giacinto Della Cananea (eds), *Research Handbook on EU Administrative Law* (Edward Elgar Publishing 2017) 92–94.

[57] Regulation (EU) 2022/123 of the European Parliament and of the Council of 25 January 2022 on a reinforced role for the European Medicines Agency in crisis preparedness and management for medicinal products and medical devices [2022] OJ L20/1; Regulation (EU) 2022/2370 of the European Parliament and of the Council of 23 November 2022 amending Regulation (EC) No 851/2004 establishing a European centre for disease prevention and control [2022] OJ L314/1; Regulation

regulations the Commission stated that structures and mechanisms set up as part of Decision No 1082/2013/EU facilitated the exchange of information on the evolution of the pandemic and supported specific national measures taken, but they could do little to trigger a timely common European level response.[58]

Therefore Regulation (EU) 2022/123 aims to ensure a high level of protection of human health by ensuring the proper functioning of the internal market for medicinal products and medical devices.[59] The Regulation establishes a framework for the monitoring and reporting of deficiencies in medicinal products and medical devices and is based on Article 114 TFEU.[60] Moreover, it aims to establish a strengthened Union framework to ensure the quality and safety of medicinal products and medical devices and is based on Article 168(4)(c) TFEU.[61]

Regulation (EU) 2022/2370 amends Regulation (EC) No 851/2004 and is based in particular on Article 168(5) TFEU. It seeks to improve the epidemiological surveillance of communicable diseases by the ECDC by enabling the use of digital technologies such as AI and computer modelling and simulation.[62] Additionally, according to the Regulation the ECDC should work on updating the EWRS to enable the use of AI technologies and interoperable and privacy-preserving digital tools.[63]

Even more important for the surveillance of communicable diseases is Regulation (EU) 2022/2371 which is also based on Article 168(5) TFEU. The regulation repeals Decision No 1082/2013/EU and seeks to create a more robust mandate for coordination at Union level.[64] Most important is a new provision in Article 14 of Regulation (EU) 2022/2371, which provides for a digital platform for surveillance. This provision refers to the EpiPulse platform that transmits the data, information, and documents of the network for the epidemiological surveillance of communicable diseases.[65] In general, it is commendable that Article 14 of Regulation (EU) 2022/2371 codifies the existence and the (technical) requirements of the platform. Previously the requirements were left entirely to the

(EU) 2022/2371 of the European Parliament and of the Council of 23 November 2022 on serious cross-border threats to health and repealing Decision No 1082/2013/EU [2022] OJ L314/26. See also Henke (n 5).

58 Commission (n 9) 4.

59 Regulation (EU) 2022/123 of the European Parliament and of the Council of 25 January 2022 on a reinforced role for the European Medicines Agency in crisis preparedness and management for medicinal products and medical devices [2022] OJ L20/1, recital 16.

60 ibid.

61 ibid.

62 Regulation (EU) 2022/2370 of the European Parliament and of the Council of 23 November 2022 amending Regulation (EC) No 851/2004 establishing a European centre for disease prevention and control [2022] OJ L314/1, recital 15.

63 ibid recital 22.

64 Regulation (EU) 2022/2371 of the European Parliament and of the Council of 23 November 2022 on serious cross-border threats to health and repealing Decision No 1082/2013/EU [2022] OJ L314/26, recital 15.

65 ibid art 14(7)(b); Kuhlmann (n 33) 734. For the operation of EpiPulse see section C.I.2.

discretion of ECDC and the European Commission.[66] However, the regulation is still very unspecific and it is unclear how the platform will use digital solutions such as AI concretely.

Overall, the legislative history—and also the new regulations for building a European Health Union—shows that the legal framework in the public health sector has only been adapted due to health crises, without a real European strategy for a common information management behind it.[67] Such a strategy not only requires a more robust mandate for coordination at Union level and the use of digital technologies but demands significant adjustments. As already pointed out by Janda, the most significant barrier to build a truly European Health Union is the absence of interoperability.[68] To change this, an expansion of European competencies in public health is necessary. Concretely, the European Union needs a shared competence for public health information management.[69]

C. Operation of the information systems for public health

At European level, information systems that transmit data on communicable diseases (section C.I) and on vaccine safety (section C.II) contribute significantly to the protection of public health. In the following sections, the operation of the information systems is explained.

I. Data on communicable diseases

For the classification of surveillance of communicable diseases, epidemiologists distinguish indicator-based surveillance from event-based surveillance.[70] Indicator-based surveillance consists of routinely collecting data about the occurrence of predefined diseases, specific pathogens, syndromes, or conditions.[71] In order to carry out indicator-based surveillance, Member States must report specific cases of detected pathogens or diseases considered important for public health to authorities or agencies via information systems.[72] In contrast to indicator-based

[66] Patrycja Dąbrowska-Kłosińska, 'Electronic Systems of Information Exchange as a Key Tool in EU Health Crisis and Disaster Management' (2019) 10 European Journal of Risk Regulation 652, 659; Kuhlmann (n 33) 734.

[67] Martins (n 29) 20.

[68] Janda (n 7) 55.

[69] Vincent Delhomme, 'Emancipating Health from the Internal Market: For a Stronger EU (Legislative) Competence in Public Health' (2020) 11 European Journal of Risk Regulation 747, 748; Calliess (n 31) 510–11; Müller (n 7) 113; Stockebrandt (n 5) 55; Gassner (n 24) 148.

[70] Andrew Amato-Gauci and Andrea Ammon, 'The Surveillance of Communicable Diseases in the European Union—A Long-Term Strategy (2008–2013)' (2008) 13 Eurosurveillance 1, 1–2.

[71] ibid.

[72] Porta (n 6) keyword: 'notifiable disease'.

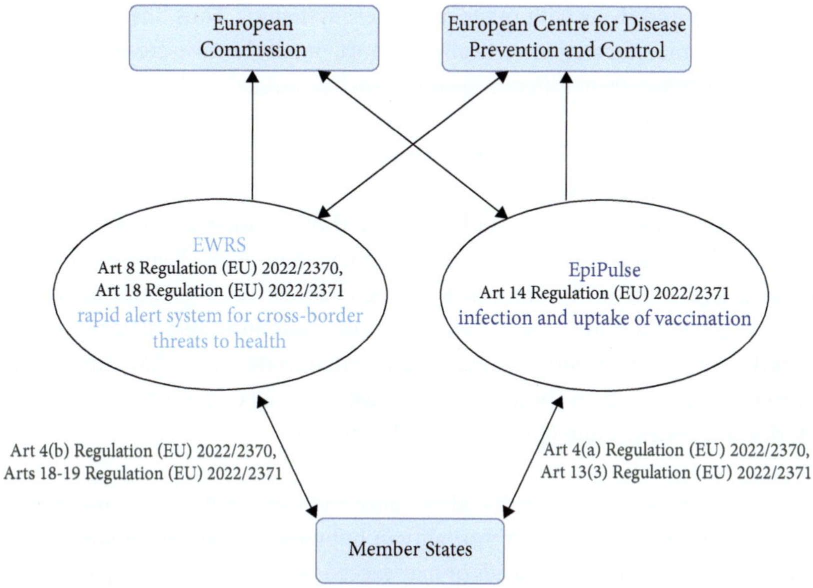

Figure 5.1 Operation of the information systems *EWRS* and *EpiPulse.*

surveillance, event-based surveillance involves searching media or information systems for events that indicate infectious diseases.[73]

The EWRS, a rapid alert system, transmits information on communicable diseases in the European Union as part of event-based surveillance (section C.I.1).[74] Besides, EpiPulse transmits information for indicator-based surveillance of communicable diseases as well as information on vaccination coverage (section C.I.2).[75]

1. The Early Warning and Response System (EWRS)

The EWRS is a rapid alert system, which tracks infections of a newly emerged disease, especially at the beginning of a pandemic. The EWRS is a web-based application. As can be seen in Figure 5.1, it enables the Commission and competent authorities responsible at national level to be in permanent communication for the purposes of alerting, assessing public health risks, and determining the measures that may be required to protect public health.[76] As public health risks do not only originate from communicable diseases, the Commission wants to link the EWRS

[73] Amato-Gauci and Ammon (n 70) 2.
[74] ibid.
[75] ibid.
[76] Regulation (EU) 2022/2371 of the European Parliament and of the Council of 23 November 2022 on serious cross-border threats to health and repealing Decision No 1082/2013/EU [2022] OJ L314/26, art 18(1); Guglielmetti and others (n 40).

efficiently and effectively with other rapid alert systems.[77] Thus, the EWRS does not only transmit information vertically and horizontally but also cross-sectoral, ie between authorities from different sectors—such as animal health, food and feed, and civil protection.

The EWRS consists of two communication channels: the general messaging channel and the selective messaging channel.[78] The general messaging channel allows Member States' competent public health authorities to send alert notifications and 'normal' information messages to other competent public health authorities, European Agencies, or the Commission. The channel transmits information regarding cross-border threats to health. Regarding communicable diseases this includes data on case numbers, hospitalization and mortality rates.[79] Member States may send an alert if a cross-border health threat meets all of the conditions set out in Article 19(1) Regulation (EU) 2022/2371. It has to

- be unusual or unexpected for the given place and time, or it has to cause or may cause significant morbidity or mortality in humans, or it grows rapidly or may grow rapidly in scale, or it exceeds or may exceed national response capacity; and
- affect or may affect more than one Member State; and
- require or may require a coordinated response at Union level.

The detection of a positive case of COVID-19 following a particular cross-border journey fulfils the criteria set out in Article 19(1) Regulation (EU) 2022/2371 as the disease may cause significant human mortality, it may spread rapidly, it affects more than one Member State, and it may require a coordinated response at Union level.[80] Accordingly, the Commission opened a COVID-19 channel as early as 9 January 2020 to inform Member States of the event and invited Member States to share any information available.[81] In the period to 11 November 2020 the platform had already processed over 2,700 COVID-19 messages.[82]

If a cross-border health threat does not meet all of the conditions set out in Article 19(1) Regulation (EU) 2022/2371, Member States' competent public health authorities may be sent a 'normal' information message.[83] In any case, the

[77] Regulation (EU) 2022/2370 of the European Parliament and of the Council of 23 November 2022 amending Regulation (EC) No 851/2004 establishing a European centre for disease prevention and control [2022] OJ L314/1, art 8(2)(c).

[78] Commission Recommendation 2012/73/EU of 6 February 2012 on data protection guidelines for the Early Warning and Response System (EWRS) [2012] OJ L36/31, 36.

[79] Janda (n 7) 61.

[80] Commission Implementing Decision (EU) 2021/858 of 27 May 2021 amending Implementing Decision (EU) 2017/253 as regards alerts triggered by serious cross-border threats to health and for the contact tracing of passengers identified through Passenger Locator Forms [2021] OJ L188/106, recital 1.

[81] Commission (n 9) 17.

[82] ibid.

[83] Commission, 'Report on the implementation of Decision No 1082/2013/EU of the European Parliament and of the Council of 22 October 2013 on serious cross-border threats to health and

authorities must send both the alert and the 'normal' information message within twenty-four hours of becoming aware of the cross-border threat to health.[84] The notification has to contain information such as the type and origin of the agent, the date and place of the incident or outbreak, and means of transmission or dissemination.[85] However, if information is missing, Member States' competent authorities may not delay notification for that reason.[86] After the authorities or the Commission sent the notification, the ECDC (or, if the health risk is not due to a communicable disease, another European agency such as the European Food Safety Authority (EFSA)) analyses it and prepares a risk assessment.[87] The Commission shall make the risk assessment available to the Member States' competent public health authorities and the Health Security Committee, established under Article 4 of Regulation (EU) 2022/2371.[88] Based on the alert notification and the risk assessment, Member States' competent authorities shall coordinate their responses.[89] If the conditions for an alert no longer exist, the Member States or the Commission must deactivate the alert.[90]

Member States' competent authorities use the second channel, the so-called selective messaging channel, if the occurrence of an event related to communicable

repealing Decision No 2119/98/EC' (Report from the Commission to the European Parliament and the Council) COM(2015) 617 final 9.

[84] Commission Implementing Decision (EU) 2017/253 of 13 February 2017 laying down procedures for the notification of alerts as part of the early warning and response system established in relation to serious cross-border threats to health and for the information exchange, consultation and coordination of responses to such threats pursuant to Decision No 1082/2013/EU of the European Parliament and of the Council [2017] OJ L37/23, art 2(1).

[85] Regulation (EU) 2022/2371 of the European Parliament and of the Council of 23 November 2022 on serious cross-border threats to health and repealing Decision No 1082/2013/EU [2022] OJ L314/26, art 19(3).

[86] Commission Implementing Decision (EU) 2017/253 of 13 February 2017 laying down procedures for the notification of alerts as part of the early warning and response system established in relation to serious cross-border threats to health and for the information exchange, consultation and coordination of responses to such threats pursuant to Decision No 1082/2013/EU of the European Parliament and of the Council [2017] OJ L37/23, art 2(4).

[87] Regulation (EU) 2022/2370 of the European Parliament and of the Council of 23 November 2022 amending Regulation (EC) No 851/2004 establishing a European centre for disease prevention and control [2022] OJ L314/1, art 8(2), 8a; Regulation (EU) 2022/2371 of the European Parliament and of the Council of 23 November 2022 on serious cross-border threats to health and repealing Decision No 1082/2013/EU [2022] OJ L314/26, art 20(1).

[88] Regulation (EU) 2022/2371 of the European Parliament and of the Council of 23 November 2022 on serious cross-border threats to health and repealing Decision No 1082/2013/EU [2022] OJ L314/26, art 20(1).

[89] art 21 ibid; Commission Implementing Decision (EU) 2017/253 of 13 February 2017 laying down procedures for the notification of alerts as part of the early warning and response system established in relation to serious cross-border threats to health and for the information exchange, consultation and coordination of responses to such threats pursuant to Decision No 1082/2013/EU of the European Parliament and of the Council [2017] OJ L37/23, art 4.

[90] Commission Implementing Decision (EU) 2017/253 of 13 February 2017 laying down procedures for the notification of alerts as part of the early warning and response system established in relation to serious cross-border threats to health and for the information exchange, consultation and coordination of responses to such threats pursuant to Decision No 1082/2013/EU of the European Parliament and of the Council [2017] OJ L37/23, art 6.

diseases with a potential Union-wide dimension requires the implementation of particular control measures, especially contact tracing measures.[91] Through this channel Member States communicate personal data, including contact and health data, only to national competent authorities involved in contact tracing measures.[92] The competent authorities must refer to the alert communicated previously through the EWRS when using the channel for selective messaging.[93] In 2021, the Commission complemented the selective messaging functionality with a platform for the exchange of Passenger Locator Forms.[94] These forms contain the data of infected passengers and persons at risk when entering another Member State.[95] Through the platform, the Member States' competent public health authorities can identify SARS-CoV-2 contacts.[96] The ECDC operates the Passenger Locator Forms exchange platform.[97] Although cross-border contact tracing during the COVID-19 pandemic requires many resources, the selective messaging functionality is overall one of the pillars of national preparedness and response strategies.[98]

2. The network for the epidemiological surveillance of communicable diseases (transmission via EpiPulse)

As Figure 1 shows, the European Commission, the ECDC, and the competent authorities at national level are in permanent communication for the transmission of data on communicable diseases within the network for the epidemiological surveillance of communicable diseases (Article 13(1) Regulation (EU) 2022/2371). Thus, the authorities mainly transmit information vertically (between Member States' competent authorities and the ECDC respectively the Commission) and horizontally (between different Member States' competent authorities). To forward information in a fully automated way, the authorities had been using the communication tool TESSy since 2008.[99] In 2021 TESSy was transferred to the newly developed European surveillance portal for infectious diseases (EpiPulse), which can be seen in Figure 5.1.[100] Via EpiPulse the Member States' competent

[91] Commission Recommendation 2012/73/EU of 6 February 2012 on data protection guidelines for the Early Warning and Response System (EWRS) [2012] OJ L36/31, 35.

[92] Regulation (EU) 2022/2371 of the European Parliament and of the Council of 23 November 2022 on serious cross-border threats to health and repealing Decision No 1082/2013/EU [2022] OJ L314/26, art 28(1).

[93] ibid art 28(3).

[94] Commission Implementing Decision (EU) 2017/253 of 13 February 2017 laying down procedures for the notification of alerts as part of the early warning and response system established in relation to serious cross-border threats to health and for the information exchange, consultation and coordination of responses to such threats pursuant to Decision No 1082/2013/EU of the European Parliament and of the Council [2017] OJ L37/23, art 2a.

[95] ibid art 1a(a).

[96] ibid art 2a(1).

[97] ibid art 2a(2).

[98] Inessa Markus and others, 'COVID-19: Cross-Border Contact Tracing in Germany, February to April 2020' (2021) 26(10) Eurosurveillance 1, 8.

[99] Ammon and Faensen (n 42) 180–81; Amato-Gauci and Ammon (n 70) 2.

[100] Janda (n 7) 61; Kuhlmann (n 33) 733.

public health authorities transmit information on the epidemiological surveillance of communicable diseases, the progression of epidemic situations, and unusual epidemic phenomena or new communicable diseases of unknown origin.[101] The ECDC and the Commission have read-only access to any information in EpiPulse but cannot write or upload any information.[102] Typically, Member States' competent authorities transmit information on the types of diseases, age, gender, birth, nationality, and the country of notification via predefined fields.[103] It is possible to add variables to the system, for example if new pathogens or diseases have to be included in the surveillance system.[104] EpiPulse makes a distinction between case-based information, which refers to an individual patient and the single occurrence of a disease, and aggregated information, which describes the total number of cases in a specific Member State and the proportion of cases with certain characteristics.[105] EpiPulse allows direct access to publicly available data without a specific request to the authority providing the data, and is therefore qualified as a database.[106]

During the COVID-19 pandemic, the national competent authorities transmit weekly case-based information on COVID-19 cases, as well as aggregated information on the number of cases, deaths, hospital and intensive care admissions, detected viral variants, and tests performed via TESSy, respectively as of 2021 via EpiPulse.[107] However, it became apparent that delays are significant and inconsistency is frequent.[108] Therefore, the information transmitted is often not comparable and its analysis is difficult.[109] To improve the quality of information, Article 14(2)(a) of Regulation (EU) 2022/2371 stipulates that EpiPulse shall enable the automated collection of surveillance and laboratory data, and use AI for data validation, analysis, and automated reporting. Moreover, it shall establish integrated and interoperable surveillance systems that enable real-time surveillance.[110] The ECDC is responsible for minimizing risks that may arise from transferring inaccurate, incomplete, or ambiguous data from one database to another, as well as establishing robust procedures for verifying data quality.[111] Additionally, the

[101] Regulation (EU) 2022/2371 of the European Parliament and of the Council of 23 November 2022 on serious cross-border threats to health and repealing Decision No 1082/2013/EU [2022] OJ L314/26, art 13(3).

[102] EDPS, *Prior Checking Opinion on the European Surveillance System ('TESSy') Notified by the European Centre for Disease Prevention and Control ('ECDC') on 22 July 2009* (EDPS 2010) 3.

[103] ibid 1.

[104] Ammon and Faensen (n 42) 179.

[105] EDPS (n 102) 2.

[106] Dąbrowska-Kłosińska (n 66) 662; Kuhlmann (n 33) 733.

[107] European Centre for Disease Prevention and Control, 'Surveillance of COVID-19' <www.ecdc.europa.eu/en/covid-19/surveillance> accessed 1 August 2023.

[108] Renda and Castro (n 38) 278; Martins (n 29) 21; Kuhlmann (n 33) 734.

[109] European Court of Auditors, *Dealing with Serious Cross-Border Threats to Health in the EU: Important Steps Taken but More Needs to Be Done* (Publications Office of the European Union 2016) 35; Martins (n 29) 2; Kuhlmann (n 33) 733–34.

[110] Regulation (EU) 2022/2371 of the European Parliament and of the Council of 23 November 2022 on serious cross-border threats to health and repealing Decision No 1082/2013/EU [2022] OJ L314/26, art 14(1).

[111] ibid.

ECDC has to establish interoperability between EpiPulse and national surveillance systems.[112] However, the ECDC does not have the authority to issue binding directives to the Member States on the basis of Article 168(5) TFEU. It therefore depends on the cooperation of the Member States.

II. Data on vaccine safety (EudraVigilance)

EudraVigilance is the information system that transmits information on vaccine safety (see Figure 5.2).

In EudraVigilance the EMA collects, manages, and analyses information on suspected adverse drug reactions to medicines authorized in the European Economic Area.[113] It contains two main modules: first, there is a EudraVigilance Clinical Trial Module for reporting suspected unexpected serious adverse reactions, which

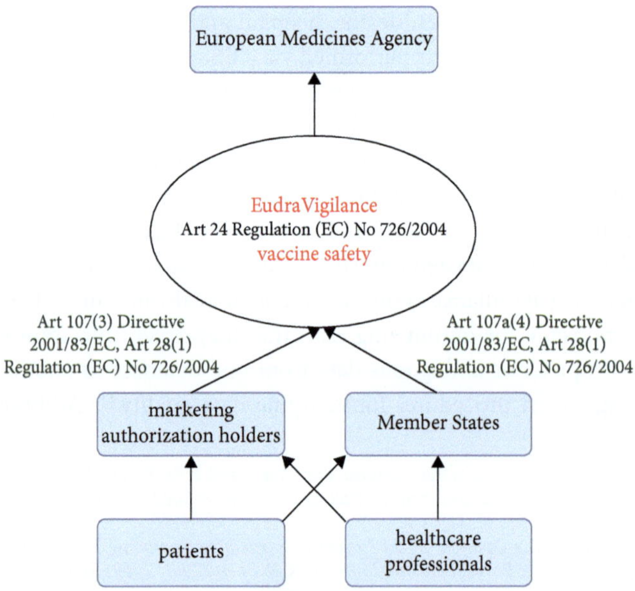

Figure 5.2 Operation of the information system EudraVigilance.

[112] ibid.

[113] Regulation (EC) No 726/2004 of the European Parliament and of the Council of 31 March 2004 laying down Community procedures for the authorisation and supervision of medicinal products for human and veterinary use and establishing a European Medicines Agency [2004] OJ L136/1, art 24; Rodrigo Postigo and others, 'EudraVigilance Medicines Safety Database: Publicly Accessible Data for Research and Public Health Protection' (2018) 41 *Drug Safety* 665, 666; Mansour Tobaiqy, Hajer Elkout, and Katie MacLure, 'Analysis of Thrombotic Adverse Reactions of COVID-19 AstraZeneca Vaccine Reported to EudraVigilance Database' (2021) 9 Vaccines 393.

derive from interventional clinical trials.[114] Second, there is a EudraVigilance Post-Authorisation Module. In the Post-Authorisation Module, healthcare professionals or patients can exchange reports from post-authorization studies and spontaneous reports that do not derive from clinical trials.[115] Spontaneous reports are of utmost importance for the safety of vaccines as active surveillance through clinical trials usually primarily focuses on assessing efficacy; safety is usually a secondary objective.[116] Furthermore, clinical trials only study a relatively small group. Therefore, only common adverse reactions related to the vaccine can be identified.[117]

Competent public health authorities of the Member States, the Commission and the EMA transmit information in EudraVigilance vertically and horizontally. They can access the database permanently.[118] As Figure 5.2 illustrates, marketing authorization holders can also access the database to the extent necessary for them to comply with their pharmacovigilance obligations.[119] It can also be seen in Figure 5.2 that healthcare professionals and patients also have appropriate levels of access to the database.[120] The EudraVigilance Access Policy specifies the extent to which each group has access to the database.[121] Moreover, information held in the EudraVigilance system are publicly available in an aggregated format together with an explanation of how to interpret the data.[122] The EMA is—either in collaboration with the marketing authorization holder or with the Member States' competent authorities that submitted an individual suspected adverse reaction report to the EudraVigilance system—responsible for operating procedures that ensure the quality and integrity of the information collected in the EudraVigilance database.[123]

D. Interoperability safeguards

This contribution has already established that data is exchanged vertically (between Member State authorities and European agencies) and horizontally (between different Member State authorities) for the cross-border governance of

[114] EMA and HMA, *Guideline on Good Pharmacovigilance Practices (GVP)—Module VI* (2017) 44.
[115] ibid.
[116] Tobaiqy, Elkout, and MacLure (n 113).
[117] ibid.
[118] Regulation (EC) No 726/2004 of the European Parliament and of the Council of 31 March 2004 laying down Community procedures for the authorisation and supervision of medicinal products for human and veterinary use and establishing a European Medicines Agency [2004] OJ L136/1, art 24(2).
[119] ibid.
[120] ibid.
[121] EMA, *European Medicines Agency Policy on Access to EudraVigilance Data for Medicinal Products for Human Use* (EMA 2019) 13–29.
[122] Regulation (EC) No 726/2004 of the European Parliament and of the Council of 31 March 2004 laying down Community procedures for the authorisation and supervision of medicinal products for human and veterinary use and establishing a European Medicines Agency [2004] OJ L136/1, art 24(2).
[123] ibid art 24(3).

communicable diseases. Moreover, authorities from different sectors (such as public health and food safety) exchange data. Therefore, interoperability among the three principles introduced at the beginning ('digital', 'cross-border', and 'interoperable') is of utmost importance for fighting the COVID-19 pandemic in the European Union. This section examines how the vertical, horizontal, and cross-sectoral interoperability of the information systems is accomplished.

The European Interoperability Framework defines interoperability as 'the ability of organisations to interact towards mutually beneficial goals, involving the sharing of information and knowledge between these organisations, through the business processes they support, by means of the exchange of data between their ICT [information and communication technology] systems'.[124] It is possible to distinguish four layers of interoperability: legal, organizational, semantic and technical layers.[125] Section D examines the main enablers and barriers to achieve the four layers of interoperability.[126] It shows that the semantic level of interoperability is especially problematic, which hinders the analysis and meaningful use of health data.[127] This can be attributed to the lack of competence of the European Union in public health information management.[128]

I. Legal layer

The legal layer of interoperability ensures that organizations which are operating under different legal frameworks, policies, and strategies are able to work together.[129] For this purpose, legislation should not block the cooperation between Member States but should be harmonized in a way that encourages cooperation.[130] Clear rules have to regulate how to deal with differences in the regulatory framework across borders.[131] Regarding information systems it is an enabler for the legal

[124] Annex 2 of Commission, 'European Interoperability Framework—Implementation Strategy' (Communication from the Commission to the European Parliament, the Council, the European Economic and Social Committee and the Committee of the Regions) COM(2017) 134 final 4–5.

[125] ibid 18. Unlike here, interoperability is also often divided into the four levels semantic, syntactic, technical, and organizational, see Caroline Stellmach, Michael R Muzoora, and Sylvia Thun, 'Digitalization of Health Data: Interoperability of the Proposed European Health Data Space' (2022) 298 Studies in Health Technology and Informatics 132, 133; Lehne and others (n 22) 79–80; Sylvia Thun, Sophie A I Klopfenstein, and Caroline Stellmach, 'Datenstandards und Interoperabilität' in Alexandra Jorzig and David Matusiewicz (eds), *Digitale Gesundheitsanwendungen (DiGA): Rechtliche Grundlagen, innovative Technologien und smarte Köpfe* (medhochzwei Verlag 2021) 230–31.

[126] For enablers and barriers for cross-border health data exchange in general, see Croatian Institute of Public Health and Aragon Health Sciences Institute, *LOST* and Found: Report on Interoperability Landscape in Europe* (2021) 25–37.

[127] Janda (n 7) 63.

[128] Section B.I.

[129] Annex 2 of Commission, 'European Interoperability Framework—Implementation Strategy' (Communication from the Commission to the European Parliament, the Council, the European Economic and Social Committee and the Committee of the Regions) COM(2017) 134 final 23.

[130] ibid 23–24.

[131] ibid 23.

layer of interoperability if information transmission is mandatory.[132] If transmission is mandatory then Member States' competent public health authorities usually transmit information more consistently than if transmission of data is voluntary.[133] Additionally, Member States often adapt their information systems to what is being requested of them when they have to transmit certain categories of information. This can facilitate horizontal, vertical, and cross-sectoral information exchange.[134]

Data collection is mandatory in all of the information systems analysed in this chapter. In the EWRS, according to Article 19(3) Regulation (EU) 2022/2371, Member States have to transmit all information that might be useful for coordinating the response to an alert. In EpiPulse Member States must transmit information on epidemiological surveillance referred to in Article 13(3) Regulation (EU) 2022/2371.[135] Also in EudraVigilance European rules specify which information Member States have to transmit.[136]

Requiring Member States' competent health authorities to adhere to the same data protection rules may also improve interoperability by allowing them to lawfully transfer information to the competent health authorities of other Member States.[137] In the EWRS Member States' competent health authorities exchange personal data via the selective messaging functionality. Article 28 of Regulation (EU) 2022/2371 regulates the protection of personal data in the selective messaging functionality. According to Article 28(6)(a) of Regulation (EU) 2022/2371 the Commission shall adopt detailed requirements necessary to ensure that the operation of the EWRS complies with the General Data Protection Regulation (GDPR)[138] and Regulation (EU) 2018/1725[139]. For the legal layer of interoperability, it is particularly helpful that the Commission will lay down the data protection requirements in the selective messaging functionality as implementing acts in the future. Up until now there has only been a Commission Recommendation for

[132] Croatian Institute of Public Health and Aragon Health Sciences Institute (n 126) 25.

[133] ibid.

[134] Croatian Institute of Public Health and Aragon Health Sciences Institute (n 126).

[135] Regulation (EU) 2022/2371 of the European Parliament and of the Council of 23 November 2022 on serious cross-border threats to health and repealing Decision No 1082/2013/EU [2022] OJ L314/26, art 14(7)(b).

[136] Directive 2001/83/EC of the European Parliament and of the Council of 6 November 2001 on the Community code relating to medicinal products for human use [2001] OJ L311/67, art 107(3) and 107a(4) in conjunction with Regulation (EC) No 726/2004 of the European Parliament and of the Council of 31 March 2004 laying down Community procedures for the authorisation and supervision of medicinal products for human and veterinary use and establishing a European Medicines Agency [2004] OJ L136/1, art 28(1).

[137] Croatian Institute of Public Health and Aragon Health Sciences Institute (n 126) 25.

[138] Regulation (EU) 2016/679 of the European Parliament and of the Council of 27 April 2016 on the protection of natural persons with regard to the processing of personal data and on the free movement of such data, and repealing Directive 95/46/EC (General Data Protection Regulation) [2016] OJ L119/1 (GDPR).

[139] Regulation (EU) 2018/1725 of the European Parliament and of the Council of 23 October 2018 on the protection of natural persons with regard to the processing of personal data by the Union institutions, bodies, offices and agencies and on the free movement of such data, and repealing Regulation (EC) No 45/2001 and Decision No 1247/2002/EC [2018] OJ L 295/39.

data protection requirements[140] that has no binding character and as such permits the different handling of personal data in different Member States. Non-binding guidelines have not led to interoperable health data.[141] On the contrary, they have been a barrier to the legal layer of interoperability.[142]

II. Organizational layer

The organizational layer of interoperability refers to the way in which public administrations align their processes, responsibilities, and expectations to achieve commonly agreed and mutually beneficial goals.[143] To work together in an efficient and effective way different administrative entities have to align their existing processes or define and establish new ones.[144]

A study commissioned by the European Parliament during the COVID-19 pandemic criticizes that public health data is very heterogeneous and that public health data collection varies widely between Member States.[145] Furthermore, it criticizes that the ECDC does not have an effective enforcement mechanism to improve compliance in the Member States.[146] In order to reduce this problem, the study demands a European strategy for communicable disease information management, which should define who does what, how, and when within the framework of European law.[147]

Regarding the organizational layer of interoperability of the EWRS, the Commission's demand that each Member State shall designate the competent authority or authorities responsible at national level for notifying alerts is therefore a step in the right direction.[148] Furthermore, the rules for notifying an alert in the EWRS are already relatively precise,[149] which promotes the vertical and horizontal interoperability of the EWRS. However, it is more difficult to ensure cross-sectoral interoperability in the system. Different Commission services manage rapid alert systems of different sectors and the systems have different contact points in the Member States.[150] For cross-sectoral interoperability it is therefore even more important to have clear organizational rules on how the Commission services and contact points

[140] Commission Recommendation 2012/73/EU of 6 February 2012 on data protection guidelines for the Early Warning and Response System (EWRS) [2012] OJ L36/31, 31.

[141] Müller (n 7) 111.

[142] Martins (n 29) 59–60.

[143] Annex 2 of Commission, 'European Interoperability Framework—Implementation Strategy' (Communication from the Commission to the European Parliament, the Council, the European Economic and Social Committee and the Committee of the Regions) COM(2017) 134 final 24.

[144] ibid 25; Lehne and others (n 22) 80.

[145] Martins (n 29) 70.

[146] ibid 21.

[147] ibid 71.

[148] Regulation (EU) 2022/2371 of the European Parliament and of the Council of 23 November 2022 on serious cross-border threats to health and repealing Decision No 1082/2013/EU [2022] OJ L314/26, art 18(3).

[149] ibid art 19.

[150] European Court of Auditors (n 109) 32.

work together. In Annex IV of Commission Implementing Decision (EU) 2017/253 the Commission defined that eleven rapid alert systems shall be progressively linked with the EWRS.[151] In spite of that, even if the Annex mentions eleven rapid alert systems which the Commission shall link to the EWRS until now it has only linked two systems to the system.[152] Organizational rules on cross-sectoral interoperability are also very scarce (Article 3 Commission Implementing Decision (EU) 2017/253). This shows that there are still major difficulties in cross-sectoral interoperability.

Concerning EpiPulse, the study commissioned by the European Parliament criticized the delays and inconsistency of information transmission.[153] Having well-organized national health information systems can help in resolving these issues as Member States' competent authorities can provide information more promptly and consistently to EpiPulse if it is already accessible at national level.[154] Accordingly, it is commendable that the ECDC supports Member States' competent authorities in their work on national health information systems.[155] The designation of a competent body in each Member State that is responsible for co-ordination between the ECDC and the Member State promotes the organizational layer of interoperability as well.[156]

Commission Implementing Regulation (EU) No 520/2012 aims to ensure the interoperability of EudraVigilance. For the organizational layer of interoperability, the Regulation defines that the national competent authorities and the Agency must have a clear distribution of tasks and responsibilities.[157] Moreover, they have to establish and use a high-quality system that is adequate and effective for the performance of their pharmacovigilance activities.[158] The Commission Implementing Regulation furthermore lays down clear procedural and responsibility rules for data management in EudraVigilance.[159] Overall, these rules enable authorities to work together efficiently and effectively in EudraVigilance.

[151] Annex IV Commission Implementing Decision (EU) 2017/253 of 13 February 2017 laying down procedures for the notification of alerts as part of the early warning and response system established in relation to serious cross-border threats to health and for the information exchange, consultation and coordination of responses to such threats pursuant to Decision No 1082/2013/EU of the European Parliament and of the Council [2017] OJ L37/23.

[152] European Commission, 'Surveillance and early warning' <health.ec.europa.eu/health-security-and-infectious-diseases/surveillance-and-early-warning_en> accessed 1 August 2023.

[153] Martins (n 29) 21; section C.I.2.

[154] Croatian Institute of Public Health and Aragon Health Sciences Institute (n 126) 29.

[155] Regulation (EU) 2022/2370 of the European Parliament and of the Council of 23 November 2022 amending Regulation (EC) No 851/2004 establishing a European centre for disease prevention and control [2022] OJ L314/1, art 5(2)(a); see also Ammon and Faensen (n 42).

[156] Regulation (EU) 2022/2370 of the European Parliament and of the Council of 23 November 2022 amending Regulation (EC) No 851/2004 establishing a European centre for disease prevention and control [2022] OJ L314/1, art 5(4).

[157] Commission Implementing Regulation (EU) No 520/2012 of 19 June 2012 on the performance of pharmacovigilance activities provided for in Regulation (EC) No 726/2004 of the European Parliament and of the Council and Directive 2001/83/EC of the European Parliament and of the Council [2012] OJ L159/5, art 14.

[158] ibid art 8.

[159] ibid art 18.

III. Semantic layer

The semantic layer of interoperability is the major problem of European public health information management. It requires that the precise format and meaning of exchanged data and information is preserved and understood.[160] In the European Interoperability Framework, the semantic layer covers both semantic and syntactic aspects. The semantic aspect refers to the meaning of data elements and the relationship between them.[161] It involves the elaboration of vocabularies and schema to describe data exchange and ensures the communicating parties understand data elements in the same way.[162] The syntactic aspect describes the exact format and structure of the information exchanged (eg an XML document).[163]

Regarding the semantic level of interoperability, the study commissioned by the European Parliament, which was mentioned earlier, points out that there are as many systems, formats, case definitions, and national and regional datasets as there are Member States in the European Union.[164] Thus, the comparability of the information is not given and the analysis of the health data is extremely difficult.[165] This is particularly problematic in indicator-based surveillance, which is the routine collection of data about the occurrence of predefined diseases, specific pathogens, syndromes, or conditions from healthcare providers.[166] EpiPulse is the information system that transmits information for indicator-based surveillance of communicable diseases.[167] But in event-based surveillance, it is also vital that the alert and information systems which will be connected to the EWRS use the same terminology and data format as the system. In particular, in emergencies that may trigger an alert (Article 19 Regulation (EU) 2022/2371) recipients must be able to read and understand the data quickly.

In order to improve the semantic layer of EpiPulse, Commission Implementing Decision (EU) 2018/945 establishes case definitions indicating which diseases and pathogens Member States must report to EpiPulse. Nevertheless, it is the Member States' competence to develop case definitions for their national information

[160] Annex 2 of Commission, 'European Interoperability Framework—Implementation Strategy' (Communication from the Commission to the European Parliament, the Council, the European Economic and Social Committee and the Committee of the Regions) COM(2017) 134 final 25.
[161] ibid 25–26.
[162] ibid 26; Lehne and others (n 22) 80.
[163] Annex 2 of Commission, 'European Interoperability Framework—Implementation Strategy' (Communication from the Commission to the European Parliament, the Council, the European Economic and Social Committee and the Committee of the Regions) COM(2017) 134 final 26; Lehne and others (n 22) 80.
[164] Martins (n 29) 14; Amato-Gauci and Ammon (n 70).
[165] Renda and Castro (n 38) 278; Kuhlmann (n 33) 735.
[166] Amato-Gauci and Ammon (n 70).
[167] Section C.I.

systems.[168] As a result, case definitions often vary.[169] Regarding COVID-19, the case definition variations were so frequent and heterogeneous that they sometimes even impaired the effective use of the information systems.[170] In addition, local testing strategy, laboratory capacity, and the efficiency of national surveillance systems influence communicable disease data and thus challenge the semantic level of interoperability.[171] Consequently, information transmitted via EpiPulse may not have the same meaning in all Member States of the European Union. The same problem arises with the syntactic aspect of interoperability. As the European Union has no competence to prescribe to the Member States which data formats they have to use, there are variations in the formats employed.[172] Thus, the ECDC cannot always decode the transmitted formats automatically. This makes it extremely challenging to enhance the semantic layer of EpiPulse without extending the competencies of the European Union.

Compared to EudraVigilance, it is striking that the European Union can, on the basis of its shared competence in public health safety, adopt rules on the terminology and formats to be used (Articles 4(2)(k), 2(2) TFEU). Accordingly, Commission Implementing Regulation (EU) No 520/2012 determines that messages have to use internationally agreed on terminology[173] and formats.[174] This shows that the European Union needs a shared competence for public health information management to set up the semantic level of interoperability in information systems.[175]

IV. Technical layer

The technical layer of interoperability covers the applications and infrastructures linking systems and services.[176] Aspects of the technical layer are interface specifications, interconnection services, data integration services, data presentation and

[168] Section B.I.

[169] European Court of Auditors (n 109) 35; Michaela Diercke and others, 'Falldefinitionen für die Surveillance meldepflichtiger Infektionskrankheiten in Deutschland, Ausgabe 2015' (2014) 57 *Bundesgesundheitsblatt* 1107, 1009; Ammon and Faensen (n 42) 181.

[170] Martins (n 29) 9.

[171] Amato-Gauci and Ammon (n 70); Kuhlmann (n 33) 734.

[172] Martins (n 29) 9.

[173] Commission Implementing Regulation (EU) No 520/2012 of 19 June 2012 on the performance of pharmacovigilance activities provided for in Regulation (EC) No 726/2004 of the European Parliament and of the Council and Directive 2001/83/EC of the European Parliament and of the Council [2012] OJ L159/5, Recital 12–13, arts 25, 29.

[174] ibid Recital 12–13, arts 26, 29.

[175] See already section B.I.

[176] Annex 2 of Commission, 'European Interoperability Framework—Implementation Strategy' (Communication from the Commission to the European Parliament, the Council, the European Economic and Social Committee and the Committee of the Regions) COM(2017) 134 final 27.

exchange, and secure communication protocols.[177] The technical layer of interoperability does not care about the meaning of information exchanged; this is a question for the semantic level.[178] With today's digital networks and communication protocols, the technical level of interoperability is usually relatively easy to achieve.[179] However, one of the key barriers to interoperability arises from legacy systems that should solve domain-specific and local problems.[180] This has led to fragmented information and communications technology islands that are a barrier to technical interoperability.[181]

Concerning the information systems analysed, Member States are at different stages of development in terms of infrastructure used and security standards.[182] Older systems are partly not configurable to add necessary additional data and functions, which can be a barrier to the technical level of interoperability.[183] This contribution analyses information systems which transfer health data from regional to Member State and to European level, in other words vertically. Thus, legacy systems developed to solve domain-specific and local problems may hinder the technical level of interoperability.

Nevertheless, as new technical solutions can raise the technical level of interoperability,[184] it is commendable that the ECDC under the Regulations for building a European Health Union shall continuously update the EWRS allowing for the use of modern technologies, such as digital mobile applications, AI models, or other technologies for automated contact tracing in the EWRS.[185] According to Article 14(6)(a) of Regulation (EU) 2022/2371, the Commission shall adopt an implementing act which lays down the technical specifications of the platform, including the electronic data exchange mechanism for exchanges with existing national systems. This will be an enabler for the technical layer of interoperability. Overall, the technical level of interoperability has been improved by the adoption of the regulations for building a European Health Union.

[177] ibid; Lehne and others (n 22) 80.

[178] Tim Benson and Grahame Grieve, *Principles of Health Interoperability: FHIR, HL7 and SNOMED CT* (4th edn, Springer 2021) 22.

[179] Lehne and others (n 22) 80.

[180] Annex 2 of Commission, 'European Interoperability Framework—Implementation Strategy' (Communication from the Commission to the European Parliament, the Council, the European Economic and Social Committee and the Committee of the Regions) COM(2017) 134 final 27.

[181] ibid.

[182] Croatian Institute of Public Health and Aragon Health Sciences Institute (n 126) 36.

[183] ibid.

[184] ibid 35.

[185] Regulation (EU) 2022/2370 of the European Parliament and of the Council of 23 November 2022 amending Regulation (EC) No 851/2004 establishing a European centre for disease prevention and control [2022] OJ L314/1, art 8(4); Regulation (EU) 2022/2371 of the European Parliament and of the Council of 23 November 2022 on serious cross-border threats to health and repealing Decision No 1082/2013/EU [2022] OJ L314/26, art 18(2).

E. Conclusion

This chapter has shown that in the field of public health most competences remain at Member State level. Although the establishment of European information systems is possible on the basis of Article 168(5) TFEU, it is problematic that the European Union cannot establish binding rules on case definitions and formats to be used in national information systems due to its lack of competences. As a result, information in EpiPulse and the EWRS is often not comparable and its analysis is extremely difficult. Regrettably, the European Union is unable to establish the semantic level of interoperability in these information systems.[186]

The situation is different when it comes to public health safety. Since the European Union has a shared competence in this area according to Article 168(4)(c) TFEU,[187] there are binding rules on which case definitions and formats Member States have to use to report adverse drug reactions to EudraVigilance.[188] Consequently, to improve the semantic layer of interoperability of EpiPulse and EWRS, the European Union would not only need a shared competence for public health safety but also for public health information management. The Regulations for building a European Health Union of 2022 do not help in this regard. Instead, in order to improve information management it is necessary to amend the Treaties.[189]

However, an amendment of the Treaties is unlikely today, in 2024, after the World Health Organization has declared an end to COVID-19 as a public health emergency.[190] An extension of the Union's competences is politically difficult to implement.[191] The division of competences between the European Union and its Member States is generally a sensitive issue. This is even more true in the health sector, where Member States want to retain their national sovereignty. Moreover, the focus on the COVID-19 pandemic has diminished meanwhile and other crises—such as the Ukraine conflict and the climate crisis—are in the spotlight. Nevertheless, we can only hope that the Member States of the European Union can agree on a treaty amendment in the form of an extension of the Union's competences. Otherwise, in the next pandemic, we will again not know how we can best fight communicable diseases via 'digital', 'cross-border', and 'interoperable' means.

[186] Section D.III.
[187] Section B.I.
[188] Section D.III.
[189] Delhomme (n 69) 748; Calliess (n 31) 510–11; Müller (n 7) 113; Stockebrandt (n 5) 55; Gassner (n 24) 148. On the difficulties of amending the treaties Leino-Sandberg and Ruffert (n 36) 434.
[190] World Health Organization, 'Coronavirus disease (COVID-19) pandemic' <www.who.int/europe/emergencies/situations/covid-19> accessed 1 August 2023.
[191] Timo Clemens and Helmut Brand, 'Will COVID-19 Lead to a Major Change of the EU Public Health Mandate? A Renewed Approach to EU's Role Is Needed' (2020) 30 European Journal of Public Health 624.

Acknowledgement

I thank all participants of the INDIGO-workshop in Freiburg on 28–30 September 2022 and especially Dr Dirk Meusel (Unit for Health Security, DG for Health and Food Safety, European Commission) for helpful comments. All remaining errors are entirely my own.

6

Smart Border is Watching You!

Fundamental Rights Implications of Automated Data Processing and Decision-Making at the EU Border

Paulina Jo Pesch and Franziska Boehm

A. Introduction

In 2013, the European Commission proposed the Smart Borders Package[1] that aims to provide for a 'modern, effective and efficient management' of the EU's external borders.[2] With the objective to fight irregular migration and overstays[3] and to strengthen internal security,[4] the Smart Borders Package comprises both: the establishment of novel tools such as the Entry/Exit System (EES) and the European Travel Information and Authorisation System (ETIAS) as well as corresponding modifications to the existing EU border framework such as the Schengen Border Code.[5] The Smart Borders Package is accompanied by the EIF that does not only establish technical interoperability of all relevant information systems[6] but also introduces novel tools such as the MID which will allow for the detection of multiple identities with the aim of improving identity checks and the fight against identity fraud.[7] The Commission has furthermore proposed a Screening Regulation to

[1] European Commission, 'Glossary, Smart border package' <https://home-affairs.ec.europa.eu/networks/european-migration-network-emn/emn-asylum-and-migration-glossary/glossary/smart-borders-package_en> accessed 20 June 2024.

[2] European Commission, 'Schengen, borders and visa, Smart Borders' <https://home-affairs.ec.europa.eu/policies/schengen-borders-and-visa/smart-borders_en> accessed 20 June 2024.

[3] European Commission, 'Glossary, Smart Borders Package' <https://home-affairs.ec.europa.eu/pages/glossary/smart-borders-package_en> accessed 20 June 2024.

[4] European Commission, 'Schengen, borders and visa, Smart Borders' <https://home-affairs.ec.europa.eu/policies/schengen-borders-and-visa/smart-borders_en> accessed 20 June 2024.

[5] Regulation (EU) 2016/399 of the European Parliament and the Council of 9 March 2016 on a Union Code on the rules governing the movement of persons across borders, amended by Regulation (EU) 2017/2225 of the European Parliament and of the Council of 30 November 2017 amending Regulation (EU) 2016/399 as regards the use of the Entry/Exit System [2017] OJ L327.

[6] The EES, the Visa Information System (VIS), ETIAS, Eurodac, the Schengen Information System (SIS), and ECRIS-TCN. For an overview over the data stored in these systems see nn 19–24.

[7] Regulation (EU) 2019/817 of the European Parliament and of the Council of 20 May 2019 on establishing a framework for interoperability between EU information systems in the field of borders and visa and amending Regulations (EC) No 767/2008, (EU) 2016/399, (EU) 2017/2226, (EU) 2018/1240, (EU) 2018/1726, and (EU) 2018/1861 of the European Parliament and of the Council and Council Decisions 2004/512/EC and 2008/633/JHA, [2019] OJ L135 (EIF Border Regulation), and Regulation (EU) 2019/818 of the European Parliament and of the Council of 20 May 2019 on

Paulina Jo Pesch and Franziska Boehm, *Smart Border is Watching You!* In: *Governance of Automated Decision-Making and EU Law.* Edited by: Herwig C.H. Hofmann and Felix Pflücke, Oxford University Press.
 DOI: 10.1093/9780198919575.003.0006

ensure the screening of all Third Country Nationals (TCNs), concerning, among other frameworks, ETIAS and the EIF.[8]

The aforementioned initiatives mark a trend towards the large-scale collection and processing of vast amounts of personal data for the purpose of performing automated risk assessments in an interoperable environment.[9] Such risk assessments are especially foreseen under ETIAS and under the EIF Framework with the MID. The Passenger Name Record (PNR) Directive[10] allows for similar data-driven risk assessments. While Smart Borders do not exclusively refer to artificial intelligence (AI) technologies,[11] such technologies—specifically models trained with machine learning algorithms (ML-trained models)—are already in use at the EU border and increasingly explored.[12]

In addition, multiple Member State and Union authorities in the areas of border control and law enforcement are provided with access rights to the various relevant information systems, creating a situation in which various authorities can influence single decisions.[13] At the same time, there are doubts about the sufficient

establishing a framework for interoperability between EU information systems in the field of police and judicial cooperation, asylum and migration and amending Regulations (EU) 2018/1726, (EU) 2018/1862, and (EU) 2019/816 [2019] OJ L135 (EIF LE Regulation), art 25(1) of each.

[8] European Commission, 'Proposal for a Regulation of the European Parliament and of the Council introducing a screening of third country nationals at the external borders and amending Regulations (EC) No 767/2008, (EU) 2017/2226, (EU) 2018/1240, and (EU) 2019/817' COM/2020/612 final.

[9] Gloria Gonzalez Fuster, 'Artificial Intelligence and Law Enforcement – Impact on Fundamental Rights' PE 656.295 (2020) European Parliament 29 f; Charly Derave, Nathan Genicot, and Nina Hetmanska, 'The Risks of Trustworthy Artificial Intelligence: The Case of the European Travel Information and Authorisation System' (2022) 13 European Journal of Risk Regulation 389, 403; Niovi Vavoula, 'Artificial Intelligence (AI) at Schengen Borders: Automated Processing, Algorithmic Profiling and Facial Recognition in the Era of Techno-Solutionism' (2021) 23 European Journal of Migration and Law 457, 458. On the international perspective Ruben Zaiotti, 'Transatlantic Journeys: Smart Borders and the Diffusion of Travelers' Screening Programs in North America and Europe' in Kiran Banerjee and Craig Smith (eds), *Understanding North American Migration Governance* (University of Toronto Press 2022).

[10] Directive (EU) 2016/681 of the European Parliament and of the Council of 27 April 2016 on the use of passenger name record (PNR) data for the prevention, detection, investigation and prosecution of terrorist offences and serious crime [2016] OJ L119 (PNR Directive).

[11] cf for international context Ana B Hinojosa, 'Smart Border Management for Seamless International Air Travel' (Uniting Aviation 2019) <https://unitingaviation.com/news/security-facilitation/smart-border-management-for-seamless-international-air-travel/> accessed 20 June 2024: "SMART borders [...] follo[w] five guiding principles: 'Secure, Measurable, Automated, Risk Management Based and Technology Driven'.

[12] Costica Dumbrava, 'Artificial Intelligence at EU borders—Overview of Applications and Key Issues' PE 690.706 (2021) European Parliament. See also European Commission, Directorate-General for Migration and Home Affairs, 'Opportunities and challenges for the use of artificial intelligence in border control, migration and security. Main report' (EU Publications Office 2020) <https://data.europa.eu/doi/10.2837/923610> accessed 12 January 2023; European Union Agency for the Operational Management of Large-Scale IT Systems in the Area of Freedom, Security and Justice (eu-LISA), 'Artificial Intelligence in the Operational Management of Large-scale IT systems—Research and Technology Monitoring Report' (eu-LISA 2020) <https://www.eulisa.europa.eu/Publications/Reports/AI%20in%20the%20OM%20of%20Large-scale%20IT%20Systems.pdf> accessed 20 June 2024.

[13] As the decision-making relies on various databases, not only the authorities responsible for the decision but also the authorities that have entered the data the decision is based on influence decisions. Also, the authorities responsible for the development of the criteria and systems for the automated processing of data impact decisions. For the MID and ETIAS see sections B.I and B.II.

human involvement in decisions that are supported by data-driven risk assessments. This is particularly dangerous where the risk assessments are not accurate or the quality of the underlying data is uncertain.[14] These reflections raise concerns especially regarding the legitimacy of decision-making processes, individual rights and access to legal remedies, and efficient independent supervision.[15]

The considerations above are the reason why we chose to analyse in particular the MID and ETIAS in more detail. Next to the functioning and the applicable EU secondary law of the MID and ETIAS, the degree of automation in decision-making and the fundamental rights concerns triggered by such automated decisions are presented. In more detail, section B provides an overview of the selected instruments that exemplify the trend towards large-scale data-driven risk assessments using highly connected information systems. Section C analyses selected fundamental rights concerns of the respective assessments and decisions, focusing especially on the degree of automation of decision-making processes. Section D draws a conclusion and provides an outlook for future work on remaining questions.

B. Functioning of EU smart border instruments

To understand the fundamental rights concerns of the EU smart border instruments it is important to explain the manner of functioning of the analysed instruments first. In particular, the methods of risk assessments and potential use cases for models trained with machine learning (ML)[16] in the context of multiple-identity detection with the MID under the EIF (section B.I.1) and in ETIAS (section B.I.2) need to be illustrated.

I. The European Interoperability Framework and the Multiple-Identity Detector

The EIF comprises four components (section B.I.1) that the European Agency for the Operational Management of Large-Scale IT Systems in the Area of Freedom, Security and Justice (eu-LISA) develops and will manage technically:[17] the

[14] On EU information systems in general section C.I.1 with n 179. On Europol section C.I.2 with n 221.

[15] See on ETIAS under secondary data protection law Paulina Jo Pesch, Diana Dimitrova, and Franziska Boehm, 'Data Protection and Machine-Learning-Supported Decision-Making at the EU Border—ETIAS Profiling Under Scrutiny' *Proceedings of the 10th Annual Privacy Forum* (APF 2022) 50.

[16] ibid 53f.

[17] See the revised development timelines for all EIF components in eu-LISA, Single Programming Document, 2024–2026, pp 9, 23: The delivery of the sBMS is planned for mid-2024; CIR and ESP are not expected before 2025, and the MID is planned to enter into operation for 2027.

European Search Portal (ESP), the Shared Biometric Matching Service (sBMS), a Common Identity Repository (CIR), and in particular, the MID,[18] which is analysed in more detail here (section B.I.2). Section B.I.3 addresses the use of ML-trained models under the EIF.

1. The four EIF components

The EIF aims to achieve interoperability between EU information systems in both the field of borders and visa on the one hand, and the field of police and judicial cooperation, asylum, and migration on the other. This concerns ETIAS,[19] SIS,[20] EES,[21] VIS,[22] Eurodac,[23] and ECRIS-TCN.[24,25] The EIF does not simply connect information systems[26] but creates centralized databases on TCNs and introduces new functionalities[27] such as multiple-identity detection (section B.I.2). It also allows for wider access to the information systems.[28] While the EIF concerns databases that store almost only[29] TCN data,[30] plans exist to extend interoperability to

[18] EIF Regulations, arts 1(2), 6(3), 12(3), 17(3).

[19] The ETIAS Central System creates and stores application files, contains the ETIAS watchlist, performs the automated part of the ETIAS risk assessment, and automatically issues a travel authorization where the automated processing does not report a hit, ETIAS Regulation, arts 6(2)(a), 19, 20, 21(1). On ETIAS see section B.II.

[20] The Schengen Information System (SIS, also referred to as SIS II) stores alerts on persons and information on objects, SIS Regulation, art 20(2).

[21] The Entry/Exit System (EES) records and stores information on entries, exits and stays of TCNs crossing the external Borders of the Schengen area and refusals of entry, EES Regulation, arts 1(1), 4(1).

[22] The Visa Information System (VIS) stores data on visa applicants and on requested, issued, refused, annulled, revoked, or extended visas, VIS Regulation, art 5(1).

[23] Eurodac comprises a central fingerprint database, storing fingerprints of applicants for international protection, and of TCNs and stateless persons crossing the borders irregularly or staying illegally in a Member State, Eurodac Regulation, arts 3(1)(a), 9, 14, 17.

[24] ECRIS-TCN refers to a centralized system for the identification of Member States holding conviction information on third-country nationals and stateless persons, ECRIS-TCN Regulation, art 1(a).

[25] EIF Regulations, art 1(1).

[26] The Commission's 2017 EIF brochure defines interoperability as 'the ability of organisations to interact towards mutually beneficial goals, . . . share . . . information and knowledge between these organisations . . ., by means of the exchange of data between their ICT systems' and does not mention any of the components. European Commission, 'New European Interoperability Framework, Promoting seamless services and data flows for European public administrations' (2017) Publications Office of the European Union.

[27] European Data Protection Supervisor, 'Opinion 4/2018 on the Proposals for two Regulations establishing a framework for interoperability between EU large-scale information systems' (2018), paras 28f.

[28] Niovi Vavoula, 'Interoperability of EU Information Systems: The Deathblow to the Rights to Privacy and Personal Data Protection of Third-Country Nationals?' (2020) 26(1) *European Public Law* 131, 148f. On access by law enforcement for the purpose of identification (EIF Regulations, art 20) Article 29 Working Party, 'Opinion on Commission proposals on establishing a framework for interoperability between EU information systems in the field of borders and visa as well as police and judicial cooperation, asylum and migration' (2018) WP266, 11; Niovi Vavoula, *Immigration and Privacy in the Law of the European Union* (Brill Nijhoff 2022) 644ff.

[29] EU citizens can appear in the files, eg as family members of a TCN, see Niovi Vavoula, 'Interoperability of EU Information Systems' (n 28) 134f (with further examples).

[30] EIF Regulations, art 1(1).

include especially Prüm[31] and Passenger Name Record (PNR) data.[32] More concretely, the EIF comprises the following four components: the European search portal (ESP), the sBMS, the CIR, and the MID.

The ESP enables Member State authorities and Union agencies to simultaneously query and access data stored in the EU information systems, Interpol databases, and Europol data.[33] For example, it allows for the automated checking of ETIAS application data against data stored in the information systems and databases according to Article 20(2) ETIAS Regulation. The sBMS stores biometric templates[34] with references to the original data record and the respective information system, and allows queries with biometric data.[35] The CIR creates and stores individual files for TCNs that are registered in the EES, VIS, ETIAS, Eurodac, or ECRIS-TCN.[36] While the sBMS stores biometric templates, the CIR stores biometrical and non-biometrical personal data.[37] In the foreseeable future each TCN is expected to have at least one file in the CIR.[38] The MID allows for the automated detection of multiple identities to improve identity checks and fight identity fraud and, for this purpose, creates and stores identity confirmation files.[39] These files consist of links among data stored in the information systems included in CIR and SIS,[40] a reference to the EU information systems the linked data is stored in, a single identification number that allows for retrieving the linked data, the authority responsible for manually verifying the different identities, and the data of the creation or any updates of the link.[41]

2. The MID

The MID allows for the automated detection of multiple identities. Automated multiple-identity detection is triggered by:

[31] See art 39 of the Proposal for a Regulation of the European Parliament and of the Council on automated data exchange for police cooperation (Prüm II). Prüm data comprise DNA profiles, fingerprint data, facial images, police and vehicle registration data, ibid art 1.

[32] See Commission EIF Proposals, COM(2017) 793 and COM(2017) 794 final, 5; Tony Bunyan, 'The Interoperability of Justice and Home Affairs Databases' (2018) Statewatch Briefing 4ff.

[33] EIF Regulations, art 6(1), (2)(a).

[34] That is, representations of biometric features that cannot be reversed to the original personal data, cf eu-LISA, Shared Biometric Matching Service (sBMS), Feasibility Study—final report, 18–20, 23. On the applicability of the GDPR to the processing EU citizens can appear in the files, eg as family members of a TCN, see Niovi Vavoula, 'Interoperability of EU Information Systems' (n 28) 141.

[35] EIF Regulations, arts 12(1), (2)(a), 13(1–2).

[36] EIF Regulations, art 17(1).

[37] cf EIF Regulations, art 18(1) in conjunction with art 5(1)(a–b), (2) of the ECRIS-TCN Regulation (Regulation (EU) 2019/816 of the European Parliament and of the Council of 17 April 2019 establishing a centralised system for the identification of Member States holding conviction information on third-country nationals and stateless persons (ECRIS-TCN) to supplement the European Criminal Records Information System).

[38] Niovi Vavoula, 'Interoperability of EU Information Systems' (n 28) 135.

[39] EIF Regulations, art 25(1).

[40] EES, VIS, ETIAS, Eurodac, ECRIS-TCN, and SIS. See for the data stored in the systems n 19–24.

[41] EIF Regulations, arts 34, 25(1)(a–e).

- the creation or update of an individual file in the EES;
- the creation or update of an application file in VIS;
- the creation or update of an application file in ETIAS;
- the creation of an alert on a person in SIS; or
- the creation or modification of an ECRIS-TCN data record.[42]

The data in the file whose creation, update, or modification has triggered the automated multiple-identity detection is, in an automated manner, checked for links with data files stored in the CIR—that contains an individual file for each TCN stored in the interoperable information systems—and in the SIS.[43] Where the file that has triggered automated multiple-identity detection contains biometric data, the sBMS compares templates of this biometric data with the biometric templates already stored in the sBMS.[44] The ESP is used to search names, places, and dates of birth, gender, and nationalities, as well as travel document data stored in the Central-SIS and CIR.[45] Where the processing does not result in any match, the creation, update, or modification of the file or data record that has triggered automated multiple-identity detection continues.[46] If there are any matches, the CIR, and, where relevant, the SIS create a link between the respective data and the data that triggered the match.[47]

The MID, in an automated manner, creates either a white or a yellow link. A white link is created if the matched data is consistent, meaning the data refers to the same person, and therefore does not indicate the use of multiple identities.[48] A yellow link is created if there is a suspicious discrepancy in the matched data, for example where the respective data files share the same biometric data but have similar[49] or different identity data.[50] In cases of yellow links, the responsible authority, for example the ETIAS Central Unit or National Unit responsible for assessing the application, manually verifies the identities the linked data refers to.[51]

Where a yellow link is created, the responsible authority[52] manually verifies the different identities in the identity confirmation file.[53] Based on the manual assessment, the responsible authority classifies the link as:

[42] EIF Regulations, art 27. For data already stored in the EES, VIS, Eurodac and SIS, the ETIAS Central Unit shall perform multiple-identity detection and manually verify links; EIF Border Regulation, arts 69(1)(2), 57(b); EIF LE Regulation, arts 65(1)(2), 58(b). See for the data stored in the different systems n 19–24.

[43] EIF Regulations, arts 27(1), 17(1).

[44] EIF Regulations, art 27(2).

[45] EIF Regulations, art 27(3).

[46] EIF Regulations, art 28(1).

[47] EIF Regulations, art 28(2–3).

[48] cf EIF Regulations, art 33(1).

[49] cf EIF Regulations, art 28(5); On the determination of what data can be considered same or similar through a delegated act by the Commission see B.I.3.

[50] EIF Regulations, art 30(1)(a).

[51] EIF Regulations, arts 30(2), 29.

[52] Where the MID is triggered by the creation or update of an ETIAS application file, either the ETIAS Central Unit or an ETIAS National Unit, EIF Regulations, arts 57(a) and 56(1)(f).

[53] EIF Regulations, art 29(1–5).

- *white*, indicating the concerned TCN is bona fide, while the linked data refers to the same person;[54] or
- *green* indicating the concerned TCN is bona fide, while the linked data refers to two different persons;[55] or
- *red* which indicates the concerned TCN uses more than one identity or somebody else's identity[56,57]

The EIF Regulations[58] list cases where links shall be classified white,[59] green,[60] or red.[61] The MID shall notify the authorities responsible for the linked data in an automated manner.[62] Further action, which can consist, for example, in the refusal of a visa or travel authorization, or in the initiation of criminal proceedings, shall be taken in accordance with Union and national law, while legal consequences for the concerned person shall only be based on the relevant data on that person and no legal consequence shall be based solely on the existence of a red link.[63]

3. Use cases for ML-trained models under the EIF

There is one definite use case for the application of an ML-trained model under the EIF. For the sBMS, eu-LISA has outsourced the development to two private companies (IDEMIA and Sopra Steria)[64] and announced that the system will comprise an ML-trained model.[65] As the sBMS is used for comparing biometric data as part of multiple-identity detection,[66] this model will affect multiple-identity detection. Where the sBMS reaches the result that biometric data in two data files match, the MID creates a link between the data.[67] Where the sBMS does not match the biometric data stored in two data files because the data is different but the files share the same identity data, this results in the creation of a yellow link.[68]

[54] cf EIF Regulations, art 33.
[55] cf EIF Regulations, art 31.
[56] cf EIF Regulations, art 32.
[57] cf Niovi Vavoula (n 30) 616, 618.
[58] EIF Border Regulation and EIF LE Regulation (n 7).
[59] EIF Regulations, art 33(1), eg if the linked data share the same biometric data and the same or similar identity data (lit. a).
[60] EIF Regulations, art 31(1), eg if two persons share the same identity data, but different biometric data, and the responsible authority concludes the data refer to two different persons (lit. a).
[61] EIF Regulations, art 32(1) eg if two persons with different biometric data use the same travel document and at least one of them uses the travel document in an unjustified manner (lit. b).
[62] EIF Regulations, art 32(6).
[63] EIF Regulations, art 32(2).
[64] IDEMIA, 'IDEMIA and Sopra Steria chosen by eu-LISA to build the new Shared Biometric Matching System (sBMS) for border protection of the Schengen Area' (IDEMIA 2020) <https://www.idemia.com/press-release/idemia-and-sopra-steria-chosen-eu-lisa-build-new-shared-biometric-matching-system-sbms-border-protection-schengen-area-2020-06-04> accessed 20 June 2024.
[65] eu-LISA, 'A deep learning solution' (the eu-LISA Bits & Bites, December 2020) <https://eulisa.europa.eu/SiteAssets/Bits-and-Bytes/002.aspx> accessed 20 June 2024.
[66] EIF Regulations, art 27(2).
[67] For example, a yellow one where the files include different identity data, art 30(1)(a) of the EIF Regulations.
[68] EIF Regulations, art 30(1)(c).

Automated multiple-identity detection itself could, in theory, also rely on an ML-trained model, namely for the distinction between same or similar and different data. The EIF Regulations do not specify the procedure for the determination of cases of same or similar data but leave the specification to delegated acts by the Commission.[69] However, the use of ML-trained models is not planned. After the European Parliament rejected the Commission's initial draft according to which eu-LISA should define an algorithm based on previously established thresholds of similarity,[70] the final versions list cases of similar identity data exhaustively.[71] Similar data such as in cases of known transliterations of names or certain inversions of names and birth dates[72] shall be detected with an algorithm developed by eu-LISA.[73]

II. ETIAS risk assessments

While the MID assesses risks of identity fraud, the European Travel Information and Authorisation System (ETIAS) shall identify security, irregular migration, or high epidemic risks posed by visa-exempt TCNs travelling to the Schengen area.[74] eu-LISA is developing the system at the time of writing[75] and will ensure its technical management.[76] ETIAS is expected to be operational by the first half of 2025.[77] The ETIAS Information System will be one of the interoperable systems managed by eu-LISA and be connected especially with the MID that is one of the four components of the EIF.[78]

69 EIF Regulations, art 28(5).

70 European Parliament, 'Objection to a delegated act Determining cases where identity data may be considered as same or similar for the purpose of the multiple identity detection pursuant to Regulation (EU) 2019/818' (European Parliament 2019) <https://www.europarl.europa.eu/doceo/document/TA-9-2022-0008_EN.pdf> accessed 20 June 2024.

71 Commission Delegated Regulation of 11 July 2022 supplementing Regulation (EU) 2019/817 of the European Parliament and if the Council as regards determining cases where identity data are considered as same or similar for the purpose of the multiple identity detection, C(2022) 4775 [2023] OJ L47, and Commission Delegated Regulation of 11 July 2022 supplementing Regulation (EU) 2019/818 of the European Parliament and if the Council as regards determining cases where identity data are considered as same or similar for the purpose of the multiple identity detection, C(2022) 4759 [2023] OJ L47.

72 ibid (both delegated regulations) annex II s 3.1(a, b, d, e), 3.2(a).

73 ibid (both delegated regulations) annex II s 2.

74 Regulation (EU) 2018/1240 of the European Parliament and of the Council of 12 September 2018 establishing a European Travel Information and Authorisation System (ETIAS) and amending Regulations (EU) No 1077/2011, (EU) No 515/2014, (EU) 2016/399, (EU) 2016/1624 and (EU) 2017/2226, PE/21/2018/REV/1 [2018] OJ L236 (ETIAS Regulation), art 1(1), rec 2.

75 See the development timelines in eu-LISA, Single Programming Document, 2022–2024, 31.

76 ETIAS Regulation, art 6(1).

77 Migration and Home Affairs of the European Commission, 'ETIAS' (European Commission) <https://home-affairs.ec.europa.eu/policies/schengen-borders-and-visa/smart-borders/european-travel-information-authorisation-system_en> accessed 20 June 2024. See also the development timelines in eu-LISA, Single Programming Document, 2022–2024, 31.

78 See section B.I.

The ETIAS Regulation requires visa-exempt TCNs to apply for a travel authorization prior to their trip, or before expiry of an existing travel authorization.[79] The travel authorization is granted or denied based on an individual risk assessment based on various personal data provided by each applicant. These comprise biographical data (including names, nationalities, travel document data), socio-economic information (such as data on education and occupation), information regarding criminal records, and the Internet protocol (IP) addresses from which the application was submitted.[80] Section B.II.1 explains the fully automated part of ETIAS risk assessments; section B.II.2. addresses manual assessments that are carried out where the automated processing has reported a hit (ie where the application file has been matched against data in the databases or risk indicators which it is compared with); and section B.II.3 describes potential use cases for ML-trained models in ETIAS.

1. The automated part of ETIAS risk assessments

In the first step of ETIAS risk assessments, the data is automatically processed.[81] That involves checks against various databases, namely:

- data stored in the ETIAS Central System, SIS, EES, VIS, Eurodac, and ECRIS-TCN; as well as
- Europol data; and
- the Interpol's databases SLTD[82] and TDAWN;[83] and
- the ETIAS watchlist, which consists of data on persons who are deemed to have committed or taken part in a terrorist or serious crime offence or are believed to do so in the future.[84]

Also, each new or updated ETIAS application file triggers automated multiple-identity detection with the MID.[85] Furthermore, the ETIAS screening rules are applied; that is, the application is compared to a set of risk indicators to be defined by the European Commission and the ETIAS Central Unit which is established within the European Border and Coast Guard Agency (Frontex).[86] As the automated risk assessment involves checks of data stored in the ETIAS Information System[87] against data stored in the other EU information systems and Europol

[79] ETIAS Regulation, arts 1(1), 15(1).
[80] ETIAS Regulation, art 17. Categorization of application data after Niovi Vavoula (n 57) 482ff.
[81] ETIAS Regulation, art 20.
[82] Stolen and Lost Travel Document Database.
[83] Travel Documents Associated with Notices Database.
[84] ETIAS Regulation, art 34(1). Similarly, SIS Regulation, art 36(3)(c).
[85] EIF Border Regulation, art 27(1)(c); On the MID see section B.I.2.
[86] ETIAS Regulation, art 33; Critical on the Commission's influence, see Pesch, Dimitrova, and Boehm (n 15) 52. For visas, a similar risk assessment takes place, VIS Regulation, art 9j; Visa Code, art 21.
[87] On the architecture ETIAS Regulation, art 6.

data, the ETIAS Regulation stipulates interoperability.[88] Where the automated processing reports no hit, a travel authorization is automatically issued.[89]

2. The manual part of ETIAS risk assessments

Where the automated processing reports at least one hit, in a second step, the data is manually processed.[90] Each hit is manually verified by the ETIAS Central Unit that either issues a travel authorization, or, where the data corresponds to the risk indicators or data in the relevant information system or there remain doubts about the applicant's identity, forwards the application to the responsible[91] ETIAS National Unit[92] for the manual risk assessment of the application.[93] For that purpose the ETIAS National Unit has access to the application file, any linked application files, and the hits triggered in the automated risk assessment.[94] Based on the manual risk assessment, the ETIAS National Unit issues or refuses a travel authorization.[95]

For certain cases, the ETIAS Regulation requires the Member States to refuse a travel authorization, namely where the travel document used by the applicant is reported lost, stolen, misappropriated, or invalidated in the SIS or there exists a SIS refusal of entry and stay alert on the applicant.[96] Otherwise the ETIAS National Unit, based on the manual risk assessment, decides to issue or refuse a travel authorization.[97] The ETIAS Regulation stipulates that the ETIAS National Unit may not automatically make a decision based on a hit against specific risk indicators but shall individually assess each case.[98] Where data entered by other Member States or Europol has triggered a hit, they shall be consulted.[99] The ETIAS Regulation does not lay down any specific rules on manual risk assessments by the ETIAS National Units,[100] especially the Regulation does not determine how much weight should be attributed to the screening rules in relation to other hits.[101]

Risk assessments are repeatedly performed also on applications that have not triggered a hit in the automated assessment or that have been manually processed already. ETIAS application data is not assessed only once after an application has

[88] ETIAS Regulation, art 11(1).
[89] ETIAS Regulation, art 21(1).
[90] ETIAS Regulation, arts 21(2), 22, 26.
[91] The responsibility is determined, where applicable, based on the responsibility for data that have triggered a hit, or the first intended stay, ETIAS Regulation, art 25(1).
[92] Each Member State designates an ETIAS National Unit, ETIAS Regulation, art 8(1).
[93] ETIAS Regulation, art 22(5).
[94] ETIAS Regulation, art 26(1).
[95] ETIAS Regulation, art 26(2).
[96] ETIAS Regulation, arts 26(3)(a), 20(2)(a, c). On the contrary, if the automated processing reports a hit against the ETIAS watchlist, the ETIAS National Unit carries out a security risk assessment and decides whether to issue or refuse the travel authorization, ETIAS Regulation, arts 20(4), 26(5).
[97] ETIAS Regulation, art 26(2)(b), (3a)(b), (4–6).
[98] ETIAS Regulation, art 26(6).
[99] ETIAS Regulation, art 28f.
[100] cf ETIAS Regulation, art 26ff.
[101] Niovi Vavoula (n 57) 509.

been filed. Instead, the data is repeatedly checked when it is entered into the relevant databases, namely when a new alert is entered in SIS, a refusal of entry is recorded in the EES, or new data is entered into the ETIAS watchlist. In these cases, a granted travel authorization can be revoked if the conditions for issuing it are no longer met.[102] ETIAS applications are processed whenever a new application is submitted.[103] In addition, the ETIAS risk assessment is repeated in cases where application files are amended, for example after a rectification request by the applicant after a travel authorization has been issued.[104]

3. (Potential) use cases for ML-trained models in ETIAS

The ETIAS Regulation stipulates the Commission shall specify many details of ETIAS through implementing[105] and delegated acts.[106,107] This regards, for example, the risks based on which the risk indicators will be determined and the technical specification of the watchlist.[108] Even though neither the ETIAS Regulation nor the implemented or delegated acts already adopted refer to the use of AI for decision-making, there are some potential use cases especially for ML-trained models.[109] As an example, ML-trained models could be used for the determination of risks based on statistics.[110] Such models can also indirectly affect automated ETIAS risk assessments, namely where entries in the relevant information systems or the ETIAS watchlist are based on risk assessments with ML-trained models. For example, decisions by Member States to enter alerts on persons with a high risk to commit future criminal offences in the SIS might be supported by an ML-trained risk assessment model. ETIAS watchlist entries on such persons might also be based on the use of such models by Europol or the Member States.[111] Europol data is especially likely to be based on the use of ML-trained models since Europol is one of the major drivers for AI in Europe,[112] and explicitly assigned a key role

[102] ETIAS Regulation, art 41(1, 3–5). For cases where a travel authorization has been issued even though the conditions for issuing have not been met, ETIAS Regulation, art 40, allows for the annulment of the travel authorization.

[103] Niovi Vavoula (n 57) 486.

[104] ETIAS Regulation, art 64(2).

[105] ETIAS Regulation, arts 15(5), 16(10), 17(9), 27(5), 33(3), 35(7), 38(3), 45(2–3), 46(4), 48(4), 59(4), 74(5), 83(4), 84(2), 92(8).

[106] ETIAS Regulation, arts 6(4), 17(3, 5–6), 18(4), 27(3), 31, 33(2), 36(4), 39(2), 54(2), 85(3).

[107] Critically Niovi Vavoula (n 57) 511f ('a violation of the rule of law').

[108] ETIAS Regulation, arts 33(2–3), 35(7).

[109] Pesch, Dimitrova, and Boehm (n 15) 54f.

[110] ETIAS Regulation, art 33(2)(a–c).

[111] ETIAS Regulation, arts 34(1), (3), 35(1).

[112] Gonzalez Fuster (n 9) 22; Europol/Frontex, 'Future Group on Travel Intelligence and Border Management' (EUROPOL 2022) <https://www.europol.europa.eu/publications-events/publications/future-group-travel-intelligence-and-border-management-presentation-0> accessed 20 June 2024; Europol Programming Document 2021–2023 and Europol Programming Document 2022–2024, especially p 11 of each. On the use of Palantir Europol, Answer to Parliamentary Question E-000951/2022 <https://www.europarl.europa.eu/RegistreWeb/search/getDocument.htm?reference=P9_RE(2022)000951&fragment=ANN02&language=XL> accessed 20 June 2024; D B C Hoek and Jill Stigter, 'Europol: An Overwhelming Stream of Big Data' (2022) 92(2/21) *Revue Internationale de Droit Pénal* 19, 39 ff.

in promoting artificial intelligence by the Regulation amending the Europol Regulation.[113]

Potential use cases for ML-trained models in the context of ETIAS, however, are not limited to the automated part of the risk assessment. Documents by eu-LISA,[114] the Commission,[115] and the Future Group (established with Europol and Frontex)[116] point out that an AI-based risk assessment system could support ETIAS National Units carrying out the manual assessment of applications for which the automated processing has reported a hit. Eu-LISA specifically refers to an 'additional risk assessment based on the data stored in the relevant systems and the historical data on the [applicant]'.[117] This implies an ML-trained model fed at least with all data used in the automated risk assessment (ie ETIAS application data, the risk indicators part of the ETIAS screening rules, the ETIAS watchlist, SIS, VIS, EES, Eurodac, Europol data, Interpol SLTD, and TDAWN). According to the report, the outcome of such a risk assessment could either consist in a binary suggestion to issue or to refuse a travel authorization, or in a risk grading.[118] The Future Group explicitly envisages an AI risk assessment model fed with data on previous case handling and other existing historical data that enables Member States to carry out checks with risk profiles, watchlists, and databases and that shall be part shall be part of common, that is, centralized, ICT components (with access management), namely the European System for Traveller Screening (ESTS).[119]

The ETIAS Regulation, however, leaves no room for the screening rules being based on an ML-trained model.[120] While, in theory, ML-trained models are feasible for risk screenings,[121] the ETIAS Regulation stipulates that the ETIAS Central

[113] Regulation (EU) 2022/991 of the European Parliament and of the Council of 8 June 2022 amending Regulation (EU) 2016/794, as regards Europol's cooperation with private parties, the processing of personal data by Europol in support of criminal investigations, and Europol's role in research and innovation [2022] OJ L169, rec 49.

[114] eu-LISA, 'Artificial Intelligence in the Operational Management of Large-scale IT systems – Research and Technology Monitoring Report' (2020) (eu-LISA AI report) 30f.

[115] Directorate-General for Migration and Home Affairs of the European Commission, 'Opportunities and challenges for the use of artificial intelligence in border control, migration and security. Main report' (EU Publications Office 2020) <https://data.europa.eu/doi/10.2837/923610> accessed 20 June 2024.

[116] Council of the European Union, Final Report Future Group on Travel Intelligence and Border Management, 6767/22 (202), 67.

[117] eu-LISA AI report (n 114), 30. On the question whether this proposal is compatible with the ETIAS Regulation see section C.I.2.

[118] eu-LISA AI report (n 114) 30.

[119] Council of the European Union (n 116) 63ff.

[120] Derave, Genicot, and Hetmanska (n 9) 391 state the use of AI for the screening rules was an open question.

[121] Richard Berk, *Criminal Justice Forecasts of Risk—A Machine Learning Approach* (Springer 2012); J Galindo and P Tamayo, 'Credit Risk Assessment Using Statistical and Machine Learning: Basic Methodology and Risk Modeling Applications' (2000) 15 Computational Economics 107; Nicola Paltrinieri, Louise Comfort, and Genserik Reniers, 'Learning About Risk: Machine Learning for Risk Assessment' (2019) 118 Safety Science 475.

Unit defines, establishes, assesses *ex ante*, implements, evaluates, revises, and deletes risk indicators.[122] This would not be possible with a self-learning model that changes whenever it is fed with new data as it implies predetermined criteria that are transparent to the authorities that apply them.[123] Even ML-trained models that provide some explainability or interpretability do not present users with a list of the criteria they apply.[124] Accordingly, Frontex is cited with the statement that the screening rules do not involve sophisticated analysis methods such as ML-trained models.[125]

C. Fundamental rights concerns

That decision-making processes are based on the large-scale processing of personal data can raise concerns about fundamental rights. As the actors involved in the data processing and decision-making in large-scale information systems at the border are Union authorities and Member States implementing Union law, they are bound by the Charter of Fundamental Rights of the European Union (CFR).[126]

ETIAS application data, data linked by the MID, and other data stored in databases relevant in the context of ETIAS and the EIF refer to identified individuals and are therefore personal data.[127] Not only the data storage and processing, especially the performance of risk assessments on the data, but also the decision-making based on such processing, as well as the data transfer[128] interfere with both the fundamental right to private life (Article 7 CFR)[129] and the fundamental right to data protection (Article 8 CFR).[130]

The interferences are particularly intense since even if single pieces of the data do not reveal much information on the concerned individuals, the data stored in

[122] ETIAS Regulation, art 33(6).

[123] See, by analogy, Case C-817/19 *Ligue des droits humains ASBL v Conseil des ministers* (2022) ECLI:EU:C:2022:491 (PNR judgment), para 194.

[124] Derek Doran, Sarah Schulz, and Tarek R Besold, 'What Does Explainable AI Really Mean? A New Conceptualization of Perspectives' (arxiv 2017) <https://arxiv.org/pdf/1710.00794.pdf> accessed 20 June 2024; Arun Rai, 'Explainable AI: From Black Box to Glass Box' (2019) 48 Journal of the Academy of Marketing Science <https://link.springer.com/article/10.1007/s11747-019-00710-5> accessed 20 June 2024.

[125] Derave, Genicot, and Hetmanska (n 9) 404.

[126] CFR, art 51(1).

[127] For the MID see section B.I, EIF Regulations, art 27. For ETIAS see section B.II, ETIAS Regulation, art 17, 20.

[128] As it enlarges group of people with access, and have negative consequences for the concerned individual, *Weber and Saravia v Germany* (2006), App No 54934/00, para 79. Such negative consequences can, for example, be the refusal of an ETIAS travel authorization, or decision following a link classified as red.

[129] On ETIAS' and the EIF's compatibility with CFR, art 7, Niovi Vavoula (n 57) 505ff, 634ff.

[130] cf Case Opinion 1/15 (2016) (PNR Opinion), ECLI:EU:C:2016:656, paras 122f, 125f with further references; Case C-817/19 *Ligue des droits humains ASBL v Conseil des ministers* (2022) ECLI:EU:C:2022:491 (PNR judgment), paras 94, 96f.

the interoperable systems combined can reveal or imply travel routes and habits,[131] relationships,[132] financial situations,[133] and health conditions[134,135] Since both multiple-identity detection and ETIAS risk assessments are performed steadily and systematically on data in the respective information systems regardless of whether there is an indication for the concerned person to pose a risk or use a false identity, they interfere seriously with Articles 7, 8 CFR.[136]

Furthermore, the outcomes of the processing can cause intense effects for concerned individuals. The automated creation of a yellow link by the MID[137] can considerably affect the concerned person as they might be stopped at the border for further checks and miss a flight.[138] Red links at least in certain cases inevitably lead not only to further checks but also adverse legal consequences for the individual concerned.[139] Where the creation of an ETIAS application file triggered the MID and a red link is associated with the application, the ETIAS National Unit responsible will most likely refuse the travel authorization or visa as there are doubts about the reliability of the applicant's statements or (travel) documents. Red links can impact different further decisions with legal consequences without sufficient individual review. For example, law enforcement agencies might base an initial suspicion that the concerned individual has forged a travel document on the existence of a red link and initiate criminal proceedings against them.[140]

Where the automated ETIAS risk assessment reports hits, this can lead to the refusal or revocation of a travel authorization.[141]

Section C.I discusses what these interferences mean for the legitimacy of the decision-making processes. Section C.II examines individual rights and legal

[131] For example based on former and current applications for visa or ETIAS travel authorizations.

[132] For example based on applications by more than one person and surnames.

[133] For example the information on the occupation or education combined with the place of residence, ETIAS Regulation, art 17(2)(f, h–i).

[134] European Data Protection Supervisor, 'Opinion 3/2017 on the Proposal for a European Travel Information and Authorisation System (ETIAS)' (2017), paras 42ff.

[135] cf in the context of PNR data Opinion 1/15 of the Court (PNR Opinion) ECLI:EU:C:2016:656, para 128; Case C-817/19 *Ligue des droits humains ASBL v Conseil des ministers* (2022) ECLI:EU:C:2022:491 (PNR judgment), para 100.

[136] Comparable is the systematic transfer of PNR data to the PIUs of PNR data Case C-817/19 *Ligue des droits humains ASBL v Conseil des ministers* (2022) ECLI:EU:C:2022:49 (PNR judgment), paras 98, 102.

[137] See section B.I.2.

[138] The European Data Protection Supervisor even assumes that the effects of yellow links are significant enough to fall under the scope of the EU data protection rules on ADM, European Data Protection Supervisor, Opinion 4/2018 on the Proposals for two Regulations establishing a framework for interoperability between EU large-scale information systems, paras 86ff.

[139] cf in the context of GDPR, art 22, CJEU Working Document, Case C-634/21—Request for a preliminary ruling (Schufa Holding). The referring court asks whether an automated credit scoring can be considered an automated decision where the score is transmitted to a third-party controller whose decision to grant or refuse a loan highly relies on the score.

[140] cf Niovi Vavoula (n 57) 647.

[141] See a brief overview of fundamental rights impacts of decisions under ETIAS Pesch, Dimitrova, and Boehm (n 15) 55ff.

remedies guaranteed by Articles 8(2), 47 CFR. Section C.III identifies practical problems of supervision (Article 8(3) CFR).

I. Legitimacy of decision-making processes

For the fundamental rights interferences to be justified, they must be founded on a clear legal basis and must be proportional; that means they must be strictly necessary to reach a legitimate purpose.[142] ETIAS pursues three purposes: public security, the prevention of illegal immigration, and the protection of public health.[143] These can be considered as objectives of general interest that can basically justify interferences.[144] The MID aims to facilitate identity checks and combat identity fraud which can also be considered legitimate purposes.[145]

The legal basis must lay down clear and precise rules and provide for sufficient safeguards to ensure that concerned individuals are effectively protected against the unlawful processing and use of their data.[146] Where personal data is subject to automated processing, particularly strong safeguards are required.[147] For a legal basis to reach sufficient clarity it must allow for the criteria and risk assessment models applied, and the data and databases concerned.[148] The automated processing must be limited to databases sufficiently specified.

Since automated risk assessments that involve the comparison of unverified personal data against predetermined criteria present a significant margin of error and consequently produce false positives, they require especially strong safeguards.[149] Such risk assessments must therefore use specific and reliable criteria,

[142] Case Opinion 1/15 (PNR Opinion), (2016) ECLI:EU:C:2016:656, paras 138ff.

[143] ETIAS Regulation, art 1(1).

[144] For public security cf Case Opinion 1/15 (2016) (PNR Opinion), ECLI:EU:C:2016:656, paras 148ff.

[145] EIF Regulations, art 25(1).

[146] Case Opinion 1/15 (PNR Opinion), (2016) ECLI:EU:C:2016:656, para 141. Joined Cases C-293/12 and C-594/12 *Digital Rights Ireland Ltd v Minister for Communications, Marine and Natural Resources and Others and Kärntner Landesregierung and Others* (2014) ECLI:EU:C:2014:238, para 54; Joined Cases C-512/18 and C-520/18 *La Quadrature du Net and Others v Premier ministre and Others* (2020) ECLI:EU:C:2020:79, para 132; *Centrum för rättvisa v Sweden* (2021), App no 35252/08, paras 246 f.; *S. and Marper v UK* (2008), App nos 30562/04 and 30566/04, para 95.

[147] cf Case Opinion 1/15 (PNR Opinion), (2016) ECLI:EU:C:2016:656 para 141; *Big Brother Watch and Others v UK* (2021), App nos 58170/13, 62322/14, and 24960/15, para 330; Joined Cases C-293/12 and C-594/12 *Digital Rights Ireland Ltd v Minister for Communications, Marine and Natural Resources and Others and Kärntner Landesregierung and Others* (2014) ECLI:EU:C:2014:238, para 55; *S. and Marper v UK* (2008), App nos 30562/04 and 30566/04 para 103; *Centrum för rättvisa v Sweden* (2021), App no 35252/08, para 244; Joined Cases C-512/18 and C-520/18 *La Quadrature du Net and Others v Premier ministre and Others* (2020) ECLI:EU:C:2020:79, para 132.

[148] Case Opinion 1/15 (PNR Opinion), (2016) ECLI:EU:C:2016:656, paras 155, 172; Case C-817/19 *Ligue des droits humains ASBL v Conseil des ministers* (2022) ECLI:EU:C:2022:49 (PNR judgment) paras 117f, 180, 187f.

[149] Case Opinion 1/15 (PNR Opinion) (2016) ECLI:EU:C:2016:656, para 169; Case C-817/19 *Ligue des droits humains ASBL v Conseil des ministers* (2022) (PNR judgment), para 107.

and reach reasonable and non-discriminatory[150] results.[151] This necessitates sufficient accuracy of the databases with which the assessed data is compared.[152] To protect concerned individuals from errors of machines and discriminatory arbitrary decisions based on such errors, positive results from automated processing must be individually reviewed[153] by non-automated means before any individual measure adversely affecting the persons concerned is taken.[154] In particular, risk assessments require an individual assessment on a case-by-case basis and must not merely rely on general assumptions.[155] For individual reviews by national authorities under the PNR Directive,[156] the CJEU has argued that the Member States must provide for clear and precise guidelines for individual reviews and objective criteria to enable agents to assess the case, and to verify the non-discriminatory nature of the automated processing and the criteria and databases used.[157]

To safeguard individual reviews it is crucial to consider the risk of decision-support systems that a sufficient individual review does not take place due to the human tendency to over-rely on the results of automated processing procedures (automation bias).[158] To avoid this, human decision-makers need sufficient training and qualification.[159] In particular, they must have a reasonable

[150] Joined Cases, C-512/18 and C-520/18 *La Quadrature du Net and Others v Premier ministre and Others* (2020) ECLI:EU:C:2020:79, para 180; Non-discriminatory in the legal sense. From a statistical point of view, risk assessments have the purpose of discrimination, cf on the discriminatory power of credit risk scorings Andreas Bloechlinger and Markus Leippold, 'Economic Benefit of Powerful Credit Scoring' (2006) 30(3) Journal of Banking & Finance 851.

[151] Case Opinion 1/15 (PNR Opinion) (2016) ECLI:EU:C:2016:656, paras 169, 172. Joined Cases C-511/18 C-512/18 and C-520/18 *La Quadrature du Net and Others v Premier ministre and Others* (2020) ECLI:EU:C:2020:79, para 180.

[152] Case Opinion 1/15 (PNR Opinion) (2016) ECLI:EU:C:2016:656, Opinion, paras 169, 172. Joined Cases C-511/18, C-512/18, and C-520/18 *La Quadrature du Net and Others v Premier ministre and Others* (2020) ECLI:EU:C:2020:79, para 180.

[153] cf the data protection provisions on ADM in GDPR, art 22(1), EUDPR, art 24(1), LED, art 11(1). In the context of EU border instruments, it is noteworthy that the Europol Regulation (Regulation (EU) 2016/794, recently amended by Regulation (EU) 2022/991) does not contain any rule on solely automated decisions. Europol Regulation, art 30(4), that covered solely automated decisions based on the processing of special categories of personal data has been deleted by the amending Regulation (EU) 2022/991.

[154] Case C-817/19 *Ligue des droits humains ASBL v Conseil des ministers* (2022) ECLI:EU:C:2022:491 (PNR judgment), para 179; Joined Cases C-511/18, C-512/18, and C-520/18 *La Quadrature du Net and Others v Premier ministre and Others* (2020) ECLI:EU:C:2020:79, para 182. cf GDPR, art 22(1), EUDPR, art 24(1), LED, art 11(1) LED.

[155] cf Case C-554/13 *Z. Zh. v Staatssecretaris van Veiligheid en Justitie and Staatssecretaris van Veiligheid en Justitie v I. O.* (2015) ECLI:EU:C:2015:377, para 50.

[156] PNR Directive, art 6(5, 6).

[157] Case C-817/19 *Ligue des droits humains ASBL v Conseil des ministers* (2022) ECLI:EU:C:2022:491 (PNR judgment), paras 205f.

[158] Kate Goddard, Abdul Roudsari, and Jeremy C Wyatt, 'Automation Bias: A Systematic Review of Frequency, Effect Mediators, and Mitigators' (2012) 19(1) Journal of the American Medical Informatics Association 121.

[159] On qualification in the context of AI tools European Data Protection Board and European Data Protection Supervisor, EDPB-EDPS Joint Opinion 5/2021 on the proposal for a Regulation of the European Parliament and of the Council laying down harmonised rules on artificial intelligence (Artificial Intelligence Act), 18 June 2021, para 59; in the context of investigation tools see Michael Fröwis and others, 'Safeguarding the Evidential Value of Forensic Cryptocurrency Investigations' (2020) 33 Forensic Science International: Digital Investigation 7.

understanding of the functioning and limitations of the decision-support systems they use.[160] This requires a realistic notion of its level of accuracy.[161]

Furthermore, decision-support systems should promote individual reviews by-design.[162] They should not only come with appropriate instructions but also be designed in a way that facilitates the critical assessment of each individual case. In particular, the user interface, the way and amount of information shown, and the presentation of processing results can reduce automation bias[163] and enable human decision-makers to assess a case carefully rather than blindly follow the suggestion of a decision-support system.[164] For probabilistic and estimation-based tools such as risk assessment systems, the level of granularity and detail of the results might impact the individual review. The presentation of results can either trigger scrutiny or create a wrong impression of certainty.[165] Where an ML-trained model is used, the lack of transparency of such models might disenable human decision-makers to scrutinize its results but explanations of the systems might reinforce automation bias.[166] To determine how decision-support systems should be designed and to which extent the logic behind them should be made transparent to the user (ie the human decision-maker), empirical studies on human oversight that are supported by automated means need to be taken into consideration.[167] Decision-support systems should be tested with real users (eg law enforcement officers or border control guards) since the optimum design to facilitate critical assessments differs based on the use case and the target user group.[168]

It should be noted that there remain general doubts about the individual review of automated processing results, as even with the best qualification and

[160] Pesch, Dimitrova, and Boehm (n 15) 60; Fröwis and others (n 159) 5, 7. In the context of data quality cf Diana Dimitrova, 'The Rise of the Personal Data Quality Principle: Is It Legal and Does It Have an Impact on the Right to Rectification?' (2021) 12(3) European Journal of Law and Technology 22; cf art 14(4) of the Artificial Intelligence Act, see European Parliament legislative resolution of 13 March 2024 on the proposal for a regulation of the European Parliament and of the Council on laying down harmonised rules on Artificial Intelligence (Artificial Intelligence Act), P9_TA(2024)0138 (AIA).

[161] Pesch, Dimitrova, and Boehm (n 15) 60; Fröwis and others (n 159) 7; cf AIA (n 160), arts 13(2), (3) (b) (ii), 14(3), (4) (a), 15(2).

[162] cf EUDPR, art 27(1), GDPR, art 25(1), LED, art 20(1) ('privacy by design').

[163] Fourough Poursabzi-Sangdeh and others, 'Manipulating and Measuring Model Interpretability', *Proceedings of the 2021 CHI Conference on Human Factors in Computing Systems* (CHI 2021).

[164] cf the human oversight requirement laid down in art 14(1) of the AIA (n 160).

[165] Pesch, Dimitrova, and Boehm (n 15) 60.

[166] Case C-817/19 *Ligue des droits humains ASBL v Conseil des ministers* (2022) ECLI:EU:C:2022:491 (PNR judgment), para 195; Pesch, Dimitrova, and Boehm (n 15) 60.

[167] cf Ben Green, 'The Flaws of Policies Requiring Human Oversight of Government Algorithms' (2021) 45 Computer Law & Security Review 105681; Maia Jacobs and others, 'How Machine-Learning Recommendations Influence Clinician Treatment Selections: The Example of Antidepressant Selection' (2021) 11 *Translational Psychiatry*; Pesch, Dimitrova, and Boehm (n 15) 60; Forough Poursabzi-Sangdeh and others, 'Manipulating and Measuring Model Interpretability', *Proceedings of the 2021 CHI Conference on Human Factors in Computing Systems* (CHI 2021).

[168] Jacobs and others (n 167).

decision-support systems, it is fundamentally questionable that human oversight over decision-support systems is feasible at all.[169]

Section C.I.1 analyses to which extent the provisions on multiple-identity detection in the EIF Regulations meet the above-mentioned requirements. Section C.I.2 examines the ETIAS Regulation.

1. Legitimacy of decision-making in the context of the MID

For the MID, the EIF Regulations specify both the data and databases to be compared against the data that triggered multiple identity-detection.[170] As the MID is an automated risk assessment system used to assess the likelihood of whether someone fraudulently uses an identity by comparing personal data[171] against other data based on predetermined criteria,[172] and automated multiple-identity detection can substantially affect concerned individuals, strong safeguards are required to ensure proportionality of interferences. In particular it should be noted that the reliability of the automated multiple-identity detection and the individual review of the results of the automated multiple-identity detection is crucial.

It remains to be seen whether the MID will reach sufficient reliability; that is, will produce reasonable results. Automated multiple-identity detection consists in the distinction of same and similar from different data. The reliability of the MID therefore depends on the performance of the algorithm for distinguishing same and similar from different data that is developed by eu-LISA based on the delegated acts by the Commission.[173] The delegated regulations[174] require eu-LISA to monitor the impact of the algorithm and to adjust it to limit the number of yellow links that are eventually classified as white.[175] However, this ensures more reasonable results only in cases in which false positives are identified in the manual verification procedure but not in cases in which the authorities responsible classify yellow links as red without sufficiently scrutinizing the MID's result.

Whether the MID reaches reasonable results is subject to the monitoring and evaluation procedures, especially to the evaluation by the Commission of the impact of the MID to the right of non-discrimination two years after its start of operations.[176] For the transitional period,[177] the EIF Regulations do not lay down any

[169] Green (n 167); Ben Green and Yiling Chen, 'The Principles and Limits of Algorithm-in-the-Loop Decision Making' (2019) 3(CSCW) Proceedings of the ACM on Human-Computer Interaction Article No 50.

[170] EIF Regulations, art 27. On the functioning of the MID see section B.I.2.

[171] In some cases unverified, eg ETIAS application data.

[172] To distinguish same and similar from different data see sections B.I.2. and B.I.3.

[173] Based on the Commission delegated acts. See section B.I.2.

[174] n 71.

[175] n 71, annex II s 2, on request of a group of experts designated by the Member States (EIF Regulations, art 73(4)).

[176] EIF Border Regulation, art 78(6); EIF LE Regulation, art 74(6).

[177] Of at least one year, up to two years and six months following notification by eu-LISA of the completion of the test of the MID, EIF Border Regulation, art 69(1), (8), EIF LE Regulation, art 65(1), (8).

rules on testing and evaluation, posing the risk that interferences with Articles 7, 8 CFR through multiple-identity detection with the MID that have not been detected in the test phase of the MID[178] will remain unnoticed until the first evaluation. The interferences of automated multiple-identity detection with Articles 7, 8 CFR will only be proportional if eu-LISA ensures sufficient testing of the MID in the development phase especially regarding accuracy and non-discrimination.

The reliability of automated identity detection could also suffer from low data quality in the databases checked for links between identity data. There are concerns about the quality of alphanumeric data in all EU information systems, for example because of spelling errors, wrong transcriptions, estimated birth dates, issues with formats, or errors due to the lack of skills or training of officers.[179]

To minimize the risk that bona fide travellers are stopped and falsely accused of identity fraud[180] individual review of the results of the automated processing is particularly important. Since in cases of yellow links the identities are manually verified,[181] the EIF Regulations formally provide for individual review. There are however doubts whether the EIF Regulations sufficiently safeguard individual review.[182]

Human decision-makers might tend to classify a link considered suspicious by the MID as red due to automation bias. In some cases, it is easier to assume that inconsistencies are based on an unjustified use of identity than to clarify them. The EIF Regulations do not lay down any specific rules on the verification of different identities and the conclusion that the respective traveller can be considered bona fide or not.[183] They do not address cases where there remain doubts, and do not require consultation with other authorities that have entered the data in the linked files. There is also the risk that decisions are taken based on red links without a sufficient individual review, for example the decision to refuse an ETIAS travel authorization. Such a refusal, formally, would not be based on the existence of a red link,[184] but on the conclusion that there remain relevant doubts about the applicant. However, there is the risk that the ETIAS National Unit simply follows the classification of the link by the ETIAS Central Unit[185] rather than making the

[178] cf EIF Border Regulation, arts 72(4)(b), 54(3); EIF LE Regulation, arts 68(4)(b), 54(3).

[179] Niovi Vavoula (n 57) 520 ff; Niovi Vavoula (n 9) 468 f with further references; European Union Agency for Fundamental Rights, *Fundamental Rights and the Interoperability of EU Information Systems: Borders And Security* (Publications Office of the European Union 2017) 20, 30; European Union Agency For Fundamental Rights, *Under Watchful Eyes: Biometrics, EU IT systems and Fundamental Rights* (Publications Office of the European Union 2018) 84; European Court of Auditors, 'Special Report, EU information systems supporting border control—a strong tool, but more focus needed on timely and complete data' (2019), EU no 20.

[180] cf Niovi Vavoula (n 57) 641f (also on the groups of travellers particularly affected by yellow links).

[181] EIF Regulations, arts 28(4), 29.

[182] Niovi Vavoula (n 57) 647.

[183] cf EIF Regulations, arts 29, 32.

[184] cf EIF Regulations, art 32(2) section B.I.2 above.

[185] EIF Border Regulation, art 29(1)(c), clarifies both the ETIAS Central Unit and the ETIAS National Units can be responsible for the verification of a link.

effort to scrutinize it. Concerned TCNs might not be able to explain the reasons for a yellow link, for example a name change after marriage, due to language barriers and time pressure at the border.[186]

The EIF Regulations neither explicitly require clear and precise guidelines for individual review, nor do they unambiguously necessitate the authorities responsible for the manual verification of identities to provide for safeguards such as clear guidelines. There are also no provisions that require sufficient training of human decision-makers and their awareness of automation bias. In light of the CFR, the assignment of the responsibility for the manual verification of identities,[187] however, must be interpreted as comprising the obligation to provide for clear guidelines and sufficient training to raise awareness of the limitations of automated multiple-identity detection and sources of error in particular.[188]

The EIF Regulations also do not lay down rules for cases where there remain doubts about the identities which might lead to a classification of links as red without substantial reasons. They furthermore do not foresee consultation with other authorities where these have entered data relevant to the assessment. From a fundamental rights perspective, it would be desirable to further detail the assessment procedures, especially because there is the risk of subsequent decisions based on red links without sufficient individual review.

To ensure the proportionality of the interferences caused by automated multiple-identity detection, eu-LISA should develop the MID and design its human–machine interface in a way that facilitate the critical assessment of the MID's results. The display of results, the wording, and a disclaimer that the MID creates yellow links also in some cases of bona fide travellers, might significantly mitigate automation bias. For this purpose, eu-LISA should carry out empirical studies and tests with real users.

Subsequent decisions such as refusals of travel authorizations or the initiation of criminal procedures are not governed by the EIF Regulations that just stipulate that no follow-up decision may be based solely on the existence of a red link.[189] Therefore, the respective Union and Member State authorities taking subsequent decisions must ensure that human decision-makers carefully assess the individual case and do not over-rely on red links.

2. Legitimacy of decision-making in ETIAS

Regarding the automated assessment, the ETIAS Regulation defines the data to be provided by applicants[190] as well as the databases and the data that the application

[186] Niovi Vavoula (n 57) 643 f.

[187] EIF Regulations, arts 56(1)(f), 57(a).

[188] See by analogy Case C-817/19 *Ligue des droits humains ASBL v Conseil des ministers* (2022) ECLI:EU:C:2022:491 (PNR judgment), paras 205f.

[189] EIF Regulations, art 32(2). Niovi Vavoula is critical on that point (n 57) 647.

[190] ETIAS Regulation, art 17.

is compared with.[191] Like the EIF Regulations, it raises concerns about the reliability of risk assessments and fails to safeguard the individual review adequately.

Like the procedure for the determination of same and similar data in the context of multiple-identity detection, the ETIAS Regulation itself does not specify the criteria of the ETIAS Screening Rules but lays down rules for the their definition to the Commission and the ETIAS Central Unit.[192] The risk indicators shall consist of information such as age range, sex, nationality, country and city of residence, level of education, and current occupation.[193] They shall be targeted, proportionate, and under no circumstances be based solely on a person's sex or age, or based on information revealing a person's colour, race, ethnic or social origin, genetic features, language, political or any other opinion, religion or philosophical belief, trade union membership, membership of a national minority, property, birth, disability, or sexual orientation.[194] But even if the screening rules do not directly rely on such information, the risk indicators might still imply such knowledge as, for example, a traveller's race might be easy to guess based on their country of residence.[195]

The risk indicators shall be based, among other things, on EES statistics on abnormal rates of refusals of entry of specific groups of travellers, ETIAS statistics indicating abnormal rates of refusals of travel authorizations due to risks associated with specific groups of travellers, and substantiated information concerning specific risk indicators or abnormal rates of overstaying and refusals of entry for specific groups of travellers by Member States.[196] That bears the risk that discriminatory historical decisions shape the risk indicators and, by this, perpetuate discrimination.[197] This would lead to unreasonable, discriminatory results and hence cause a disproportionate interference with Articles 7, 8 CFR.

The same could hold true for checks against the ETIAS watchlist, where entries on the watchlist are not reliable. The reliability of watchlist entries is particularly questionable for the most problematic type of entries, namely entries for persons that are believed to commit terrorist offences or other serious crimes in the future.[198] For the underlying risk assessments, it is unclear whether their accuracy is sufficiently tested. The ETIAS Regulation states without specification of criteria that entries shall be based on factual indications or reasonable grounds.[199]

[191] ETIAS Regulation, art 30(2).
[192] ETIAS Regulation, art 33(2–4).
[193] ETIAS Regulation, art 33(4).
[194] ETIAS Regulation, art 33(5).
[195] Niovi Vavoula (n 9) 473.
[196] ETIAS Regulation, art 33(2)(a–b, d–e).
[197] cf European Union Agency for Fundamental Rights (FRA), *Bias in Algorithms, Artificial Intelligence and Discrimination—Report* (Publications Office of the European Union 2022) (FRA AI Bias report) p 29ff. (on feedback loops); Niovi Vavoula (n 9) 471f.
[198] ETIAS Regulation, art 34(1).
[199] ETIAS Regulation, art 34(1); The ETIAS Regulation also does not specify what can be considered terrorism, Vavoula is critical on that point (n 57) 526.

Member States and Europol shall bear responsibility for the accuracy of watchlist entries.[200] The ETIAS Regulation requires Europol and the Member States to ensure (continued) accuracy of entries.[201] From a fundamental rights perspective, a clear legal requirement to demonstrate accuracy levels based on metrics would be desirable.[202] If watchlist entries—or other data such as SIS alerts—are based on unreliable risk assessments, this causes unreliable results of ETIAS risk assessments and hence disproportionate interferences with Articles 7, 8. Also, ETIAS risk assessments can lead to unreasonable results where other data that applications is checked against lack data quality.[203]

While travel authorizations are automatically issued where the automated processing of an application reports no hit,[204] the ETIAS Regulation, in cases of hits, formally provides for an individual review before the decision to refuse or revoke a travel authorization is made.[205] However, there is the concern that human decision-makers in the ETIAS National Units do not get meaningfully involved in the decision-making.[206]

Human decision-makers might not sufficiently get involved in the decision-making insofar as they over-rely on the results of the automated part of the ETIAS risk assessment, and the data stored in the relevant information systems.[207] This concerns not only the risk indicators but also the ETIAS watchlist and databases that ETIAS applications are checked against. That the ETIAS Regulation does not lay down detailed rules on the manual assessment and the weight of the screening rules and other factors contributes to the risk of automated decision-making (ADM).[208] There remains a risk that data entered by other Member States or Europol are not sufficiently scrutinized. Data might not allow for a critical assessment without further information. Even if another Member State or Europol has entered the relevant data and is consulted,[209] the further information provided might be ambiguous due to language barriers or different interpretation of legal terms.[210]

[200] ETIAS Regulation, arts 34(1), 35(4–6).

[201] ETIAS Regulation, art 35(1), (4).

[202] The AIA explicitly requires such testing and transparency of the accuracy level to users, AIA (n 160), arts 9(7), 13(3)(b)(ii), (3)(d), 15(2).

[203] On EU information systems in general see section C.I.1 with n 179. On Europol see next para with n 221.

[204] ETIAS Regulation, art 21(1).

[205] ETIAS Regulation, arts 21(2–4), 22(5), 26(2)(b), 41.

[206] Timo Zandstra and Evelien Brouwer, 'Fundamental Rights at the Digital Border—ETIAS, the Right to Data Protection, and the CJEU's PNR Judgment' (*Verfassungsblog*, 2022) <https://verfassungsblog.de/digital-border/> accessed 20 June 2024.

[207] On Member States relying on other Member States' and Third Countries' information in the context of SIS Evelien Brouwer, 'Schengen and the Administration of Exclusion: Legal Remedies Caught in between Entry Bans, Risk Assessment and Artificial Intelligence' (2021) 23 European Journal of Migration and Law (2021) 485, 490.

[208] See section B.II.2.

[209] ETIAS Regulation, art 28f.

[210] Pesch, Dimitrova, and Boehm (n 15) 61. cf Roy D Ingleton, Mission Incomprehensible: The Linguistic Barrier to Effective Police Cooperation in Europe (Multilingual Matters 1994).

Also such information can be incomplete, for example where the data is based on risk assessments themselves and the underlying criteria and reasoning are non-transparent. An example is data on the watchlist, as in cases of hits against the watchlist the travel authorization is not necessarily refused but the risk assessment by the ETIAS National Unit is decisive.[211]

The data that human decision-makers consider and might not scrutinize can even be based on automated processing without an individual review of processing results. This especially holds true for ETIAS watchlist. The ETIAS Regulation does not specify the assessments on which watchlist entries are based.[212] It especially does not impose the requirement of an individual review of entries. Both the Member States or Europol can enter data.[213] For Europol, the Europol Regulation lays down an autonomous data protection framework that does not address ADM.[214] Europol is not only a main driver for AI in the EU[215] but is also explicitly assigned a key role in promoting artificial intelligence by the Regulation amending the Europol Regulation.[216] After the Court of Justice of the European Union (CJEU) has approved the retention of vast amounts of data by the Member States to avert serious threats to national security,[217] the Member States provide Europol with huge amounts of data for the fight against terrorism.[218] Europol is known to use Palantir's 'AI ready operating system'[219] called Gotham.[220] Watchlist entries by Europol are therefore likely to be based on big data analytics that might involve ML-trained models. This is worrying, as Europol data has been found not be of high quality[221] and this raises concerns about transparency.[222] The European Data

211 ETIAS Regulation, arts 20(4), 26(5).

212 ETIAS Regulation, art 34f.

213 ETIAS Regulation, art 34(3).

214 n 153.

215 n 112.

216 Regulation (EU) 2022/991 of the European Parliament and of the Council of 8 June 2022 amending Regulation (EU) 2016/794, as regards Europol's cooperation with private parties, the processing of personal data by Europol in support of criminal investigations, and Europol's role in research and innovation [2022] OJ L169, rec 49.

217 cf Joined Cases C-512/18 and C-520/18 *La Quadrature du Net and Others v Premier ministre and Others* [2020] ECLI:EU:C:2020:79, para 137; Case C-623/17 *Privacy International v Secretary of State for Foreign and Commonwealth Affairs and Others* (2020) ECLI:EU:C:2020:790, para 74; Hoek and Stigter (n 112) 25 take a critical view; Monika Zalnieriute, 'The Future of Data Retention Regimes and National Security in the EU after the Quadrature Du Net and Privacy International Judgments' (2020) 24(28) American Society of International Law.

218 Hoek and Stigter (n 112) 25f.

219 Palantir, Gotham <https://www.palantir.com/platforms/gotham/> accessed 20 June 2024.

220 European Parliament, 'Parliamentary question E-000173/2020(ASW), Answer given by Ms Johansson on behalf of the European Commission' (European Parliament, 2020) <https://www.europarl.europa.eu/doceo/document/E-9-2020-000173-ASW_EN.html> accessed 20 June 2024.

221 Especially as the data is likely to be biased, Hoek and Stigter (n 112) 27 with reference to the remark of Clare Daly (MEP), Brussel (Europol mandate), 24 February 2021. Also, the data delivered by the Member States is based on discriminatory and racist policing practices, ibid with reference to Dietrich Oberwittler and Sebastian Roché, *Police Citizen Relations Around the World—Comparing Sources and Contexts of Trust and Legitimacy* (Routledge 2017).

222 Brouwer (n 207) 491.

Protection Supervisor has furthermore stated that the sheer volume of data that Europol receives makes it impossible to assess its data protection compliance.[223] Also, the European Data Protection Supervisor—before the amendment of the Europol Regulation—has found Europol to unlawfully process huge amounts of data that lacked data subject categorization,[224] and requested the CJEU to annul provisions of the amended Europol Regulation that retroactively legalize[225] the processing of that data.[226]

To ensure proportionality of the interferences caused particularly by ETIAS risk assessments and refusal decisions, the Member States whose ETIAS National Units are responsible for the manual assessment must provide clear guidelines and ensure sufficient training that raises awareness of automation bias in particular. eu-LISA should also ensure in the development of the ETIAS System and, if applicable, additional risk assessment systems,[227] that the individual review is safeguarded by design based on tests with real users.

Furthermore, where data in the relevant databases are not reliable,[228] the ETIAS National Units might simply not have enough information to scrutinize hits that such data has triggered. If the National Units obtain further information by consulting other authorities mistakes might occur due to the language barrier and different interpretations of legal terms.[229] Data by Europol in particular might be hard to scrutinize as its background lacks transparency.[230] The interferences with Articles 7, 8 CFR caused by the ETIAS risk assessments will be proportional only if the involved authorities can demonstrate that the databases are accurate and allow for meaningful individual reviews.

[223] European Data Protection Supervisor, 'Decision on the own initiative inquiry on Europol's big data challenge', C 2019-0370 (2020) para 4.7.

[224] European Data Protection Supervisor, Decision on the retention by Europol of datasets lacking Data Subject Categorisation, Cases 2019-0370 and 2021-0699.

[225] Critical Statewatch, 'EU: Europol: "Significant progress" on legalising illegal data practices' (Statewatch 2022) <https://www.statewatch.org/news/2022/january/eu-europol-significant-progress-on-legalising-illegal-data-practices/> accessed 20 June 2024 and Statewatch, 'Europol: Council Presidents proposes workaround for illegal data processing' (Statewatch 2022) <https://www.statewatch.org/news/2022/january/europol-council-presidency-proposes-workaround-for-illegal-data-processing/> accessed 20 June 2024. In that context, also see open letter by twenty-three human rights organizations. Civil society urges European policy-makers seriously to reconsider the expansion of Europol's data processing capacities. Statewatch, 'EU: Legislators must put the brakes on big data plans for Europol' (Statewatch 2022) <https://www.statewatch.org/news/2022/february/eu-legislators-must-put-the-brakes-on-big-data-plans-for-europol/> accessed 20 June 2024.

[226] European Data Protection Supervisor, 'EDPS takes legal action as new Europol Regulation puts rule of law and EDPS independence under threat' (2022) <https://edps.europa.eu/press-publications/press-news/press-releases/2022/edps-takes-legal-action-new-europol-regulation-puts-rule-law-and-edps-independence-under-threat_en> accessed 20 June 2024.

[227] See section B.II.3 on the proposed additional risk assessment system.

[228] On EU information systems in general see section C.I.1 with n 179. On Europol see next para with n 221.

[229] Pesch, Dimitrova, and Boehm (n 15) 61. cf Ingleton (n 210).

[230] Brouwer (n 207) 491. Section C.II, last para.

It is particularly questionable whether an ML-trained model supporting the ETIAS National Units with the manual assessment, as suggested by eu-LISA, the Commission, and the Future Group established by Europol and Frontex,[231] is compatible with fundamental rights. Such models pose two problems: first, they can lack reliability; secondly, they might hinder human decision-makers from individually reviewing their results if they are non-transparent.

ML-trained models do not reach sufficient reliability if they are fed with discriminatory or non-representative historical data.[232] As usually the development of such models is outsourced and the models are trained with datasets that are kept secret, the training of the models is non-transparent.[233] That the models are not biased and sufficiently accurate must be ensured with sufficient tests with representative unbiased data. Such tests require clear and strict guidelines.[234]

Even accurate and unbiased models might not allow for the individual review of their results. As the CJEU has pointed out in the context of the PNR Directive, the use of non-transparent ML-trained risk assessment systems that do not provide for interpretability or explainability[235] of their results might not allow for an individual review, since human decision-makers cannot comprehend the reasoning of such models.[236]

It is questionable whether the ETIAS Regulation allows for the use of such models in the first place. eu-LISA, the Commission, Europol, and Frontex plan to include an additional layer of automated assessment to support the manual processing of applications.[237] The ETIAS Regulation clearly defines the automated processing of application files[238] and explicitly requires the manual processing of applications for which the automated processing has reported a hit.[239] These rules

[231] Section B.II.3.
[232] Julia Angwin and others, 'There's Software Used Across the Country to Predict Future Criminals. And It's Biased Against Blacks' (ProPublica 2016) <https://www.propublica.org/article/machine-bias-risk-assessments-in-criminal-sentencing> accessed 20 June 2024; Rachel Courtland, 'Bias Detectives: The Researchers Striving to Make Algorithms Fair' (2018) Nature <https://www.nature.com/articles/d41586-018-05469-3> accessed 20 June 2024; on biased AI FRA AI Bias report (n 197); Michelle Seng Ah Lee and Jatinder Singh, 'Risk Identification Questionnaire for Detecting Unintended Bias in the Machine Learning Development Lifecycle' in Marion Fourcade, Benjamin Kuipers, Setz Lazar, and Deirdre Mulligan (eds) *Proceedings of the AAAI/ACM Conference on AI, Ethics, and Society* 704 (2021); Ninareh Mehrabi and others, 'A Survey on Bias and Fairness in Machine Learning' (2021) 54(6) ACM Computing Surveys Article 115; Eirini Ntoutsi and others, 'Bias in Data-Driven Artificial Intelligence Systems—An Introductory Survey' 2020 10(3) WIREs e1356; Pesch, Dimitrova, and Boehm (n 15) 53; Niovi Vavoula (n 57) 528.
[233] Pesch, Dimitrova, and Boehm (n 15) 64.
[234] ibid 64.
[235] n 124.
[236] Case C-817/19 *Ligue des droits humains ASBL v Conseil des ministers* (2022) ECLI:EU:C:2022:491 (PNR judgment), para 194.
[237] See section B.II.3.
[238] ETIAS Regulation, art 20.
[239] ETIAS Regulation, arts 21(2), 22(6), 26.

must be interpreted as precluding automated decision-support tools in the manual assessment of applications by the ETIAS National Units. The interpretation of legal terms is based on the one hand on their meaning in everyday language and, on the other, on the context and purpose of the norm.[240] The term 'manual' refers to an assessment by non-automated means. The context of the ETIAS Regulation that clearly differentiates the automated and manual assessment also argues for this understanding. Furthermore, the requirement of the manual processing must be interpreted in the light of Articles 7, 8 CFR as safeguarding the individual review. An assessment supported by an ML-trained model can hardly fulfil this purpose. Instead of safeguarding the protection of individual rights, the use of further automated risk-assessments—based on the same or similar historic data—would pose the same risks as the automated processing before and reinforces automation bias.[241] Such an additional layer of automation would require a clear legal basis with specific safeguards. For ML-trained models, additionally, the AIA should apply without exception[242] to safeguard human oversight and sufficient transparency to users.[243]

3. Deficits of the EIF and the ETIAS Regulations

To summarize the analysis of the legitimacy of decision-making processes, both the EIF Regulations and the ETIAS Regulation lack clear safeguards with regard to both the reliability of the automated risk assessments, and the individual review of the risk assessment results. To ensure the proportionality of the interferences caused by the MID on the one hand and ETIAS risk assessments on the other, the responsible authorities must fill the regulatory gap. Concretely, the authorities responsible for the decisions must ensure the individual review of risk assessment results through clear guidelines and sufficient trainings for human-decision makers. Furthermore, the risk assessment systems should not only be subject to thorough accuracy tests but also be designed in a way that is proven to facilitate human oversight.

Apart of the abovementioned aspects, the justification of the interferences caused by multiple-identity detection with the MID, and ETIAS risk assessments

[240] Case C-554/13 *Z. Zh. v Staatssecretaris van Veiligheid en Justitie and Staatssecretaris van Veiligheid en Justitie v I. O.* (2015) ECLI:EU:C:2015:377, para 42.

[241] cf Case C-817/19 *Ligue des droits humains ASBL v Conseil des ministers* (2022) ECLI:EU:C:2022:491 (PNR judgment), para 194.

[242] cf the exemption in AIA (n 160), arts 111(1), Annex X. Critical on the exemption in the context of the AIA proposal, Statewatch, 'Joint Statement: The EU Artificial Intelligence Act Must Protect People on the Move' (Statewatch 2022) <https://www.statewatch.org/news/2022/december/joint-statement-the-eu-artifical-intelligence-act-must-protect-people-on-the-move/> accessed 20 June 2024; Access Now and others, 'Uses of AI in Migration and Border Control: A Fundamental Rights Approach to the Artificial Intelligence Act' (Access Now 2021) <https://www.accessnow.org/cms/assets/uploads/2022/05/Uses-of-AI-in-migration-and-border-control.pdf> accessed 20 June 2024; Access Now, 'The EU AI Act Proposal: A Timeline' (Access Now 2023) <https://www.accessnow.org/the-eu-ai-act-proposal-a-timeline/> accessed 20 June 2024.

[243] cf AIA (n 160), arts 13, 14.

is uncertain insofar as the necessity[244] of the measures has not yet been sufficiently substantiated through impact assessments.[245]

II. Individual rights and legal remedy

As there is the risk that human decision-makers in the context of the EIF and under ETIAS do not individually review the results of the automated processing, they might fail to sufficiently explain decisions to the concerned individuals. That touches upon both the right to good administration (Article 41 CFR) and the right to legal remedy (Article 47) CFR. The latter is especially interrelated to the fundamental right to data protection that explicitly guarantees access and rectification rights (Article 8(2) CFR).[246]

The right to remedy not only requires that individuals can challenge decisions concerning them but also obtain information or data on which decisions are based.[247] Where decision-making processes lack transparency, challenging decisions can be impossible.[248] Therefore transparency, especially the individual right of data subjects to access their personal data, is a prerequisite for the exercise of further individual rights and legal remedy.[249] Article 47 CFR requires legislation to provide for legal remedy to enforce individual rights to access, rectification, and erasure of data and restriction of its processing.[250]

The judicial review granted by Article 47 CFR must assess the legality of decisions and take into account all relevant aspects.[251] It is only effective where the concerned individual is enabled to understand the reasons for decisions concerning them, either because the reasons are included in the decision or on request.[252] This

[244] *Big Brother Watch and Others v UK* App nos 58170/13, 62322/14 and 24960/15, paras 333f.

[245] Article 29 Working Party, 'Opinion on Commission proposals on establishing a framework for interoperability between EU information systems in the field of borders and visa as well as police and judicial cooperation, asylum and migration' (2018) WP266, 5 (on the CIR, in the MID context, cf EIF Regulations, art 19(2)). On the lack of elaboration on the extent of the problem of identity fraud European Data Protection Supervisor, Opinion 4/2018 on the Proposals for two Regulations establishing a framework for interoperability between EU large-scale information systems, para 146. In the context of ECRIS-TCN see Brouwer (n 207) 506; European Data Protection Supervisor, 'Opinion 3/2017 on the Proposal for a European Travel Information and Authorisation System (ETIAS)' (2017), paras 49, 56, 59; Niovi Vavoula (n 57) 512ff.

[246] Angela Ward in Steve Peers and others (eds), *The EU Charter of Fundamental Rights—A Commentary* (2nd edn, Bloomsbury 2021) 47.02, and Herke Kranenborg, ibid 08.75.

[247] cf Case C-300/11 *ZZ v Secretary of State for the Home Department* (2013) ECLI:EU:C:2013:363, para 53.

[248] European Data Protection Supervisor, 'Opinion 3/2017 on the Proposal for a European Travel Information and Authorisation System (ETIAS)' (2017), para 79.

[249] cf Niovi Vavoula (n 57) 535.

[250] Case C-362/14 *Maximillian Schrems v Data Protection Commissioner* (2015) ECLI:EU:C:2015:650, para 95.

[251] Joined Cases C-225/19 and C-226/19 *R.N.N.S. and K.A. v Minister van Buitenlandse Zaken* (2020) ECLI:EU:C:2020:951 (in the context of the Visa Code), para 48.

[252] In the context of the Visa Code Joined Cases C-225/19 and C-226/19 *R.N.N.S. and K.A. v Minister van Buitenlandse Zaken* (2020) ECLI:EU:C:2020:951, para 43.

is because understanding the reasons for a decision concerning them puts the individual in a position to defend their rights and decide with full knowledge whether to apply to a court.[253] For individual risk assessment criteria and systems applying the criteria, the CJEU has clarified that the authorities must enable the concerned individual to understand how those criteria and programs work and, by this, to decide with full knowledge of the relevant facts whether they seek legal remedy to challenge the unlawful, for example discriminatory, nature of the criteria.[254]

The following sections, based on this jurisdiction, analyse individual rights and remedies in the contexts of the MID and ETIAS. Section C.II.1 outlines the legal provisions on transparency, individual rights, and legal remedy under both the EIF Regulations with respect to the MID and the ETIAS Regulation. Section C.II.2 identifies concerns about individual rights under both frameworks in practices.

1. Provisions on individual rights in the EIF Regulations and the ETIAS Regulation

The EIF Regulations address transparency and individual rights. Referring to transparency provisions under EU data protection law,[255] they require that concerned individuals are informed about the storage of their personal data in the sBMS, CIR, or MID. For multiple-identity detection with the MID, the EIF Regulations require information on the creation of red links in particular. Where links are classified as red based on the manual verification of identities for links created by the MID,[256] the concerned person must be informed of this and provided with a single identification number which allows for retrieving the linked data from the corresponding information systems as well as information on the authority responsible for the manual verification.[257] The information shall be given through a standard form to be designed by the Commission.[258] Furthermore, data subjects have a right to information regarding personal data stored in the sBMS, the CIR, or the MID.[259] For the information to be provided, the EIF Regulations refers to the respective provisions in the EU Data Protection Regulation (EUDPR), General Data Provision Regulation (GDPR), and the Law Enforcement Directive (LED).[260]

The EIF Regulations furthermore clarify that individuals have the rights of access to, and rectification and erasure of personal data stored in the MID,[261] and

[253] In the context of the Visa Code ibid.

[254] Case C-817/19 *Ligue des droits humains ASBL v Conseil des ministers* (2022) ECLI:EU:C:2022:491 (PNR judgment), para 210 with reference, by analogy, to Joined Cases C-225/19 and C-226/19 *R.N.N.S. and K.A. v Minister van Buitenlandse Zaken* (2020) ECLI:EU:C:2020:951, para 43.

[255] EIF Regulations, art 47(1), with reference to GDPR, arts 13f; LED, arts 12f; EUDPR, arts 15f.

[256] On the types of links and the manual verification of identities see section B.I.2.

[257] EIF Regulations, art 32(4).

[258] EIF Regulations, art 32(5) (by means of an implementing act).

[259] EIF Regulations, art 47.

[260] EIF Regulations, art 47(1), with reference to GDPR, arts 13f; LED, arts 12f; EUDPR, arts 15f.

[261] EIF Regulations, art 48.

shall make their requests through a web portal established for the purpose of facilitating the exercise of their rights.[262] Individuals exercising their rights from the GDPR, EUDPR, or LED can request access, rectification, and erasure from any Member State. Where another Member State or the ETIAS Central Unit is responsible for the verification of different identities in cases of erasure or rectification requests, the other Member State is contacted, further examines the case, and decides about the request, or the requested Member State obtains the opinion of the ETIAS Central Unit before making a decision.[263] For cases in which the Member State does not agree with the request, it needs to issue an administrative decision explaining in writing to the concerned individual why their data are not rectified or erased, and the 'possibility to challenge the decision . . . and, where relevant, information how to bring an action or a *complaint before the competent authorities or courts*, and any assistance, including from supervisory authorities'.[264]

The ETIAS Regulation includes transparency requirements and addresses individual rights and the right to appeal. The ETIAS Regulation stipulates that the ETIAS Central Unit shall provide certain information to the public.[265] This information comprises, among other things, the facts that applicants must be notified about the decisions concerning their applications and that they have the right to appeal in cases of refusals of travel authorizations.[266]

Where an ETIAS travel authorization has been refused, annulled, or revoked, the ETIAS Regulation grants the concerned individual the right to appeal.[267] The right to appeal is flanked by the notification requirements.[268] A clear statement that the respective decision has been taken, a reference to and contact of the ETIAS National Unit responsible for the decision, and a statement of grounds are all required.[269] The latter requirement, however, refers to the list of general reasons for refusal such as 'poses a security risk'.[270] The statement of grounds consequently just consists of selecting one of the listed reasons but does not provide for enough transparency of the reasoning.

The ETIAS Regulation addresses access, rectification, completion, and erasure rights for data stored in the ETIAS Central System.[271] The ETIAS Regulation does not establish these rights but refers to the respective rights laid down in the EUDPR

[262] EIF Regulations, art 49.
[263] EIF Regulations, art 48(3–5), (7).
[264] EIF Regulations, art 48(7, 8), emphasis added.
[265] ETIAS Regulation, art 71.
[266] ETIAS Regulation, art 71(h).
[267] ETIAS Regulation, arts 37(3), 40(3), 41(7).
[268] For refusal decisions ETIAS Regulation, art 38(2), for cases of annulment or revocation ETIAS Regulation, art 42.
[269] ETIAS Regulation, art 38(2)(a–c), art 42(a–c).
[270] ETIAS Regulation, art 37(1)(b). Also see art 1(1), annexes I–III of the Commission Implementing Decision (EU) 2022/102 of 25 January 2022 laying down forms for refusal, annulment, or revocation of a travel authorisation [2022] OJ L17.
[271] ETIAS Regulation, art 64.

and the GDPR. Applicants may address with their request either the ETIAS National Unit responsible for their application, or the ETIAS Central Unit.[272]

2. Practical concerns about the exercise of individual rights and legal remedy
The main problem for the exercise of individual rights and the right to legal remedy in context of ETIAS and the MID is the limited transparency of decisions, as the information that concerned individuals are provided with do not reflect the reality of highly interoperable systems with many authorities involved. There is the concern that not only the authorities involved in the decision-making and the data decisions are based on but also the applied criteria remain non-transparent due to the complicated and interlinked design of such procedures[273]. This could have a chilling effect on individuals to exercise their rights and seek legal remedy.

The rules laid down in the EIF Regulations and in the ETIAS Regulation[274] do not make sure that individuals can directly identify all controllers and that they are informed about all data and criteria that decisions concerning them are based on. For the MID, the information about red links allows for retrieving the linked data. This enables data subjects to identify the authorities that have entered the respective data. However, the exercise of rights regarding this data and subsequent decisions might be impaired as 'the data' refers to the whole data file in the respective database, not the concrete pieces of data the link is based on (eg the biometric data contained in the file).[275] Additionally, individuals are not informed about the conclusion that has led to the classification of the link as red[276] and much less about the reasoning underlying that conclusion.

Regarding the information of concerned individuals about the creation of red links, the EIF Regulations allow for limitations necessary to protect security and public order, prevent crime, and guarantee that no national investigation will be jeopardized. Indeed, data subjects' interests in transparency must be balanced with public interests in secrecy.[277] It remains to be seen in which way authorities will invoke this rather wide exemption.[278]

Where the responding Member State decides against erasing or rectifying the data, it must adopt an administrative decision in writing with an explanation.[279]

[272] ETIAS Regulation, art 64(2).
[273] See sections B.I and B.II.
[274] See section C.II.1.
[275] cf EIF Regulations, art 32(1)(a–d).
[276] cf ibid.
[277] In the surveillance context, the data subject must not be informed until the information does no longer liable to jeopardize the investigations, Joined Cases C-511/18, C-512/18, and C-520/18 *La Quadrature du Net and Others v Premier ministre and Others* (2020) ECLI:EU:C:2020:79, para 66; Case Opinion 1/15 (PNR Opinion), (2016) ECLI:EU:C:2016:656, para 220; *Segerstedt-Wiberg and Others v Sweden* (2006), App no 62332/00 para 102; also see *Metanovic v Croatia* (2017), App no 2742/12, para 152.
[278] Niovi Vavoula (n 57) 648.
[279] EIF Regulations, art 48(7).

While both the information and the explanation requirement in the EIF Regulations do not explicitly require a substantiated explanation of the decisions and the specification of the data and other authorities involved,[280] these requirements must be interpreted in light of the CFR requiring such specific information. A parallel can be drawn to the CJEU's judgment on visa refusal decisions that are based on the objection of other Member States: the court required the decision to indicate the identity of the respective Member State, specify the grounds for refusal, and, where appropriate, the essence of the reasons for the objection to enable the concerned individual to seek legal remedy also regarding the objection of the other Member State, as this enables the individual to seek legal remedy against both Member States and hence at both courts responsible.[281]

Notifications on refusal, revocation, or annulment decisions under ETIAS may also include incomplete information. They do include a reason for refusal, revocation, or annulment (eg the conclusion that an applicant poses a security risk) and do not reveal the underlying reasoning and the relevant data or criteria.[282] Also, they do include information about the ETIAS National Unit responsible for the decision (and the manual processing) but not about the other authorities responsible for the data on which the decision is based.[283] Consequently, the notification requirements under ETIAS[284] must be interpreted in light of the CFR as requiring substantiated explanations that specify the data and the criteria the decision is based on, as well as information on the other authorities that have entered data in the respective databases.

The ETIAS Regulation neither requires that the concerned individual is informed about entries in the ETIAS watchlist at any point nor does it grant any individual rights in that respect. This would result in a situation where individuals cannot challenge watchlist entries with the risk of being denied travel authorizations in the future. Therefore, individuals should be informed about their data being stored in the watchlist where the application has reported a hit against the watchlist, and a travel authorization is then refused due to a high security risk.

For risk assessment criteria and models, it is problematic to determine how much information must be revealed. This holds true especially for the right of access to the decision-making logic.[285] The GDPR and EUDPR require the controller to inform data subjects 'if automated decision-making, including profiling' takes place, and to provide data subjects 'at least in those cases' with meaningful information on the decision-making logic and consequences for the data subject. The

[280] Section C.II.1.
[281] Joined Cases C-225/19 and C-226/19 *R.N.N.S. and K.A. v Minister van Buitenlandse Zaken* (2020) ECLI:EU:C:2020:951 (in the context of the Visa Code), paras 51 ff, especially 56.
[282] Brouwer takes a critical view (n 207) 503; European Data Protection Supervisor, 'Opinion 3/2017 on the Proposal for a European Travel Information and Authorisation System (ETIAS)' (2017), para 78.
[283] See section C.II.1.
[284] ETIAS Regulation, arts 38(2), 42.
[285] EUDPR, art 15(2)(f); GDPR, art 15(1)(h).

wording 'at least in those cases' implies that the obligation to reveal the decision-making logic is not limited to cases of automated decisions but also to some cases of profiling that decisions are not solely based on.[286] The intensity of the interferences of multiple-identity detection with the MID and of ETIAS risk assessments with Articles 7, 8 CFR argues for the controllers' obligation to reveal the decision-making logic also to secure the right to legal remedy (Article 47 CFR) as decisions might, in fact, be based solely or mainly on this logic.[287] It remains unclear how much information on risk assessment algorithms and models themselves must be revealed.[288] To exercise their rights, the individual concerned (and the responsible court) must be enabled to assess the lawfulness of decisions concerning them, including the sufficient individual review of processing results and the non-discriminatory nature of the decision-making logic.[289] This especially comprises information about the factors taken into account and their respective weight.[290]

It could be argued that revealing the risk indicators that the ETIAS screening rules are based on to an individual leads to the risk of circumvention of the risk indicators, and therefore the public interest to keep them secret out-balances the concerned individual in transparency. However, at least, during the judicial review by a court, such criteria must be revealed to check their legality.

If ML-trained risk assessment models are used, as eu-LISA, the Commission, Europol, and Frontex envisage for ETIAS risk assessments,[291] revealing underlying criteria could be impossible if such systems are non-transparent. In the PNR judgment, the CJEU has stressed that non-transparent ML-trained models that make an appropriate individual review of their results impossible may also undermine the right to an effective legal remedy.[292]

[286] Pesch, Dimitrova, and Boehm (n 15) 62; Sebastião Barros Vale and Gabriela Zanfir-Fortuna, 'Automated Decision-Making Under the GDPR: Practical Cases from Courts and Data Protection Authorities' (Future of Privacy Forum 2022) 18; Gianclaudio Malgieri and Giovanni Comandé, 'Why a Right to Legibility of Automated Decision-Making Exists in the General Data Protection Regulation' (2017) 7(4) International Data Privacy Law 250 f, assume the phrase 'at least' just points to voluntary information by the controller.

[287] Pesch, Dimitrova, and Boehm (n 15) 62.

[288] ibid 62.

[289] cf ibid 62.

[290] Article 29 Working Party, 'Guidelines on Automated individual decision-making and Profiling for the purposes of Regulation 2016/679' (2018) wp251rev_01 p 27. On a right to explanation of individual decisions see Diana Dimitrova, *Data Subject Rights: The Rights to Access and Rectification in the Area of Freedom, Security and Justice* (PhD Dissertation at the Vrije Universiteit Brüssel, 2021); Margot E Kaminski, 'The Right to Explanation, Explained' (2019) 34 Berkeley Technology Law Journal 189; Sandra Wachter, Brent Mittelstadt, and Luciano Floridi, 'Why A Right to Explanation of Automated Decision-Making Does Not Exist in the General Data Protection Regulation' (2017) 7(2) International Data Privacy Law 76, 79ff argue a right to explanation does not exist under the GDPR; Andrew D Selbst and Julia Powles 'Meaningful Information and the right to explanation' (2017) 7(4) International Data Privacy Law 233; Gianclaudio Malgieri, 'Automated Decision-Making in the EU Member States: The Right to Explanation and Other "Suitable Safeguards" in the National Legislations' (2019) 35(5) International Data Privacy Law 243.

[291] See section B.II.3.

[292] Case C-817/19 *Ligue des droits humains ASBL v Conseil des ministers* (2022) ECLI:EU:C:2022:491 (PNR judgment), para 195; also cf Desara Dushi, 'Human Rights in the Era of Automated Decision

Even under the assumption that sufficient transparency is provided for, it might be difficult for individuals to exercise their rights. The probabilistic nature of ETIAS risk assessments affects the enforcement of rectification requests as, for probabilistic results, the determination of accuracy is difficult.[293] For probabilistic data to be accurate, their probabilistic nature must be apparent from the data.[294] To be processed lawfully, data must furthermore be based on a probabilistic method that is sufficiently reliable and that leads to reasonable results.[295] Otherwise the processing of the data cannot be considered necessary for the intended purpose[296] and creates a disproportionate interference with Articles 7, 8 CFR.[297] In accordance with the accountability principle,[298] the data must allow for assessing these requirements.[299] In practice, even with complete information it is hard for TCNs to prove that the underlying risk assessment criteria such as the MID algorithm[300] or the ETIAS screening rules[301] are not sufficiently reliable.

Summarizing the above, there are doubts about the exercise of individual rights and the effectiveness of legal remedies, particular because the EIF Regulations and the ETIAS Regulation do not explicitly require sufficient information for TCNs about decisions concerning them, specifically the relevant data, applied criteria, substantiated reasons, and authorities that have influenced a decision. In practice, TCNs might not be able to obtain information that they understand due to language barriers.

III. Independent supervision

An effective supervision in data protection law is crucial for both, enabling data subjects to exercise their individual rights and ensuring the protection of personal data where individuals themselves do not exercise their rights. Article 8(3) CFR, as well as Articles 39 of the Treaty on European Union (TEU), 16(2) of the Treaty on the Functioning of the European Union (TFEU), require an independent

Making and Predictive Technologies' (*Asia-blogs* 2022) <https://asia-blogs.org/2022/04/11/human-rights-in-the-era-of-automated-decision-making-and-predictive/> accessed 20 June 2024; Danielle Keats Citron, 'Technological Due Process' (2008) 85(6) Washington University Law Review 1249, 1298ff.

[293] Pesch, Dimitrova, and Boehm (n 15) 63. On the applicability of the accuracy principle to non-factual data see Dimitrova (n 160) 4f.

[294] Pesch, Dimitrova, and Boehm (n 15) 63; Fröwis and others (n 159) 5.

[295] Pesch, Dimitrova, and Boehm (n 15) 63.

[296] ibid 63.

[297] See section C.I.

[298] GDPR, art 5(2); EUDPR, art 4(2); LED, art 4(4).

[299] Pesch, Dimitrova, and Boehm (n 15) 63; Fröwis and others (n 159) 5.

[300] See section B.I.3.

[301] See section B.II.1.

authority to control data protection compliance. Effective, independent supervision forms an essential part of data protection.[302]

Because, in the context of ETIAS and the EIF, multiple authorities are involved in the data processing, the processing and the decision-making based on it are subject to supervision by multiple authorities. For ETIAS, national data protection authorities (DPAs) supervise the ETIAS National Units, and the European Data Protection Supervisor supervises the ETIAS Central Unit, eu-LISA, and Europol.[303] For the personal data processing by the Member States under the EIF, the National DPAs are responsible.[304] For the data processing by eu-LISA, the ETIAS Central Unit and Europol, the EIF Regulations require audits by the European Data Protection Supervisor,[305] who is the responsible for the supervision of the agencies.[306] All information systems under the scope of the EIF are subject to coordinated supervision by the European Data Protection Supervisor and the national supervisory authorities.[307] Coordinated supervision requires the cooperation of the authorities which involves agreeing on harmonized proposals for solutions for any problems.[308] The European Data Protection Board (EDPB) has created[309] the Coordinated Supervision Committee (CSC)[310] that consists of the European Data Protection Supervisor, twenty-seven Member State DPAs, and three supervisory authorities of non-EU Schengen members (Iceland, Liechtenstein, and Norway).[311]

While the harmonized interpretation and application of data protection law is desirable and coordinated supervision promotes that goal, coordinated supervision does not solve the problem of delineating the supervisory authorities'

[302] Case C-518/07 *European Commission v Federal Republic of Germany* (2010) ECR-I-01885, para 23; Case C-614/10 *European Commission v Republic of Austria* (2012) ECLI:EU:C:2012:631, para 37; Case C-362/14 *Maximillian Schrems v Data Protection Commissioner* (2015) ECLI:EU:C:2015:650, para 41.

[303] ETIAS Regulation, arts 66(1), (3), 67.

[304] EIF Regulations, art 51(1).

[305] EIF Regulations, art 52.

[306] EUDPR, art 52(2); Regulation (EU) 2018/1726 of the European Parliament and of the Council of 14 November 2018 on the European Union Agency for the Operational Management of Large-Scale IT Systems in the Area of Freedom, Security and Justice (eu-LISA), and amending Regulation (EC) No 1987/2006 and Council Decision 2007/533/JHA and repealing Regulation (EU) No 1077/2011 (2018) OJ L295, art 35; Regulation (EU) 2019/1896 of the European Parliament and of the Council of 13 November 2019 on the European Border and Coast Guard and repealing Regulations (EU) No 1052/2013 and (EU) 2016/1624 (2019) OJ L295, art 86(1); Europol Regulation, art 43.

[307] ETIAS Regulation, art 68(1); EIF Regulations, art 53(1), (2); EUDPR, art 62, just as VIS Regulation art 43, SIS Regulation art 71, Eurodac Regulation art 32, ECRIS-TCN Regulation, art 30, EES Regulation, art 57, Europol Regulation, art 44.

[308] cf ETIAS Regulation, art 68(2); EUDPR, art 62(2).

[309] In accordance with EUDPR art 62(3).

[310] cf Coordinated Supervision Committee, 'Rules of Procedure of the Coordinated Supervision Committee' (CSC2019) (CSC RoP), art 1.

[311] cf CSC RoP (n 310), art 2(1); European Data Protection Board, 'Members—Coordinated Supervision Committee' (EDPB) <https://edpb.europa.eu/csc/about-csc/members-coordinated-supervision-committee_en> accessed 20 June 2024.

responsibilities regarding the data processing and decision-making in the context of large-scale information systems. In cases of coordinated supervision, it is still required that the supervisory authorities each act within the scope of their respective competences and within the framework of their responsibilities.[312] Which supervisory authority is responsible for the data processing and decision-making in the context of the MID or ETIAS depends on the responsibilities of the authorities involved in the data processing and decision-making. This conglomerate of different supervisory authorities makes supervision highly complicated and possibly non-transparent for the individual.

Albeit both the ETIAS Regulation and the EIF Regulations specify the responsibilities of the involved authorities, neither of the regulations addresses the problem of ADM and the involvement of multiple authorities in the relevant systems. Where an individual complains about a decision, the supervisory authorities must be able to assess their responsibility and the lawfulness of the decision. Like the exercise of rights, this requires transparency of the data used, the authorities who have entered the data, and the criteria applied, and risk assessment systems used.

Even with full transparency, however, it can be difficult to determine the authorities responsible in certain cases. For example, where in the context of multiple-identity detection a decision is based on the automated processing with the MID and the sBMS, the European Data Protection Supervisor as the supervisor of eu-LISA might also bear responsibility, as eu-LISA is responsible for the technical development of both components.[313] For cases where the automated ETIAS risk assessment reports a hit, the ETIAS National Unit bears the responsibility for both, examining the application and the decision to issue or refuse a travel authorization.[314] However, due to the influence of the data stored in the relevant databases, the ETIAS screening rules, and possibly further risk assessment systems, multiple supervisory authorities can be responsible. The ETIAS Central Unit is responsible for the definition of the specific risk indicators, that is, the screening rules.[315] For the ETIAS watchlist, Europol and the Member States are each responsible for the data they enter into the watchlist.[316]

Connecting large-scale information systems that multiple authorities are responsible for does not only make the delineation of responsibilities difficult, but also confronts supervision with more complexity.[317] Like in other areas such as the financial sector, supervision can only tackle the complexity of increasingly

[312] EUDPR, art 62(1, 2); EIF Regulations, art 53(1, 2); ETIAS Regulation, art 68(1).
[313] EIF Regulations, arts 54(3), 55(1).
[314] ETIAS Regulation, art 8(2)(a).
[315] ETIAS Regulation, art 7(2)(c).
[316] ETIAS Regulation, arts 34(3), 35(4).
[317] European Data Protection Supervisor, 'Opinion 4/2018 on the Proposals for two Regulations establishing a framework for interoperability between EU large-scale information systems' (2018), paras 22f.

connected systems with sufficient human and financial resources[318] and appropriate supervisory instruments.

D. Conclusion and outlook

Both risk assessments with the MID and in ETIAS automate decisions, at least to some extent. While it is currently impossible to assess the reliability of the risk assessment criteria and systems that are still in development, there are doubts about the quality of data used in the assessments and for the specification of risk assessment criteria. The legal frameworks lack clarity and safeguards with regard to the individual review of the results of automated risk assessments (section C.I). The authorities responsible for the decision-making must therefore fill the regulatory gaps with clear guidelines on the manual assessment of automated processing results and provide for sufficient training of human decision-makers to counterbalance the intense interferences with the fundamental rights to privacy and data protection (Articles 7, 8 CFR). The development of the risk assessment systems should not only comprise thorough accuracy testing based on clear guidelines and accuracy metrics but also empirical studies with real users to design the systems in a way that safeguards the individual review of processing results. This requires sufficient transparency of the risk assessment criteria and relevant data to human decision-makers. The authorities will furthermore have to provide concerned individuals with more information than the legal frameworks explicitly require (section C.II). In particular, they need to give substantiated reasons for their decisions to enable individuals to exercise their rights and seek legal remedy (Articles 8(2), 47 CFR). There remain practical concerns about the exercise of rights especially with regard to language barriers, and rectification rights for which it can be difficult to prove that data is inaccurate and processed unlawfully. At the same time, the complexity of the systems and the number of authorities involved can impede effective supervision (section C.III).

If non-transparent ML-trained risk assessment models are used to support decisions, this might impair the legitimacy of the decision-making procedure with regard to the individual review of the risk assessment results (section C.I) and the right to legal remedies (section C.II). We have argued that the ETIAS Regulation must be interpreted as precluding the use of automated risk assessment systems to support the ETIAS National Units' manual assessments, as eu-LISA, the Commission, Europol, and Frontex have proposed (section C.I.2).

Our analysis discussed selected fundamental rights concerns. The EIF components and ETIAS risk assessments can also conflict with other aspects of the

[318] ibid para 23.

fundamental right to data protection (Article 8 CFR), such as data retention[319] and purpose limitation,[320] and with other provisions of the Charter, especially the right to good administration (Article 41 CFR) and the non-discrimination principle (Article 21 CFR). Also, the analysis covers MID and ETIAS risk assessments, while other instruments in the context of Smart Borders may raise similar problems. This is subject to further research and particularly regards the planned screenings based on the Commission's Proposal for a Screening Regulation, risk assessments based on PNR data, and screenings in VIS.

Against the background of ever increasing technological complexity, ensuring fundamental rights protection at smart borders is only possible with an ongoing interdisciplinary debate. To protect the especially vulnerable group of TCNs, the public, supervisory authorities, and jurisdiction must pay keen attention to the practices of the authorities involved and hold them continually accountable for ensuring fundamental rights compliance. Regular checks, impact assessments, and the overview of testing phases belong to this process.

[319] cf Article 29 Working Party, 'Opinion on Commission proposals on establishing a framework for interoperability between EU information systems in the field of borders and visa as well as police and judicial cooperation, asylum and migration' (2018) WP266, 10.

[320] Niovi Vavoula, 'Interoperability of EU Information Systems' (n 28) 147f; European Data Protection Supervisor, 'Opinion 4/2018 on the Proposals for two Regulations establishing a framework for interoperability between EU large-scale information systems' (2018), para 62; Article 29 Working Party, 'Opinion on Commission proposals on establishing a framework for interoperability between EU information systems in the field of borders and visa as well as police and judicial cooperation, asylum and migration' (2018) WP266, 11.

7

Between Humans and Machines

Judicial Interpretation of the Automated Decision-Making Practices in the EU

Sümeyye Elif Biber

A. Introduction

In the European Union (EU), recent judicial rulings have provided more precise interpretations of automated decision-making (ADM) practices. The right not to be subject to automated decisions, as described in Article 22 of the General Data Protection Regulation (GDPR),[1] was brought to the Court of Justice of the European Union (CJEU) on 16 March 2023, making the first instance of such consideration.[2] The case concerns credit scoring used in Germany, known as 'Schufa', and whether credit scoring can be considered an automated decision. Additionally, another significant case related to Article 22 of the GDPR came out in the Netherlands. The Court of Appeal in Amsterdam (*Gerechtshof Amsterdam*) found that several automated processes, including assigning rides, calculating prices, rating drivers, calculating 'fraud probability scores', and deactivating drivers' accounts in response to suspicions of fraud on Uber's and Ola platforms, are considered as automated decisions.[3]

In light of these contemporary examples within the EU, this chapter aims to systematize the ADM practices and explores the role of judicial interpretation in defining these activities and involvement of humans in decision-making processes. The chapter is divided into three sections focusing on machines, humans, and courts. It begins by exploring the concrete uses of ADM in the EU (section B. Machines). From there, it delves into how these systems are currently being utilized by taking into account two official reports published by the EU institutions. The

[1] Regulation (EU) 2016/679 of the European Parliament and of the Council of 27 April 2016 on the protection of natural persons with regard to the processing of personal data and on the free movement of such data, and repealing Directive 95/46/EC (General Data Protection Regulation) (2016) OJ L119/1.

[2] Opinion of Advocate General Pikamäe, *OQ v Land Hesse*, Joint Party: Schufa Holding AG, Case 634/21, 16 March 2023.

[3] Amsterdam Court of Appeal (*Gerechtshof Amsterdam*), ECLI:NL:GHAMS:2023:796, Case No 200.295.747/01, 4 April 2023; ECLI:NL:GHAMS:2023:793, 200.295.742/01, 4 April 2023; ECLI:NL:GHAMS:2023:804, Case No 200.295.806/01, 4 April 2023.

Sümeyye Elif Biber, *Between Humans and Machines* In: *Governance of Automated Decision-Making and EU Law.*
Edited by: Herwig C.H. Hofmann and Felix Pflücke, Oxford University Press. © Sümeyye Elif Biber 2024.
DOI: 10.1093/9780198919575.003.0007

objective is to provide nuanced insights into the current applications of ADM systems, avoiding overly broad generalizations. Following this analysis, the research identifies the socio-technical quality of ADM practices and argues how this quality necessitates meaningful human participation in decision-making processes. The chapter then examines the human-centric provisions of the relevant EU legal instruments surrounding ADM systems and targeting human participation (section C. Humans). Finally, it examines four judicial cases which surfaced public and private contexts in the Netherlands, Italy, and Germany (section D. Courts). In conclusion, the chapter identifies three key aspects of judicial interpretation regarding ADM practices: (i) epistemic; (ii) substantial, encompassing socio-technical and legal dimensions; and (iii) methodological. It argues that these aspects prove the pivotal role of judicial interpretation in comprehending the technical aspects of automation and ensuring meaningful human participation in decision-making processes.

B. Machines: The first instances

In the artificial intelligence (AI) age, the decision-making landscape is undergoing a profound transformation. Significant decisions about modern life are increasingly delegated from human hands to algorithmic machines.[4] Algorithms are 'a series of instructions that instruct a software package to take a dataset and learn a model or discover some underlying pattern'.[5] An ADM system 'augments or replaces human decision-making by using computational processes to produce answers to questions either as discrete classifications or continuous scores'.[6] Such decision-making has been implemented in complex areas involving public and private contexts, including social benefits, migration and border control, and loan or mortgage applications. As such systems become more prevalent in modern life, it is important to consider the complexities they introduce to decision-making and to examine their social and legal impacts thoroughly.

However, as noted by an Italian court in 2019, ADM systems possess the quality of 'multidisciplinary characterization' (*caratterizzazione multidisciplinare*), requiring not only legal, but technical, computer, and statistical skills.[7] This situation makes it even more difficult to understand the complexities posed by such

[4] Karen Yeung, 'The New Public Analytics as an Emerging Paradigm in Public Sector Administration' (2022) 27(2) Tilburg Law Review 1–32.

[5] David Leslie and others, 'Artificial Intelligence, Human Rights, Democracy, and the Rule of Law: A Premier' (2021) Council of Europe and Alan Turing Institute, 36 https://edoc.coe.int/en/artificial-intelligence/10206-artificial-intelligence-human-rights-democracy-and-the-rule-of-law-a-primer.html accessed 10 October 2023.

[6] ibid 36.

[7] Consiglio di Stato, Sec IV, n 2270, 8 April 2019, para 8.3.

systems. Therefore, legal scholars resort to analogical thinking and explore the similarities first between the new digital technology in question and the previous ones. However, the use of analogy in those examples has demonstrated that it does not sufficiently meet the nature of what a particular technology is, and thus misses many of its unique features.[8] It is important to note that incorrect conceptualizations of technologies which often rest on the use of analogy can lead to incorrect normative results in the legal sphere, as also recognized by a recent judgment of the District Court of the Hague (*Rechtbank Den Haag*), which argues that if we base our knowledge of technologies on properties and use terms such as 'self-learning', and make wrong analogies between the human person and a new technology, we are then unable 'to properly justify actions and to properly substantiate decisions' in an administrative system.[9]

Considering this issue, this chapter takes into account two official reports published by the EU institutions which provide empirical research on the current uses of automated systems used by the public sector: 'Getting the Future Right: Artificial Intelligence and Fundamental Rights' published by the Fundamental Rights Agency in 2020[10] (hereafter Report I) and 'AI Watch Artificial Intelligence in Public Services: Overview of the Use and Impact of AI in Public Services in the EU' published by the Joint Research Centre in 2020 (hereafter Report II).[11] The purpose is to be concrete on the current uses of ADM systems and to avoid examining the systems at stake on an overgeneralized fashion. Considering the two reports, the most critical examples used in the public sector are observed in the fields of social benefits and biometrics.

The Organisation for Economic C-operation and Development (OECD) defines social benefits as 'current transfers received by households intended to

[8] On the controversial analogies between states and social platforms see Kate Klonick 'The New Governors: The People, Rules, and Processes Governing Online Speech' (2017) 131 Harvard Law Review 1599–603.

[9] The Hague District Court (*Rechtbank Den Haag*), ECLI:NL:RBDHA:2020:865, Case No C-09-550982/HA ZA 18-388, 5.2.2020, at para 6.46, stating from the opinion of the Advisory Division: 'The term "self-learning" is confusing and misleading: an algorithm does not know and understand reality. There are predictive algorithms which are fairly accurate in predicting the outcome of a court case. However, they do not do so on the basis of the substantive merits of the case. They can therefore not substantiate their predictions in a legally sound manner, while that is required for all legal proceedings for each individual case. . . . The reverse also applies: the human user of such a self-learning system does not understand why the system concludes that there is a link. An administrative organ that partially bases its actions on such a system is unable to properly justify its actions and to properly substantiate its decisions.'

[10] European Union Agency for Fundamental Rights (FRA), 'Getting the Future Right: Artificial Intelligence and Fundamental Rights' (2020) (Report I) https://fra.europa.eu/sites/default/files/fra_uploads/fra-2020-artificial- intelligence_en.pdf accessed 13 July 2023.

[11] European Commission (EC), 'AI Watch Artificial Intelligence in Public Services: Overview of the Use and Impact of AI in Public Services in the EU' (2020) Science for Policy Report by the Joint Research Centre (Report II) https://publications.jrc.ec.europa.eu/repository/handle/JRC120399 accessed 13 July 2023. At the civil society level, see also EDRi, 'Use Cases: Impermissible AI and Fundamental Rights Breaches' (2020) https://edri.org/wp-content/uploads/2021/06/Case-studies-Impermissible-AI-biometrics-September-2020.pdf accessed 13 July 2023.

provide for the needs that arise from certain events or circumstances, for example, sickness, unemployment, retirement, housing, education or family circumstances'.[12] The Report I underlines that automated systems used in public administration include areas such as benefit calculations, fraud prevention and detection, eligibility assessments, and risk scoring.[13] The purpose of governments is to enhance the efficiency of decision-making on these issues. In the context of social benefits, the Report I explains two important areas where ADM systems are used for decisions—housing and unemployment benefits.[14] In these areas, rule-based decision-making is applied, defined based on 'if–then rules'.[15] For instance, a person will be eligible for a certain income if she/he has an income below a certain threshold.[16] Table 7.1 sketches three artificial intelligence (AI) practices in the field of social benefits, defining their purposes, data sources, and 'black-box' aspects.[17]

Table 7.1 ADM systems in the field of social benefits.[18]

ADM Systems in the Area of Social Benefits	Purpose	Data Source	Techniques—The 'Black Box' Aspects
Deciding on Housing Benefits (Report I)	Efficiency (to speed up tasks)	**Internal database** containing data on benefit application processes Data is pseudonymized	**Processing applications** **Rule-based decision-making** Decision-tree model following the rules In particular, 'a simple statistical model (linear regression) is used where the input is the income and the cost limits, and the outcome is the amount of benefit'.[19]

[12] OECD, Glossary of Statistical Terms, Social Benefits Definitions, https://stats.oecd.org/glossary/detail.asp?ID=2480 accessed 13 September 2023.
[13] Report I (FRA) (n 10).
[14] ibid. It is worth noting that according to the report, the organization used this AI system has firstly used image processing to process applications in order to decide on such social benefit applications.
[15] ibid 27.
[16] ibid.
[17] The data is collected from Report I (FRA) (n 10) and Report II (EC) (n 11). The table is generated by the author.
[18] The data is collected from Report I (FRA) (n 10) and Report II (EC) (n 11). The table is created by the author.
[19] Report I (FRA) (n 10).

Table 7.1 Continued

ADM Systems in the Area of Social Benefits	Purpose	Data Source	Techniques—The 'Black Box' Aspects
Deciding on Unemployment Benefits (Report I)	Efficiency	**Various databases** containing the population register and tax authorities' databases to obtain information about salaries and work experiences	**Processing applications** **Rule-based decision-making:** 'if all conditions are fulfilled, the system calculates the period of payments and the amount of benefits in the light of the period of payments and the average daily salary'.[20]
Automating Various Social Assistance Decisions (Report II)[21] Processing applications on homecare, sickness benefits, unemployment benefits, and taxes	Efficiency	Personal data through the self-service portal	Robotic Process Automation (RPA)[22] Rule-based decision-making

In this field, these systems include processing the applications first and deciding on these applications second. Due to the complexity of the systems used, the techniques on decision-making should be considered as the 'black-box' aspects of the ADM practice at stake, meaning that such systems are producing results without clear or understandable explanations of how the results have been reached.[23] This quality is particularly significant because, as the Hague Court highlighted, citizens could neither anticipate the intrusion into their private life nor can they guard themselves against it.[24]

All three practices are developed as rule-based decision-making. In the last practice, robotic process automation (RPA) has been used in the municipality of

[20] Report I (FRA) (n 10).

[21] Report II notes that this system is used in Trelleborg, Sweden in 2015. As of 2020, 75 per cent of the citizens use the online platform to access welfare payments. See the Report II (EC) (n 11) 43–44.

[22] Report II does not provide sufficient information about this system. It only considers this system as an 'automated decision-making system' in n 11. Therefore, this part of the research is conducted through the report of the 'Algorithm Watch', which reported this issue in 2020. See in Katarina Lind and Leo Wallentin, 'Central Authorities Slow to React as Sweden's Cities Embrace Automation of Welfare Management' (2020) https://algorithmwatch.org/en/trelleborg-sweden-algorithm/ accessed 13 July 2023.

[23] Frank Pasquale, *The Black Box Society: The Secret Algorithms That Control Money and Information* (Harvard UP 2015).

[24] The Hague District Court, Case No C/09/550982/HA ZA 18-388, 5 February 2020, para 6.65.

Trelleborg, Sweden, since 2016, noted by Report II.[25] Despite in-depth conversations in major media outlets, neither the public officials or the company which developed the system have provided satisfactory answers regarding how the system works, nor how it makes decisions.[26] Furthermore, such a system makes decisions on the basis of its data sources. It is therefore necessary to take into consideration the fact that the data source may not provide sufficient, necessary, or even correct information. This critical observation emphasizes the importance of human intervention in these areas.

In the case of biometrical systems, two fields are prominent in public use: predictive policing and migration and border control management. Table 7.2 sketches the two use cases in this area based on Report I[27] and Report II,[28] defining their purposes, data sources, and 'black-box' aspects.

Table 7.2 ADM systems in the field of biometrics (law enforcement).[29]

ADM systems in the Area of Biometrics—Law Enforcement	Purpose	Data Source	Techniques—The 'Black-Box' Aspects
Predictive Policing (mapping crime patterns, detecting online hate speech,[30] preparing risk assessment on gender-based violence) (Report I)	Efficiency (to speed up tasks) Security	**Historical crime and police data** (containing crime reports, witness statements, suspect declarations)	**Data mining and machine learning processes and predictive analytics, simulation, and data visualization** Analysing data to identify common patterns and trends and creating models on the basis of this analysis to predict crimes, perpetrators, or victims

[25] Report II (EC) (n 11).

[26] Lind and Wallentin (n 21). It is worth noting that a journalist, Freddi Ramel, lodged an appeal to the Administrative Court of Appeal under the Sweden's Freedom Information Act to see the code of the system. Trelleborg argued that the code was a trade secret. However, the Court decided that the code of the system is a public document and therefore 'the source code has to be made accessible to the public and is fully included in the principle of public access'. Available in Anne Kaun, 'Suing the Algorithm: The Mundanization of Automated Decision-Making in Public Services through Litigation' (2021) Information, Communication & Society 1–17.

[27] Report I (FRA) (n 10).

[28] Report II (EC) (n 11).

[29] The data is collected from the Report I (FRA) (n 10). The table is created by the author.

[30] According to Report I (FRA) (n 10), a public agency uses an AI system to detect online hate speech.

Table 7.2 Continued

ADM systems in the Area of Biometrics—Law Enforcement	Purpose	Data Source	Techniques—The 'Black-Box' Aspects
		Environmental data such as population density, the presence of certain public places and services, and major events or holidays **Personal data** (real-time and historical data used) in predicting potential perpetrators and victims (including criminal records, addresses, phone numbers, location data)	Creating a 'heat map' outlining the prevalence of certain crimes in certain areas In the case of gender-based violence, the AI system produces a 'risk score' on the basis of the risk of repetition that is evaluated by the police in the light of the level of gravity and the nature of threats (Report I)
Migration and Border Control Management	Efficiency and Security	**Personal data** evaluating facial expressions and behaviours	Biometric identification, biometric categorization, and emotion recognition system

Both Report I and Report II do not provide any specific use case about the AI-driven ADM systems used for migration and border control management. However, newer AI techniques are being developed to control borders and to provide a decision support system for border authorities.[31] Moreover, this area is particularly significant as all the three systems of biometrics mentioned in the table, biometric identification, categorization, and emotion recognition systems, can be used in this area.[32] According to a recent empirical study, the existing uses of digital technologies across European immigration and asylum systems include forecasting tools, processing of short- and long-term residency and citizenship applications, risk assessment and triaging systems, speech recognition, distribution of welfare benefits, matching tools, mobile phone data extraction, and electronic

[31] The project of iBorderCtrl at https://perma.cc/L7KM-TPFK accessed 13 July 2023.

[32] New technologies serving in this area are categorized within the area of 'smart borders' technologies. See Javier Sánchez-Monedero and Lina Dencik, 'The Politics of Deceptive Borders: "Biomarkers of Deceit" and the Case of iBorderCtrl' (2022) 25(3) Information, Communication & Society 414. See also the UK's smart border technology to detect deception at https://post.parliament.uk/research-briefings/post-pn-375/ accessed 16 September 2023. See also the US version called 'AVATAR', an automated lie detector and a deception detection technology based on eye tracking at https://discernscience.com/avatar/ accessed 16 September 2023.

monitoring.[33] Due to such a rich variety of advanced technological systems, this field is called a 'human laboratory',[34] where people are used as 'test subjects' for such systems.

As a case study, the 'iBorderCtrl' project funded under EU Horizon 2020 over a thirty-six-month period can be considered in this regard. The main objective of this project is 'to enable faster and thorough border control for third country nationals crossing the land borders of EU Member States (MS), with technologies that adopt the future development of the Schengen Border Management'.[35] The project brings together many technologies including biometric verification, automated deception detection, document authentication, and risk assessments in one system.[36] The project team evaluated these technologies with the border control officers' assistance from Hungary, Latvia, and Greece, who were the three end-users of the project.[37] However, the project has received severe criticism from digital rights journalists,[38] scholars,[39] and civil society organizations.[40] They have highlighted concerns regarding the technology's accuracy as well as issues related to bias, discrimination, privacy, due process, and procedural fairness.

Furthermore, in 2018, 'Homo Digitalis', an organization focusing on the protection of digital rights in Greece and a member of European Digital Rights, filed a petition to the Greek Parliament regarding the pilot implementation of the iBorderCtrl project on the Greek border.[41] They underlined the concerns

[33] Derya Ozkul, 'Automating Immigration and Asylum: The Uses of New Technologies in Migration and Asylum Governance in Europe' (Refugee Studies Center, Oxford 2023) 5–6 https://www.rsc.ox.ac.uk/publications/automating-immigration-and-asylum-the-uses-of-new-technologies-in-migration-and-asylum-governance-in-europe accessed 27 October 2023.

[34] EDRi, 'Technological Testing Ground: Migration Management Experiments and Reflections from the Ground Up' (2020) 16, https://edri.org/our-work/european-court-supports-transparency-in-risky-eu-border-tech-experiments/ accessed 18 September 2023.

[35] The project's website is https://www.iborderctrl.eu/The-project accessed 6 October 2023. See also European Commission, 'Intelligent Portable Border Control System: Periodic Reporting for Period 2—iBorderCtrl (Intelligent Portable Border System) https://cordis.europa.eu/project/id/700626/reporting accessed 6 October 2023.

[36] See the details of the project at https://cordis.europa.eu/project/id/700626/reporting (accessed on 3 July 2024).

[37] European Commission, 'Intelligent Portable Border Control System' (2023) n 35.

[38] Ryan er and Ludovica Jona, 'We Tested Europe's New Lie Detector for Travelers – and Immediately Triggered a False Positive' (2019) The Intercept https://theintercept.com/2019/07/26/europe-border-control-ai-lie-detector/ accessed 6 October 2023 (quoting Ray Bull, professor of criminal investigation at the University of Derby: 'The technology is based on a fundamental misunderstanding of what humans do when being truthful and deceptive.').

[39] Dimitri Van Den Meerssche, 'Virtual Borders: International Law and the Elusive Inequalities of Algorithmic Association' (2022) 33(1) European Journal of International Law 171–204; Niahm Kinchin and Davoud Mougouei, 'What Can Artificial Intelligence Do for Refugee Status Determination? A Proposal for Removing Subjective Fear' (2022) 34(3–4) International Journal of Refugee Law 373–97; Sánchez-Monedero and Dencik (n 32) 413–30.

[40] Petra Molnar, 'Technological Testing Grounds: Migration Management Experiments and Reflections from the Ground Up' (European Digital Rights Refugee Law Lab 2020) https://edri.org/our-work/regulating-migration-tech-how-the-eus-ai-act-can-better-protect-people-on-the-move/ accessed 18 September 2023.

[41] Eleftherios Chelioudakis, Homo Digitalis, EDRi, 'Greece: Clarifications Sought on Human Rights Impacts of iBorderCtrl' https://edri.org/our-work/greece-clarifications-sought-on-human-rights-impacts-of-iborderctrl/ accessed 18 September 2023.

regarding the lack of transparency and trust in the actual capabilities of the AI systems employed in the project. The petition also underscored the high risk of discrimination against individuals based on specific categories of personal data.[42] However, the 'black-box' aspects of the project have not been unlocked. The project was filed before the CJEU to disclose information about the ethics reports and the legal assessments regarding the technological system concerned and how it works.[43] The General Court argued that the public interest justifies the disclosure of the relevant documents:

> there is a public interest in participating in an informed, open, and democratic debate regarding the question, whether control technologies, as the one mentioned, are desirable, if they should be funded via public money, and that this public interest must be duly respected.[44]

However, the Court arguably concluded that the public interest in disclosing information should begin only after the completion of research.[45] It is also important to note that in the case of an ADM use with law enforcement purposes such as prevention, detection, or prosecution of criminal offences, that ADM is subject to the Law Enforcement Directive[46] (*lex specialis*) which provides lower standards compared to the General Data Protection Regulation (GDPR) in terms of transparency and data protection rights.[47]

I. ADM systems as socio-technical systems

The use cases examined above have proved that ADM systems are more than just technological systems. They are social systems that mediate social institutions and structures.[48] They are used in different social, public, and human services. In

[42] ibid.

[43] CJEU, *Breyer v REA*, Case T-158/19, 15 December 2021.

[44] ibid para 200 stating the importance of democratic oversight of such technologies, in verbatim, '[es besteht] ein Interesse der Öffentlichkeit daran . . . an einer informierten öffentlichen und demokratischen Diskussion über die Frage teilzunehmen, ob Kontrolltechnologien wie die in Rede stehenden wünschenswert sind und ob sie durch öffentliche Gelder finanziert werden sollen, und dass dieses Interesse gebührend gewahrt werden muss'.

[45] ibid paras 200203. On 7 September 2023, the CJEU upheld this decision in C-135/22P, 7 September 2023, paras 64–112.

[46] Directive (EU) 2016/680 of the European Parliament and the Council of 27 April 2016 on the protection of natural persons with regard to the processing of personal data by competent authorities for the purposes of the prevention, investigation, detection or prosecution of criminal offences or the execution of criminal penalties, and on the free movement of such data, and repealing Council Framework Decision 2008/977/JHA, OJ L119/89, 4 May 2016.

[47] Teresa Quintel, Data Protection, *Migration and Border Control: The GDPR, The Law Enforcement Directive and Beyond* (Hart 2022)

[48] Nathalie Smuha and others, 'How the EU can Achieve Legally Trustworthy AI: A Response to the European Commission's Proposal for an Artificial Intelligence Act' (2021) LEADS Law, University of Birmingham for a Legal, Ethical and Accountable Digital Society, 12 https://papers.ssrn.com/sol3/pap

particular, AI-driven ADM systems for deciding on social benefits, making risk assessments and producing risk scores of individuals, and identifying, categorizing, and detecting individuals and their behaviours or their emotions[49] clearly affect and form social structures and institutions.

In the field of philosophy of technology, the social aspect of AI-driven ADM systems is identified through the notion of relational ethics.[50] According to the relational understanding of AI, AI is able to recognize the interaction between people and technology, and how complex infrastructures are affected by society and by human behaviours. In other words, AI-driven ADM systems have an impact on people, interpersonal interactions, and society as a whole because they are able to recognize these social components of their environment. Therefore, the notion of relational ethics proposes that AI should be considered as a *socio-technical* system that is much more than an automation technique. In this regard, it suggests an investigation within the dynamics of the situation in which the decision is taken to see what is 'right'.[51]

The relational understanding of AI helps separate the technical and social aspects of AI, although the two are closely intertwined. While the technical aspect is related to the black-box aspects or decision trees of an AI system, thereby presenting an epistemic problem, the social aspect is related to the data it collects. Indeed, the data possesses a social dimension, given that it originates from societal sources. The AI systems examined above obtain social data, such as social expressions, behaviours, events, emotional reactions, and common patterns or mistakes. This overview underscores a crucial aspect of AI systems: namely, individuals are not only subjected to their own data regarding their own actions and choices but also to the aggregated data that is collected from similarly situated individuals and weaves social contexts of individuals. In the context of AI systems used in the field of migration and border control, this social context is widely built, including different publics coming from different countries.

In other words, the judging framework of AI-driven ADM systems is built on the basis of actions and behaviours not attributable to a single individual. This situation means that the outcome of an ADM system examined above will never be a personal decision but a social one that encompasses not only a single social community but diverse communities. Therefore, it is necessary to protect not

ers.cfm?abstract_id=3899991 accessed 13 July 2023 (stating that such systems cannot be considered solely as consumer or technical products).

49 See an interesting discussion stating that emotion AI systems detect physical signals or muscle movements not emotions in Lisa Feldman Barrett, 'Darwin was Wrong: Your Expressions Do Not Reveal Your Emotions' (2022) Scientific American https://www.scientificamerican.com/article/darwin-was-wrong-your-facial-expressions-do-not-reveal-your-emotions/ accessed 4 October 2023.

50 Virginia Dignum, 'Relational Artificial Intelligence' (2022) arXiv:2202.07446, 2022, https://arxiv.org/abs/2202.07446 accessed 16 September 2023.

51 However, it is not an easy task as it requires multidisciplinary and multi-stakeholder participation.

only individual interests but also collective interests.[52] This situation proves that such systems have the potential to produce significant consequences for individuals, minorities, and society in general. They are particularly sensitive in terms of the protection of fundamental rights and can pose life-changing social consequences.[53] Therefore, it is imperative to engage human input in decision-making processes to avert such outcomes. This situation necessitates a critical assessment of the human-centric provisions of the relevant EU legal instruments to understand whether they adequately facilitate human participation in decision-making processes.

C. Humans: 'Human intervention' and 'human oversight'

European legal instruments on digital technologies acknowledge the importance of the human factor in the era of automation.[54] Despite being in its early stages, European digital legal framework is strongly committed to ensuring that humans play an active role in decision-making. This human-centric approach sets Europe apart on a global scale, distinguishing it from the United States and China.[55] While the United States is adopting a market-driven approach and China is promoting a state-driven approach, the EU is pursuing a rights-driven human-centric approach.[56] On 26 January 2022, the Commission also published the European Declaration on Digital Rights and Principles for the Digital Decade defining the European position on digital transition as 'putting people at the centre' which emphasizes that rights and freedoms should be duly respected online—just as they are offline.[57]

The reflection forms of this perspective and its connection with ADM systems can be found both in the GDPR and the draft AI Act. Under Article 22

[52] Such a conclusion necessitates the full consideration of the existing formulations of the rule of law, as some approaches solely focus on protecting individual interests. See a relevant discussion on this issue in Anuj Puri, 'Rule of Law, AI, and the 'Individual' (*Verfassungsblog*, 2022) https://verfassungsblog.de/roa-individual/ accessed 27 August 2023.

[53] Sümeyye Elif Biber, 'Machines Learning the Rule of Law: EU Proposes the World's First Artificial Intelligence Act' (*Verfassungsblog*, 13 July 2021) https://verfassungsblog.de/ai-rol/ accessed 27 August 2023.

[54] It is impossible to cite here all European legal instruments surrounding digital technologies. However, the most prominent legal instruments are the GDPR (Regulation (EU) 2016/179, OJ L119/1), the Digital Services Act (DSA) Regulation (EU) 2022/2065, OJ L277/1, the draft AI Act (European Commission, COM/2021/206 final), and the Consolidated Working Draft of the Framework Convention on Artificial Intelligence, Human Rights, Democracy and the Rule of Law (CAI(2023)18).

[55] Anu Bradford, *Digital Empires: The Global Battle to Regulate Technology* (OUP 2023).

[56] Anu Bradford, 'The Race to Regulate Artificial Intelligence: Why Europe has an Edge over America and China' Foreign Affairs (27 June 2023) https://www.foreignaffairs.com/united-states/race-regulate-artificial-intelligence?utm_medium=promo_email&utm_source=lo_flows&utm_campaign=registered_user_welcome&utm_term=email_1&utm_content=20231106 accessed 9 August 2023.

[57] European Declaration on Digital Rights and Principles for the Digital Decade, Brussels, 26.1.2022 COM(2022) 28 final.

of the GDPR,[58] data subjects have the right not to subjected to decisions with legal and 'significant effects' 'based solely on automated decision-making' or profiling.[59] This means that the GDPR prohibits *in general* automated decision-making that does not involve meaningful human intervention. It only allows such decision-making in specific circumstances, according the conditions set in the second paragraph: (i) if it is necessary for contractual aims, (ii) if it is authorized by Union or Member State law, or (iii) if it is based on the data subject's explicit consent. When automated decisions are exceptionally allowed in one of these described circumstances, the data controller shall implement safeguarding measures for the data subject, such as the right to be informed, the right to obtain human intervention, and the right to challenge the decision.[60] Furthermore, the GDPR also limits the use of sensitive data in ADM systems to mitigate potential discriminatory effects. Processing such kind of data[61] is only permissible with the explicit consent of the data subject or a substantial public interest.[62]

However, legal scholarship has underlined that the wording of Article 22 leaves an extensive room for interpretation, and that interpretation plays a key role in clarifying its scope.[63] In particular, the question of whether there is a meaningful human intervention in an ADM process that can circumvent the prohibition defined in Article 22 can only be understood on a case-by-case basis.[64]

While this situation poses a critical challenge for judges in terms of setting clear and consistent interpretations, the very fact that their interpretations hold decisive authority reveals the significance of judicial interpretation on this issue.

[58] GDPR (n 1).

[59] Art 22 of the 2016 GDPR is the main EU legal norm on the right not to be subject to automated decision-making. However this right is not a recent development in the EU. It is first recognized in French Law in art 2 of the 1978 French Law on Data Processing, Data Files and Individual Liberties (Loi no 78-17 du 6 janvier 1978 relative à l'informatique, aux fichiers et aux libertés, at https://www.legifrance.gouv.fr/loda/id/LEGIARTI000006528060/1978-07-23/#LEGIARTI000006528060), and then respectively reflected in arts 12 and 15 of the 1995 'Directive 95/46/EC on the protection of individuals with regard to the processing of personal data and on the free movement of such data' (OJ L281/31), art 6 of the 1981 'Council of Europe Convention for the Protection of Individuals with regard to Automatic Processing of Personal Data' (ETS 108), and finally art 22 of the GDPR (n 1).

[60] Art 22(3) of the GDPR (n 1). It is important to note that this provision must be systematically read in line with the transparency rights described in arts 13 and 15 and Recital 71 of the GDPR.

[61] Art 9 of the GDPR (n 1).

[62] Art 22(4) and (a) and (g) paragraphs of Art 9(2) of the GDPR (n 1).

[63] Frederike Kaltheuner and Elettra Bietti, 'Data is Power: Towards Additional Guidance on Profiling and Automated Decision-Making in the GDPR' (2018) 2(2) Journal of Information Rights, Policy and Practice 10; Reuben Binns and Michael Veale, 'Is That Your Final Decision? Multi-Stage Profiling, Selective Effects, and Article 22 of the GDPR' (2021) 11(4) International Data Privacy 319–32.

[64] Sebastião Barros Vale and Gabriela Zanfir-Fortuna, 'Automated Decision-Making under the GDPR: Practical Cases from Courts and Data Protection Authorities' (2022) Future Privacy Forum, 28 https://fpf.org/blog/fpf-report-automated-decision-making-under-the-gdpr-a-comprehensive-case-law-analysis/ accessed 27 August 2023.

Another critical legal instrument of the EU, the draft AI Act,[65] also mandates 'human oversight' requirements to ensure that fundamental rights of individuals are protected:[66]

> Human oversight shall aim at preventing or minimising the risks to health, safety or fundamental rights that may emerge when a high-risk AI system is used in accordance with its intended purpose or under conditions of reasonably foreseeable misuse, in particular when such risks persist notwithstanding the application of other requirements set out in this Chapter.[67]

Moreover, in the fourth paragraph of this provision, the draft AI Act recognizes individual autonomy by authorizing the human person who is responsible for human oversight to 'decide, in any particular situation, not to use the high-risk AI system or otherwise disregard, override or reverse the output'.[68]

However, the normative power of the Article is not sufficient to achieve this purpose, as it does not consider the difference between AI-driven ADM systems and human beings in terms of 'cognition'.[69] It is obvious that humans are not capable of examining the whole entire data mining process nor validating the outputs of AI systems in a meaningful way.[70] The human person might only detect obvious failures. This situation also makes it difficult to detect human gender bias replicated in the ADM system.[71] Therefore, human oversight provisions alone cannot be considered as an effective resort for the fundamental rights challenges that ADM systems pose. Alone, they can neither legitimate the use of the ADM system nor the decisions that the system takes. In fact, the system cannot be considered a

[65] Proposal for a Regulation of the European Parliament and of the Council Laying Down Harmonised Rules on Artificial Intelligence (Artificial Intelligence Act) and amending certain Union Legislative Acts COM(2021) 206 final.

[66] The human oversight requirement is applied in Germany in a different way. German approach excludes the use of automated systems for administrative acts requiring the use of discretion. This approach means that only humans can exercise discretion. See a comment on this issue in Paul Nemitz and Eike Grzäf, 'Artificial Intelligence Must Be Used According to the Law, or Not at All' (*Verfassungsblog*, 2022) https://verfassungsblog.de/roa-artificial-intelligence-must-be-used-according-to-the-law/ accessed 17 September 2023.

[67] Art 14 of the draft AI Act (n 65).

[68] Art 9/4(d) of the draft AI Act (n 65).

[69] Manuel Alfonseca and others, 'Superintelligence Cannot be Contained: Lessons from Computability Theory' (2020) 70 Journal of Artificial Intelligence Research 1–7.

[70] See an excellent empirical study on the inadequacy of human oversight in Ben Green, 'The Flaws of Policies Requiring Human Oversight of Government Algorithms' (2022) 45 Computer Law & Security Review 1–22. (demonstrating that people are unable to perform the desired oversight function, and proposing institutional oversight). See also Ben Green and Amba Kak, 'The False Comfort of Human Oversight as an Antidote to AI Harm' (2021) Future Tense, https://slate.com/technology/2021/06/human-oversight-artificial-intelligence-laws.html accessed 17 August 2023.

[71] World Wide Web Foundation, 'Policy Brief W20 Argentina, Artificial Intelligence: Open Questions about Gender Inclusion' (2018) http://webfoundation.org/docs/2018/06/AI-Gender.pdf accessed 17 September 2023.

legitimate device in a democratic society unless its use is proven legal, necessary, and proportionate.[72]

However, the human oversight requirement is still crucial and can be advanced as one of the ways for humanizing the digital government. Indeed, the proposal warns the human person who is responsible for the oversight to be 'aware of the possible tendency of automatically relying or over-relying on the output produced by a high-risk AI system'.[73] This tendency refers to 'undue deference to automated systems by human actors that disregard contradictory information from other sources or do not (thoroughly) search for additional information',[74] known as 'automation bias'.[75] It is promising that the proposal is aware of this tendency.[76] Still, other aspects must be considered. In future iterations, the AI Act should also consider that the excessive digitalization of government services and the automation of decision-making might exclude the unique human feature of forgiving trivial mistakes, such as misspelling names or dates when filling out benefit applications or tax returns.[77] Overall, a rigorous approach must consider that the system itself might have bias, the human person who is reviewing the system might also have bias ('automation bias'), and the individual who is subject to the system might make trivial mistakes due to, for instance, digital illiteracy or ignorance. The

[72] Art 52 of the EU Charter, which provides that 'any limitation on the exercise of the rights and freedoms recognised by this Charter must be provided for by law and respect the essence of those rights and freedoms. Subject to the principle of proportionality, limitations may be made only if they are necessary and genuinely meet objectives of general interest recognised by the Union or the need to protect the rights and freedoms of others'.

[73] Art 14(4)(b) of the draft AI Act (n 65).

[74] Saar Alon-Barkat and Madalina Busuioc, 'Human–AI Interactions in Public Sector Decision-Making: "Automation Bias" and "Selective Adherence" to Algorithmic Advice' (2022) Journal of Public Administration Research and Theory 7–8 https://papers.ssrn.com/sol3/papers.cfm?abstract_id=3794660 accessed 17 August 2023 (discussing that there are two reasons for this bias, namely 'the perceived inherent superiority of automated systems by humans' and 'cognitive laziness' referring to 'human reluctance to engage in cognitively demanding mental process'). It is important to note that the 'cognitive laziness' of the human person who is examining the system cannot be an excuse for an unfair situation created by an ADM system. After all, the system must pass the necessity test, and cannot serve the purpose of exacerbating injustice in society.

[75] ibid.

[76] Indeed, the over-reliance on the outputs of a high-risk AI system is extremely dangerous. Spanish government, for instance, used an AI system called 'VioGén' to estimate the risk of recidivism in gender violence. According to the Algorithmic Watch, however, the system failed in its predictions. Fourteen out of the fifteen women who were killed in a domestic violence incident in 2014, having reported their aggressor before, had been classified by the system as being at low or non-specific risk. See in Algorithmic Society Report, 'Algorithmic Society' (2020) 227, https://automatingsociety.algorithmwatch.org/wp-content/uploads/2020/12/Automating-Society-Report-2020.pdf accessed 13 July 2023 See also the news on this issue reported by *El Mundo*, 'Las asesinadas que denunciaron se valoraron como "riesgo bajo o nulo"' https://www.elmundo.es/espana/2014/12/09/54861553ca4741734b8b457e.html accessed 13 July 2023. See also an article on the function of the system in José Luis González Álvarez et al, 'Integral Monitoring System in Cases of Gender Violence VioGén System' (2018) 4(1) Behavior & Law Journal http://www.interior.gob.es/documents/642012/1626283/articulo+violencia+de+genero/fd0e7095-c821-472c-a9bd-5e6cbe816b3d accessed 13 July 2023.

[77] Sofia Ranchordás, 'Empathy in the Digital Administrative State' (2022) 71 Duke Law Journal 1341–89 (discussing this issue within the concept of 'empathy' as a key value of administrative law).

current version of the proposal is far from addressing this standard as it does not sufficiently consider the first and last points presented here. However, in the following section, the chapter explains that judicial interpretation plays a critical role in providing guidance for such concerns.

D. Courts: Between humans and machines

In this section, the chapter focuses on four leading judgments on the concrete ADM practices that have been observed in the EU Member States. The purpose is not to discuss all the ADM-related cases observed in the EU but rather shed light on the role of courts in clarifying the socio-technical and legal aspects of automation and the human factor in decision-making processes. In this regard, the section examines the *SyRI*, *Buona Scuola*, *Schufa*, and *Uber* cases, respectively, which surfaced public and private contexts in the Netherlands, Italy, and Germany.

I. The *SyRI* case

The *SyRI* case from the Netherlands stands out as one of the most significant tech-related cases in the world.[78] It provides a clear example of the global trend towards the digitalization of the welfare state and the legal concerns surrounding it. As the UN Special Rapporteur on extreme poverty and human rights noted in 2019, the 'welfare state is gradually disappearing behind a webpage and an algorithm, with significant implications for those living in poverty'.[79]

The Dutch government is the first government in the EU to have applied AI-driven digital welfare technologies and, as a result, to have violated the rights of individuals. On the 5 February 2020, the District Court of the Hague (*Rechtbank Den Haag*) ruled that the use of the SyRI algorithm system ('System Risk Indication'), a digital welfare fraud detection system applied by the Dutch government, violated Article 8 of the European Convention of Human Rights (ECHR),[80] which guarantees the right to respect for private and family life, home and correspondence.[81]

According to the Dutch Legislator, SyRI was a technical infrastructure linking and analysing data anonymously, with the ability to generate risk reports that

[78] The Hague District Court (*Rechtbank Den Haag*), ECLI:NL:RBDHA:2020:865, Case No C-09-550982/HA ZA 18-388, 5.2.2020, at paras 6.1–6.118.

[79] UN Human Rights Council (2019) 'Visit to the United Kingdom of Great Britain and Northern Ireland: Report of the Special Rapporteur on extreme poverty and human rights', A/HRC/41/39/Add.1', 23 April, https://ap.ohchr.org/documents/dpage_e.aspx?si=A/HRC/41/39/Add.1 accessed 13 October 2023.

[80] European Convention on Human Rights, 4 November 1950, 213 UNTS 221.

[81] The *SyRI* case (n 78) paras 6.1–6.118.

address legal or natural persons considered 'worthy of investigating with regard to possible fraud, unlawful use and non-compliance with legislation'.[82] Certain bodies of the Dutch government applied this algorithm in collaboration by exchanging data to identify the perpetrators of related abuses.

The claimants, several human rights activists and non-governmental organizations, stated that the national legislation on SyRI does not have sufficient safeguards for the protection of private life, with the result that its binding effect was deemed invalid. The District Court of the Hague reviewed the algorithm's legislation and the usage of the algorithm by the Dutch government mainly based on Article 8 of the ECHR, the Charter of Fundamental Rights of the European Union (CFR), and the principles established in the GDPR, particularly the principle of transparency, the principle of purpose limitation, and the principle of data minimization. In this context, the Court analysed the 'extent and seriousness of the interference' with Article 8 of the ECHR based on the SyRI Legislation and the information about the algorithm provided by the State.[83]

To identify the scope of interference, the Court focused mainly on the functioning of the algorithm. The Court concluded that the SyRI legislation did not provide sufficient information about the functioning of the system particularly related to the risk models consisting of risk indicators, risk analysis methods applied in the system, and the generation of the decision trees. Therefore, the Court found a violation under Article 8 of the ECHR on the basis of lacking information about the system in the SyRI legislation.[84] The main problem, which led to a violation of the Convention, is that the function of the SyRI has remained opaque in the legislation. The problem of lack of transparency in the legislation also illustrates the concentration of private power behind the system.[85]

The claimants also referred to Article 22 of the GDPR. They argued that 'the submission of a risk report . . . can be considered a decision with legal effect, or at least a decision that affects the data subjects significantly in another way, and that this decision is taken on the basis of automated individual decision-making within the meaning of Article 22 GDPR, which is prohibited'.[86] The Court agreed

[82] ibid para 3.2.

[83] It is important to note that the Hague Court highlighted the special responsibility of the state when applying to such kind of technologies and their extensive and increasing interference with the right to respect for private life in the light of the case of *S. and Marper v the United Kingdom* of the European Court of Human Rights, para 6.84.

[84] The *SyRI* case (n 78) paras 6.1–6.118.

[85] Matteo Turilli and Luciano Floridi, 'The Ethics of Information Transparency' (2015) 11 Ethics and Information Technology 105 (defining transparency as a pro-ethical condition for enabling or impairing other ethical principles or practices); Jenna Burrell, 'How the Machine Thinks: Understanding Opacity in Machine Learning' (2016) 3(1) Big Data and Society, January–June 2016, 1 (according to the author, opacity might stem from three forms, namely state or corporate secrecy, technical illiteracy, and from the characteristics of machine learning algorithms and the scale required to apply them usefully). See also Mireille Hildebrandt, 'The Dawn of a Critical Transparency Right for the Profiling Era' in Jacques Bus and others (eds), *Digital Enlightenment Yearbook* (IOS Press 2012) 41.

[86] The *SyRI* case (n 78) para 6.57.

with the claimants that a risk report had a '"significant effect" on the private life of the person to whom the risk report pertains'.[87] However, it noted that such a risk report did not have the legal effect. The Court did not 'give an opinion on whether the exact definition of automated individual decision-making in the GDPR and, insofar as this is the case, one or more of the exceptions to the prohibition in the GDPR have been met. That is irrelevant in the context of the review by the court whether the SyRI legislation meets the requirements of Article 8 ECHR.'[88] To conclude, the Dutch Court in its SyRI judgment clarified that legislation on ADM systems should articulate the functioning of ADM systems in clear terms.

II. The *Buona Scuola* case

Another significant judicial case on ADM systems has been observed in Italy. The ADM practice was concerned with using a teacher placement algorithm (known as '*algoritmo della buona scuola*', 'good-school algorithm' in English),[89] which sparked extensive public debate and prompted public administrative decisions in 2019.[90] In this case, the Italian Ministry of Education used software to make efficient and swift decisions on the placements of newly selected teachers and process the mobility requests of already employed teachers. According to the Mobility Rankings 2016, the algorithm made structural mistakes by assigning thousands of teachers[91] to incorrect professional placements in practice.[92] Furthermore, according to the Algorithm Watch, the system automictically compelled some teachers with autistic children to relocate from the southern region of Calabria to Prato, in the northern region of Tuscany.[93]

Two critical judgements on this issue have offered significant legal interpretations making concrete the principle of transparency and the human factor. First, in April 2019, the Italian Council of State (*Consiglio di Stato*) found that 'the use of "robotic" procedures cannot justify circumventing the principles that shape our

[87] ibid para 6.59.

[88] ibid para 6.60.

[89] Marcia de Angelis, 'Algoritmi nei concorsi pubblici: il caso dei docenti che fa "scuola"' *Ius in Itinere*' (3 October 2019) <https://www.iusinitinere.it/algoritmi-nei-concorsi-pubblici-il-caso-dei-docenti-che-fa-scuola-23299> accessed 15 October 2023.

[90] Stefano Civitarese Matteucci, '"Umano troppo umano". Decisioni amministrative automatizziate a principio di legalità (2019) (1) Dritto Pubblico Il Mulino, January–April 4–41.

[91] According to Repubblicca, at least 10,000 teachers are affected: 'Scuola, trasferimenti di 10 mila docenti lontano da casa. Il Tar: "L'algoritmo impazzito fu contro la Costituzione"', https://www.repubblica.it/cronaca/2019/09/17/news/scuola_trasferimenti_di_10mila_docenti_lontano_da_casa_il_tar_l_algoritmo_impazzito_fu_contro_la_costituzione_-236215790/ accessed 15 October 2023.

[92] Fabio Chiusi, 'Italy/Contextualization: A Lauder Conversation, but mostly around "AI"' in 'Automating Society Report 2020', Algorithm Watch, https://automatingsociety.algorithmwatch.org/report2020/italy/ accessed 15 October 2023.

[93] ibid.

legal system and regulate the conduct of administrative activities'.[94] In this regard, the algorithm, which has a legal value, must comply with the general principles of administrative activity, such as transparency, reasonableness, and proportionality.[95] Furthermore, the Council of State interpreted the transparency principle that requires 'the full knowability of any rules expressed in a language other than the judicial one'.[96] This 'full knowability' ('*piena conoscibilità*') includes the decision-making procedure and the relevant data of that system in order to verify whether the outcomes of the 'robotic procedure' comply with the legal requirements.[97] It is crucial to emphasize that the Council of State does not advocate for the complete disclosure of the system's code in question. Instead, it calls for a clear explanation of its 'technical formula' that both judges and citizens can comprehend.[98]

In September 2019, the second key judgment came on this issue from the Administrative Court of Lazio (*Tribunale Amministrativo Regionale del Lazio*). The Court focused on the human factor and pointed out that human judgment is irreplaceable, and automation may only play 'a merely auxiliary and instrumental role', rather than taking a 'dominant or surrogate' position within the administrative process:[99]

> informatics procedures, even when they reach their highest level of precision and even perfection, they can never fully replace, truly supplant, the cognitive, inquisitive, and judgmental activities that only an inquiry entrusted to a physical person is capable of performing.[100]

According to the Lazio Court, this interpretation is in line with the Italian Constitution and Article 6 of the ECHR,[101] which prevents a 'deleterious Orwellian perspective' where the decision-making is entirely handed over to machines.[102] While the Lazio Court did not concretize Article 6 of the ECHR concrete in the

[94] Consiglio di Stato, Sec IV, n 2270, 8 April 2019, para 8.2: 'L'utilizzo di procedure 'robotizzate' non può, tuttavia, essere motivo di elusione dei princìpi che conformano il nostro ordinamento e che regolano lo svolgersi dell'attività amministrativa'.

[95] The *Buona Scuola* case (Consiglio di Stato) (2019) (n 94) para 8.2.

[96] ibid para 8.3: 'il meccanismo attraverso il quale si concretizza la decisione robotizzata (ovvero l'algoritmo) deve essere "conoscibile", secondo una declinazione rafforzata del principio di trasparenza, che implica anche quello della *piena conoscibilità* di una regola espressa in un linguaggio differente da quello giuridico'. The italic emphasis made by the author.

[97] The *Buona Scuola* case (Consiglio di Stato) (2019) (n 94) para 8.3.

[98] ibid.

[99] TAR Lazio-Roma, Section 3rd-Bis, n 10964, 10–13 September 2019.

[100] ibid. It states verbatim: 'le procedure informatiche, finanche ove pervengano al loro maggior grado di precisione e addirittura alla perfezione, non possano mai soppiantare, sostituendola davvero appieno, l'attività cognitiva, acquisitiva e di giudizio che solo un'istruttoria affidata ad un funzionario persona fisica è in grado di svolgere'.

[101] ECHR (n 80).

[102] The *Buona Scuola* case (TAR Lazio-Roma) (2019) (n 99).

present case, the 'principle of good governance' is considered in the case law of the Strasbourg Court:

> the principle of 'good governance' requires that where an issue in the general interest is at stake it is incumbent on the public authorities to act in good time, in an appropriate manner and with utmost consistency.[103]

To conclude, considering these arguments, the Lazio Court underlined that algorithms should serve as supporting tools in public decision-making rather than assuming a primary role.

III. The *Schufa* case

The right not to be subject to automated decisions was considered for the first time in the *Schufa* case before the CJEU on 16 March 2023. The Schufa is a private German credit information agency responsible for evaluating the trustworthiness of customers seeking any contractual relationship including loans, mortgages, or house rentals through profiling their financial behaviours.[104] Based on that profiling, Schufa issues a certificate with a score and provides a positive or negative result about the person applied.[105] However, the company offers no reasonable or understandable reasoning about its evaluation. In other words, it does not disclose how the score is calculated.[106]

In 2018, an applicant who received a negative score requested Schufa to provide additional information about the negative result. Considering the underlying logic of their automated system as commercial and industrial secrecy, Schufa provided only the basic functioning of its automated system. The applicant waited for information about Schufa's profiling for two years despite filing a complaint with the German Data Protection Authority. Subsequently, the applicant appealed the decision before the Administrative Court of Wiesbaden (*Verwaltungsgericht Wiesbaden*). In October 2021, the Wiesbaden Administrative Court ('referring court') stayed the administrative proceedings and referred to the CJEU two questions regarding the interpretation of Article 22 of the GDPR, the right not to be

[103] ECtHR, *Moskal v Poland*, App No 10373/05, 15 September 2009, para 51.

[104] Opinion of Advocate General Pikamäe, *OQ v Land Hesse*, Joint Party: Schufa Holding AG, Case 634/21, 16 March 2023. Schufa describes its activities as follows: 'Credit scoring is all about the question of how probable it is that a person will meet their payments. This is very important information for companies or banks. It provides a data basis to help decide whether to provide credit or purchases on account. Thus reducing the risk of a default.' See at https://www.schufa.de/schufa-en/scores-data/scoring-at-schufa/#532026 accessed 23 October 2023.

[105] Currently, Schufa provides five score classes, namely 'insufficient', 'sufficient', 'acceptable', 'good', and 'excellent'. See https://www.schufa.de/scoring-daten/hilfe-ihrem-schufa-score/ (23 October 2023).

[106] The *Schufa* Case (AG) (2023) (n 104) para 2.

subject to automated decision-making which is granting data subjects the right 'not to be subject to a decision based solely on automated processing, including profiling, which produces legal effects concerning him or her or similarly significantly affects him or her'.[107] Hence, the German Administrative Court initiated the first example of such consideration before the CJEU.

The first matter focuses on clarifying the financial activity conducted by Schufa and questions whether credit scoring is an automated decision. Before analysing the matter, however, the Advocate General (AG) first emphasizes the distinctive character of Article 22(1) and states that that provision 'establishes a *general prohibition* on decision of the kind described' rather than a right to be invoked by the data subject.[108] In terms of interpretating Article 22 GDPR the AG suggests that:

> [t]he automated establishment of a probability value concerning the ability of a data subject to service a loan in the future constitutes a decision based solely on automated processing, including profiling, which *produces legal effects* concerning the data subject or *similarly significantly affects* him or her, where that value, determined by means of personal data of the data subject, is transmitted by the controller to a third-party controller and the latter, in accordance with consistent practice, *draws strongly on that value* for its decision on the establishment, implementation or termination of a contractual relationship with the data subject.[109]

In this regard, the AG argues that the scoring is considered as *profiling* within the meaning of Article 4(4) of the GDPR since the procedure in question 'uses personal data to evaluate certain aspects concerning their economic situation, reliability and probably behaviour'.[110] Secondly, the AG argues that the refusal of a credit has both *legal* and *significant* effects on the data subject since the data subject can no longer benefit from a contractual relationship with the financial institution and is affected significantly from a financial point of view.[111] This means that the action in question may have an impact that is not only legal but also economic and social.[112]

[107] Art 22 of the GDPR, n 1.

[108] The *Schufa* case (AG) (2023) (n 104) para 31. This interpretation aligns with the 2018 opinion of the European Data Protection Board, which endorsed the views presented in the Article 29 Working Part Guidelines, stating that '[t]he term "right" in the provision does not mean that Article 22(1) applies only when actively invoked by the data subject. Article 22(1) establishes a general prohibition for decision-making based solely on automated processing. This prohibition applies whether or not the data subject takes an action regarding the processing of their personal data.' In 'Article 29 Data Protection Working Party: Guidelines on Automated individual decision-making and Profiling for the purposes of Regulation 2016/679', WP251REV.01, 6 February 2018, 19.

[109] The *Schufa* case (AG) (n 104) para 59. The author has indicated emphasis through the use of italics.

[110] ibid para 33.

[111] ibid para 35.

[112] ibid para 38.

Thirdly, the AG questions what is the relevant 'decision' in the case at issue and underlines that in the decision-making process, there are multiple phases such as profiling, the establishment of the score, and the actual decision on the grant of credit.[113] He then highlights that the scoring by Schufa is a 'decision' within the meaning of Article 22(1) of the GDPR since it 'tends to *predetermine* the financial institution's decision to grant or refuse the credit to the data subject, such that this position must be considered only to have purely formal character in the process'.[114] According to the AG, the crucial factor is the effect that the 'decision' has on the data subject.[115] Considering that a negative score alone may produce negative impact on data subjects by restricting their freedoms and stigmatizing them in society, it makes sense to qualify that score as a 'decision' when a financial institution gives it paramount importance in the decision-making process.[116]

He concludes that in such circumstances, 'credit applicants are affected from the stage of the evaluation of their creditworthiness . . . not only at the final stage of the refusal to grant credit, where the financial institutions is merely applying the result of that evaluation to the specific case'.[117] It is also worth noting that the referring court states similar aspect: 'experience from the data protection supervision carried out by the authorities shows that the score plays the *decisive role* in the granting of loans'.[118]

He further considers the purpose of the EU Legislator through Article 22, which is to protect the rights of data subjects, and states that a restrictive interpretation of that provision would create a gap in legal protection where data subjects cannot exercise their rights and freedoms, particularly described in Articles 15(1)(h), 16, and 17 of the GDPR.[119]

Furthermore, the AG clarifies the content of Article 15(1)(h) regarding the obligation to provide 'information about logic involved'. He states that this information covers the calculation method used by a credit information agency unless there are no conflicting interests that are worthy of protection such as the right to protection of intellectual property under Article 17(2) of the CFR.[120] In light of joint reading of Recitals 58 and 63 and Article 12(1) of the GDPR, the AG concludes that 'the obligation to provide 'meaningful information about the logic involved' must be understood to include sufficiently detailed explanations of the method used to calculate the score and the reasons for a certain results'.[121] Moreover, considering the complexity of algorithms, the AG emphasizes that the principle of transparent information and communication in Article 12 of the GDPR does not establish any

113 ibid para. 40.
114 ibid para 47.
115 ibid para 43.
116 ibid para 43.
117 ibid para 43.
118 ibid para 46.
119 ibid paras 48–50, namely the right to information, the right to rectification and the right to erasure.
120 ibid para 54.
121 ibid para 58.

obligation for the controller to disclose the algorithm since there is no benefit of commutating a complex formula without providing a necessary explanation.[122]

Finally, to reply to the second question posed by the referring court, the AG explains that Article 6(1) and Article 22 do not prevent domestic legislation from profiling as long as it falls outside the scope of Article 22 of the GDPR. However, in this case, the national court must comply with the requirements outlined in Article 6 of the GDPR which includes relying on an appropriate legal basis. The AG Opinion holds notable importance as it marks the initial judicial interpretation of the legal term 'automated decision', clarifying that if an algorithm predominantly influences decision-making, the activity of that algorithm qualifies as an 'automated decision' within the meaning of Article 22 of the GDPR.

IV. The *Uber* case

On 4 April 2023, the Court of Appeal in Amsterdam (*Gerechtshof Amsterdam*) found that several automated processes including assigning rides, calculating prices, rating drivers, calculating 'fraud probability scores', and deactivating drivers' accounts in response to suspicions of fraud on Uber's and Ola platforms are considered as automated decisions in three judgments.[123] In particular, the Court's judgment on the deactivation decisions taken against Uber drivers has been crucial with regard to ADM systems and human participation. In this case, the Dutch Court has argued whether the deactivation decision taken against Uber drivers, which means they can no longer work through Uber, are automated decisions.[124]

First, the Court has considered the privacy statement of the company, which confirms that Uber makes an 'automated decision' when deactivating users 'who are identified as having engaged in fraud'.[125] Secondly, Uber has explained that Uber's Risk Team relies on software to automatically detect various fraudulent activities, such as when a driver repeatedly cancels rides within a short time period, which may suggest 'cancellation fraud'.[126] According to the Court of Appeal, this example has showed that Uber 'involves automated processing of personal data of drivers whereby certain personal aspects of them are evaluated on the basis of that data, with the intention of analysing or predicting their job performance, reliability and behaviour. As such, this processing meets the definition of profiling as contained in Article 4(4) of the GDPR.'[127] Thirdly, the Court has considered that the deactivation decisions addressed to drivers are worded in a very general

[122] ibid para 57.

[123] Amsterdam Court of Appeal (*Gerechtshof Amsterdam*), ECLI:NL:GHAMS:2023:796, Case No 200.295.747/01, 4.4.2023; ECLI:NL:GHAMS:2023:793, 200.295.742/01, 4.4.2023; ECLI:NL:GHAMS:2023:804, Case No 200.295.806/01, 4.4.2023.

[124] Amsterdam Court of Appeal (*Gerechtshof Amsterdam*), ECLI:NL:GHAMS:2023:793, 4.4.2023,

[125] The *Uber* case (n 124) para 3.21.

[126] ibid para 3.21.

[127] ibid para 3.21.

manner without mentioning any concrete conduct that forms the basis of decisions.[128] Furthermore, the Court found that the limited human intervention in Uber's automated decisions to dismiss workers was not 'much more than a purely symbolic act' considering also the fact that the Risk Team of the company is based in Kraków, Poland.[129] In other words, the Dutch Court clarified that human intervention should have a meaningful contribution to the decision-making process rather than a simply symbolic participation. Table 7.3 sketches all four cases examined in this chapter and illustrates the key legal provisions and their findings.

Table 7.3 Judicial interpretation of the ADM practices.[130]

Judicial Cases	Technical Framework of the ADM systems	Key Legal Provisions	Judicial Interpretation
The SyRI Case (The Netherlands) The Hague District Court	**Fraud detection system:** Generating risk reports about legal and natural persons considered worthy of investigating with regard to possible fraud	Article 8 of the ECHR	Legislation should articulate the functioning of an algorithm in clear terms.
The Buona Scuola Case (Italy) The Council of State & the Administrative Court of Lazio	**Teacher placement system:** Assigning thousands of teachers to an incorrect professional placement	Article 6 of the ECHR	Algorithms should serve as supporting tools in public decision-making rather than assuming a primary role
The Schufa Case (Germany) Advocate General Pikamäe	**Credit scoring system:** Providing its clients with information on the creditworthiness of consumers and producing a prediction on the basis of a mathematical statistical method of the probability of future behaviour, such as the repayment of credit	Article 22(1) of the GDPR Article 15(1) (h) of the GDPR	If an algorithm plays a primary role in decision-making, the activity of that algorithm is considered as an 'automated decision' within the meaning of Article 22 of the GDPR
The Uber Case (The Netherlands) The Court of Appeal	**Predicting job performance:** deactivating drivers' accounts in a generalized framework	Article 22(1)	Human intervention should have a meaningful contribution to the decision-making process rather than a simply symbolic participation

[128] ibid para 3.21.
[129] ibid para 3.24.
[130] The table is created by the author with the intention of summarizing the key aspects of the judicial cases examined in this chapter.

E. Concluding remarks

Similarly to the *bricolage* activity, judicial interpretation involves navigating a complex landscape of normativities that may not always appear seamlessly fused or unified.[131] When judges engage in interpreting laws, regulations, and legal principles, they often encounter a mosaic of norms and precedents, each with its own distinct nuances and interpretations. This process provides for making concrete the relevant legal norms and clarifies their rules.[132] The integration of algorithms into public and private decision-making processes and the mosaic landscape of Article 22 of the GDPR covering both public and private decision-makers have cascaded the complexity of this task, necessitating an intricate interplay between technological and legal components.

The judicial cases examined in this chapter have evinced that judicial interpretation is highly crucial for understanding both the socio-technical, and legal aspects of automation and the human factor in decision-making processes. Ultimately, the chapter has identified three aspects of judicial interpretation on ADM practices: (i) epistemic, (ii) substantial including socio-technical and legal aspects, and iii) methodological.

From an epistemic point of view, in all four cases judges struggled to describe the functioning and the purpose of the algorithm at stake. They tried to understand where, how, and for what purpose ADM systems have been used by the relevant public or private actors rather than understanding technical or computer science-related features of a particular system. In this sense, their judicial interpretation had started from defining the digital system at stake, namely defining the functioning of fraud detection, credit scoring, teacher placement, and dismissing workers, in the cases examined in this chapter.

From a substantial point of view, the courts have clarified socio-technical and legal aspects of automation and the human factor in decision-making-processes.

[131] For the use of '*bricolage*' in legal context, see Mark Tushnet, 'The Possibilities of Comparative Constitutional Law' (1999) 108 Yale Law Journal 1285–86. See also the definition of this activity in Claude Lévi-Strauss, *The Savage Mind* (University of Chicago Press 1966) 17–18. According to Lévi-Strauss there is a distinction between engineering and bricolage. The engineer approaches to a task with a predefined project in mind and works with the materials available to achieve it. The bricoleur, in contrast, makes do with 'whatever is at hand', with a set of tools and materials. Tushnet uses this term to explain the work of interpreters as they find themselves in an intellectual world that 'provides them with a bag of concepts "at hand", not all of which are linked to each other in some coherent way'.

[132] Friedrich Müller, *Arbeitsmethoden des Verfassungsrechts*' in *Enzyklopädie der Geisteswissenschaftlichen Arbeitsmethoden* (R. Oldenburg Verlag 1971) 123–90 (discussing that the process of making concrete legal norms involves extensive engagement with legal materials, including doctrines, commentaries, case law, comparative legal documents, and numerous texts that are not *identical* with the respective legal norm text); Friedrich Müller and Ralph Christensen, *Juristische Methodik—Band I—Grundlegung für die Arbeitsmethoden der Rechtspraxis* (11th edn, Dunker & Humblot 2013) 263; Matthias Klatt, *Making the Law Explicit: The Normativity of Legal Argumentation* (Hart Publishing 2008) 54–56 ('the text is only a "guideline", as such it has no claim to normativity . . . the rule is not the beginning, but the product of the process of the application of the law').

On the socio-technical side, the courts have demonstrated that it is necessary to have clear legislations on the functioning of ADM practices to ensure that the system at stake is explainable to human persons. In the *SyRI* case, the Dutch court has found that the relevant legislation did not provide sufficient information about the functioning of the fraud detection system particularly related to the risk models consisting of risk indicators, risk analysis methods, and the generation of the decision trees. It is also worth noting that understanding the basic functioning of the algorithm has become highly significant to determine the 'extent and seriousness' of individual rights interferences by ADM systems.

The Italian courts have also highlighted similar concerns in the *Buona Scuola* case regarding the teaching placement algorithm. The Italian Council of State has underlined the need for a clear explanation regarding the 'technical formula' of a particular ADM system to ensure the general principles of an administrative activity, such as transparency, reasonableness, and proportionality. On the same issue, the Lazio Court focused on the human factor and underlined that automation can only play an auxiliary role in decision-making rather than a dominant position. In this sense, both the *SyRI* and the *Buona Scuola* cases have clarified that (i) legislation should articulate the functioning of an algorithm in human-readable terms rather than complex computer codes, and (ii) algorithms should serve as supporting tools in public decision-making rather than assuming a primary role. The two arguments prove that in both cases involving public uses of ADM systems, the courts have largely emphasized public law principles while assessing the ADM system at stake such as the principles of legality and transparency.

From a legal perspective, the AG in the *Schufa* case and the Dutch Court in the *Uber* case have focused on the meaning of the 'automated decision' and the human intervention measure. In the *Schufa* case, the AG has clarified that 'credit scoring' is an 'automated decision' within the meaning of Article 22 of the GDPR when a financial institution gives it *paramount importance* in the decision-making process. In the *Uber* case, the Dutch Court has underlined that the deactivation decisions addressed to drivers are worded in a general manner without mentioning any concrete conduct that forms the basis of decisions and the limited human intervention in Uber's automated decisions to dismiss workers was not 'much more than a purely symbolic act'. In this sense, both aspects have clarified that (i) if an algorithm plays a primary role in decision-making, the activity of that algorithm is considered as 'automated decision' within the meaning of Article 22 of the GDPR, and (ii) the human intervention should have a meaningful contribution to the decision-making process rather than a simply symbolic participation. Both arguments demonstrate that in instances involving private uses of ADM systems, the courts have predominantly focused on elucidating how the ADM system in question was employed in decision-making by private entities.

From a methodological point of view, the judges' inquiry regarding automation and meaningful human participation has presented an interactional legal ground where the relevant normative actors interact with one another. The courts have considered the normative aspect of automation, the relevant provisions of the ECHR, the GDPR, and the relevant domestic legislation to clarify the roles of automation and humans in decision-making processes. In this sense, their reasoning has not been limited to scope of national legislation, but also included supranational and international legal provisions.

Ultimately, the three aspects of judicial interpretation, epistemic, substantial, and methodological, have proved the pivotal role that judges play in comprehending automation and ensuring meaningful human participation in decision-making processes. In doing so, judges have not only narrowed the divide between machines and humans but also law and digital society.

8

Freedom of Political Speech Lost in Translation?

The Four Regulatory Frames of Automated and Targeted Political Advertising in EU Law

Sam Wrigley, Miikka Hiltunen, and Päivi Leino-Sandberg

A. Introduction

A core function of advertising is to persuade viewers, listeners, and readers that a certain thing is desirable or true. Some advertisements, for example, try to persuade the audience that they should buy a certain product or take out a certain service, others that a certain issue is particularly important, and the individual should regard it in a certain way, and some others that a certain political party or politician would best represent the individual's interests is elected. However, not everybody is the same; some people find some messages more persuasive than others while some find different ways of presenting those messages more persuasive than others. It is here that targeted advertising comes into play. Alongside the growth of social media we have also seen a growth of interest in a more precise form of targeted and tailored political advertising: that of online targeted adverts, also referred to as micro-targeted adverts. Such adverts have been described as involving three main stages: '1) collecting personal data, 2) using those data to identify groups of people that are likely susceptible to a certain message, and 3) sending tailored online messages [to those groups]'.[1]

As technology has developed so too have the concerns about that technology. If such adverts have the potential to change our political beliefs and opinions, this will have an inevitable consequence for our democratic society. Following this line of reasoning, the European Parliament (EP) has explicitly called for strong regulation of such adverts, stating that they intend to defend citizens' rights 'to be treated fairly and equally [and] not to be manipulated'.[2] Indeed, the Parliament has warned that targeting:

[1] Tom Dobber, Ronan Ó Fathaigh, and Frederik J Zuiderveen Borgesius, 'The Regulation of Online Political Micro-Targeting in Europe' (2019) 8(4) Internet Policy Review, https://doi.org/10.14763/2019.4.1440, 3.

[2] European Parliament, *Transparency and targeting of political advertising: Amendments adopted by the European Parliament on 2 February 2023 on the proposal for a regulation of the European Parliament*

Sam Wrigley, Miikka Hiltunen, and Päivi Leino-Sandberg, *Freedom of Political Speech Lost in Translation?* In: *Governance of Automated Decision-Making and EU Law.* Edited by: Herwig C.H. Hofmann and Felix Pflücke, Oxford University Press.
 DOI: 10.1093/9780198919575.003.0008

> enables a fragmentation of the public debate about important societal issues, predatory voter analysis, selective outreach and, ultimately, the manipulation of the electorate. It also increases the risk of spreading of disinformation, and has been used for foreign electoral interference especially by non-democratic foreign entitles. Misleading or obscure advertising for political purposes is a risk because it influences the core mechanisms that enable the functioning of our democratic society. All this takes place despite already existing conditions for the processing of personal data, including for targeting and ad delivery, provided for in [the GDPR].[3]

The Parliament further argues that tailoring and targeting 'are subject to systemic abuse . . . which cannot be solved under the current framework'[4] and notes that 'strict limitations' are required to prevent the 'influencing [of a person's] democratic choices and their involvement in the public debate, as well as to protect democracy and the integrity of elections'.[5]

However, evidencing the harm created by online targeted political advertising may be harder than initially assumed. While the European Commission has asserted that 'the *Cambridge Analytica* scandal . . . revealed a need to address this phenomenon', this assertion was supported with references to commercial, rather than political, advertising.[6] Equally, while Cambridge Analytica was very boastful about the power of its advertising,[7] there is evidence that its involvement in recent electoral twists was (at best) rather exaggerated, at least within the context of Donald Trump's 2016 presidential election campaign[8] and the UK Brexit referendum.[9] While, therefore, there seems little doubt that Cambridge Analytica was selling its ability to manipulate voters and distort the democratic process,[10] it is very difficult to determine what impact online targeted political advertising actually had in these scandals—and therefore how large a threat that particular advertising approach might actually pose to the democratic process.

and of the Council on the transparency and targeting of political advertising (COM(2021)0731—C9-0433/2021—2021/0381(COD)), P9_TA(2023)0027 (2 February 2023), recital 47.

[3] ibid.

[4] ibid recital 47a.

[5] ibid recital 47d.

[6] European Commission, *Proposal for a Regulation of the European Parliament and of the Council on the transparency and targeting of political advertising*, COM(2021) 731 final ('Commission Proposal for Political Advertising Regulation'), 3–4.

[7] See eg Alexander Nix, 'The Power of Big Data and Psychographics' (Concordia Annual Summit, New York, 19 September 2016) <https://youtu.be/n8Dd5aVXLCc> accessed 1 June 2022.

[8] Jessica Baldwin-Philippi, 'The Myths of Data-Driven Campaigning' (2017) 34 Political Communication 627, 630.

[9] Letter from the Information Commissioner's Office to Julian Knight, MP (2 October 2020) <https://ico.org.uk/media/action-weve-taken/2618383/20201002_ico-o-ed-l-rtl-0181_to-julian-knight-mp.pdf> accessed 10 March 2023.

[10] See eg Channel 4 News, 'Cambridge Analytica Uncovered: Secret Filming Reveals Election Tricks' (19 March 2018) <https://www.youtube.com/watch?v=mpbeOCKZFfQ> accessed 10 March 2023.

Scientific evidence is equally divided on the issue. A study by Zarouali and others,[11] for example, created a fake social media site for students and profiled users according to the Big Five personality dimensions model.[12] The authors then targeted users who had been scored with a high extraversion trait and found that an advert tailored to that trait was more effective at changing voting intentions for those users than one which was not.[13] In another study, Papakyriakopoulos and others also found that it was possible to build personality models for users in Germany using only information obtained through Facebook.[14] However, social media did not necessarily reflect real life and that 'political preferences appearing on social media platforms cannot be assumed to be the same for the actual electorate'.[15] There is evidence that microtargeted voters were likely to be more loyal to their current party affiliations, finding that they were '7.8% less likely to change their mind [about voting intentions] during [a] campaign'.[16] Equally, targeted advertising can have an effect on voter turnout, with one study finding that a Facebook banner can be somewhat more persuasive at getting people to vote if it shows pictures of the user's close friends who have already voted.[17] While the banner only influenced roughly 0.14 per cent of the voting population, this could be as many as 340,000 votes,[18] and it is possible that more aggressive targeting could have increased this number. At the same time, however, another study has found that social media usage reduces turnout.[19] There is, then, at least some evidence that targeted advertising will affect voters, even if it remains difficult to say how effective such adverts actually are and what impact they actually have on users.[20]

11 Brahim Zarouali and others, 'Using a Personality-Profiling Algorithm to Investigate Political Microtargeting: Assessing the Persuasion Effects of Personality-Tailored Ads on Social Media' (2022) 49(8) Communication Research 1066.

12 The five personality dimensions in this model are extraversion, agreeableness, conscientiousness, neuroticism, and openness/intellect. More information about this model can be found at, for example, Jacob B Hirsh, Sonia K Kang, and Galen V Bodenhausen, 'Personalized Persuasion: Tailoring Persuasive Appeals to Recipients' Personality Traits' (2012) 23(6) Psychological Science 578, 579, citing Lewis R Goldberg, 'An Alternative "Description of Personality": The Big-Five Factor Structure' (1990) 59 Journal of Personality and Social Psychology 1216. It is also interesting to note that Cambridge Analytica used a substantially similar model, albeit renamed the 'OCEAN model'.

13 Zarouali and others (n 11).

14 Orestis Papakyriakopoulos and others, 'Social Media and Microtargeting: Political Data Processing and the Consequences for Germany' (2018) (2) Big Data & Society doi:10.1177/2053951718811844.

15 ibid 3.

16 Mathieu Lavigne, 'Strengthening Ties: The Influence of Microtargeting on Partisan Attitudes and the Vote' (2021) 27(5) Party Politics 965, 970.

17 Bond and others, 'A 61-Million-Person Experiment in Social Influence and Political Mobilization' (2012) 489 Nature 295. It must be noted that, at least in percentages, the number of affected users was not particularly high; turnout for users who received a banner displaying images of their friends were 0.39 per cent higher than turnout for users who received either no banner, or simply received a generic banner with no pictures. ibid 296.

18 ibid 297.

19 Federica Liberini and others, 'Politics in the Facebook Era: Evidence from the 2016 US Presidential Elections' (2018) University of Warwick Working Paper No 389, 27.

20 Papakyriakopoulos and others (n 14) 3; Thomas Christiano, 'Algorithms, Manipulation, and Democracy' (2022) 52(1) Canadian Journal of Philosophy 109, 110; Katharina Baum and others,

These uncertainties also affect possible regulatory design. When it comes to the regulation of online targeted political advertising, there are a number of different perspectives that the law could take. One option is to regulate such adverts through the regulation of personal data; since the actual acts of targeting and of tailoring require profiling, and that profiling requires personal data, a control on how one can use personal data will operate as a control on how one can use these types of adverts. Equally, we may look at the regulation of these adverts on a more general level, looking not at the regulation of online targeted political adverts *per se* but rather at online targeted adverts as a whole. Another option is to regulate from the perspective of the freedoms of expression and information; since such adverts involve political expression, and the receipt of political information, we may wish to regulate such adverts directly, with a view to respecting human rights. Finally (at least for our purposes), we may consider the regulation from the perspective of the market; while politicians, activists, or other political actors may want to use these adverts to spread a certain message, the creation and distribution of these adverts is itself also a business, and a regulation of how that business operates is one way to control these adverts.

Each of these approaches can be identified in EU and/or European Convention on Human Rights (ECHR) law, whether as something which has already been implemented, something that has been recently approved, or as a logical extension of other regulatory rules. Each are also examples of framing, defined by Windsor as 'the idea that the way a problem is presented can impact how that problem is understood and resolved'.[21] Each approach frames the topic in a very different way and, therefore, creates rules that build on different background assumptions and promote very different interests. Further, each approach is implemented and enforced by actors with different missions and tasks. This chapter will look at these different regulatory framings, identify some of the rules that have been created under those approaches, and consider how the law risks distorting the issue of online targeted political advertising. We do not necessarily call for a unified, *sui generis* or *lex specialis* law which will act as the singular and authoritative word on online targeted political advertising. However, we do wish to highlight how the choice of frame affects the emphasis of regulation and the outcome of its implementation. While much of the regulation is new, it is already evident that the regulatory framework lacks a unified perspective and consistent policy approach to online targeted political advertising throughout the law.

'Do They Really Care About Targeted Political Ads? Investigation of User Privacy Concerns And Preferences' (27th European Conference on Information Systems—Information Systems for a Sharing Society, Stockholm and Uppsala, Sweden, June 2019) 4; Jessica Baldwin-Philippi, 'Data Ops, Objectivity, and Outsiders: Journalistic Coverage of Data Campaigning' (2020) 27(4) Political Communication 468, 469.

[21] On this see Matthew Windsor, 'Expertise as Framing' in Emilia Korkea-aho and Päivi Leino-Sandberg (eds), *Law, Legal Expertise and EU Policy Making* (CUP 2022) 43–54.

To do this, this chapter will first look at the regulation of online targeted political advertising under the General Data Protection Regulation (GDPR).[22] As this is a general law, and many provisions may apply to such adverts depending on the precise circumstances, it will focus in particular on the rules relating to the processing of special category personal data, and then briefly consider the law's overall approach to protecting such data. Having done this, we will then look at the regulation under the Digital Services Act (DSA),[23] which does not provide special mention for political adverts *per se* but does prohibit certain types of platforms from using profiles based on special category personal data to target. Next, we consider how a fundamental rights perspective might differ from the above. While the European Court of Human Rights (ECtHR) has not yet explicitly ruled on the issue, there is existing case law which can indicate how the Court may view restrictions on the ability to target online political adverts—and, particularly, how such restrictions must be justified so as to be compatible with the ECHR. Finally, we will consider the regulation of such adverts under the new EU Political Advertising Regulation. This Regulation is not limited to targeted political adverts, but it does contain special rules for such adverts—rules which, notably, differ from those ultimately settled on under the DSA. Having reviewed these different legal approaches, this chapter will then pull together the different strands and illustrate why the choice of frame is decisive for the outcome.

B. The first approach: Regulation under the General Data Protection Regulation

The targeting and tailoring of political adverts will, inevitably, involve the use of personal data. In some cases, this may involve very little information (perhaps even just the viewer's name), while in others this may involve elaborate profiles built on huge datasets. In either case, this inherent use of personal data means that when discussing the regulation of online targeted political adverts, the GDPR is often a good place to start. As indicated by its name, the GDPR does not contain any specific provisions for online targeted political advertising. Rather, it is a very wide law that, aside from certain narrow exemptions,[24] applies to any operation or

[22] Regulation (EU) 2016/679 of the European Parliament and of the Council of 27 April 2016 on the protection of natural persons with regard to the processing of personal data and on the free movement of such data, and repealing Directive 95/46/EC (General Data Protection Regulation) [2016] OJ L119/1.

[23] Regulation (EU) 2022/2065 of the European Parliament and of the Council of 19 October 2022 on a Single Market For Digital Services and amending Directive 2000/31/EC (Digital Services Act) [2022] OJ L277/1.

[24] For some of these exemptions, see eg the GDPR art 2(2). The Court of Justice has consistently held that, since the protection of personal data is a fundamental right under the Charter of Fundamental Rights and Freedoms [2012] OJ C326/391, art 8, these exemptions must be interpreted narrowly. See eg C-212/13 *Ryneš v Úřad pro ochranu osobních údajů*, ECLI:EU:C:2014:2428, para 29.

set of operations performed on any information relating to an identified or identifiable natural person.[25] Nevertheless, the law does provide extra protections to certain types of personal data which it deems particularly sensitive—so-called special category personal data, as defined by GDPR, Article 9—which is particularly relevant for targeted political advertising.

'Personal data' is defined in GDPR, Article 4(1) as 'any information relating to an identified or identifiable natural person' (that person then being referred to as a 'data subject'). As indicated by the use of the word 'any' this is an incredibly broad term.[26] This definition is then complemented by the idea of special category personal data, defined under GDPR, Article 9(1) as:

> personal data revealing racial or ethnic origin, political opinions, religious or philosophical beliefs, or trade union membership, and the processing of genetic data, biometric data for the purpose of uniquely identifying a natural person, data concerning health or data concerning a natural person's sex life or sexual orientation.

As with the definition of bare personal data, this provision is interpreted widely; the Court of Justice of the European Union (CJEU) has held that it covers both data which explicitly falls under one of those categories and also any personal data which 'indirectly' reveals such information, including where that revelation is only as a result of 'an intellectual operation involving deduction or cross-referencing'.[27] The width of these definitions is important as it means that information required to target adverts in general will inevitably fall under 'personal data' (if no personal data were involved at all, it would not be possible to identify the user for targeting) while information required to target political adverts may well qualify as 'special category personal data'.

On the topic of special category personal data, then, most online targeted political adverts would seem likely to include information about a person's political beliefs. This could, for example, include an advert about a particular issue that is shown to a particular user because the advertiser knows that this user cares about that topic, or where an advert for a particular party or candidate is shown to somebody who is already a known supporter. In both cases, the advert is targeted on the basis of information which directly reveals political opinions, and therefore is

[25] GDPR arts 2(1), and 4(1) and (2).

[26] See eg Article 29 Working Party, *Opinion 4/2007 on the concept of personal data*, WP 136 (20 June 2007); Nadezhda Purtova, 'The Law of Everything. Broad Concept of Personal Data and Future of EU Data Protection Law' (2018) 10(1) Law, Innovation & Technology 40; and Michèle Finck and Frank Pallas, 'They Who Must Not Be Identified—Distinguishing Personal from Non-Personal Data under the GDPR' (2020) 10(1) International Data Privacy Law 11.

[27] See eg C-184/20 *OT v Vyriausioji tarnybinės etikos komisija*, ECLI:EU:C:2022:601, paras 123–128.

targeted on the basis of special category personal data. However, this is not the only possible form of online targeted political advertising.

During a speech about Cambridge Analytica's marketing strategy, the CEO of that company boasted that they could tailor their advertisements to a user's personality so as to get the best possible results. One example which he gave was about adverts relating to gun control. A person who they had profiled as neurotic and conscientious, he claimed, would receive an advert that focused on the defensive capabilities of guns. Meanwhile, he said, a person who had been profiled as being closed and agreeable would receive an advert that focused on tradition and the idea of guns and hunting as something passed from father to son.[28] Neither of these adverts necessarily use a person's political opinions about gun control and could (in theory) be created without needing any data that actually relates to a person's political views. We could, therefore, argue that such a targeted advert would not involve processing of special category personal data, simply the processing of non-special-category personal data which is then applied to a political context.

On the other hand, we could also argue that by using the data for a targeted political advert, we place that personal data in a political context which then brings the data within the scope of the GDPR, Article 9(1). It seems reasonable that the concept of a 'political opinion' should include not just the conclusion but also the beliefs and reasoning used to reach that conclusion; political opinions are more nuanced than simply 'gun control is good' or 'gun control is bad', but also include opinions like 'self-defence is a more persuasive justification for less gun control'. Under this line of reasoning, even if the general profile may not include any special category personal data ('this person is persuaded by messages emphasizing self-defence'), the linking of that profile to the political context ('and therefore will be best persuaded to vote against gun control by an advert which emphasizes that message') inherently brings that profile within the scope of political opinions, which means that we are now dealing with special category personal data.

Of the two, this second interpretation would seem to be more strongly supported by the existing guidance. In case of *OT*, and as already noted, the CJEU indicated that something could be considered special category personal data if someone could use that data to infer, *inter alia*, information about a person's political beliefs through deduction or cross-referencing.[29] Importantly, we also know that inaccurate or false personal data still qualifies as personal data[30] and there

[28] Nix (n 7) 3:52ff.
[29] C-184/20 *OT v Vyriausioji tarnybinės etikos komisija*, paras 123–128.
[30] European Data Protection Board, *Guidelines 8/2020 on the targeting of social media users*, version 2.0 (13 April 2021) para 123. See also GDPR art 16 (the right to rectification), which states that data subjects have the right to correct 'inaccurate personal data'. While the GDPR arts 4(1) or 9(1) do not explicitly say whether or not personal data must be true in order to fall under the GDPR, the existence of this right inherently supports the idea that untrue information about a person is still considered personal data and therefore falls under the law.

is nothing to indicate that this would be limited to non-special-category personal data. Therefore, where political opinions (eg this person believes that gun control is best justified by self-defence) can be inferred from data which would otherwise have nothing to do with political opinions (eg this person is best persuaded by messages emphasizing self-defence), the data which permits those inferences should still gain protection under GDPR Article 9, even if the inferences are wrong (eg a message emphasizing self-defence would not, in actual fact, persuade the data subject to vote for less gun control).

This interpretation is also supported in the guidance from the European Data Protection Board (the EDPB), which generally supports a wide interpretation of 'special category personal data'.[31] As a starting point, it does not necessarily matter how the personal data is categorized or labelled; provided that the personal data 'enables targeting based on special category data', that is sufficient.[32] The guidance also supports the idea that mere inference is enough to place data within the scope of Article 9(1). For example, the EDPB notes that an interest in 'mind, body and spirit movement' can qualify as special category personal data, even if 'no explicit statement on philosophical belief is provided'.[33] In the example of an advert for gun control, then, the fact that a profile never explicitly says 'This person's view on guns will be that self-defence is the most reasonable justification for looser gun control', and the fact that this opinion never explicitly appears in the dataset does not prevent the profile from being special category personal data. Importantly, the EDPB does note that simply because an inference is possible, it does not necessarily mean that the information shall be considered special category personal data.[34] However, for the EDPB, this would require that the controller has 'taken measures to prevent that such data can be inferred *or used for targeting*'.[35] In the case of targeted political advertising, then, this exemption would seem to be relatively narrow.

Finally, it is interesting to remember that targeted political adverts are used because the advertiser believes that, after seeing the advert, the viewer will be more likely to hold a certain opinion or belief. If we follow the logic of both the EDPB's guidelines and *OT*, this belief is, arguably, an inference which reveals a person's political opinions (whether or not it is true), and therefore may qualify as special category personal data under the GDPR, Article 9(1).

Ultimately, then, it seems likely that online targeted political advertising will involve the use of special category personal data. However, this does not mean that such advertising is prohibited (at least, as far as the GDPR is concerned). While Article 9(1) does contain a *prima facie* ban on the processing of special category personal data, Article 9(2) sets out a number of conditions under which it can be

[31] European Data Protection Board, *Guidelines 8/2020 on the Targeting of Social Media Users*, 31ff.
[32] ibid para 123.
[33] ibid 33.
[34] ibid para 124.
[35] ibid emphasis added.

lawfully processed. Particularly for our purposes, special category personal data can be processed if the data subject has provided their explicit consent.[36]

Even once processing has been legitimized under one of these grounds, the advertising must still comply with the other provisions within the GDPR. For example, the controller must also legitimize the processing under the GDPR, Article 6(1). This ground may raise particular questions for online targeted advertising, including online targeted political advertising. For example, under GDPR, Article 6(1)(f), it is possible for a controller to justify direct advertising (in general) on the ground that the processing of personal data is necessary for their legitimate interest and where that legitimate interest is not overridden by the data subject's interests or fundamental rights and freedoms.[37] However, the CJEU has expressed doubts that targeted advertising in particular could be justified by this ground, arguing that, at least in the context of an online social network such as Facebook, users 'cannot reasonably expect that the operator the social network will process [their] personal data, without his or her consent, for the purposes of personalised advertising'.[38] Further, the CJEU has noted that where the data gathering is 'particularly extensive', then this may 'give rise to the feeling that [the data subject's] private life is being continuously monitored'.[39] These are important observations, since the data subject's reasonable expectations is explicitly noted by the GDPR as one of the elements to be considered when performing the legitimate interest balancing test.[40] While the considerations mentioned by the Court may not apply to all online targeted political advertising, the use of special category personal data may also make it very difficult to satisfy the balancing act under the GDPR, Article 6(1)(f). This is particularly true where the sensitive nature of such data, and/or the sensitive nature of the adverts themselves, contribute to the feeling of being inappropriately monitored or surveilled, or if a data subject may be surprised by the use of information which they considered to be unconnected to their political opinion is now being used to try and profile their political tendencies. As a result, most controllers wishing to deploy such adverts may therefore be limited to processing that is justified on the basis of the data subject's consent under GDPR, Article 6(1)(a) and Article 9(2)(a).

Further, the processing must be sufficiently fair and transparent,[41] data subjects must be given certain information about the processing (including who is using their data and what they are using it for)[42] and, depending on how the processing

[36] GDPR art 9(2)(a).
[37] Where such processing involves special category personal data, it must typically also have been manifestly made public by the data subject under the GDPR art 9(2)(e). This, in itself, contains a number of further requirements and conditions, including those set out by the CJEU in C-252/21 *Meta Platforms Inc v Bundeskartellamt*, ECLI:EU:C:2023:537, paras 74–85.
[38] ibid para 117.
[39] ibid para 118.
[40] GDPR recital 47.
[41] GDPR art 5(1)(a).
[42] GDPR arts 12–15.

is justified, data subjects may either be able to withdraw their consent[43] or object to the processing's continuation.[44] Equally, controllers must make sure that any personal data is sufficiently accurate[45] and deleted when no longer necessary,[46] comply with principles like data protection by design and default (ideally using as little data as possible to achieve the purpose of the processing),[47] and must ensure that the processing is properly secured.[48] This is not a complete list and each of these provisions also apply to bare personal data. However, the CJEU has noted that the provisions of the GDPR must be interpreted so as to achieve its goals—and that one of the law's goals is to give particularly strong protection to special category personal data.[49] Following both this and the GDPR's risk-based approach in general,[50] these provisions may then be given a particularly protective interpretation where special category personal data is being utilized. This idea can also be seen in the GDPR's enforcement provisions, with Article 83(2)(g) noting that the 'categories of personal data affected' by a GDPR breach can influence the size of the fine levied.

The GDPR does also place some additional specific protections for special category personal data. One example of this is GDPR, Article 22, which restricts the ability to subject data subjects to sufficiently significant decisions that are based solely on automated decision-making, with further restrictions in place where that automated decision-making involves special category personal data. Equally, data protection impact assessments are 'in particular' required if a controller performs large-scale processing of special category personal data[51] and companies are required to hire a data protection officer if their core activities consist of such large-scale processing.[52]

The GDPR, then, contains many rules which may be relevant to online targeted political advertising. However, these rules are neither designed specifically for, nor expressed in terms of, such advertising. Rather they simply require that the targeting and tailoring of the adverts (as with any uses of personal data) is done in a way that respects the fundamental right to the protection of personal data. While the rules will cover online targeted political advertising, any limitations imposed by the GDPR will predominantly be designed to prohibit abuses of personal data,

[43] GDPR art 7(3).
[44] GDPR art 21.
[45] GDPR art 5(1)(d).
[46] GDPR art 5(1)(e).
[47] GDPR art 25. See also the data minimization principle in GDPR art 5(c).
[48] GDPR art 32.
[49] C-184/20 *OT v Vyriausioji tarnybinės etikos komisija*, paras 121 and 125–126. This is also supported by GDPR recital 51.
[50] For a discussion of this approach, see eg Claudia Quelle, 'Enhancing Compliance under the General Data Protection Regulation: The Risky Upshot of the Accountability—and Risk-based Approach' (2018) 9(3) European Journal of Risk Regulation 502.
[51] GDPR art 35(3)(b).
[52] GDPR art 37(1)(c).

rather than abuses of online targeted political advertising *per se*. Data protection law, then, may be able to protect against some of the potential harms associated with online targeted political advertising, such as the creation and deployment of abusive and manipulative profiles. However, there are some associated harms, such as a potential fracturing of debate or use of tailored adverts to make inconsistent promises to different voters, which are unconnected with personal data *per se* and so will be outside of the reach of data protection law.

Finally, it is worth observing the nature of balancing in the GDPR. The GDPR does recognize and reflect that 'the right to the protection of personal data is not an absolute right [and] it must be considered in relation to its function in society and be balanced against other fundamental rights'.[53] One way in which the GDPR attempts to enable this balancing act is by employing a principles-[54] and risk-based[55] approach to its rules. Equally, the GDPR contains an explicit exception for the freedom of expression, requiring that Member States implement laws to reconcile the two rights.[56] Nevertheless, it must be remembered that the law—and particularly specific terms under that law, such as the definition of 'special category personal data'—will typically be interpreted in line with the overarching purpose of data protection, rather than through any other particular lens. Both when interpreting data protection law in isolation and when balancing data protection provisions against other rights and interests, the CJEU has tended towards a very strong, pro-data protection approach.[57] While this, in theory, provides strong protection for data subjects and personal data rights, it is also something to be considered when thinking about how the regulatory approach taken by data protection law may balance against, complement, or conflict with the other regulatory approaches discussed below.

C. The second approach: Regulation under the Digital Services Act

Another approach to the regulation of online targeted political advertising in the EU centres the new advertising ecosystem, and the techniques that are enabled by the online environment and personal data processing. More specifically, following

[53] GDPR recital 4.
[54] See eg GDPR art 5.
[55] See eg GDPR arts 32 and 35.
[56] GDPR art 85(1).
[57] See eg C-73/07 *Tietosuojavaltuutettu v Satakunnan Markkinapörssi Oy*, ECLI:EU:C:2008:727; [2008] ECR I-09831, C-28/08 P *Commission of the European Communities v The Bavarian Lager Co. Ltd.* [2010] ECR I-06055, C-131/12 *Google Spain SL v Agencia Española de Protección de Datos (AEPD)*, ECLI:EU:C:2014:317, C-582/14 *Breyer v Bundesrepublik Deutschland*, ECLI:EU:C:2016:779, T-639/15 to T-666/15 and T-94/16 *Psara v European Parliament*, and C-345/17 *Buivids*, ECLI:EU:C:2019:122; Case C-439/19 *B v Latvijas Republikas Saeima*, ECLI:EU:C:2021:504.

the changes in the internet infrastructure,[58] this increasingly directs our attention to so-called online platforms. In the EU, the regulation of online platforms and other Internet 'intermediary services' relies primarily on the new Digital Services Act (DSA),[59] which updates and extends the old electronic service regulation in the e-Commerce Directive adopted in 2000.[60] Maintaining the underlying foundations of the Directive intact, the DSA slightly modifies the conditions for the liability exemption of various online services providers over illegal information circulating online.[61] To assure service providers of the continuing legal support of the liability exemption, the DSA also provides that various own initiative efforts to manage information do not lead by themselves to the loss immunity as long as these efforts are carried out 'in good faith and in a diligent manner'.[62] More importantly, it adds on the liability provisions a tiered regulatory structure of extensive transparency and due diligence obligations regulating the flow and presentation of paid and unpaid information online.[63] While the DSA provisions do not target specifically political adverts, as a horizontal online service regulation the DSA obligations on online advertising more generally are highly relevant for political advertising as well.

As already noted, the DSA focuses on so-called intermediary services. For our purposes, the most important of these is the 'hosting service' category, which is often the relevant for advertising service providers.[64] However, the DSA also introduces legal definitions of 'online platform' and 'online search engine'. An online platform is defined as

> a hosting service that, at the request of a recipient of the service, stores and disseminates information to the public, unless that activity is a minor and purely ancillary feature of another service or a minor functionality of the principal service and, for objective and technical reasons, cannot be used without that other

[58] Anne Helmond, 'The Platformization of the Web: Making Web Data Platform Ready' (2015) July–December Social Media + Society 1, doi:10.1177/2056305115603080; and more generally, Thomas Poell, David Nieborg, and José van Dijck, 'Platformisation' (2019) 8(4) Internet Policy Review 1.

[59] Regulation (EU) 2022/2065 of the European Parliament and of the Council of 19 October 2022 on a Single Market For Digital Services and amending Directive 2000/31/EC (Digital Services Act) [2022] OJ L277/1.

[60] Directive 2000/31/EC of the European Parliament and of the Council of 8 June 2000 on certain legal aspects of information society services, in particular electronic commerce, in the Internal Market ('Directive on electronic commerce') [2000] OJ L178/1.

[61] DSA ch II and recital 16.

[62] DSA art 7. On this encouragement of own initiative content moderation effort, see Aleksandra Kuczerawy, 'The Good Samaritan That Wasn't: Voluntary Monitoring under the (Draft) Digital Services Act' (*Verfassungsblog*, 12 January 2021) <https://verfassungsblog.de/good-samaritan-dsa/> accessed 30 August 2023.

[63] DSA, ch III.

[64] Joined Cases C-236/08 to C-238/08, *Google France and Google Inc v Louis Vuitton Malletier and others* [2010] ECR I-2417, paras 116–117; and Case C-18/18, *Eva Glawischnig-Piesczek v Facebook Ireland Limited*, EU:C:2019:821, para 22.

service, and the integration of the feature or functionality into the other service is not a means to circumvent the applicability of this Regulation.[65]

The core distinctive feature of an online platform, being the dissemination of hosted information to the public, is then separately defined as 'making information available, at the request of the recipient of the service who provided the information, to a potentially unlimited number of third parties'.[66]

The DSA also contains some obligations which only apply to the most widely used services, which the DSA refers to as 'very large online platforms' and 'very large online search engines', 'which have a number of average monthly active recipients of the service in the Union equal to or higher than 45 million'.[67] The DSA outlines a specific process for the designation of very large online platforms and search engines,[68] but the category includes the most well-known online political advertising service providers such as Facebook and several Google services.[69]

Most of the DSA's provisions that govern the circulation of information via intermediary services have relevance for political advertising, since the line between paid and unpaid 'user-generated' messages is porous at best. While advertisers generally have slightly more control over the presentation of information than normal end-users, adverts can (usually) also be 'liked' and shared as any other user-generated content.[70] Similarly, the affordability and usability of platform advertising tools have made advertising more accessible for new actors, and the increasingly popular 'influencer marketing'—which can be used for promoting political or non-political views—complicates the division even further.[71] Lastly, as with other content on such platforms, advertising is governed through 'content moderation' practices that rely on user reporting and, increasingly, automated detection and/or intervention.[72]

[65] DSA art 3(i).

[66] DSA art 3(k) and recitals 13–14.

[67] DSA art 33(1).

[68] DSA art 33(4).

[69] See European Commission, 'Supervision of the designated very large online platforms and search engines under DSA' (updated 17 May 2024) <https://digital-strategy.ec.europa.eu/en/policies/list-designated-vlops-and-vloses> accessed 30 May 2024.

[70] Tarleton Gillespie, *Custodians of the Internet: Platforms, Content Moderation, and the Hidden Decisions That Shape Social Media* (Yale UP 2018) 203.

[71] Giovanni De Gregorio and Catalina Goanta, 'The Influencer Republic: Monetizing Political Speech on Social Media' (2022) 23 German Law Journal 204, 207–11; and on regulatory problems around influencers more generally, Catalina Goanta and Sofia Ranchordás (eds), *The Regulation of Social Media Influencers* (Edward Elgar Publishing 2020).

[72] DSA defines content moderation in art 3(t) broadly as 'the activities, whether automated or not, undertaken by providers of intermediary services, that are aimed, in particular, at detecting, identifying and addressing illegal content or information incompatible with their terms and conditions, provided by recipients of the service, including measures taken that affect the availability, visibility, and accessibility of that illegal content or that information, such as demotion, demonetisation, disabling of access to, or removal thereof, or that affect the ability of the recipients of the service to provide that information, such as the termination or suspension of a recipient's account'.

The DSA contains a number of due diligence obligations for hosting services, intended to make content moderation more transparent and accountable to the newly envisioned regulators and to platform users (ie the public) at large.[73] These protections will apply as much to actors seeking to disseminate paid political messages as they would to those seeking to disseminate purely commercial messages. For instance, if a political advert is removed from a hosting service, the advertiser may attain 'a clear and specific statement of reasons' for the removal.[74] The advertiser can also have the removal decision reviewed within an online platform's internal complaint handling system[75] and/or by an out-of-court dispute settlement.[76] However, it is important to note that these rules largely codify the content moderation practices that the service providers had already developed.[77] It therefore remains unclear to what extent the new legal obligations will transform the status quo in practice.

The most directly relevant DSA article for online political advertising is Article 26, which specifically regulates advertising on online platforms and thus excludes micro and small businesses that do not operate very large online platforms. Paragraph 1 of that article requires that adverts be accompanied by a label disclosing that the message is an advert, the actor on whose behalf the advertisement is presented and who paid for it, and why the advert was targeted to that recipient and how the relevant parameters might be changed. This should, in theory, help to distinguish adverts from 'normal' posts on such platforms. However, for our purposes, it is important to note that adverts do not need to identify themselves as being political or not. While, in some cases, this may be readily apparent (eg where the advert is presented on behalf of a particular political party or candidate), this will not apply to all adverts. Paragraph 2 of DSA Article 26, meanwhile, requires that online platforms create a system whereby users can flag themselves as uploaders of content that 'is or contains commercial communications' (including adverts). Where they do so, the platform operator is then responsible for labelling these users as such.

Finally, paragraph 3 of Article 26 is probably the most consequential DSA provision for political advertisers seeking to disseminate their messages on online platforms. This paragraph prohibits online platform providers from presenting adverts, political or otherwise, to their users if that presentation is based on a profile that uses special category personal data. This provision, then, forges an innate

[73] Marta Maroni, '"Mediated Transparency": The Digital Services Act and the Legitimisation of Platform Power' in Päivi Leino-Sandberg, Maarten Hillebrandt, and Ida Koivisto (eds), *(In)visible European Government: Critical Approaches to Transparency as an Ideal and a Practice* (Routledge 2023).

[74] DSA art 17.

[75] DSA art 20.

[76] DSA art 21.

[77] Maroni (n 73). On the development of platform content moderation practices, see Kate Klonick, 'The New Governors: The People, Rules, and Processes Governing Online Speech' (2018) 131 Harvard Law Review 1598, 1616–29.

link between the DSA and the GDPR, relying on the GDPR's definitions of profiling and special category personal data. As already stated, data revealing political opinions comprise special category personal data, and the term is understood very widely under that law. The discussion on the GDPR emphasized that while online political targeted regulation would fall under the scope of GDPR Article 9(1), it may otherwise be permitted if it complied with GDPR provisions and was done in a way that respected the right to the protection of personal data. Under the DSA, however, these options do not exist, and, on the relevant online platforms, online political targeted regulation which falls under that scope is simply prohibited altogether. This is important as the scope of 'special category personal data' was interpreted within the context of the GDPR and its exceptions and rules—and one may wonder if it would have been interpreted as widely had the GDPR contained an equally total prohibition. This is not to say that all online targeted political advertising is prohibited under the DSA. As a starting point, this prohibition only applies to online platforms; online targeted political advertising on other services is not affected. Equally, as micro and small businesses[78] are exempted from the prohibition if they do not provide a very large online platform service, wider targeting could remain available for (political) advertisers via niche platforms. The availability of such advertising routes, however, does still assume that they will be in compliance with the Political Advertising Regulation and that they fulfil the data protection requirements set out in the GDPR.

As already mentioned, another layer of online platform regulation is imposed on very large online platforms and search engines under Section 5 of the DSA. These services have been argued to pose 'systemic risks' for the online ecosystem and societies more widely.[79] The providers of these platforms and search engines are required to 'diligently identify, analyse and assess any systemic risks in the Union stemming from the design or functioning of their service and its related systems'.[80] The DSA outlines four types of systemic risks in somewhat abstract terms, but the risks that the EU has most intimately associated with political advertising are 'any actual or foreseeable negative effects on civic discourse and electoral processes, and public security'.[81] '[S]ystems for selecting and presenting advertisements' are also mentioned as a factor influencing the systemic risks.[82]

Risks must not only be identified and studied but must also be mitigated. For example, service providers are informed that this may include 'adapting their advertising systems and adopting targeted measures aimed at limiting or adjusting

[78] As defined in Commission Recommendation of 6 May 2003 concerning the definition of micro, small and medium-sized enterprises, OJ L124/36.

[79] DSA, recitals 75–76. On the notion of systemic risk see, Julie E Cohen, 'The Regulatory State in the Information Age' (2017) 17 Theoretical Inquiries in Law 369, 389–95.

[80] DSA art 34(1).

[81] DSA art 33(1)(c).

[82] DSA art 33(2)(d).

the presentation of advertisements in association with the service they provide'.[83] Due to the abstract formulations of all these provisions, the DSA foresees Commission guidelines and co-regulatory codes of conducts as a way to provide more specific details in the future.[84] Indeed, as the Commission has already facilitated the recently updated Code of Practice on Disinformation,[85] which contains several commitments regarding political advertising, the DSA is clearly meant to bring the Code and other similar Union co-regulatory efforts under its umbrella, highlighting the nature of the DSA as a wide horizontal framework. However, the practical implications of all these provisions for online political advertising remain unclear.

In addition to the systemic risk regulation, the DSA mandates very large online platforms and search engines to provide 'at least one option for each of their recommender systems which is not based on profiling'.[86] As the delivery of information, including adverts, currently relies heavily on various recommender systems that draw upon user profiling,[87] the provision could significantly alter the presentation of any adverts on platforms—and may, at least in principle, empower users to influence how and what information they receive online. Moreover, 'additional advert transparency' imposed on very large online platforms foresees a publicly available advertisement repository or 'ad bank'.[88] Finally, online platforms' self-regulation continues to play a role in political advertising on online platforms, starting from the fact that a platform operator may still prohibit the dissemination of paid political messages on their service altogether.[89]

What emerges from our analysis in this section is a complex and interlinked regulatory framework constructed around online platforms. We have seen that the DSA builds on definitions set out and interpreted in data protection law, most notably those of 'special category personal data' and 'profiling' in the GDPR. However, the DSA itself has also clearly been meant as a reference point for other regulation such as the Code of Practice on Disinformation and, as will be discussed below, the Political Advertising Regulation. The monitoring and enforcement structure is correspondingly complex and networked. The DSA distributes new powers to the

[83] DSA art 35(1)(e).

[84] DSA arts 35(3), 45(2), and 46. Code of conducts are mentioned as a risk mitigation measure of their own in DSA art 35(1)(h).

[85] European Commission, '2022 Strengthened Code of Practice on Disinformation' (16 June 2022) <https://digital-strategy.ec.europa.eu/en/library/2022-strengthened-code-practice-disinformation> accessed 21 March 2023.

[86] DSA art 38. Again, the DSA references GDPR art 4(4) for the definition of profiling.

[87] Jennifer Cobbe and Jatinder Singh, 'Regulating Recommending: Motivations, Considerations, and Principles' (2019) 10(3) European Journal of Law and Technology 1, 2.

[88] DSA art 39. On ad banks as a form of transparency regulation see Paddy Leerssen and others, 'Platform Ad Archives: Promises and Pitfalls' (2019) 8(4) Internet Policy Review 1.

[89] Google, for example, currently has detailed country-specific restrictions on 'political content'. See Google Advertising Policies Help, 'Political Content' (2023) <https://business.twitter.com/en/help/ads-policies/ads-content-policies/political-content.html > accessed 30 November 2023.

Commission and to the new Digital Service Coordinators and the European Board for Digital Services. In addition to this, it also seeks to mobilize various other actors for assistance with monitoring and enforcement, including online platform operators themselves, independent auditors, researchers, trusted flaggers, out-of-court dispute resolution providers, and even ordinary service users. The fact the DSA has only just entered into force, not to mention the complex web of interdependencies it weaves, makes it hard to see all the consequences for online political advertising that will eventually emerge. Nevertheless, it is already clear that the DSA significantly complicates and restricts those advertising practices.

D. The third approach: Regulation under the Freedom of Expression and Information

Freedom of expression and information, protected under both the Charter Article 11 and the ECHR Article 10, is unlike the others discussed in this chapter in one key way: while the others view online targeted political advertising as a risky activity, or as a problem to be restrained and controlled, freedom of expression is concerned with the exact opposite—protecting the ability to distribute political messages, including (presumably) the ability to use such adverts. At the same time, these rights also protect the other side of the equation: the right for members of the public to receive information, including (arguably) the ability to receive the information communicated in such adverts.[90]

The existence of a freedom of expression does not altogether prevent the law from placing restrictions or limitations on the use of online targeted political adverts. The Charter Article 52 states that such limitations may be imposed, but that they 'must be provided for by law and respect the essence of those rights and freedoms', and that 'subject to the principle of proportionality, limitations may be made only if they are necessary and genuinely meet objectives of general interest recognised by the Union or the need to protect the rights and freedoms of others'. This provision is significantly more open-ended than the equivalent section under the ECHR; still, ECHR Article 10(2) states that the freedom of expression 'may be subject to such formalities, conditions, restrictions or penalties as are prescribed by law', provided that such restrictions are for one of the reasons explicitly set out in that provision. Of these reasons, the ECtHR has previously held that 'preserving the impartiality of broadcasting on public interest matters and, thereby, of protecting the democratic process . . . corresponds to the legitimate aim of protecting

[90] This right to receive information is explicitly stated in the Charter, art 11. Meanwhile, the ECHR and the jurisprudence of the ECtHR emphasize that art 10 also includes a broader notion of 'freedom to receive information'. See eg *Tarsaság a Szabadságjogokért v Hungary* App no 37374/05 (ECHR, 14 April 2009), para 35.

the "rights of others".[91] We can, therefore, reasonably assume that the protection of the democratic process could be used to justify a limitation of online targeted political advertising under both the Charter and the ECHR—if such limitations can be shown to be necessary for and proportionate to that goal. The freedom of expression, as a right, must also be balanced against other rights protected under the Charter and the ECHR, such as the rights to privacy and the protection of personal data.

When thinking about a limitation on the right to access information, the ECtHR has placed particular emphasis on whether access to the information is, in some manner, in the public interest. For our purposes, one particularly important way in which access can gain such a status is if access 'provides transparency on the manner of conduct of public affairs and on matters of interest for society as a whole and thereby allows participation in public governance by the public at large'.[92] The ECtHR's definition of a public interest is context-bound, but it

> relates to matters which affect the public to such an extent that it may legitimately take an interest in them, which attract its attention or which concern it to a significant degree, especially in that they affect the well-being of citizens or the life of the community. This is also the case with regard to matters which are capable of giving rise to considerable controversy, which concern an important social issue, or which involve a problem that the public would have an interest in being informed about. . . . In this connection, the privileged position accorded by the Court in its case-law to political speech and debate on questions of public interest is relevant.[93]

Consequently, the exceptions to the freedom to receive information have been interpreted narrowly. Further, while striking the balance will clearly depend on a case-by-case analysis, it would appear that political messages (including those contained in political advertising) would often be considered information the access of which is in the public interest.

So far, the ECtHR has not issued any rulings about the freedom of expression's effect on online targeted political advertising. It has, however, addressed questions involving political advertising more generally, including the use of paid televised advertising, the use of mobile phone apps to share political news and pictures, and the distribution of digital leaflets—and, in each case, found that they could be protected under ECHR Article 10 as a form of political speech.[94] Further, the idea

[91] *Animal Defenders International v United Kingdom* App no 48876/08 (ECHR, 22 April 2013), para 78, citing *VgT Verein gegen Tierfabriken v Switzerland* App no 24699/94 (ECHR, 28 September 2001), para 62 and *TV Vest AS v Norway* App no 21132/05 (ECHR, 11 March 2009), para 78.

[92] *Magyar Helsinki Bizottsag v Hungary* App No 18030/11 (ECHR 8 November 2016), para 161.

[93] ibid paras 162–163.

[94] Dobber, Ó Fathaigh, and Zuiderveen Borgesius (n 1) 7–8.

that paid televised advertising should be considered as political speech, and the ECtHR's 'broad notion of what constitutes an exercise of freedom of expression' leads to the conclusion that online targeted political advertising should be protected under ECHR, Article 10, notwithstanding the lack of direct case law on the point.[95] It is also notable that, in many cases where the ECHR was asked if a limitation on political advertising was compatible with the ECHR, the Court explicitly noted that political advertising was vital for political parties to spread the word and participate in the democratic process.[96]

Compared to the position under the GDPR or the DSA, then the starting point for our analysis under the freedom of expression is very different. While a person's first mental image of online targeted political advertising might be a manipulative advert, intended to trick someone into voting against their interests, our current perspective emphasizes a different angle: rather than being seen as a threat to democracy, online targeted political advertising is actually a way for people to participate more efficiently and effectively in democracy. It must be remembered that 'targeting' is not necessarily a particularly high barrier. It could, for example, include something as innocuous (and even desirable) as people trying to spread their political message to people who might want to see it without having to waste resources on people who will never vote for them anyway.

This provokes an interesting contrast with the approach taken by, for example, the fundamental right to the protection of personal data. With the GDPR, online targeted political advertising is prohibited unless they complied with data protection law—the default, under Article 9(1), is that the processing is unlawful, unless an exception applies.[97] Here, the approach is the opposite: that online targeted political advertising should be permitted, unless reasons for prohibition or limitation can be properly established. Further, as was discussed in the Introduction, it is quite difficult to evidence the impact of online targeted political advertising (at least in any conclusive manner). Attempts to limit the use of online targeted political advertising on the basis that it distorts the electoral process and undermines democracy may, therefore, be hard pushed to produce evidence of those claims. On the other hand, limitations to the freedom of expression justified by a conflict with the protections of privacy and personal data may be easier to advance, relying as they do on a (more familiar) balancing of two human rights, rather than difficult-to-produce evidence as to the harm of online targeted political adverts on the political process.

[95] ibid.

[96] See eg *VgT Verein gegen Tierfabriken v Switzerland*, App no 24699/94 and *TV Vest AS v Norway*, App no 21132/05.

[97] This approach of 'prohibited, except where exceptions apply' was also heavily emphasized by Advocate General Bobek in the context of bare personal data: C-13/16 *Valsts policijas Rīgas reģiona pārvaldes Kārtības policijas pārvalde v Rīgas pašvaldības SIA (Rīgas satiksme)*, Opinion, ECLI:EU:C:2017:43, para 38.

The focus on proportionality and the justifiability of a limitation should not be seen as a barrier to the protection of democracy, voter freedom, and the democratic process. Even beyond this, it would seem very easy to blame certain 'wrong' electoral outcomes on online targeted political advertising, alleging that those outcomes arose because such adverts manipulated voters into making a poor decision. While this may well be true in some cases, there is also a risk that online targeted political adverts become a distraction from other issues, whether those issues are fundamental threats to the functioning of democracy and elections or whether those issues are wider, societal problems that need to be addressed, beyond the online environment, in appropriate democratic processes.

Finally, even within the human rights framework, it still matters which court rules on the subject. Like the ECtHR, the CJEU has not yet explicitly addressed the relationship between online targeted political advertising and freedom of expression. Nevertheless, the European Commission has explicitly recognized that 'a limitation of targeting techniques could impact freedom of expression'[98] and we can probably assume that, as under the ECHR, online targeted political adverts will attract protection under the Charter. However, this is not the only consideration, and there is no guarantee that the ECtHR and the CJEU would actually interpret that protection (and the ways that it can be limited) in the same way. Article 52(3) of the Charter does say that Charter rights which 'correspond to rights guaranteed' by the ECHR shall have the same 'meaning and scope of those rights shall be the same as those laid down by the said Convention'. This article does not stop EU law from providing more extensive protection, but, as a matter of principle, this overlap of rights should lead to significant reference to ECtHR cases when looking at the scope and meaning of the freedom of expression under the Charter.[99] Yet the requirement of 'corresponding rights' leaves a great degree of discretion, as the wording and structure of the Charter provisions are often very different from their ECHR counterparts. Indeed, many examples can be identified in the relevant CJEU's case law where the ECHR has not been considered at all.[100]

While the Court acknowledges the value of publicity as an objective of general interest and the importance of finding the appropriate balance between rights, to our knowledge there are no cases where freedom of expression and information would actually have conquered over data protection. At the same time, it is not difficult to identify cases where the CJEU has chosen to emphasize data protection rights over the publication of data to the public, and, as noted above, the Court

[98] Commission Proposal for Political Advertising Regulation, 12.

[99] See eg C-555/19 *Fussl Modestraße Mayr GmbH v SevenOne Media GmbH*, ECLI:EU:C:2021:89 para 81 et seq and Lorna Woods, 'Article 11' in Steve Peers and others (eds), *The EU Charter of Fundamental Rights: A Commentary* (Hart 2014).

[100] Bruno de Witte, 'The Use of the ECHR and Convention Case Law by the European Court of Justice' in Patricia Popelier, Catherine van de Heyning, and Piet van Nuffel (eds), *Human Rights Protection in European Legal Order: The Interaction between the European and the National Courts* (Intersentia 2011) 25.

has tended to prefer the protection of personal data over other grounds.[101] One recent case concerned a Luxembourg law adopted in 2019 establishing a Register of Beneficial Ownership and providing that a whole series of information on the beneficial owners of registered entities must be entered and retained in that register.[102] Some of that information was made accessible to the general public, in particular through the Internet. The Court's Grand Chamber held that in light of the Charter, the provision of the anti-money laundering directive whereby Member States must ensure that the relevant information is accessible in all cases to any member of the general public is invalid. For the Court, the general public's access to information on beneficial ownership constitutes a serious interference with the fundamental rights to respect for private life and to the protection of personal data.[103] Another recent example is the case of *OT*, referenced above. In this case, the CJEU was asked to consider legislation which required that certain declarations of private interests, made by certain people working in the public service and by the heads of certain bodies which received public funds, be published online with a view of preventing corruption from emerging and spreading in the public service. While the argumentation of the Court in this case may be somewhat more balanced than in a number of earlier cases, the CJEU did find such national legislation contrary to the GDPR, including because the data contained information about those individuals' partners' names, and because this information would reveal information about those people's sexual orientation.[104]

It is evident that this emphasis on data protection and privacy, then, is likely to affect the significance of freedom of expression and information in the EU context, and therefore the regulation of online targeted political advertising.

E. The fourth approach: Regulation under the Political Advertising Regulation

The final approach to be considered is that in the new European Political Advertising Regulation. Trilogue agreement on the Regulation was reached on 6 November 2023 and a part of the obligations became applicable for 2024 European Parliament elections.[105] The most predominant feature of the regulation is that the

[101] See eg C-73/07 *Tietosuojavaltuutettu v Satakunnan Markkinapörssi Oy*; C-28/08 P *Commission of the European Communities v The Bavarian Lager Co. Ltd.*; C-131/12 *Google Spain SL v Agencia Española de Protección de Datos (AEPD)*; T-639/15 to T-666/15 and T-94/16 *Psara v European Parliament*; and C-345/17 *Buivids*, ECLI:EU:C:2019:122.

[102] Joined Cases C-37/20 *Luxembourg Business Registers* and C-601/20 *Sovim*, ECLI:EU:C:2022:912.

[103] Joined Cases C-37/20 *Luxembourg Business Registers* and C-601/20 *Sovim*, ECLI:EU:C:2022:912, para 44.

[104] Case C-184/20 *OT v Vyriausioji tarnybinės etikos komisija*, ECLI:EU:C:2022:601.

[105] Regulation (EU) 2024/900 of the European Parliament and of the Council of 13 March 2024 on the transparency and targeting of political advertising [2024] OJ L2024/900.

regulatory approach is specifically aimed at political advertising, unlike data protection (which views the issue through a lens of personal data and privacy) and the DSA (which views the issue through a lens of non-specific advertising on online platforms). However, unlike the regulatory approach embodied by the freedom of expression, the regulatory approach taken under the Political Advertising Regulation unambiguously views targeted political advertising as a problem to be tackled; the law imposes strict limitations on the use of online targeted political advertising.[106] In the absence of a specific legal basis, the Union competence for regulating political advertising was found jointly in Articles 16 (data protection) and 114 (internal market) of the Treaty on the Functioning of the European Union, and the use of latter was justified in terms of harmonizing the internal market of political advertising services.[107] However, the content of the Regulation itself focuses mainly on the protection against problematically viewed political advertising. While the new Regulation does contain specific regulation for online targeted political advertising (albeit as part of what it calls political adverts subject to 'targeting and ad delivery of online political advertising'), the majority of it looks at political advertising as a whole.[108]

The Regulation contains two main regulatory points: one limiting the use of types of personal data and one imposing greater transparency and notice obligations. In many ways, the Regulation mirrors a 'notice and consent' model, where data subjects are given enough information to make an informed decision about their personal data and then have the choice as to whether or not to let the processing take place. However, this model has been somewhat controversial in data protection contexts.[109] It is therefore important to consider how this regulatory approach would operate within the context of online targeted political advertising.

The Regulation introduces stringent restrictions on the use personal data for the targeting of political advertising. First, the use of special category data for the targeting of political advertising is prohibited altogether if that targeting is based on profiling within the meaning of the GDPR.[110] In addition, targeting on the basis of non-special category personal data comes with restrictions as well. The personal data must be explicitly provided by the data subject for the purposes of targeting

[106] Political Advertising Regulation art 18.
[107] Commission Proposal for Political Advertising Regulation, 5–6. On the competence of the Political Advertising Regulation see Miikka Hiltunen and Sam Wrigley, '"Why Am I Seeing This Regulation"? Exploring Underlying Issues from the Proposed Political Advertising Regulation' (2023) 48 The European Law Review 312, 314–17.
[108] Political Advertising Regulation art 1. In the Regulation, ch II relates to transparency and due diligence obligations for all political advertising services, ch III relates to the targeting and delivery of political advertising, and ch IV relates to supervision and enforcement, with ch V setting out final provisions.
[109] See eg Neil Richards and Woodrow Hartzog, 'The Pathologies of Digital Consent' (2019) 96 Washington University Law Review 1461; or Fred H Cate and Viktor Mayer-Schönberger, 'Notice and Consent in a World of Big Data' (2013) 3(2) International Data Privacy Law 67.
[110] Political Advertising Regulation art 18(1)(c).

and the targeting needs to be based on consent specifically and explicitly obtained for those targeting activities.[111] There are also other more specific restrictions such as a ban to use minors' data for targeting.[112] However, certain traditional communications from political parties, foundations or other non-governmental organizations to their members, such as internal newsletters, are excluded from the scope of the targeting restrictions.[113] Also, unsponsored journalistic content and communications concerning the organization of elections are outside the remit of the Regulation altogether.[114] Finally, a ban on political advertising by non-European sponsors was added to the Regulation during the trilogue negotiation phase. During a three-month period before a referendum or elections, third-country entities are prohibited from sponsoring political advertising in the EU.[115]

One particularly apparent feature of this Regulation is the partial overlap with DSA Article 26. Under that law, online platforms (including major advert networks like Facebook) were prohibited from any targeted advertising (political or otherwise) that involved the use of special category personal data. However, as regards targeted political advertising on online platforms, the Political Advertising Regulation brings in even further restrictions from the DSA. Targeting of political advertising on online platforms that is based on non-special category data will also need to comply with the other restrictions set in Political Advertising Regulation such as the requirement of explicit purpose-specific consent. Thus, as this brief outline already makes plain, it seems that only a very limited targeting of political adverts will be legally available through online platforms such as Facebook. Finally, the new regulation may expand slightly on the transparency requirements for targeted advertising.[116]

Bringing this together with the other justifications, the regulatory approach taken by the Union in the Political Advertising Regulation seems very much to be the use of prohibitions and strict limitations to push advertisers from online targeted political advertising to contextual-based advertising. However, it remains to be seen to what extent the Regulation will eventually change or reduce targeted online political advertising. In terms of the targeting restrictions, the enforcement of the Regulation will be entrusted to national data protection authorities—a decision that furthers stresses the importance of the data protection frame.[117] In turn, more discretion is provided to Member States for designating supervisory authorities for the transparency obligations.[118]

[111] Political Advertising Regulation art 18(1)(a–b).
[112] Political Advertising Regulation art 18(2).
[113] Political Advertising Regulation art 18(3).
[114] Political Advertising Regulation arts 1(2) and 2(2)(i–iii).
[115] Political Advertising Regulation art 5(2).
[116] Political Advertising Regulation arts 7, 8, 11, 12, 13, 14 and 19.
[117] Political Advertising Regulation art 22(1–2).
[118] Political Advertising Regulation art 22(3–4).

It is important to note that the approaches taken in the DSA and the Political Advertising Regulation are relatively well aligned. Both laws rely heavily on the use of special category personal data (with both laws importing the concept wholesale from data protection law), with both declaring a total ban on the use of special category personal data within the relevant form of targeted advertising. When looking at this alignment, however, we may ask ourselves if the overlap is because of the area being regulated (ie there is something particular about both targeted political advertising and targeted advertising on online platforms that makes the use of special category personal data inappropriate) or whether the overlap is because of the subject-matter being regulated (ie regardless of the context, the European Union believes that we should not use special category personal data in targeted advertising, and it is simply that we have not yet seen a general regulation on this point).

It is, further, very interesting that the idea of 'special category personal data', and particularly the idea of special category personal data as defined under data protection law, is such a frequently used concept in this topic. It must be noted that the use of legal concepts across laws is not necessarily that uncommon, nor is it necessarily problematic. Indeed, the cross-pollination of laws in this way can be very helpful for legal consistency and can save on redundant or unnecessary duplication of jurisprudence. The difficulty here is that the framings of the different laws involved are radically different. As discussed above, data protection law takes a very broad view of 'special category personal data', interpreting the term widely so as to bring as much data as possible within the scope of Article 9 and the extra protections provided in the GDPR. In particular, as discussed above, it is arguable that, at least within the GDPR's framing, any personal data used to target online political advertising may be considered special category personal data, even if that data by itself has no relevance to political opinions.

However, this view may not be shared by the other approaches. It is apparent in the Political Advertising Regulation that the Union legislators do not believe that using otherwise non-special-category personal data as part of targeting a political advert is necessarily enough to turn that personal data into special category personal data. This belief can be seen in the substantive provisions, which explicitly includes rules for the use of non-special-category personal data in targeted advertising, while the use of special category personal data is entirely prohibited. When the issue is framed in this way, it seems reasonable to distinguish between, on the one hand, personal data which is so sensitive that it should never be used and, on the other, personal data which can be used under certain conditions, and the law is clearly intended to draw such a dividing line.

While the above has focused on the Political Advertising Regulation, the discussion is equally applicable to the prohibition on certain targeted advertising within the DSA. This then leads to a number of problems for the legal regulation of online targeted political advertising as a whole. As a first issue, we may ask how a court would respond when the interpretation of 'special category personal data' is appropriate in one frame but inappropriate in the other, and how far and in what way it would be appropriate for the CJEU to (for example) consider the implications on the political advertising regime while deciding a data protection case. As a second issue, we may also ask how it is possible to fully evaluate the political advertising rules (particularly as to their necessity and proportionality) when the interpretation of key provisions in that regime depend on terms that are controlled by other legal implements.

F. Conclusion

This chapter has examined a number of different approaches to the regulation of online targeted political advertising. Each of these approaches demonstrates a different way of framing the issue, sometimes in ways that compliment other framings and sometimes in ways which contrast with other framings.

The GDPR's approach to the issue was explored primarily through the concept of special category personal data, as defined in GDPR Article 9(1). This term, as was demonstrated above, is interpreted widely, bringing as much data into the scope of protection as possible. However, under the GDPR, this did not necessarily prohibit the data from being used, but simply required that it be used in certain ways or under certain conditions. We also noted that, due to its framing, this law had the potential to stop online targeted political advertising which involved the abuses of personal data, but was not useful for preventing online targeted political advertising which involved other kinds of abuses (eg threats to the democratic process).

The DSA's approach, meanwhile, focuses on adverts on certain online platforms. The regulation does not look at political adverts in particular but instead imposes a broad imposition on any targeted advertising distributed through such platforms if that targeting is based on special category personal data. Similarly, the Political Advertising Regulation imports the same concept to impose a ban on the targeted political advertising if that targeting is based on special category personal data. This use of special category personal data is interesting because it means that, at least to some extent, the lines of the prohibition are defined by data protection law, and that definition will inherently be drawn from that law's perspective.

Finally, and unlike the other approaches identified here, the framing embodied by the freedom of expression and information looks at online targeted political advertising as something to be protected rather than as something to be guarded against. However, this protection is not absolute and must be balanced against other interests, including the protection of democracy and the democratic process, and the protection of personal data. Proving limitations justified on the former may be difficult (though certainly not impossible), as it is very hard to actually gather evidence as to the impact of online targeted political advertising on the democratic process. For the latter, however, the CJEU has demonstrated an extremely pro-data protection stance, and we can ask how any balancing of interests will actually play out in practice. In this respect, its balance is fundamentally different from that promoted by the ECtHR, which suggests that online targeted political advertising should be permitted, unless reasons for prohibition or limitation can be properly established. The EU framework rather presumes such harm to exist instead of engaging with discussing its existence or limits.

While it is clear that the different approaches do (in practical terms) present different framings of the issues, the data protection perspective remains dominant. Indeed, one could argue that, while the theoretical or nominal frame of each approach is different, in practice, each of the approaches effectively adopt the GDPR's framing, as demonstrated by (for example) the wholesale importation of special category personal data and the CJEU's apparent preference for balancing in favour of data protection issues. We argue that data protection is incapable of regulating all aspects of online political targeted advertising because at least some of the associated risks, harms, and benefits were relatively unconnected to that approach's core concern: the protection of personal data. This chapter does not endorse such a strong position for data protection. It is also clear that this wide emphasis on data protection law, and its framings, may lead to internal conflicts when imported into the other approaches, and these conflicts will need to be resolved as these laws begin to take effect. Equally, it will be important to think not only about how the legislation itself is framed but also how any bodies which are responsible for interpreting and implementing those pieces of legislation will, in turn, frame their work. The mandate of a Digital Service Coordinator, for example, is different from that of a Data Protection Supervisory Authority, much as the mandates of a human rights court differ from those of the European Board for Digital Services or the EDPB. Each primarily interprets the legal framework that constitutes their offices, with the view of fulfilling their overall mission—and, in doing so, may and even should also reframe the issues as part of their interpretation.

In this process of framing and reframing there is a risk that the ability to distribute political messages and the right to receive such messages, which both constitute a vital part of democratic society, are downgraded and ultimately lost. Data protection takes over a significant field of democratic debate, even in matters that have a distant (if any) connection to the aims of the protection of personal data. This should be a source of worry, especially since evidencing the harm created by online targeted political advertising is significantly harder than initially assumed.

9

The Interplay Between Lawfulness and Explainability in the Automated Decision-Making of EU Administration

Davide Liga

A. Introduction

Automated decision-making (ADM) refers to the use of technology to make automatic or semi-automated decisions, in other words make decisions with limited or no human intervention.[1] The increasing availability of data, combined with more powerful computing capabilities, recently opened a new era of artificial intelligence (AI) and machine learning (ML), and this was accompanied with a significant increase in the use of ADM systems.

As the use of ADM systems continues to grow, there are also growing ethical concerns being raised around the fairness and transparency of these artificial systems and around the potential for unintended biases or dangerous misuses. These ethical concerns directly affect the legal dimension and the necessity to regulate these technologies appropriately.

While these ethical and legal concerns can be considered crucial in any automated context, their importance is even greater when the automated decision is generated by a public body or institution. This chapter focuses on this aspect, considering the use of ADM systems in the context of European administrative law. In section B, we will refer to some related studies. Then we will discuss the concept of explainability in section C, showing why this concept is often connected or overlapped with a range of other concepts, some of which are particularly important in the legal domain. In section D we will describe how the concept of 'explanation' is instantiated in the context of AI models. In section E, we will instantiate the previously discussed concepts in the context of EU law, describing the interplay between AI explainability and lawfulness. In section F, we will describe some famous

[1] This work was supported by the project INDIGO, which is financially supported by the NORFACE Joint Research Programme on Democratic Governance in a Turbulent Age and co-funded by AEI, AKA, DFG, FNR, and the European Commission through Horizon 2020 under grant agreement No 822166.

Davide Liga, *The Interplay Between Lawfulness and Explainability in the Automated Decision-Making of EU Administration*
In: *Governance of Automated Decision-Making and EU Law*. Edited by: Herwig C.H. Hofmann and Felix Pflücke,
Oxford University Press. © Davide Liga 2024. DOI: 10.1093/9780198919575.003.0009

methods of eXplainable artificial intelligence (XAI), showing how some of the most popular methods work from a technical point of view, and try to describe what are the outcomes and limitations of such approaches.

B. Related studies

In recent years a growing number of studies has been dedicated to the field of explainability and XAI, due to the increasing relevance of AI systems in people's life. Moreover, due to the increasingly important role of so-called black-box models (models which are intrinsically opaque), a huge portion of these studies has been dedicated to understanding how to treat these models and make sense of their predictions and behaviours. Under this growing need of explainability, some popular XAI methods emerged, such as LIME (local interpretable model-agnostic explanations)[2] and Shapley additive explanations (SHAP).[3] However, due to the ambiguous and versatile nature of the word 'explanation', many scholars have been proposing different interpretations of explainability, with the consequence that a lot of different taxonomies have been proposed to define and classify XAI methods. In this regard, an ambitious work has been proposed by Speith,[4] which tries to make sense of the various taxonomies and classifications of XAI methods. In our chapter, we will start from this definitional level of analysis, trying to further clarify what is an explanation, and why there has been so much confusion and overlap between explainability and other concepts. We will also see how this idea of explainability is connected to more specific concepts which are crucial in the legal domain and in legal XAI.

With regard to this intersection between XAI and law, there have been only a few studies which analysed the intersection between explainability and law in the field of ADM and EU administration. In this regard, a crucial work has been proposed by Fink and Finck,[5] which has been of great inspiration for our work and describes ADM in EU administration[6] by showing the most important legal basis concerting ADM for EU bodies, focusing on both primary and secondary legislation. Some previous studies have been dedicated to shedding some light on a similar direction,

[2] Marco Tulio Ribeiro, Sameer Singh, and Carlos Guestrin, '"Why Should I Trust You?" Explaining the Predictions of Any Classifier' (2016) Proceedings of the 22nd ACM SIGKDD International Conference on Knowledge Discovery and Data Mining 1135–44.

[3] Scott M Lundberg and Su-In Lee, 'A Unified Approach to Interpreting Model Predictions' (2017) 30 Advances in Neural Information Processing Systems.

[4] Timo Speith, 'A Review of Taxonomies of Explainable Artificial Intelligence (XAI) Methods' (2022) ACM Conference on Fairness, Accountability, and Transparency 2239–50.

[5] M Fink and M Finck, 'Reasoned AI Administration: Explanation Requirements in EU Law and the Automation of Public Administration' (2022) 47(3) European Law Review 376–92.

[6] HC Hofmann, 'An Introduction to Automated Decision-Making (ADM) and Cyber-Delegation in the Scope of EU Public Law' University of Luxembourg Law Research Paper (2021-008).

like the one proposed by Hacker and Passoth[7] and another by Bibal and others.[8] However, we believe that more effort is needed to address the interconnection between law and XAI methods, especially because these methods are increasing in number and variety and show different ways in which explainability can be addressed. For this reason, this chapter is an attempt to offer some steps in this direction, trying to connect legal requirements with some specific XAI techniques.

C. Explanation and explainability

One of the problems in the field of XAI is defining what explainability means and what is its relationship to other related terms such as 'understandability', 'interpretability', and 'transparency'.

The *Oxford English Dictionary* defines 'explanation' as 'a statement or account that makes something clear'. Etymologically, the word 'explain' is associated with the Latin verb '*explanare*' which is composed of the prefix 'ex' (ie out) and 'planus' (ie plain), which refers to the idea of making things plain. This is contextual with regards to XAI, as the underlying aim of this field is to make the decisions of AI systems clear or understandable to humans.

However, the scientific community proposed different meanings for the term 'explanation'.[9] Moreover, the word 'explainability' is often used in reference to (or even in place of) other close or overlapping concepts. When talking about explainability in the legal context, the term can be even associated with specific goals such as 'justification', 'accountability', 'fairness', and 'privacy'. We argue that the reason why the term 'explainability' is often used in combination or in reference to other concepts is this multidimensional nature of the explainability.

I. Explanation and its dimensions

The ambiguous use of the term 'explainability' is somehow due to the fact that explanation is in itself a multidimensional concept whose dimensions can be intertwined. From a very general and abstract perspective, an explanation implies that there is an interaction between a source (delivering some piece of information, ie the explanation) and a destination (receiving the explanation), a target (the object

[7] P Hacker and J-H Passoth, 'Varieties of AI Explanations Under the Law. From the GDPR to the AIA, and Beyond' in A Holzinger and others (eds) *International Workshop on Extending Explainable AI Beyond Deep Models and Classifiers* (Springer 2020) 343–73.

[8] A Bibal and others, 'Legal Requirements on Explainability in Machine Learning' (2021) 29 Artificial Intelligence and Law 149–69.

[9] R Guidotti and others, 'A Survey of Methods for Explaining Black Box Models' (2018) 51(5) ACM Computing Surveys (CSUR) 1–42.

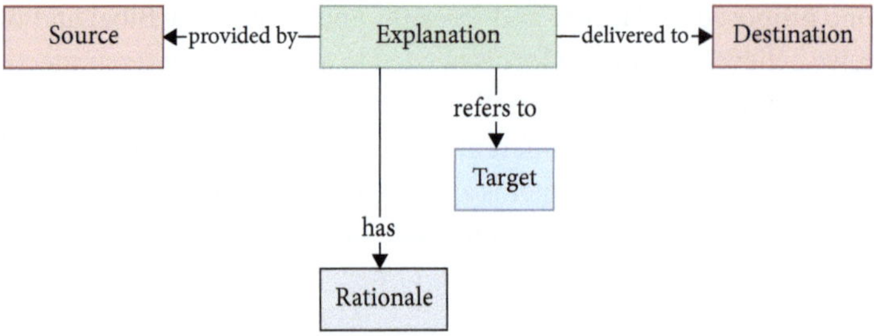

Figure 9.1 The main dimensions of an explanation.

of the explanation), and a rationale (the reasons and the goals of the explanation) (see Figure 9.1).

At the most abstract level, explanations have at least one rationale, namely providing some clarity about the explanation target;[10] we can see this as the very basic rationale of any explanation. In other cases, the rationale can be more specifically related to the context of the explanation: for example, in the context of ADM in EU administration, the rationale of an explanation might be that of providing some kind of assessment with regard to the fairness of an automated decision. In other words, the rationale can be very simple and basic (aiming at providing just clarity) or more complex (being directly connected to the aims or goals of a given explanation). We will clarify this aspect further in the following sections.

II. Types of explainability

If an explanation is an exchange of information which has the goal to clarify some target, explainability is the capacity of some target to be explainable. By definition, something is explainable if it can be explained, where the word 'can' usually refers to the intrinsic capability of the target or to an extrinsic possibility.[11] Moreover, the explainability of a target can be seen in a multifaceted way since it reflects the multidimensional nature of the word 'explanation'. We argue that there are four notions of explainability: it can be acquired, intrinsic, external, and contextual.

For example, one can refer to the explainability provided by the source (we call it acquired explainability). Supposing that an EU body is using an XAI method to provide an explanation of a specific automated decision from an AI system

[10] It is important to note that sometimes the clarifying information is not needed (what we call 'destination' might not need such information to have a better understanding of the target).

[11] Adjectives with the suffix -able/-ability (adjectives denoting ability) are multifaceted by nature, since the potentiality channelled by their suffixes may convey different meanings (possible, capable of, suitable for, allowed to, causing/resulting in). The meaning of -able adjectives depends on the context, on the nature of the adjective itself, and on the object modified by the adjective.

employed by the EU body itself. In this scenario, some explainability will be provided by the relative XAI algorithm (in this sense, the XAI method/algorithm will be the source of the explanation).

Another notion of explainability is referred to the nature of the target itself (this is intrinsic explainability). For example, supposing that we are using an AI model or algorithm to produce a specific automated decision, our artificial model or algorithm will have a specific level of explainability depending on its nature (eg depending on whether it is a transparent model or a black-box model). This explainability is not acquired from the explanatory process (ie by an explanation's source), instead it is an intrinsic quality of the target.

A further notion of explainability is referred to the destination's capability of understanding the target (external explainability). As an example, suppose that a decision made by a deep learning algorithm has to be evaluated by people who have no knowledge about AI. In this scenario, we might refer to a lack of explainability of the algorithm's decision because of the illiteracy of the destination. In other words, in this case our notion of explainability will be directly connected to what we called the explanation's destination.

Finally, explainability can also depend on the specific kind of explanation which is acceptable in a specific context (contextual explainability). This notion of explainability is very much dependent on the underlying rationale of the context in which the explanation is envisaged. For example, one might say that there is a lack of explainability because a specific rationale is not satisfactorily explained (see Figure 9.2).

In other words, the explainability can depend on each one of four dimensions surrounding the concept of explanation, as illustrated in Figure 9.1. Consequently, all these notions of explainability can coexist in the same scenario, showing different analytical angles for the explanation (see Figure 9.2).

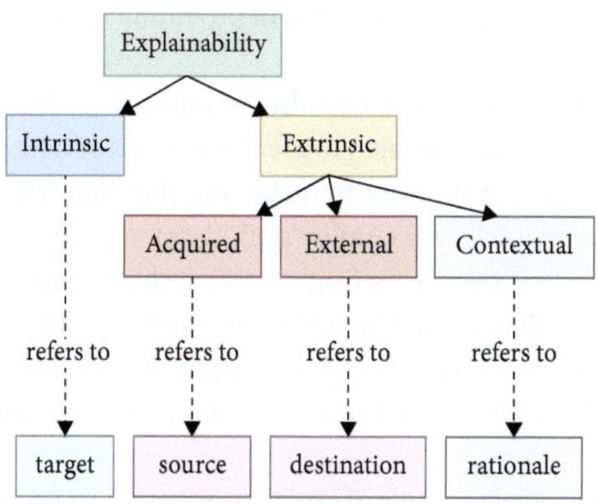

Figure 9.2 Four different notions of explainability.

For example, suppose that we are dealing with an AI system used by a European administration and that we are interested in understanding why the system took a very specific decision. In this scenario, the acquired explainability might be provided by an XAI method and is instantiated by the information provided by the XAI method itself. The intrinsic explainability will be determined by the kind of algorithm used by the AI system to produce the decision (is it a transparent AI system, or a black-box system?). The external explainability will be related to the agents who will receive the explanation (are they capable of understanding the explanation?). The contextual explainability will be related to the specific rationale of the explanation (eg there might be a requirement to provide an assessment that the decision to be explained was fair and not discriminatory). In this scenario, the explainability of the system will be the result of these different interconnected analytical angles.

To sum up, we can reformulate our previous definition of explainability: explainability is the intrinsic or acquired capacity of something to be explained (with some purposes or rationales) to some agent.

III. An explanations' rationales and transparency

As mentioned earlier, the rationale of an explanation can deeply determine what can be acceptable as an explanation. While the basic rationale of an explanation is to provide some clarity, understandability, or interpretability (ie making the target clear, understandable, or interpretable by the destination), in some context, this basic clarification is just one of the steps toward a more complex rationale.

In this regard, the rationale can be very much specific to the context in which the automated decision is taken. For example, in some context, we might want our systems to be capable to explain why their automated decisions are aligned to principles such as 'privacy', 'fairness', and 'accountability'. Other rationales can instead be very abstract and general, like that of providing trust (ie making the target trustworthy).

In the field of XAI, explanations can also be referred to data, which means we can have specific rationales dedicated to the dimensions of data. For example, one might want to explain data in order to make sure that they are 'relevant' (for the task of the AI system which will employ such data), or 'representative' (to avoid discriminatory or biased outcomes from the AI system which will leverage such data). In this sense, 'relevance' and 'representativeness' are other kind of rationales.

In other words, the explainability can be connected to different concept because the underlying explanation can be aimed towards different goals (ie it can have different rationales).

Transparency A special example of explanation rationale is transparency, which is an instance of complex rationale, since it is a concept which can have different meanings. For example, according to Lipton,[12] there are different notions of transparency in the field of AI:

- Simulatability
- Decomposability
- Algorithmic transparency

Simulatability emphasizes the ease of mentally reproducing the model's decision process. Decomposability highlights the ability to dissect and understand the model's components. Algorithmic transparency focuses on the clarity of the underlying algorithm.

In the context of ADM, especially in EU administration, EU bodies are required to exert their power by fostering transparency in order to grant citizens with a sufficient amount of information such that they are able not only to comprehend their position after the decision is made but also to challenge the decision itself before the institutions. Therefore, an automated system used by an EU administration to perform automated decisions should be capable of providing some degree of transparency for its decisions, assessing whether an AI system has an acceptable level of transparency with regard to one or more of the three kinds of transparency mentioned earlier, depending on the given context. Moreover, transparency is a complex rational because its scope often overlaps with the scope of other rationales such as 'accountability', 'trust', and so on. In fact, crucially for ADM in EU administration:

- Transparency ensures that the EU bodies are accountable for their actions. It allows the public to verify that EU institutions are functioning properly and are not abusing their power. This also includes how EU bodies use and manage personal and data information.
- Transparency fosters trust. When the public can see how decisions are made this helps to build confidence in the EU bodies and administration.
- Transparency supports the principle of participatory democracy. When information is freely available, citizens are better equipped to engage in dialogue and decision-making processes.
- Transparency is a hallmark of good governance. It contributes to efficiency, effectiveness, and rule of law. It allows for scrutiny, which ensures that best practices are being followed, and can act as a deterrent to corruption. When there is a high level of transparency it is more difficult for unethical behaviour to go unnoticed.

[12] Zachary T Lipton, 'The Mythos of Model Interpretability: In Machine Learning, the Concept of Interpretability is Both Important and Slippery' (2018) 16(3) Queue 31–57.

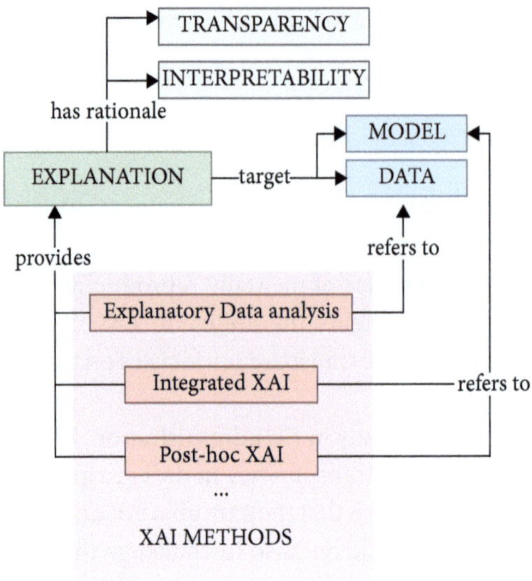

Figure 9.3 XAI's explanation scope.

Moreover, the European Treaties foster the EU institutions to conduct their work as openly and as closely as possible to the citizen, for which transparency is an essential requirement.

It should also be remarked that transparency is very much related but not equal to interpretability, although some studies (like the one by Lipton) use these terms almost in an interchangeable way. In the context of explainability, we think that interpretability should be more related to the subjective capacities of the destination, while transparency should be more related to the objective intrinsic qualities of the target. Similarly, 'transparent' is not equal to 'understandable'.

As an example, we might consider a very transparent ML algorithm like a decision tree. Decision trees are generally considered intrinsically transparent and interpretable 'white-box' models because one can see exactly what there is in each of their branches. However, they can also be very complex in their structure or in the interpretation of what each branch represents, which would make them less interpretable for some people. In this sense, even if their intrinsic (objective) transparency would not be contested, their interpretability might still be contested (subjectively) because of their complex structure.

D. eXplainable AI

Another source of confusion in the field of XAI is related to the different ways of categorizing XAI methods. As we mentioned, XAI methods can be applied to both AI

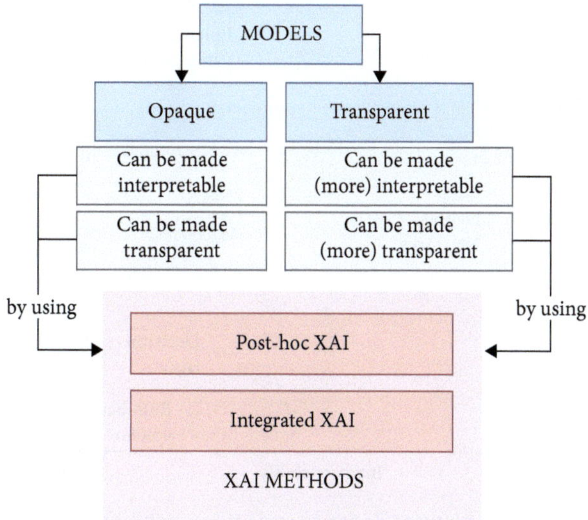

Figure 9.4 XAI methods can be used both on opaque and on already transparent models.

models and data. A famous example of XAI method applied to data is so-called explanatory data analysis (EDA), which focuses on providing useful insights about data and datasets (as we will see later in this chapter, this is an important aspect for the lawfulness of AI systems). However, most of the studies on XAI are currently focusing on AI models, either to provide these models with some post-hoc explainability (ie providing an explanation for the models' decisions) or to provide integrated explainability (ie creating models which are intrinsically designed to be more interpretable or more transparent).[13] These different aspects are shown in Figure 9.3.

Therefore, it is important to notice that XAI methods are not just used to deal with black-box (ie opaque) models. Instead, XAI methods have the more comprehensive goal of enhancing transparency and interpretability of any AI model, even those which are possibly already intrinsically transparent. In fact, 'transparent' is not synonyms of 'understandable'. Transparent models might still need some XAI method to make them more understandable (see Figure 9.4).

I. Trade-offs in XAI

Explainability cannot be accurately characterized as a binary attribute: 'explainable' vs 'not explainable'. The attribution of explainability is more similar to a

[13] It can be useful to remark that the former are related to the external explainability mentioned earlier, while the latter are related to the intrinsic explainability.

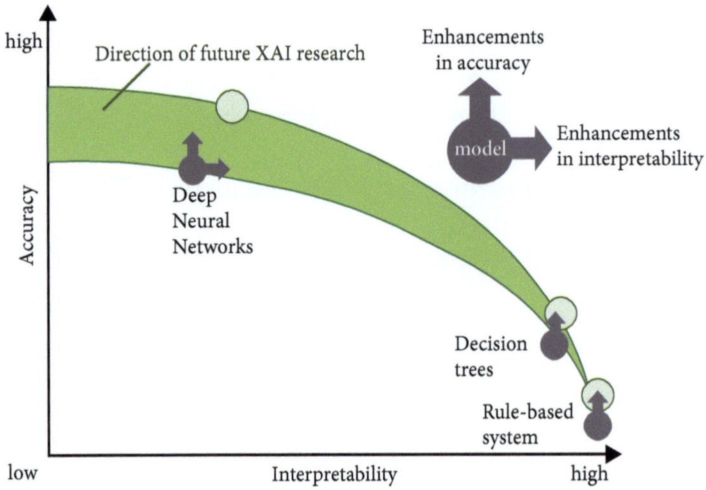

Figure 9.5 The trade-off between accuracy and interpretability for some types of AI systems.

gradient or spectrum of values ranging from high to low, rather than a dichotomous discrete categorization.

Moreover, explainability is often a compromise, since more explainable systems can have less performative outcomes. Highly complex models (like deep learning, random forests, or gradient-boosting machines) often give better predictive performance but have a low interpretability because they involve many parameters and complex structures. On the other hand, simpler models (like linear or logistic regression) are easily interpretable but might not perform as well on complex tasks. Figure 9.5 is inspired by a well-known graph proposed by Arrieta and others[14] and shows how the field of XAI tries to find the right compromise in this trade-off between performance/accuracy and explainability/interpretability.

Apart from the above-mentioned trade-off between prediction accuracy vs interpretability, there are other important trade-offs to consider in the field of XAI.

An important trade-off is transparency vs usability/scalability. In fact, full transparency might require disclosing all aspects of an AI model, which could affect usability by overwhelming non-expert users with unnecessary details. Additionally, creating fully transparent models could require significant computational resources, challenging scalability or efficiency.

Another important trade-off is privacy vs explainability: providing detailed explanations may also risk disclosing sensitive details from the training data, causing

[14] AB Arrieta and others, 'Explainable Artificial Intelligence (XAI): Concepts, Taxonomies, Opportunities and Challenges Toward Responsible AI' (2020) 58 Information Fusion 82–115.

privacy concerns. On the other hand, obscur\ing this element for the sake of privacy can compromise the system's explainability.

A further kind of trade-off is explainability vs time and computer resources, since acquiring highly interpretable models or explanations can be computationally intensive and time-consuming.

II. Categories of XAI methods

To the best of our knowledge, the most complete and comprehensive categorization of XAI methods is the one proposed by Speith,[15] which shows the most common ways in which scholars classify XAI methods.

Inspired by Speith, Figure 9.6 shows an illustration of different ways in which XAI methods can be categorized.

Stage One of the main categorization is related to the 'stage' on which the XAI method is dedicated: some XAI methods focus on the 'post-hoc' stage (the stage which occurs *after* the model's output or automated decision), while other XAI methods focus on the 'ante-hoc' stage (the stage which occurs *before* the automated decision). Post-hoc methods are becoming very popular due to the necessity of explaining black-box models such as those based on deep neural networks (DNNs).

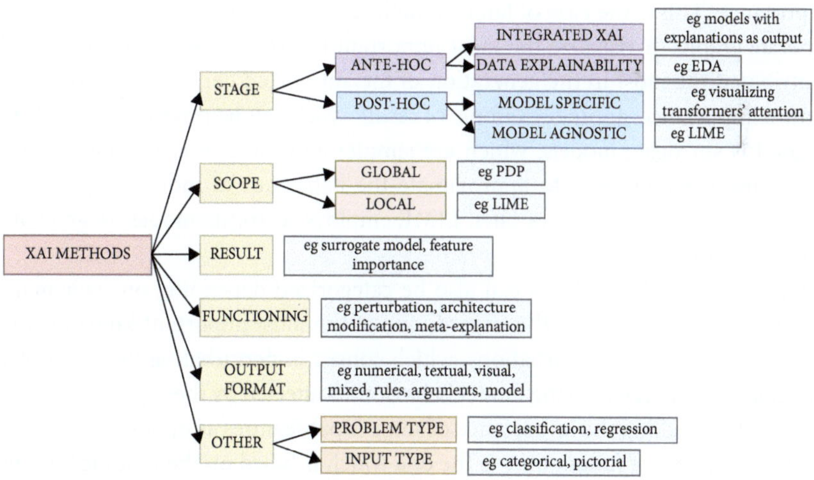

Figure 9.6 Taxonomy of explainable methods.

15 Speith (n 4).

Since these models are intrinsically opaque, post-hoc XAI methods tries to shed some light on their behaviour by analysing their output. Post-hoc methods can, in turn, be categorized by whether their applicability is model-specific (ie whether the XAI methods can only work for specific models) or model-agnostic (ie whether the XAI methods can work for any models). For example, explanations based on the visualization of the attention mechanism can be applied only with neural networks which employs the attention mechanism (eg transformers). On the other side, methods such as LIME[16] and SHAP[17] can be applied to any model. As far as ante-hoc methods are concerned, they can either be dedicated to the explanation of data (as with EDA) or to improve the transparency and interpretability of models directly at the modelling stage (which is what we call integrated XAI).

Scope Another important way of categorizing XAI methods is by referring to whether the produced explanations have a local or global scope. On the one hand, local explanations provide explainability about why an AI model made a specific single prediction, for example by focusing on how features contributed to that particular outcome. A global explanation, on the other hand, describes the overall behaviour of the model, providing a general understanding of how the model makes predictions based on all the features across all instances. A famous example of XAI method which provides local explanations is LIME, while an example of XAI method which provides global explanations is partial dependency plots (PDPs). We will have a look to these methods in section F.

Results XAI methods can be categorized depending on the kind of output they generate. For example, some XAI methods provide explanations in terms of feature importance. This is the case of famous methods such as LIME and SHAP, which generate graphs to visualize the most important features (ie which features have contributed the most in the generation of the automated decisions). Apart from feature importance, another example of result which can be produced by an XAI method is surrogate models, which are simpler and more interpretable models which are generally used to approximate the behaviour of more complex and opaque models (as we will see later, LIME employs surrogate models to generate its explanations).

Functioning XAI methods can also be categorized depending on their main underlying functioning. In this regard, one of the most important kinds of XAI approach is based on perturbations, which consist in perturbating the input of a model in order to see how the model behaviour is affected by these perturbations, potentially signalling the importance of some input features as opposed to others. Another example of functioning is the one which is based on the modification of the model's architecture.[18] XAI methods functioning in this way simplify complex

[16] Ribeiro, Singh, and Guestrin (n 2).
[17] Lundberg and Lee (n 3).
[18] Arrieta and others (n 14).

models by altering their architecture. A further example of functioning are explanations based on previous explanations, also called meta-explanations.[19] Another category functioning is based on leveraging the structure of the model to provide explanations (eg using the gradients of a DNN).[20]

Output format Another way of categorizing XAI methods is by simply referring to what kind of outputs they provide. Some XAI methods provide numerical values, other methods provide textual values, and others provide visual representations such as graphs or diagrams. There are also models which combine different options providing mixed outputs. Other kinds of input types are rules, arguments, and even other models.

Other Apart from the above-mentioned taxonomies, there are other ways of classifying XAI methods. As noticed by Speith,[21] another potential way of categorizing models concerns for which kind of problem the XAI method is conceived (eg regression, classification). Another way of categorizing XAI methods is by referring to the type of input data the method employs.

E. Lawful explanations

In this section, we discuss explainability and lawfulness. We will describe some legal basis which regulate explainability in EU administration and ADM. At the same time, we will show how these legal provisions are met by current XAI methods.

I. Duty to give reasons

In the context of ADM in EU administration, there are 'long-standing and deeply rooted explanation duties in administrative law'.[22] A pillar of EU administrative law is in fact the duty to give reasons. According to this duty, EU bodies are requested to provide reasons for their decisions.

The duty to give reasons is rooted in different legal basis. For example, Article 296 Treaty on the Functioning of the European Union (TFEU) states that legal acts 'shall state the reasons on which they are based'. Moreover, Article 41 of the Charter of Fundamental Rights (CFR), which is focused on the procedural side, describes a range of rights to ensure the more general right to good administration, stating that there is an 'obligation of the administration to give reasons for its decisions'.

[19] Wojciech Samek and Klaus-Robert Müller, 'Towards Explainable Artificial Intelligence' (2019) Explainable AI: Interpreting, Explaining and Visualizing Deep Learning 5–22.
[20] ibid.
[21] Speith (n 4).
[22] Fink and Finck (n 5).

Furthermore, the duty to give a reason is well rooted also as a general principle of law, and the Court of Justice of the European Union (CJEU) often refers to the duty to give a reason, which is seen both as a way for EU bodies to exert their power to review the legality of decisions and as a way for citizen to have enough information to assess whether the decisions affecting their lives are well founded (possibly challenging them if that is not the case).

More precisely, the duty to give reasons requires a decision-making authority to state the facts and the most decisive legal considerations that were brought to bear when a decision was being made, also mentioning relevant counterarguments to that decision. According to the CJEU, the reasons provided by the EU bodies must be appropriate to the content of the decision and to the interests of the individuals affected by such decision, which means that decisions having negative and important consequences on an individual require more explanations.

Giving reasons with XAI The problem here is that for an EU body to provide reasons for an automated decision generated by an AI system, the AI system must have some degree of explainability. Moreover, as noticed by Fink and Finck,[23] 'the fact that AI is used may actually be a reason to increase the decision-maker's reasoning obligations'. Given that one of the key aspects mentioned by the CJEU in reference to the requirements of the statement of reasons provided by EU bodies is that these reasons have the crucial goal of allowing decision review, a crucial XAI dimension to consider is the one related to the scope of the XAI methods. In fact, in case an EU body is requested to review a decision made about a single individual, the provided explanation will probably need a local scope through which the EU body can say why the automated decision had some given outcomes. Moreover, the EU body will probably need to assess the global scope of the AI system too, especially in cases where the local explanation led the EU bodies to judge the automated decision negatively (eg unfair or discriminatory). In this scenario, a global explanation could be used to determine whether the AI system tends to reproduce the same unfair or discriminatory automated decision with regard to more individuals, especially if they belong to a minority or to some potentially discriminated group.

Moreover, supposing that global explanation methods show that the AI system addresses a specific group of individuals unfairly, this could mean that the underlying data on which the AI system was trained on was not sufficiently accurate, relevant, or representative. In this regard, according to the Article 10(3) of the recent AI Act, 'training, validation and testing data sets shall be relevant, representative, free of errors and complete'. In this scenario, another group of XAI methods which will be relevant for addressing and evaluating the (unfair) automated decision is be the one we defined as data explainability methods, whose goal is to provide explainability at the level of data (such as EDA).

[23] ibid.

II. Right to an explanation

In the last few years, a huge topic of debate has been related to the existence of a right to an explanation. This debate raised from the interpretation of Article 22 of the European General Data Protection Regulation (GDPR). Article 22 introduces a prohibition on the use of 'solely automated decision-making', stating some exceptions on Article 22(3), paragraph 3. For these exceptions, a 'right to an explanation' is envisaged in recital 71. The problem here is that the Legislator has decided to add this statement in a recital, that is in a non-legally binding provision. This opened a huge debate among legal experts in the attempt to determine whether or not such a right actually exists.[24,25,26]

As far as the ADM in EU administration is concerned, the GDPR does not actually apply in the context of EU administration. In the context of EU administration, the relevant law is Regulation 2018/1725 (the European Union Data Protection Regulation (EUDPR)), which regulates how EU institutions, bodies, and agencies should process personal data. However, the provisions related to the right to an explanation mentioned for the GDPR are identical to those in the EUDPR: Article 22 and recital 71 of the GDPR are equivalent to Article 24 and recital 43 of the EUDPR. This means that GDPR and EUDPR share a common ambiguous formulation for the alleged, previously mentioned 'right to an explanation'.

As clarified by Fink and Finck,[27] only case law from the CJEU will clarify whether and to what extent such a right exists. However, since this right is defined explicitly (although in a non-legally binding way), it can be inferred that it has at least a 'political' or symbolic nature, aiming at shaping some future directions both in terms of legislation and in terms of case law.

Right to an explanation using XAI In case the enforceability of a right of an explanation is defined by the CJEU, this right would certainly make the use of XAI methods even more important in the data protection procedures where decision-making is totally automated. In practice, this would mean that XAI methods would be required to provide explanations in the context of data protection for the exceptions specified in Article 24 EUDPR. These explanations would aim, for example, at describing how an AI system processes data and for what purposes.

24 Bryce Goodman and Seth Flaxman, 'European Union Regulations on Algorithmic Decision-Making and a "Right to Explanation"' (2017) 38(3) AI Magazine 50–57.

25 Sandra Wachter, Brent Mittelstadt, and Luciano Floridi, 'Why a Right to Explanation of Automated Decision-Making Does Not Exist in the General Data Protection Regulation' (2017) 7(2) International Data Privacy Law 76–99.

26 Fink and Finck (n 5).

27 ibid.

III. AI Act requirements

The recent AI Act (AIA) is another important piece of law for the scope of this work since it is also applicable in the context of EU administration and it fosters the enforcement of explainability for AI systems. More precisely, the AIA proposed a risk-based approach to regulate the use of AI systems. The deployment of AI systems which are considered at higher levels of risk is subject to stricter requirements and obligations. Among these requirements, a crucial role is played by transparency: the higher the risks of the use of an AI system the higher the level of required transparency.

The AIA is very much focused on the concept of transparency. For example, in Article 52, a right to be informed is defined, stating that 'AI systems intended to interact with natural persons' must be 'designed and developed in such a way that natural persons are informed that they are interacting with an AI system'. In other words, Article 52 creates a simple duty to inform the user about the fact that they are interacting with an artificial system, which is quite similar to other analogous provisions in product liability law (where products are required to have some informative statements). Article 13 of AIA is probably more relevant for the scope of our work since it directly addresses the need to provide explainability (not just informative statements). The article states that 'high-risk AI systems shall be designed and developed in such a way to ensure that their operation is sufficiently transparent to enable users to interpret the system's output and use it appropriately'.

It is relevant that the legislator decided to say 'sufficiently', showing that transparency (similarly to explainability) is a gradual continuous value and not a discrete dichotomous categorization. It is also relevant that the envisaged goal is to 'enable users to interpret the system', acknowledging the subjective counterpart of the term 'transparency', usually referred to as 'interpretability'.

Going further into the details of Article 13, there is an obligation for the providers of high-risk AI systems to provide instructions containing 'characteristics, capabilities and limitations of performance of the high-risk AI systems', which includes among other things the intended purpose of the AI system, as well as the level of accuracy, robustness, and cybersecurity. Moreover, the instructions must also include 'the performance as regards the persons or groups of persons on which the system is intended to be used' and 'when appropriate, specifications for the input data, or any other relevant information in terms of the training, validation and testing data sets used, taking into account the intended purpose of the AI system'.

Importantly, the requirements set out in Article 13 are not to be interpreted as a right to an explanation (mentioned in the previous section) but rather as an obligation of explainability, which must be addressed by AI system providers.

The providers of AI systems must ensure a certain degree of explainability for their systems, which they can achieve through the use of XAI methods.

XAI methods for the AIA XAI methods can be useful to facilitate the compliance with the requirements set out by AIA. In this regard, XAI methods can be used by providers of high-risk AI systems to generate some of these informative instructions. For example, this might be the case for the requirement related to the performance with regards to specific groups of people, since some features of the data can be shown to be relevant for the robustness of the model with regard to specific data points. In this sense, a combination of local and global methods would be needed, similar to what we said earlier with regard to the duty to give reasons.[28]

Another important aspect in this regard concerns the previously mentioned requirements in terms of input data, including training and validation datasets. To understand this requirement better, recital 44 can be a complementary source of information since it specifies that data must be 'relevant, representative and free of errors' as well as 'complete in view of the intended purpose of the system'. Moreover, requirements are further specified in Article 10(2) of AIA, related to 'data and data governance', where some requirements are laid out which concern the practices that data governance should employ. These practices should concern, for example, data collection, design choices, and any relevant data preparation and manipulation. Moreover, data governance and management should concern 'a prior assessment of the availability, quantity and suitability of the data sets that are needed' and 'examination in view of possible biases'.

In this regard, data explainability (like EDA) can surely be used to describe the relevance of data with respect to the intended goals of the system. In other words, to comply with these requirements, providers of high-risk AI systems will probably need to address different XAI methods, both those related to the explainability of the underlying models (eg integrated XAI, post-hoc XAI) and those related to the explainability of the employed data (eg EDA).

This obligation of explainability set out in Article 13 is even more important when considering point (e) of Article 13(3), which states that the information should include 'the expected lifetime of the high-risk AI system and any necessary maintenance and care measures to ensure the proper functioning of that AI system, including as regards software updates'. This requirement is closely connected to data governance since some AI systems might require a periodic update of the underlying training data, which means that data explainability will be periodically needed.

[28] The duty to give reason in administrative law is very much related to the obligation to an explainability of the AI Act, even if the former is intended for EU bodies only, while the latter includes EU bodies as well as private stakeholders.

IV. XAI as a compromise

It is important to underline that the legal framework described so far seems to give an important role to the performance of the models. For example, we mentioned the 'the performance as regards the persons or groups of persons', which seems to be a reference to the risk of some systems to be unfair, discriminatory, or simply non-representative with respect to specific groups. However, this is where it becomes clear that in some cases AI providers will need to face a compromise, given the trade-off between explainability and performance mentioned in section D.I and described in Figure 9.5. For example, we might have cases in which the contested opacity of some AI system might be justified by a higher capacity of such a system to be fair. Similarly, we might have cases in which the required transparency of some high-risk AI system might produce a lower capacity of such a system to generate fair decisions. In these cases, the compromise will probably require AI providers to use a combination of different XAI methods, tackling explainability from different perspectives at the same time, including the modelling stage (integrated XAI), the post-modelling stage (post-hoc XAI), as well as data explainability.

F. Methods of XAI

We will now describe some popular methods of XAI. In particular, we will describe two famous model-agnostic XAI methods, namely LIME and SHAP. Moreover, we will describe a well-known XAI method for global explanations called PDPs. While describing these methods, we will discuss how they can meet the legal requirements set out in the previous section.

I. LIME

LIME[29] is a method for explaining the predictions made by any ML model. LIME creates interpretable explanations by approximating the prediction surface locally, around the outcome to be explained. To do this, LIME generates a new dataset of perturbed samples, obtains the predictions for these from the original model, and then applies a simple model (eg a linear model) to these samples. The coefficients of the simpler model serve as the explanation and can help in understanding how each feature affects the prediction for the specific instance to be explained. The advantage of LIME is that it provides model-agnostic and locally faithful explanations, helping to interpret complex models (see Figure 9.7).

[29] Ribeiro, Singh, and Guestrin (n 2).

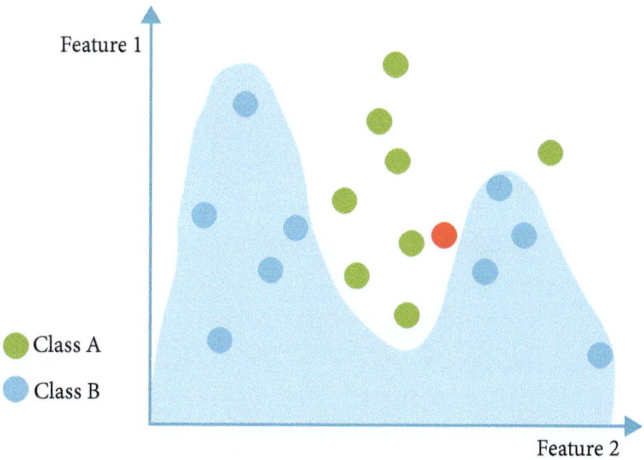

Figure 9.7 Illustrative example of a non-linear decision boundary of a complex (black-box) model. The red data point is the one for which we want an explanation.

To understand how LIME works, suppose we have a black-box model which generates some complex (non-linear) decision boundary on our data points. To keep this scenario simple, we can consider a simple binary classification. The decision boundary might look similar to the one depicted in Figure 9.7, and we might have a data point for which we want to know why a decision has been made. For example, in Figure 9.7, the red data point is classified as belonging to class A (green), because it falls outside the decision's 'blue area', which represents our decision boundary (we coloured the point red just to show that it is the data point we want to target). Intuitively, this target data point could be seen as the single automated decision which a citizen might want to have an explanation for.

To give some explanations about why a decision was taken (ie why the red dot was classified under class A), LIME will focus on the local boundary in the proximity of the targeted data point, as illustrated in Figure 9.8. This is crucial because by zooming in the vicinity of a specific data point we can approximate a linear decision boundary, which is more explainable than the complex non-linearity of the global model.

As can be seen from Figure 9.8, LIME roughly performs four steps:

- It focuses on the vicinity of the targeted data point;
- It creates some perturbation on the data points (the yellow dots);
- It weights the data points depending on their vicinity to the target;
- It creates a surrogate linear model which approximate the behaviour of the complex model.

Since LIME creates a linear surrogate model which approximates the (local) behaviour of the complex black-box model, it generates numerical coefficients which

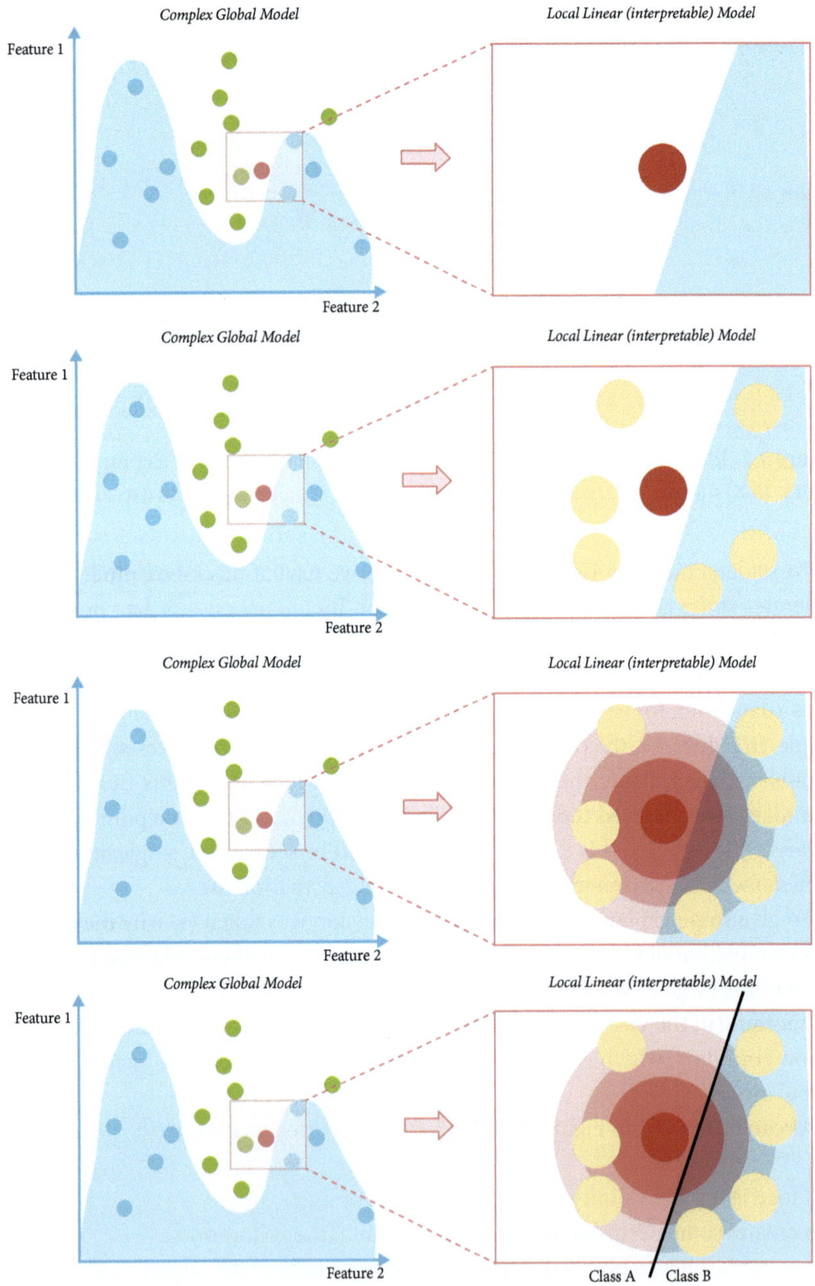

Figure 9.8 Illustrative example of the local boundary targeted by LIME.

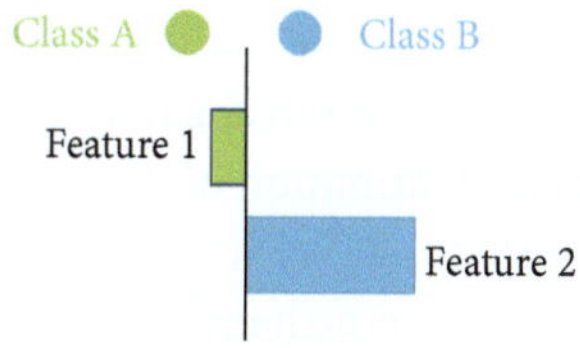

Figure 9.9 Example of visualization of feature importance showing that feature 2 contributed significantly towards the prediction.

can explain the contribution of each feature in determining why the data point fall on one side of the decision boundary as opposed to the other side. In this scenario, LIME will generate some visualizations which indicate the contribution of each feature (ie the feature importance) in the prediction of our targeted data point, as illustrated in Figure 9.9.

As we can see, LIME employs some of the aspects mentioned in the previous sections: perturbations (as a way of functioning), surrogate models (which is an intermediate result), feature importance (which is the final result), and visualization (which is the type of output) (see Figure 9.9).

LIME and its usefulness for legal XAI From the point of view of the legal requirements we described in the previous section, LIME can certainly be helpful in meeting the legal requirements of the current legal framework governing ADM in EU administration. Since LIME provides local explanations it is particularly suitable to address those situations in which an individual wants to exert their right to contest an automated decision which significantly affected them. In this scenario, the EU bodies might want to use LIME to address what features determined the given decision, as a step towards the clarification of the righteousness of the automated decision. Importantly, while this might provide the targeted decision with additional explainability, potentially meeting the previously mentioned duty to give reasons, this local explainability might not be sufficient, or even not significant. In fact, one of the criticisms of LIME is that it lacks consistency. Specifically, LIME does not guarantee that if the model changes such that it relies more on a feature, the attributed importance for that feature should not decrease. This means that LIME's local explanations are sometimes uninformative, and this could and should push an EU body to search for complementary explanatory insights through the use of other XAI methods.

II. SHAP

Another very famous method which recently achieved enormous success is SHAP,[30] which is a unified measure of feature importance that assigns each feature

[30] Lundberg and Lee (n 3).

an importance value for a particular prediction. SHAP values are based on the concept of a Shapley value from cooperative game theory. Their main characteristic is that they represent a fair distribution of the contribution of each feature to the prediction for a specific instance.

To understand this concept, it can be helpful to consider that the features employed in an ML algorithm have both an individual contribution towards the achievement of a specific prediction and a 'collective' contribution (in the sense that their contribution is not just individual but also correlated to the presence of other features).

Metaphorically, we can think of features as single individuals of a team. This team of individuals might have achieved a specific result (ie the prediction) and we might want to know which is a fair distribution of the merit for each individual (ie which is a fair distribution of the contribution). Shapley values answer this question by providing the so-called marginal contribution. This term refers to the additional benefit or value that is gained from increasing a particular input or factor while keeping all other factors constant.

SHAP employs this concept by considering different coalitions of inputs and by calculating the marginal contribution for all of them. The intuition behind this process, described in the previous metaphor, is illustrated in Figure 9.10.

To calculate the contributions of each feature, SHAP divides features into coalitions, where each coalition is a subset of features. This is particularly important, because some features achieve better results when they are together (while perhaps their contribution is negligible when only one of them is employed). To stick with the previous metaphor, supposing we have a team like the one on the top of Figure 9.10; it might be the case that the green individual and the grey individual have the greatest contribution in the achievement of the prize when they operate together, while they might have a negligible contribution in case they operate separately.

For each coalition (ie for each subset of features) SHAP compares the difference in the prediction when removing a single element of the coalition (ie a single features). In this way, it is possible to calculate all marginal contributions of the features, having as a result a numerical representation visualized in a graph where we can see which features contributed the most in a specific prediction.

Although SHAP, like LIME, is mostly thought as a local method (since we are trying to explain single predictions), it can also be used with a global scope by aggregating local explanations, which is one of the advantages of SHAP with regard to LIME.

SHAP and its usefulness for legal XAI While both SHAP and LIME are frequently employed, SHAP has some characteristics that make it more suitable in certain contexts:

- **Consistency:** The main advantage of SHAP over LIME is consistency. SHAP values are consistent in their explanations, which means that if we change a

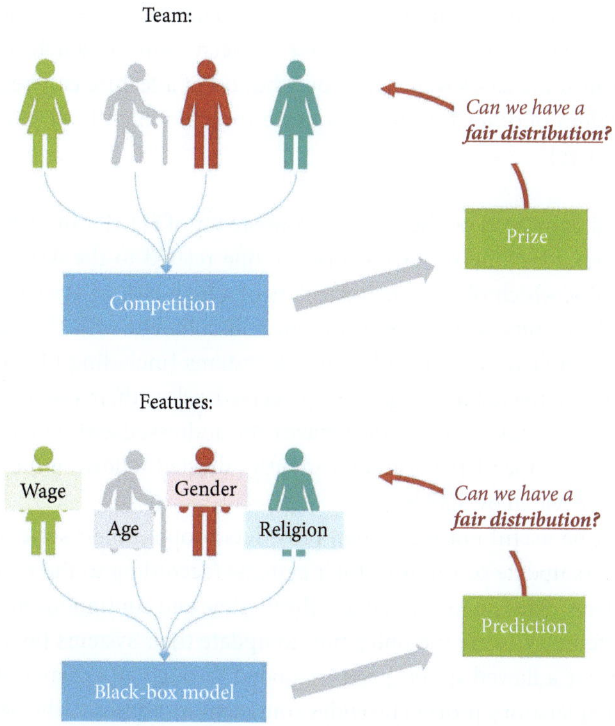

Figure 9.10 Shapley values, from game theory, address the problem of how to find a fair distribution of contribution. SHAP translates this concept in XAI in order to find the features' contribution for a specific prediction.

model to rely more on a feature, the attributed importance for that feature should not decrease. This consistency is lacking in LIME.

- **Game theoretic approach:** SHAP is based on game theory, which provides a more solid theoretical foundation and justification for the calculated importance values. This arguably makes SHAP's interpretability stronger as compared to LIME.
- **Global interpretability:** Along with local interpretability (explaining individual predictions), SHAP also provides global interpretability (which can describe the behaviour of the whole model).
- **Superior model agnosticity:** While both LIME and SHAP are model agnostic XAI methods, LIME has been criticized for the fact that the reliability of its results depends too much on the selected neighbourhood size (which determines the weighting process described in Figure 9.8), which is in turn a factor that is strongly affected by the underlying model. SHAP, instead, does not have this problem, since it is based on the above-mentioned game theoretic approach.

- **Handling feature interactions:** another consequence of SHAP's game theoretic nature is that SHAP handles interactions between features, which is extremely important in some cases where the contribution of a feature can be correlated with the values of other features (ie in case there is a high level of correlation among features).

From the legal point of view, the superior consistency of SHAP can certainly make it more suitable for some scenarios, like the one related to the AIA's obligation of explainability, which obliges the providers of a high-risk AI systems to ensure levels of explainability which are consistent and coherent with the purposes of the AI system. In fact, providers of high-risk systems (including EU bodies) will presumably be motivated to mitigate the perceived risk of their systems, therefore trying to show that their design choices have been addressed with a look to specific numerical values which have been consistently adjusted following the numerical explanations provided by SHAP.

This might be useful not only when providers propose their systems but also when providers update or improve their systems (according to the requirements set out in Article 13 of the AIA, related to the lifetime and continuous maintenance of the AI systems). Clearly the obligation to update their systems (as well as any need to improve a flawed system) can be guided through an explanatory process only if such explanatory process provides consistent responses to the newly introduced integrations.

III. PDPs

PDPs[31] offer a way to visually explore the relationship between a small number of input variables and the predictions made by a model. Similarly to LIME and SHAP, PDPs are model-agnostic (they can be used on any model). However, contrarily to LIME, PDPs operate on a global scope, that is they are a global XAI method. A PDP shows the marginal effect of a feature on the predicted outcome of a model, taking into account the average effect of all other features (this is why PDPs are a global XAI method). This is accomplished by systematically varying the values of the feature of interest, while holding all other features constant at their average values, and plotting the effect on the prediction. PDPs are particularly useful for visualizing interactions between features and their impact on the prediction, and can be used with any type of ML model.

For example, we might have a series of predictions generated by our model and we might want to know more about the relation between these predictions and

[31] Jerome H Friedman, 'Greedy Function Approximation: A Gradient Boosting Machine' (2001) Annals of Statistics 1189–232.

the input features on which our model was trained, from a global point of view. Suppose, for example, that our predictions are related to court decisions in the field of criminal law, where the prediction is 'approved' or 'rejected', and suppose we have some features (eg we might have both legal aspects and factual aspects). In this scenario, our features might be the nullity of the hearing (legal factor), the suspected criminal organization of the defendant (legal factor), and the number of years the defendant has been already in detention (factual factor). In this example, we might have a list of predictions made by our model, which might look like Table 9.1 and which we might want to explain from a global point of view.

For example, we might want to see what the global behaviour of our model's prediction is with regard to Feature 3 (the number of years the defendants already passed in detention in the past). In this scenario, we will follow the following simple steps:

- Choosing a set of fixed values for the selected feature (eg from 0 to the maximum value found in our dataset, say 12).
- For each fixed value, we will create a modified dataset where all instances have the same fixed value for the selected feature while keeping the original values for the other features.
- We will run the model's predictions for each modified dataset.
- We will calculate the average prediction for each unique fixed value of the selected feature, plotting it on a graph.

A drawback of PDPs is that they can be misleading when there are strong interactions or correlations between features or when missing data is not handled correctly.

PDPs and their usefulness for legal XAI Being a very intuitive and easily understandable method of global XAI, PDPs can be particularly useful for the purposes of the obligation of explainability. However, it is important to noticed that this method of XAI should be employed in context in which there is not a strong

Table 9.1 Prediction examples. *Feature 1 = nullity, Feature 2 = suspected criminal organization, Feature 3 = years in detention.*

Feature 1	Feature 2	Feature 3	Result
no	Camorra	2	approved
yes	Cosa Nostra	12	rejected
yes	'Ndrangheta	0	rejected
...	...	...	...

correlation between features because it could be a weakness in the robustness of the provided explainability.

Moreover, this method can arguably be useful to meet the duty to give reasons for the automated decisions performed by EU bodies and affecting single individuals (although in this case, reasons should probably be accompanied with some complementary local explanations directly connected to the single decision which affected the individual). In other words, also in this case, we can see that each method has advantages and limitations, and the optimal solution is often a combination of different XAI approaches.

G. Conclusions

This chapter tackles two issues. On the one hand it tries to shed some light on the interconnection between explainability and other related terms such as 'interpretability' and 'transparency'. In this regard, we showed why explainability is often used in combination or even in overlap with other terms, arguing that this versatility is somehow justified by the intrinsic multidimensional nature of the concept 'explanation'. On the other hand, this chapter shows how explainability is practically instantiated in the context of ADM for EU administration by referring to the legal basis which currently dominates the explainability requirements for automated systems in EU bodies. In this regard, we showed some of the most important obligations and rights which EU bodies must address when using ADM systems, considering more specifically how XAI methods can fit these obligations. Furthermore, we discussed why EU bodies are likely to need to address explainability requirements by employing different XAI methods in order to tackle different explanatory angles, given that there is no approach that is ideal for each and every scenario.

10

Interoperability in the EU

Paving the Way for Digital Public Services

Felix Pflücke

A. Introduction

Interoperability is a principle that has gained increasing importance in the context of the European Union's (EU) efforts to harmonize digital services and foster the Digital Single Market.[1] The EU's fundamental freedoms, namely the free movement of goods, services, capital, and people, form the core link to interoperability. Developing digital services that enable a seamless exchange of information and services between public service providers (PSP) across different Member States is essential to realizing these freedoms. Enhancing interoperability also supports the principle of good administration under Article 41 of the EU Charter. The EU and its Member States can foster a more efficient and less cumbersome regulatory environment by avoiding the unnecessary burden of repeatedly gathering and supplying information.

In recent years, the EU has placed a central focus on interoperability, undertaking numerous initiatives since the 1980s to address this critical aspect. However, the recent emergence of planned large-scale adoption of interoperability holds significant implications. This development bears the potential to propel innovation forward while fostering heightened efficiency and effectiveness within public services, for instance regarding automated decision-making (ADM). As a result, policy-makers, researchers, and practitioners alike have turned their attention towards this crucial area of interest.

The chapter begins by introducing the core principles and objectives underlying the EU's interoperability policy, emphasizing its transformative potential for diverse sectors and industries. It highlights the need for a coordinated and harmonized approach to interoperability, considering the complexities arising from varying national frameworks and diverging practices. Next, the chapter delves into the historical evolution of the EU's interoperability policy, tracing its roots back to the developments of the 1980s and 1990s. It explores critical milestones that have shaped the interoperability landscape, culminating in establishing a

[1] Commission, '2030 Digital Compass: The European way for the Digital Decade' COM(2021) 118 final, ss 3.4 and 5.2.

Felix Pflücke, *Interoperability in the EU* In: *Governance of Automated Decision-Making and EU Law.* Edited by: Herwig C.H. Hofmann and Felix Pflücke, Oxford University Press. © Felix Pflücke 2024.
DOI: 10.1093/9780198919575.003.0010

comprehensive European interoperability policy. It also discusses the significance of the European Interoperability Frameworks and the Tallinn Declaration of 2017, which emphasized digital transformation and interoperability in the Digital Single Market. The chapter then examines the European Commission's Interoperable Europe Act Regulation Proposal (the Proposal). It explores the Proposal's origins, ambitions, and the driving forces behind its formulation. The Proposal's impact on cross-border interoperability and public-sector cooperation in the EU is under analysis. The chapter also discusses the framework for future interoperability cooperation and the mechanisms to guide this collaborative endeavour. The chapter evaluates the progress towards achieving effective and efficient interoperability within the EU, considering challenges and opportunities related to technological advancements, governance structures, and legal frameworks. It concludes by emphasizing the significance of interoperability within the EU and presenting prospects and recommendations for realizing a genuinely interoperable Europe.

B. The EU Interoperability Policy

The EU Interoperability Policy has emerged as a dynamic and rapidly evolving policy field within the EU. Initially rooted in sectoral European and national initiatives, it has swiftly become one of the EU's most pressing and significant policy priorities. This section offers a comprehensive and critical examination of the origins and future trajectory of the EU Interoperability Policy. It aims to shed light on this policy domain's multifaceted nature and evolving landscape by delving into its historical development and exploring its potential future directions.

I. Early developments in the 1980s and 1990s

Early developments of a EU Interoperability Policy emerged during the 1980s and 1990s. One notable initiative during this period was the programme for using telematics in Community information systems, the CADDIA (Cooperation in the Automation of Data and Documentation for Imports-Exports and Agriculture) programme, specifically focusing on imports and exports and the management and control of agricultural market organizations.[2] A study conducted as part of

[2] It was initially created for two years by Council Decision (EEC) 85/214 of 26 March 1985 concerning the coordination of the activities of the Member States and the Commission related to the implementation of a long-term programme for the use of telematics for Community information systems concerned with imports/exports and the management and financial control of agricultural market organizations [1985] OJ L96/35 and renewed for another five years by Council Decision (EEC) 87/288 of 1 June 1987 concerning the extension of the period of validity of Decision 85/214/EEC and 86/23/EEC [1987] OJ L145/86. Eurofi Plc, *1992-Planning for the Information Technology Industries* (Butterworths and Eurofi Plc 1989) 108.

the CADDIA programme recommended adopting a ten-year development programme to be implemented by the European Commission and the competent national authorities.[3] The objective was to analyse telematics' feasibility, costs, and benefits for processing data and documentation in the mentioned areas. CADDIA included the development of coordinated and computerized administrative procedures,[4] and was also closely linked to the INSIS (Community Inter-Institutional Information System) programme[5] and the TEDIS (Trade Electronic Data Interchange) programme.[6]

To prepare for the implementation of the CADDIA programme, the European Commission collaborated with a so-called User Advisory Committee and engaged in preparatory activities with the Member States.[7] Within a year, the Commission presented a report to the Council and the European Parliament, accompanied by proposals for adopting a long-term development programme to be implemented jointly with relevant stakeholders.[8] This development marked an essential step in the early development of a European Interoperability Policy. Nonetheless, the scope of CADDIA was relatively narrow as it only concerned the customs, agricultural, and statistical sectors.[9]

The 1994 White Paper of the outgoing Delors administration addressed the need to expand interoperability further.[10] The White Paper emphasized the importance of achieving interconnection and interoperability to promote economic cooperation, growth, and international competitiveness.[11] It acknowledged that complete interoperability had yet to be achieved, particularly in sectors such as

[3] Commission, 'Long-term programme (EEC) for the use of telematics for Community information systems concerned with imports-exports and the management and control of agricultural market organizations (CADDIA)—Preparatory activities, 1982–1983' [1982] OJ L247—23:08:1982. Johannes Frerich and Gernot Müller, *Politisch-ökonomische Rahmenbedingungen, Verkehrsinfrastrukturpolitik* (De Gruyter 2010) 527.

[4] Council Decision (EEC) 86/23 of 4 February 1986 relating to the coordinated development of computerized administrative procedures (CD project) [1986] OJ L33/28. Eurofi Plc (n 2) 109.

[5] Proposal for a Council Decision on the coordination of the activities of the Member States and Community institutions with a view to setting up a Community inter-institutional information system (INSIS) COM(84) 380 final [1986] OJ C247/3, adopted by the Council on 22 December 1986 (session 1136). For a comment on the policy background see eg Hans R Hansen, *GI/OCG/ÖGI-Jahrestagung 1985* (Springer Publishing 1985) 276.

[6] Council Decision (EEC) 87/499 of 5 October 1987 introducing a communications network Community programme on trade electronic data interchange systems (TEDIS) [1987] OJ L285/35. Eurofi Plc (n 2) 109.

[7] Commission (n 3) para 4.

[8] ibid.

[9] As highlighted in Eurofi Plc (n 2) 108.

[10] Commission, 'Growth, competitiveness, employment—The challenges and ways forward into the 21st century: White paper' (European Commission Publications Office, 1994) <https://op.europa.eu/en/publication-detail/-/publication/0d563bc1-f17e-48ab-bb2a-9dd9a31d5004#> accessed 20 March 2023. The role of Europe in the global information society was highlighted in the Bangemann report, see Commission, 'Bangemann report: Europe and the global information society' (European Commission Publications Office, 1994) <https://cordis.europa.eu/article/id/2730-bangemann-report-europe-and-the-global-information-society> accessed 20 March 2023.

[11] ibid 90–94.

electronic images and mail and traffic management systems.[12] The report highlighted the need for additional efforts to achieve seamless interoperability 'to provide greater access to a wide range of interactive services and create a common information area'.[13]

As a result of the Delors White Paper, the EU adopted the Interchange of Data between Administrations (IDA) programme.[14] The IDA programme aimed to enhance interoperability and facilitated cooperation across European administrations from 1995 to 1999. The Standards Directive was also established, further advancing technical standards and regulations.[15]

The 1980s and 1990s witnessed significant progress in developing a sectoral EU Interoperability Policy. The CADDIA programme and subsequent initiatives like the IDA programme and the Standards Directive laid the groundwork for future advancements in interoperability within the EU. These initiatives set the tone for further integration in the following decade. Nonetheless, the EU promoted interoperability only in a few sectors, which, as depicted below, changed in the following decades.

II. Towards a more comprehensive European Interoperability Policy

Between 1999 and 2004, the European Interoperability Policy advanced by implementing the follow-on programme called IDA II, aiming to increase the efficiency of online public services.[16] The Stockholm European Council in 2001[17] and the eGovernment conference in Como in 2003[18] provided platforms for further expanding the EU Interoperability Policy. It led to the adoption of the Interoperable Delivery of European eGovernment Services to Public Administration, Business and Citizens (IDABC) programme,[19] which operated from 2005 to 2009 and took the evaluations from IDA II into account.[20]

[12] ibid 25, 30.

[13] ibid 25.

[14] Council Decision (EC) (95/468 of 6 November 1995 on a Community contribution for telematic interchange of data between administrations in the Community (IDA) [1995] OJ L269/23.

[15] Directive (EC) 98/34 of 22 June 1998 laying down a procedure for the provision of information in the field of technical standards and regulations [1998] OJ L204/37.

[16] Decision (EC) 1719/1999 of the European Parliament and of the Council of 12 July 1999 on a series of guidelines, including the identification of projects of common interest, for trans-European networks for the electronic interchange of data between administrations (IDA) [1999] OJ L203/1; Decision (EC) 1720/1999 of the European Parliament and of the Council of 12 July 1999 adopting a series of actions and measures in order to ensure interoperability of and access to trans-European networks for the electronic interchange of data between administrations (IDA) [1999] OJ L203/9.

[17] Commission, 'Network and Information Security: Proposal for A European Policy Approach' COM (2001) 298 final, 2–4.

[18] Commission, 'The Role of eGovernment for Europe's Future' COM (2003) 567 section 4.2.6.

[19] Decision (EC) 2004/387 of 21 April 2004 on the interoperable delivery of pan-European eGovernment services to public administrations, businesses and citizens (IDABC) [2004] OJ L144/62.

[20] Commission, 'Report on the Evaluation of the IDA II programme' COM (2005) 493 final.

IDA II and IDABC paved the way for establishing ISA[21] and ISA^2.[22] ISA, a targeted action programme, aimed to facilitate the development of efficient electronic cross-border public services, ensuring interoperability for citizens and businesses. It provided a comprehensive approach for European public administrations to collaborate and establish interoperable electronic services across borders. ISA^2, the successor to ISA, continued the efforts from 2010 to 2015, focusing on coordinating interoperability activities at the EU level, developing solutions aligned with the needs of businesses and citizens, and introducing key instruments such as the revised EIF,[23] the European Interoperability Strategy (EIS),[24] the European Interoperability Reference Architecture (EIRA),[25] and the European Interoperability Cartography (EIC)[26] to boost interoperability both at the EU and national levels.

III. The European Interoperability Frameworks

The EIF contain recommendations to promote interoperability solutions across the EU public services, which have evolved through different versions and updates over the years. The initial versions include EIF Version 1 in 2004, under the IDABC programme,[27] and EIF Version 2 in 2010, under the ISA programme.[28] However, the most recent significant development in the EIF is the release of the New EIF in light of ISA^2 in 2017.[29] This version introduces forty-seven recommendations—the previous version only contained twenty-five—aimed at promoting interoperability within the EU's and Member States' digital public services. Notably, the EIF operates voluntarily, meaning that its recommendations are optional but serve as guidance for achieving interoperability.

The EIF plays a crucial role in establishing a framework for interoperability between EU information systems, encompassing various fields such as borders and

[21] Decision (EC) 922/2009 of 16 September 2009 on interoperability solutions for European public administrations (ISA) [2009] OJ L260/20.

[22] Decision (EU) 2015/2240 of 25 November 2015 establishing a programme on interoperability solutions and common frameworks for European public administrations, businesses and citizens (ISA2 programme) as a means for modernising the public sector [2015] OJ L318/1.

[23] Commission, 'European Interoperability Framework—Implementation Strategy' COM (2017) 134 final.

[24] Commission, 'Towards interoperability for European public services' COM(2010) 744 final.

[25] Decision (EU) 2015/2240 (n 22).

[26] ibid.

[27] Commission, 'European Interoperability Framework for Pan-European eGovernment Services Version 1.0' (Commission, 2004) <https://joinup.ec.europa.eu/sites/default/files/custom-page/attachment/2021-11/EIF%20V1.0.pdf> accessed 12 May 2023.

[28] Commission, 'Towards interoperability for European public services' COM(2010) 744 final, Annex 2.

[29] Commission, 'European Interoperability Framework—Implementation Strategy' COM(2017) 134 final, including Annex 1 and 2 (New EIF).

visas, police and judicial cooperation, asylum, and migration. It addresses three main areas: administration to administration, administration to business, and administration to citizens.[30] It covers public service governance and interoperability's legal, organizational, semantic, and technical aspects.[31]

Legal interoperability ensures that public administrations operating under different legal frameworks can work together to provide European public services, requiring the identification of interoperability barriers, evaluation of legislation coherence, consideration of information and communications technology (ICT) impact, and maintenance of legal value and data protection across borders through additional agreements if necessary.[32] Organizational interoperability involves aligning business processes and establishing clear relationships between different administrative entities to achieve commonly agreed goals, ensuring services are user-focused and accessible, and formalizing mutual assistance and joint actions.[33] Semantic interoperability ensures the accurate preservation and shared understanding of data and information through the development of vocabularies, schemas, and information management strategies while facing challenges due to linguistic, cultural, legal, and administrative differences among Member States.[34] Technical interoperability within the EIF involves linking systems and services through interface specifications, interconnection services, data integration, presentation, exchange, and secure communication protocols, addressing challenges posed by legacy systems and emphasizing the use of formal technical specifications to promote interoperability.[35]

The future of interoperability lies in continuous improvement and adaptation. Regular assessments and updates ensure that the EIF remains relevant and effective. By promoting interoperability, the EIF contributes to developing digital public services and facilitates the efficient delivery of European public services. As shown below, the EIF will be crucial in the proposed Interoperable Europe Action Regulation.

IV. The Tallinn Declaration and the road to full public sector interoperability

The Tallinn Declaration of 2017 marked a fundamental turning point in advancing interoperability in the EU.[36] This ministerial declaration on eGovernment

[30] ibid s 1.3.1 of Annex 2.
[31] ibid s 3 of Annex 2.
[32] ibid s 3.3 of Annex 2 and Recommendation 27.
[33] ibid s 3.4 of Annex 2 and Recommendations 28 and 29.
[34] ibid s 3.5 of Annex 2 and Recommendations 30–32.
[35] ibid s 3.3 of Annex 2 and Recommendation 33.
[36] Commission, 'Tallinn Declaration on eGovernment at the ministerial meeting during Estonian Presidency of the Council of the EU on 6 October 2017' (Commission, 6 October 2017) <https://ec.europa.eu/newsroom/document.cfm?doc_id=47559> accessed 15 May 2023.

introduced the principle of interoperability by default and called for greater national-level initiatives to promote interoperability.[37] Member State ministers articulated their expectations for EU institutions and outlined actions to be taken. The declaration was built upon earlier initiatives, such as the Malmö Declaration of 2009 which loosely advocated for increased interoperability.[38]

At the national level, the Tallinn Declaration outlined three essential actions.[39] First, Member States committed to improving the reuse and implementation of joint solutions under programmes like the Connecting Europe Facility. The stakeholders will make an effort to prevent duplicate service infrastructures and encourage collaboration across sectors. Secondly, Member States promised to increasingly adopt open-source solutions and open standards, mitigating vendor lock-in and fostering interoperability. EU programmes for interoperability and standardization, such as ISA^2, played a supportive role in this regard. Thirdly, Member States aimed to make ICT solutions developed for or owned by public administrations more accessible for re-use in the private sector and civil society, promoting innovation and collaboration.

In addition to national-level actions, the Member States called upon EU institutions and the European Commission to take four steps.[40] First, the Commission urged institutions to implement the EIF and the Interoperability Action Plan, encompassing all Commission services and emphasizing cross-border services within the Single Market.[41] Secondly, the Commission was requested to engage in discussions and pursue agreements on cross-border interoperability principles with global partners, particularly focusing on the Electronic Identification, Authentication and Trust Services (eIDAS) framework for mutual recognition of electronic identities and trust services. Thirdly, the Commission must propose effective integration of digital considerations into the EU's external development policy support instruments with EU frameworks and standards.

While early interoperability efforts were sector-specific, the expanding competence of the EU and the need for seamless collaboration across the entire public sector propelled the concept of full public sector interoperability. [42] Recognizing the challenges posed by fragmented public administrations and cross-border

[37] ibid s 5.

[38] se2009.eu, 'Ministerial Declaration on eGovernment approved unanimously in Malmö, Sweden, on 18 November 2009' (se2009.eu, 18 November 2009) <https://www.aoc.cat/wp-content/uploads/2014/09/declaracio-malmo-1.pdf> accessed 15 May 2023.

[39] S 5 of the Tallinn Declaration 2017.

[40] ibid.

[41] The Commission set the implementation target for the end of 2021.

[42] Further examples of interoperability are discussed in Francesco Contini and Giovan Francesco Lanzara (eds), *The Circulation of Agency in E-Justice: Interoperability and Infrastructures for European Transborder Judicial Proceedings* (Springer 2013).

interactions, the EU sought to establish a comprehensive framework for interoperability, leading to the proposal of the Interoperable Europe Act Regulation.[43]

As depicted above, interoperability efforts were concentrated within specific sectors, targeting improvements in efficiency and service delivery. These early initiatives laid the groundwork for the development of broader interoperability frameworks. However, as the importance of seamless cooperation across the entire public sector became evident, the EU recognized the need for a comprehensive interoperability framework. The European Commission proposed the Interoperable Europe Act to strengthen cross-border interoperability and cooperation within the public sector in response to this need. The Act envisions a network of interconnected digital public administrations facilitating seamless data exchange and collaboration across borders, sectors, and organizational boundaries. Leveraging open-source software, guidelines, frameworks, and information technology (IT) tools, the Act aims to enhance the effectiveness and efficiency of public services.

The path to achieving full public sector interoperability takes time and effort. Fragmentation, diverse legal and technical frameworks, and varying levels of digital maturity across Member States present hurdles. However, these challenges also offer innovation, collaboration, and knowledge-sharing opportunities. The Interoperable Europe Act seeks to bridge these gaps through structured EU cooperation, mandatory assessments of IT system changes, and the sharing and reuse of solutions via an interoperability portal. The Act also emphasizes the importance of public sector innovation and public–private collaboration through GovTech projects and regulatory sandboxes.

The Tallinn Declaration and the subsequent Interoperable Europe Act have played critical roles in advancing interoperability in the EU. They have driven the transition from sector-specific initiatives to the pursuit of full public sector interoperability. By promoting seamless collaboration and data exchange, these milestones have laid the foundation for an interconnected European public sector. The Interoperable Europe Act, in particular, represents a significant step towards establishing a comprehensive framework that addresses challenges and unlocks the potential benefits of interoperable public services.

C. The European Commission's Interoperable Europe Act Regulation Proposal

The European Commission presented the Interoperable Europe Act Regulation Proposal in November 2022, marking a significant milestone in pursuing a more

[43] Proposal of 18 November 2022 for a Regulation laying down measures for a high level of public sector interoperability across the Union (Interoperable Europe Act) COM (2022) 720 final (the Proposal).

connected and cooperative EU.[44] Accompanied by an explanatory memorandum, the Proposal seeks to foster increased cross-border interoperability and enhance public sector cooperation within the EU. This section of the chapter delves into the origins and aspirations of the Interoperable Europe Act Regulation Proposal, shedding light on its contents and exploring the transformative effects it aims to bring about. By delving into the intricacies of this ground-breaking Proposal, the chapter provides a comprehensive understanding of the path towards a more digital, interconnected, and cohesive Europe.

I. Origin and ambitions of the Proposal

The Commission justifies the Proposal because achieving the 2030 Digital Targets[45] is necessary as it saves time and costs for citizens and businesses.[46] For instance, interoperability on the EU level currently exists in the form of the EU Digital COVID-19 Certificate[47] and the voluntary EIF.[48] The EU Digital COVID-19 Certificate quickly gained recognition and became mandatory across the EU, serving as a vital digital document to facilitate safe and secure travel amidst the COVID-19 pandemic. The EIF, on the other hand, operates as a voluntary framework, offering Member States the opportunity to enhance their communication and collaboration efforts within the EU.

The European Commission proposed adopting a Regulation on Interoperability following Article 172 of the Treaty on the Functioning of the European Union (TFEU),[49] which provides a legal basis for 'the establishment and development of trans-European networks in the areas of transport, telecommunications and energy infrastructures'.[50] The nature of the instrument, a regulation, will ensure complete harmonization in the EU Member States.[51] This choice is supported by Article 172 of the TFEU and by the *ex-post* evaluations, impact assessments,

[44] ibid.

[45] Commission, '2030 Digital Compass: the European way for the Digital Decade' COM(2021) 118 final, ss 3.4 and 5.2.

[46] Commission, 'Press Release: New Interoperable Europe Act to deliver more efficient public services through improved cooperation between national administrations on data exchanges and IT solutions' (Commission, 21 November 2022) <https://ec.europa.eu/commission/presscorner/detail/%20en/ip_22_6907> accessed 20 February 2023.

[47] Regulation (EU) 2021/953 of 14 June 2021 on a framework for the issuance, verification and acceptance of interoperable COVID-19 vaccination, test and recovery certificates (EU Digital COVID Certificate) to facilitate free movement during the COVID-19 pandemic [2021] OJ L211/1.

[48] Commission, 'European Interoperability Framework in detail' (Commission, 2023) <https://joinup.ec.europa.eu/collection/nifo-national-interoperability-framework-observatory/european-interoperability-framework-detail> accessed 28 April 2023.

[49] Consolidated version of the Treaty on the Functioning of the European Union (TFEU) [2012] OJ C326.

[50] TFEU art 170(1).

[51] TFEU art 288.

and stakeholder consultations accompanying the Proposal for the Interoperable Europe Act Regulation.[52] The *ex-post* evaluations drew on the fitness check of the voluntary EIF, revealing that cross-border interoperability is more efficient and effective on the EU than the national level,[53] also supported by the impact assessments.[54] The stakeholder consultations further revealed a need for consistent alignment with other EU policy areas.[55] According to the Commission, the Proposal also ensures compliance with fundamental rights, particularly Articles 8 (the right to protection of personal data) and 22 (the right to linguistic diversity).[56]

II. Contents and effects of the Proposal

As pointed out in the previous section, this proposed Regulation aims to establish a robust European network that promotes cross-border interoperability, ensuring seamless information exchange and collaboration among public sector bodies (PSBs) across Member States and EU institutions. The proposed Regulation consists of twenty-two provisions divided into six chapters that address various aspects of interoperability and support the implementation of interoperable solutions within the public sector.

1. General provisions

Chapter 1 focuses on the obligation of PSBs to perform interoperability assessments and support the sharing of interoperability solutions. PSBs must evaluate their current systems and processes through interoperability assessments[57] and actively facilitate sharing and reusing interoperability solutions.[58] This obligation applies to PSBs of Member States and institutions, bodies, and agencies of the EU involved in network or information system provision or management.[59] Article 2 of Chapter 1 provides essential definitions, thus establishing a harmonized standard across the EU.[60] Being a Regulation, this instrument guarantees a consistent understanding and interpretation of these terms across the EU,

[52] Proposal (n 43) s 2. The complete account is provided in Commission, 'Impact Assessment Report Accompanying the Document: Proposal for a Regulation of the European Parliament and of the Council laying down measures for a high level of public sector interoperability across the Union (Interoperable Europe Act)' (2022) SWD 721 final.
[53] Proposal (n 43) s 3 ('Ex-post evaluations/fitness checks of existing legislation').
[54] ibid s 3 ('Impact Assessment').
[55] ibid s 3 ('Stakeholder consultations').
[56] ibid s 3 ('Fundamental Rights').
[57] ibid art 3.
[58] ibid art 4.
[59] ibid art 1.
[60] Art 2 of the Proposal (n 43) defines the following terms: 'cross-border interoperability' (1), 'network and information system' (2), 'interoperability solution' (3), 'public sector body' (4), 'data' (5), 'machine-readable format' (6), 'GovTech' (7), 'standard' (8), and 'highest level of management' (9).

ensuring coherence and clarity in their application. The approach of complete harmonization is appreciated considering the need for standardized practices across Europe.

2. Interoperability solutions

Chapter 2 emphasizes establishing interoperability solutions and adopting recommendations provided by the Interoperable Europe Board based on the EIF. Although non-mandatory, the Chapter encourages PSBs to implement these solutions to enable seamless information exchange and collaboration across borders, especially when Member States adopt national interoperability frameworks and other domestic policies.[61] Article 5 states that the European Commission will publish Interoperable Europe solutions and the EIF in open, machine-readable formats on the Interoperable Europe portal. Furthermore, the Interoperable Europe Board is responsible for monitoring the coherence of the developed solutions and proposing measures to ensure compatibility with other interoperability solutions.[62]

Article 6 introduces the EIF, which provides legal, organizational, semantic, and technical interoperability recommendations, as discussed above. The Interoperable Europe Board may also develop specialized interoperability frameworks targeting specific sectors or administrative levels based on the EIF.[63] Article 7 empowers the Interoperable Europe Board to recommend and publish interoperability solutions for cross-border network and information systems that provide or manage public services.

The Interoperable Europe portal, as described in Article 8 of the Proposal, serves as a central access point for information related to cross-border interoperability. It provides access to Interoperable Europe solutions,[64] other interoperability solutions,[65] ICT technical specifications,[66] and information on data processing in regulatory sandboxes.[67] The portal also facilitates knowledge exchange,[68] stakeholder feedback,[69] and interoperability-related monitoring data access.[70] In addition, the Interoperable Europe Board can propose publishing additional interoperability solutions on the portal, subject to certain conditions such as alignment with Interoperable Europe solutions and open-source licensing.[71] PSBs or institutions

[61] ibid art 6(4).
[62] ibid art 5(2).
[63] ibid art 6(3).
[64] ibid art 8(1)(a).
[65] ibid art 8(1)(b).
[66] ibid art 8(1)(c).
[67] ibid art 8(1)(d).
[68] ibid art 8(1)(e).
[69] ibid art 8(1)(g).
[70] ibid art 8(1)(f).
[71] ibid art 8(2).

with similar portals must ensure interoperability with the Interoperable Europe portal.[72] The European Commission has the authority to issue guidelines on interoperability for other portals with similar functions, ensuring a coherent EU-wide application.[73]

3. Interoperable Europe Support Measures

Chapter 3 of the proposed Regulation details the support measures for Interoperable Europe. It introduces policy implementation support projects, which aim to assist PSBs in digitally implementing EU 'policies ensuring the cross-border interoperability of network and information systems which are used to provide or manage public services to be delivered or managed electronically'.[74] These projects outline the necessary Interoperable Europe solutions for meeting policy requirements.[75] They identify any missing interoperability solutions that need development and recommend additional support measures, like 'trainings or peer-reviews'.[76] After consulting the Interoperable Europe Board, the European Commission specifies 'the scope, the timeline, the needed involvement of sectors and administrative levels and the working methods of the support project'.[77] When creating the support project, it must consider the outcome of any previously conducted and published interoperability assessment.[78] These checks and balances are necessary and welcomed.

Another noteworthy feature is that the Interoperable Europe Board may propose the establishment of a regulatory sandbox to reinforce the policy implementation support project.[79] The outcome of a policy implementation support project, including any developed interoperability solutions, must be open access and published on the Interoperable Europe Portal.[80] Article 10 then focuses on innovation measures to support developing and adopting innovative interoperability solutions within the EU. The Interoperable Europe Board can propose these measures, which contribute to developing existing or new Interoperable Europe solutions,[81] involving GovTech actors.[82] To support the development of innovation measures, the Interoperable Europe Board may propose the establishment of a regulatory sandbox.[83] The European Commission is responsible for making the results of the

[72] ibid art 8(3).
[73] ibid art 8(4).
[74] ibid art 9. Referred to as 'policy implementation support projects'.
[75] ibid art 9(2).
[76] ibid art 9(2)(c).
[77] ibid art 9(3).
[78] ibid art 9(3).
[79] ibid art 9(4).
[80] ibid art 9(5).
[81] ibid art 10(1).
[82] ibid art 10(2)(b).
[83] ibid art 10(3).

innovation measures openly available on the Interoperable Europe portal to foster information exchange and constructive dialogue.[84]

Article 11 provides details about the establishment of regulatory sandboxes. These sandboxes create controlled environments 'for the development, testing and validation of innovative interoperability solutions supporting the cross-border interoperability of network and information systems'.[85] Participating PSBs operate regulatory sandboxes.[86] Relevant national authorities or the European Data Protection Supervisor (EDPS) supervise the processing of personal data by EU institutions, bodies, and agencies.[87] Establishing a regulatory sandbox aims to foster innovation, facilitate cross-border cooperation, develop an open European GovTech ecosystem, enhance understanding of cross-border interoperability opportunities or barriers, and contribute to creating or updating Interoperable Europe solutions.[88] Cooperation with authorities in the regulatory sandbox is necessary to improve legal certainty and ensure compliance with the Regulation and other EU and Member States' legislation.[89] The Commission, after consulting the Interoperable Europe Board and, if personal data processing is involved, the EDPS, authorizes the establishment of a regulatory sandbox upon joint request from at least three participating PSBs. The sandbox supports interoperability solutions that enable EU institutions, bodies, or agencies to use network and information systems across borders, with or without the participation of PSBs.[90]

Article 12 outlines participation in the regulatory sandboxes. Participating PSBs must ensure the involvement of national data protection authorities and other national authorities responsible for supervising access to data if the innovative interoperability solution involves personal data processing or falls under their supervisory remit.[91] Participation in the regulatory sandbox is time-limited, depending on the complexity and scale of the project.[92]

Despite the involvement of the EDPS regarding data protection and data quality, crucial aspects need to be thoroughly addressed within the interoperability framework. The potential consequences of data linkage (Article 5 of the General Data Protection Regulation (GDPR)), context removal, and the degradation of data quality over time are pertinent issues that could impact the credibility and integrity of shared data.

[84] ibid art 10(4).
[85] ibid art 11(1).
[86] ibid art 11(2).
[87] ibid art 11(2).
[88] ibid art 11(3).
[89] ibid art 11(4).
[90] ibid art 11(5).
[91] ibid art 12(1). For an overview on interoperability in the GDPR framework, especially data portability, see eg Paul De Hert and others, 'The Right to Data Portability in GDPR: Towards User-Centric Interoperability of Digital Services' (2018) 34(2) Computer Law & Security Review 193.
[92] Proposal (n 43) art 12(2).

4. Governance of cross-border interoperability

Chapter 4 of the proposed Regulation focuses on the governance of cross-border interoperability, outlining the role and responsibilities of the Interoperable Europe Board, the Interoperable Europe Community, national competent authorities, and interoperability coordinators for institutions, bodies, and agencies of the Union.

Article 15 establishes the Interoperable Europe Board, a platform for strategic cooperation and information sharing on cross-border interoperability. The Board comprises representatives from each Member State, the Commission, the Committee of the Regions, and the European Economic and Social Committee (EESC).[93] The Commission chairs the Board and may grant observer status to countries in the European Economic Area and candidate countries.[94] The Board is responsible for adopting decisions by consensus or, if necessary, by a simple majority vote.[95] It has various tasks, including supporting the implementation of national interoperability frameworks, adopting guidelines on interoperability assessments, proposing measures to foster the sharing and re-use of interoperable solutions, monitoring overall coherence, and proposing Interoperable Europe solutions.[96]

Article 16 establishes the Interoperable Europe Community, which contributes expertise and advice to the Interoperable Europe Board. Stakeholders from public and private entities in the Member States can register as members of the Community through the Interoperable Europe portal.[97] Members can contribute to the portal's content, participate in working groups, and engage in peer reviews.[98]

Article 17 focuses on national competent authorities responsible for implementing the Regulation within each Member State. Each Member State designates the competent authorities and has various tasks, including appointing a member to the Interoperable Europe Board, coordinating national questions related to the Regulation, supporting interoperability assessments, fostering the sharing and re-use of interoperable solutions, and facilitating cooperation with other Member States.[99] To ensure effective task completion, competent authorities in Member States must have the necessary competencies and resources,[100] as well as establish cooperation structures with other national authorities involved in implementation.[101]

93 ibid art 15(2).
94 ibid art 15(3).
95 ibid art 15(3).
96 ibid art 15(4).
97 ibid art 16(2).
98 ibid art 16(4).
99 ibid art 17(2).
100 ibid art 17(3).
101 ibid art 17(4).

Article 18 mandates the designation of interoperability coordinators within institutions, bodies, and agencies of the Union that provide or manage network and information systems for delivering or managing public services electronically. The interoperability coordinators, overseen by the highest management level, are responsible for supporting departments in implementing interoperability assessments and ensuring compliance with the proposed Regulation.

5. Interoperable Europe planning and monitoring

Chapter 5 of the proposed Regulation highlights the significance of aligning EU funding programmes to maximize synergies in digitalization efforts. It underscores the importance of planning, coordinating, monitoring, and evaluating interoperability initiatives within the public sector while emphasizing the need for effective monitoring and evaluation mechanisms to assess the impact and progress of interoperability measures.

Article 19 outlines the Interoperable Europe Agenda, developed annually by the Interoperable Europe Board, after a public consultation. The agenda aims to plan and coordinate priorities for cross-border interoperability of network and information systems to deliver or manage public services electronically, considering long-term digitalization strategies, existing EU funding programmes, and ongoing policy implementation.[102] The Interoperable Europe Agenda includes the identification of needs for interoperability solutions, continuing and planned support measures, proposed actions for innovation measures, and synergies with other relevant EU and national programmes.[103] The European Commission publishes the agenda on the Interoperable Europe portal but does not impose financial obligations.[104]

Article 20 focuses on monitoring and evaluation. The European Commission is responsible for monitoring the progress of cross-border interoperable public services within the Union.[105] Specific monitoring areas include the implementation of the EIF by Member States, the uptake of interoperability solutions across sectors and at different levels, and the development of open-source solutions, public sector innovation, and cooperation with GovTech actors in cross-border public services.[106] Additionally, the Commission is required to present a report on the application of the proposed Regulation to the European Parliament and the Council.[107] This constant supervision will ensure continuous improvement of how the proposed Regulation is applied.

[102] ibid art 19(1).
[103] ibid art 19(2).
[104] ibid art 19(3).
[105] ibid art 20(1).According to art 20(3), the Interoperable Europe portal publishes monitoring results; whenever feasible, they are available in a machine-readable format.
[106] ibid art 20(2).
[107] ibid art 20(4).

6. Progress and controversies in the legislative progress

The proposed Regulation is currently undergoing legislative discussions in the Council, and soon the European Parliament[108] and various institutions have provided their opinions on the existing draft. The EDPS, the EESC, and the Committee of the Regions have all responded to consultations initiated by the European Commission regarding the Regulation, highlighting some of the shortcomings of the current draft.

The EDPS acknowledges the potential benefits of increased interoperability and emphasizes the importance of upholding data protection principles, particularly the principle of purpose limitation when addressing technical barriers to information exchange.[109] The EDPS positively welcomes the provision in the Proposal that requires consultation with the EDPS before authorizing the establishment of regulatory sandboxes.[110] However, the Supervisor proposes a change in the wording of this provision.[111] The focus of the opinion revolves around the provisions related to processing personal data in regulatory sandboxes, and the EDPS offers five targeted and actionable recommendations. First, they recommend evaluating the necessity of use cases for regulatory sandboxes and suggest removing the legal basis for personal data processing if they cannot identify suitable use cases.[112] Secondly, the EDPS suggests further defining the respective objectives of public interest within the proposed Regulation and further specifying it concerning restrictions in pursuance of public authorities' interests under Article 23(1) of the GDPR and Article 25(1) of the European Union Data Protection Regulation (EUDPR).[113] Thirdly, the EDPS proposes amending Article 12(6)(f) of the proposed Regulation, recommending that sandbox participants be required to establish effective technical and organizational arrangements to fulfil data subjects' rights.[114] Fourthly, the EDPS advises modifying Article 12(6) to prohibit any subsequent change of purpose to

[108] EUR-Lex, 'Procedure 2022/0379/COD' (*EUR-Lex*, 2023) <https://eur-lex.europa.eu/legal-content/EN/HIS/?uri=CELEX:52022PC0720#OPCOR_OPI_byCOR1> accessed 13 June 2023.

[109] The European Data Protection Supervisor, 'Opinion 1/2023 on the Proposal for an Interoperable Europe Act' (*The European Data Protection Supervisor*, 13 January 2023) <https://edps.europa.eu/system/files/2023-01/2022-1196_d0089_opinion_en.pdf> accessed 30 May 2023. The EDPS has already commented on the debate in 2018, see The European Data Protection Supervisor, 'EDPS calls for wider debate on the future of information sharing in the EU' (*The European Data Protection Supervisor*, 18 April 2018) <https://edps.europa.eu/press-publications/press-news/press-releases/2018/edps-calls-wider-debate-future-information-sharing_en> accessed 30 May 2023.

[110] Arts 11(2), (5), 12(3), and (6) of the proposed Interoperability Europe Act Regulation (2022). European Data Protection Supervisor Opinion 1/2023 (n 109) s 4.

[111] ibid s 6.

[112] ibid s 6(1).

[113] ibid s 6(2). Regulation (EU) 2016/679 of 27 April 2016 on the protection of natural persons with regard to the processing of personal data and on the free movement of such data, and repealing Directive 95/46/EC [2016] OJ L119/1 (General Data Protection Regulation, short GDPR); Regulation (EU) 2018/1725 of 23 October 2018 on the protection of natural persons with regard to the processing of personal data by the Union institutions, bodies, offices and agencies and on the free movement of such data, and repealing Regulation (EC) No 45/2001 and Decision No 1247/2002/EC [2018] OJ L295/39 (EUDPR).

[114] European Data Protection Supervisor Opinion 1/2023 (n 109) s 6(3).

ensure that test data used in the sandboxes do not become part of the production environment.[115] Finally, the EDPS suggests amending another provision on regulatory sandboxes, namely Article 11(5), dealing with the role of the EDPS and data protection rules.[116] This includes clearly 'defining the purpose of the processing, the actors involved, their roles, the categories of data concerned, their source(s) and the envisaged retention period'.[117] The EDPS also recommends that a data protection impact assessment be in progress or completed. The proposed changes put forth by the EDPS appear to have a common objective of enhancing transparency, accountability, and data protection measures within the proposed Interoperability Regulation.[118]

The EESC shares the Commission's view that achieving interoperability among public services is a fundamental requirement for establishing digital public services.[119] However, the EESC emphasizes that this objective should not come at the expense of in-person services or neglecting vulnerable population groups.[120] Contrary to the notion of reducing personnel with digitalization, the EESC asserts that developing and operating digital services will initially create a demand for additional personnel, highlighting that adequate staffing is essential for a successful digital transformation of public services.[121] Regarding governance, the EESC welcomes the proposed model, comprising the Interoperable Europe Board and the Interoperable Europe Community, as leading bodies to oversee and facilitate this policy.[122] Furthermore, the EESC expresses appreciation for the provision in the proposed Regulation that enables the development of experimental solutions through collaborations between the public sector, innovative technology companies, and start-ups.[123] Regarding funding programmes, the EESC suggests that future funding for interoperability projects should be contingent upon adopting the principles and structures advocated by the EIF.[124] This approach promotes consistency and coherence in public service digitalization initiatives. Amid the process of digitalization, the EESC acknowledges concerns about specific technological solutions being highly energy-intensive.[125] Therefore, balancing digital progress and environmental impact requires careful consideration. The

[115] ibid s 6(4).
[116] ibid s 6(5).
[117] ibid s 6(5).
[118] The comments also partly reflect the academic debate. See eg Evelien Brouwer, 'Large-Scale Databases and Interoperability in Migration and Border Policies: The Non-Discriminatory Approach of Data Protection' (2020) 26(1) European Public Law 71.
[119] Opinion of the European Economic and Social Committee of 25 May 2023 on the 'Proposal for a Regulation of the European Parliament and of the Council laying down measures for a high level of public sector interoperability across the Union (Interoperable Europe Act)' [2022] OJ C60/17.
[120] ibid ss 1.2 and 3.3.
[121] ibid s 1.3.
[122] ibid s 1.5.
[123] ibid s 1.6.
[124] ibid s 1.7.
[125] ibid s 1.8.

EESC opinion also addresses data protection concerns, stressing that data protection should not hinder the development of interoperable solutions for public services or impede access to data for individuals, businesses, or other public services.[126] It also proposes implementing different authorization levels for data access to ensure confidentiality and limit disclosure to strictly necessary information.[127] In summary, the EESC underscores the importance of a comprehensive but balanced approach to digital transformation, encompassing in-person services and the protection of vulnerable population groups while fostering collaboration, upholding data protection principles, and prioritizing sustainability in the creation of interoperable solutions for public services.

The Committee of the Region also issued their opinion on the proposed Regulation.[128] The Committee of the Regions acknowledges that certain aspects of the Proposal must be strengthened and refined, especially concerning the new responsibilities assigned to subnational authorities. It emphasizes the importance of providing these authorities with adequate resources to implement interoperability solutions swiftly and effectively. Additionally, the Committee stresses the need for a balanced governance structure that upholds the principle of subsidiarity and respects the diverse governance models within the Member States. It also emphasizes the importance of granting local and regional authorities a voice in determining the implementation pace and extent of interoperability solutions. The Committee recognizes that developing and implementing common interoperability solutions will involve significant financial and staffing costs for local and regional authorities. It highlights the need for funding sources, such as the Digital Europe programme, to assist these authorities in covering the associated expenses. This includes investing in new interoperable solutions or transforming existing systems. The Committee calls on the Interoperable Europe Board to provide specific information on the timing of mandatory interoperability assessments and the factors that may trigger such reviews, particularly about public procurement. It stresses that the evaluations should only be compulsory once the Interoperable Europe Board has adopted the relevant guidelines. Furthermore, the Committee reiterates the critical importance of interoperability for the digital resilience and strategic independence of the EU. It stresses that ensuring interconnected services and systems is essential to prevent potential digital pandemics from major cyberattacks on vulnerable network points.[129]

[126] ibid s 1.8.1.

[127] ibid s 1.8.2.

[128] The Committee of the Region, 'Opinion Factsheet CDR 152/2023: Interoperable Europe Act' (*The Committee of the Region*, 24 May 2023) <https://cor.europa.eu/en/our-work/Pages/OpinionTimeline.aspx?opId=CDR-152-2023> accessed 29 June 2023.

[129] The issues of data protection and cybersecurity are critical regarding interoperable regulatory technologies that operate in real-time. See Herwig CH Hofmann, Dirk A Zetzsche, and Felix Pflücke, 'The Changing Nature of "Regulation by Information": Towards Real-time Regulation?' (2023) 28(4–6) European Law Journal 172.

In conclusion, various institutions have responded to and are currently debating the progress and controversies surrounding the legislative process of the proposed Regulation in the Council and European Parliament. The EDPS highlights the need for upholding data protection principles and offers targeted recommendations to enhance transparency and accountability in the Regulation. On the other hand, the EESC stresses the importance of a balanced approach to digital transformation, considering in-person services and the needs of vulnerable population groups while advocating for adequate staffing, collaborative partnerships, and funding programmes aligned with the EIF. The Committee of the Regions echoes some of the remarks of the EDPS and EESC. The Committee emphasizes the need for strengthened subnational authorities' responsibilities, sufficient resources, and a governance structure that respects subsidiarity and allows local and regional authorities to influence interoperability implementation. In light of the critical role interoperability plays in the EU's digital resilience and strategic independence, the Committee of the Regions calls for mandatory interoperability assessments and highlights the benefits of open-source solutions. These opinions collectively aim to enhance transparency, protect data, and promote consistency in public service digitalization efforts, and they will likely also shape the legislative debate.

III. Steering the future Interoperability Cooperation Framework

The interoperability cooperation framework established by this proposed Regulation draws on lessons from previous initiatives. It will play a crucial role in shaping the future of interoperability within the European public sector. Recognizing the necessity for mandatory cooperation at the EU level,[130] the Interoperable Europe Board will oversee the framework, an essential entity responsible for strategic coordination, decision-making, and information sharing about cross-border interoperability.

As highlighted in the previous section, the Interoperable Europe Board comprises representatives from each Member State, the European Commission, the Committee of the Regions, and the EESC.[131] Chaired by the Commission, the Board operates based on consensus or, if necessary, a simple majority vote.[132] Several essential tasks have been entrusted to it, which contribute to advancing interoperability across borders.

First, the Interoperable Europe Board will support and guide the implementation of national interoperability frameworks.[133] These frameworks serve as roadmaps for Member States to enhance their interoperability capabilities and

[130] Proposal (n 43) s 1.4.3 of the Annex ('Lessons learned from similar experiences in the past').
[131] ibid art 15(2) and (3).
[132] ibid art 15(3).
[133] ibid art 15(4)(a).

align their practices with European standards. The Board's expertise and coordination will ensure the coherence and effectiveness of these frameworks, promoting a harmonized approach to interoperability across the Union.

Moreover, the Board will adopt guidelines on interoperability assessments, offering clear instructions and best practices for PSBs to evaluate their systems and processes.[134] These assessments will play a crucial role in identifying strengths, weaknesses, and areas for improvement regarding public service interoperability. The Board will help ensure a consistent and comprehensive approach by monitoring interoperability across Member States.[135]

Another vital responsibility of the Interoperable Europe Board is to propose measures that foster the sharing and re-use of interoperable solutions.[136] The Board will identify areas where interoperability solutions can be developed, harmonized, and shared across borders by leveraging the EIF as a foundation.[137] These proposed solutions, known as 'Interoperable Europe solutions', will be published on the Interoperable Europe portal, serving as valuable resources for PSBs seeking interoperable solutions endorsed and recommended at the European level.[138]

In addition to its coordination role, the Interoperable Europe Board will collaborate with other relevant bodies and stakeholders, ensuring alignment and synergy in interoperability initiatives. It will work closely with the European Data Innovation Board to address data-related challenges and opportunities, fostering a comprehensive approach to interoperability that encompasses both technical and data aspects.[139] By engaging in strategic partnerships and collaboration, the Board will maximize the impact and effectiveness of its initiatives.

Furthermore, the Interoperable Europe Board will actively engage with the Interoperable Europe Community, which comprises registered members from public and private entities in the Member States.[140] This community provides a platform for knowledge exchange, peer reviews, and collaboration. By fostering active participation and involving stakeholders from various sectors, the Board will tap into a wealth of expertise and diverse perspectives, further enhancing the development and implementation of interoperability solutions.

Through its collective efforts and expertise, the Interoperable Europe Board will drive the future of interoperability within the European public sector. By setting strategic priorities, providing guidance, fostering collaboration, and proposing interoperable solutions, the Board will enable seamless information exchange, enhance public services, and contribute to a more digitally connected and efficient EU.

[134] ibid art 15(4)(b).
[135] ibid art 15(4)(d).
[136] ibid art 15(4)(c).
[137] ibid art 15(4)(f) and (g).
[138] ibid art 15(4)(h) and (i).
[139] ibid art 15(4)(q).
[140] ibid art 15(4)(r).

D. Towards effective and efficient interoperability?

The European public sector's journey towards effective and efficient interoperability is undoubtedly underway, fuelled by the proposed Interoperability Europe Act Regulation and the comprehensive interoperability cooperation framework it establishes. The Proposal outlines regulatory measures that aim to drive substantial progress in achieving interoperability goals by promoting cross-border collaboration, enabling seamless information exchange, and adopting interoperable solutions. It will allow for a variety of public services, including automated decision-making.

One of the fundamental aspects contributing to interoperability's effectiveness and efficiency is the obligation imposed on PSBs to perform interoperability assessments.[141] These assessments systematically evaluate current systems and processes, enabling PSBs to identify areas that require improvement and take necessary measures to enhance interoperability.[142] By actively facilitating the sharing and reusing of interoperability solutions, PSBs can leverage existing best practices, reducing duplication of efforts and promoting efficiency in deploying interoperable solutions.[143]

Furthermore, establishing the Interoperable Europe Board as the steering body for the interoperability cooperation framework is a significant step towards achieving effective and efficient interoperability. The Board, composed of representatives from Member States, the Commission, the Committee of the Regions, and the EESC,[144] fosters strategic coordination, decision-making, and information sharing.[145] With its guidance and expertise, the Board ensures a harmonized and efficient approach to interoperability across the EU.

The proposed Regulation also emphasizes the importance of interoperability solutions and the adoption of recommendations provided by the Interoperable Europe Board, based on the EIF.[146] While these recommendations to the European Commission are not mandatory,[147] they provide valuable guidance for PSBs to enable seamless information exchange and collaboration across borders. By promoting the implementation of interoperability solutions and adopting the EIF,[148] the Regulation encourages a harmonized approach to interoperability, fostering efficiency and effectiveness in delivering public services.

Additionally, the support measures outlined in the Regulation, such as policy implementation support projects and innovation measures, contribute to

[141] ibid art 3.
[142] ibid art 3(1) and (2).
[143] ibid art 4.
[144] ibid art 15(2) and (3).
[145] ibid art 15(1).
[146] ibid arts 6(2) and 15(4).
[147] ibid s 5 ('Other Elements').
[148] ibid art 15(4)(f) and (g).

advancing interoperability. These measures provide targeted assistance to PSBs, helping them implement Union policies, develop innovative interoperability solutions, and address specific interoperability challenges. By providing tailored support and facilitating collaboration among stakeholders, these measures enhance the effectiveness and efficiency of interoperability efforts.

Moreover, the emphasis on monitoring, evaluation, and reporting outlined in the proposed Regulation is pivotal in ensuring continuous improvement and progress towards effective and efficient interoperability.[149] The European Commission's responsibility for monitoring progress, assessing the implementation of the EIF by the Member States, and publishing monitoring results on the Interoperable Europe portal fosters transparency and accountability.[150] The periodic reporting to the European Parliament and the Council also enables comprehensive evaluation and identification of areas that require further attention and improvement.[151]

As pointed out in section C.II of this chapter, various institutions, including the EDPS, the EESC, and the Committee of the Regions, have provided responses and recommendations regarding the proposed Regulation on data protection and digital transformation, focusing on transparency, data protection, and accountability. These opinions will shape the legislative debate and aim to enhance consistency and accountability in public service digitalization efforts.

While the proposed Regulation and the interoperability cooperation framework provide a solid foundation for effective and efficient interoperability, the journey towards its realization is ongoing. Continuous collaboration, knowledge exchange, and stakeholder engagement will address emerging challenges, foster innovation, and drive further improvements. The system is strengthened through constant monitoring, evaluations, sandboxes, and peer reviews, ensuring its robustness. By remaining committed to the principles and objectives outlined in the proposed Regulation, the European public sector can progress towards a future where interoperability becomes a seamless reality, enabling effective and efficient delivery of digital public services across borders.

E. Conclusion

The European Interoperability Policy has evolved into a comprehensive framework for seamless integration and collaboration within the EU. Various programmes and initiatives, such as IDA, IDABC, ISA, and ISA^2, have significantly enhanced interoperability. The EIF has played a crucial role in guiding member

149 ibid art 20.
150 ibid art 20(3).
151 ibid art 20(4).

states and promoting interoperability, providing recommendations and guidance for achieving interoperability goals.

The Tallinn Declaration of 2017 marked a significant milestone in the policy's development, introducing the principle of 'Interoperability by default' and calling for actions at both national and EU levels. The Member States are committed to improving the reuse of joint solutions, adopting open source solutions and open standards, and facilitating the accessibility of ICT solutions developed by public administrations for reuse in the private sector and civil society. The EU institutions were urged to implement the EIF and the Interoperability Action Plan, engage in discussions for cross-border interoperability principles, and integrate digital considerations into EU development policy.

The European Interoperability Policy has emerged as a dynamic and ever-evolving field. From national initiatives, it has become a top priority within the EU. The policy has progressed towards achieving seamless interoperability across various sectors, shaping the future landscape of collaboration and integration. As technology advances and new challenges arise, the policy will continue to adapt and address emerging needs, such as EU-wide automated decision-making.

The Interoperable Europe Act Regulation Proposal further advances interoperability and public sector cooperation within the EU. With a focus on achieving the 2030 Digital Targets and reducing time and costs for citizens and businesses, the Proposal builds upon existing initiatives and the voluntary EIF. It establishes obligations, provides guidance, and offers support to foster collaboration and enhance the digital transformation of the public sector.

The Proposal outlines the legal basis, evaluations, impact assessments, and stakeholder consultations that support its implementation. It covers various aspects of interoperability and support measures within the public sector, including the obligation to perform interoperability assessments, sharing interoperability solutions, and the role of the Interoperable Europe Board in providing recommendations and monitoring coherence. The Proposal also emphasizes support measures, policy implementation projects, innovation measures, regulatory sandboxes, and effective planning, coordinating, monitoring, and evaluating interoperability initiatives.

The European public sector is making significant strides towards achieving effective and efficient interoperability, driven by the proposed Interoperability Europe Act Regulation and the comprehensive interoperability cooperation framework. The regulatory measures outlined in the Proposal, such as interoperability assessments and sharing solutions, are expected to lead to substantial progress in cross-border collaboration and seamless information exchange. Establishing the Interoperable Europe Board as the steering body ensures strategic coordination and a harmonized approach to interoperability across Member States. The emphasis on adopting recommendations and the EIF further promotes a unified approach. Support measures, monitoring, and evaluations contribute to continuous improvement and accountability.

In conclusion, the Interoperable Europe Act Regulation Proposal is a significant step towards achieving effective and efficient interoperability within the EU. By establishing obligations, providing guidance, and offering support, the Proposal aims to foster collaboration, facilitate seamless information exchange, and enhance the efficiency and effectiveness of public services. The Proposal and the comprehensive interoperability cooperation framework provide a solid foundation for the continued progress towards a future where interoperability becomes a seamless reality, enabling effective and efficient delivery of public services across borders.

11

Automated Decision-Making in EU Public Law and Governance

Herwig C.H. Hofmann and Felix Pflücke

A. Governance of automated decision-making and EU law

This book is about exploring the impact of the rapid development of innovative information technologies on the processes of public decision-making in the scope of EU law. What are the ramifications for EU constitutional principles and values? How can it be ensured that the rule of law is upheld allowing democratically legitimate legislation to steer reality in the age of artificial intelligence (AI)-based automated decision-making (ADM) systems? ADM poses some essential challenges to the fabric of public decision-making procedures and for judicial review and other accountability mechanisms of the executive branch of powers in Europe. Throughout its chapters, this volume develops approaches to regulating the transformation administrative implementation of EU policies. It does so from multiple angles, studying *inter alia* regulatory changes in financial regulation, integration of procedural requirements into executive action, digitalized governance of the single market, algorithmic processes in administrative procedures, and the influence of targeted political advertising on democratic processes.

B. What we have learnt—towards a new perspective on AI regulation in the public sphere

Illustrating risks and possibilities of AI-based ADM in EU public law this book's first chapter analyses the evolution of decision-making procedures in view of the rise of automated decision-making systems. It asks whether it is necessary to re-evaluate constitutional concepts in light of ADM's transformative impact. The chapter suggests that a key distinction consists between the role of ADM's de facto executive rule-making and its role in individual decisions. This fundamental distinction leads to differing considerations as to the legality and accountability of acts. In order to guarantee that constitutional values are respected, IT-based rule-making systems must adhere to the principles of procedural and administrative justice, the rule of law, and democratic accountability.

Herwig C.H. Hofmann and Felix Pflücke, *Automated Decision-Making in EU Public Law and Governance* In: *Governance of Automated Decision-Making and EU Law*. Edited by: Herwig C.H. Hofmann and Felix Pflücke, Oxford University Press.
 DOI: 10.1093/9780198919575.003.0011

Chapter 1 outlines that these principles must be embedded in the design and development of the systems so that they remain consistent with the EU's constitutional value system. Additionally, the design of these systems must consider the potential impacts on fundamental rights, including the right to privacy, data protection, and non-discrimination. As such, it is necessary to strike a balance between the interests of the state and those of the individual, ensuring that the use of ADMs does not undermine the protection of fundamental rights. These are the normative underpinnings of the development of the chapters following in this book. One of the key features of ADM-supported procedures, the first chapter argues, is a change in information management. An increase in the amount of information taken into account and the speed of decision-making combined with direct access to the information of market participants may, practically, in some areas, lead towards real-time regulation.

Chapter 2 of the book then continues by developing criteria of cyber-delegation in the face of evolving concepts of how to ensure accountability of such ADM in EU public law. Can concepts developed for the control of delegated powers be made useful in the context of the empowerment of public bodies to design decision-making procedures supported by ADM systems? Concepts of establishing criteria for empowering public bodies to decide with the support of ADM systems as well as *ex-post* review under criteria of the duty of care are central elements for holding ADM in public decision-making to account.

Chapter 3 gives an overview of AI utilization within the EU Administration, bringing to light several important case studies and use scenarios. Limited availability of information regarding existing AI use cases in the EU Administration due to the absence of a centralized repository for such information poses a significant challenge in comprehensively understanding the scope and nature of AI implementation. Changing this visibility problem by showing real-life scenarios is a central element of understanding legal implications. The chapter underscores the potential benefits of AI in improving administrative functions, strengthening control measures, and facilitating decision-making processes within the EU Administration. It emphasizes the transformative power of AI technologies and their opportunities to enhance operational efficiency and effectiveness. By addressing these essential aspects, Chapter 3 provides a comprehensive analysis of AI utilization within the EU Administration, offering valuable insights into the current landscape, challenges, and potential avenues for further development in this domain. The chapter primarily examines the crucial role of administrative procedure in the current debate on algorithmic accountability in the public sector. It proposes some basic distinctions concerning the use of algorithms and suggests certain procedural adaptations to avoid the risks that such use may entail. Particular attention is paid to the principles to be drawn from EU law and the activities of the EU Administration in the light of a case study carried out in recent months and summarized in the Annex. The chapter then critically examines the AI

Act,[1] highlighting its predominant emphasis on regulating AI in the private sector while neglecting the specificities of AI use within the public sector. This oversight necessitates an examination of the implications and requirements of AI deployment by public authorities. In recognizing a positive development, establishing a centralized database within the Commission to document existing AI use cases is acknowledged. However, the chapter argues for including all AI systems employed by public authorities, not solely those categorized as high risk. A comprehensive database would provide a more accurate and holistic understanding of AI usage within the EU Administration. Furthermore, the chapter highlights the authority of the European legislator to regulate the utilization of AI by the EU Administration itself. This authority plays a crucial role in shaping the framework and governance of AI applications within the public sector. By shedding a light on the current state of AI implementation, the chapter also reveals that it is primarily driven by individual initiatives rather than a centralized policy. This decentralized approach raises questions about coherence, standardization, and potential inconsistencies in AI adoption across different departments and entities within the EU Administration. The chapter also explores the common practice of outsourcing AI implementation raising further questions of public–private relations.

Chapter 4 looks at collaborative governance of the EU Digital Single Market established by the Digital Services Act (DSA), focusing on decision-making procedures implementing EU policies for the Digital Single Market. A key infrastructure of the EU Digital Single Market consists of online platforms and other intermediary services provided by private operators. Very large online platforms (VLOPs) as well as very large online search engines (VLOSEs) perform gatekeeper functions concerning access to the EU Digital Single Market, including ever-increasing communication on social media. This chapter shows that recent EU legislation, in particular the DSA, builds upon the mentioned gatekeeper function of VLOPS and VLOSEs, including their ADM systems. It also establishes a regulatory framework for a legitimate and accountable exercise of this private gatekeeper function and the use of respective ADM systems. This combination of outsourcing certain public policing functions concerning the Digital Single Market with due diligence obligations or accountability structures for VLOPS, VLOSEs, and other intermediary services enforced by various administrative and supervisory authorities qualifies as a complex arrangement of collaborative governance. Another focus of this chapter concerns legal instruments established by the DSA to cope with various knowledge gaps concerning the concrete impact of ADM systems used by intermediary service providers in general and especially of VLOPs and VLOSEs on public values such as democracy and free speech.

[1] On the basis of the European Commission's Proposal for a Regulation Laying Down Harmonised Rules on Artificial Intelligence (Artificial Intelligence Act) and Amending Certain Union Legislative Acts COM (2021) 206 final (hereafter AI Act proposal).

Various chapters on policy-specific areas follow and illustrate the issues contained in the book. Chapter 5 focuses on the competencies and challenges related to public health in the EU. The chapter analyses the existing framework and identifies areas where improvements are needed for effective information management and interoperability in the field of public health. Currently, most competencies in public health remain with the Member States, resulting in a decentralized approach to public health governance within the EU. This fragmentation poses challenges when comparing and analysing information from national information systems, such as EpiPulse and EWRS (Early Warning and Response System). This chapter critically examines the governance of communicable diseases within the EU. Information systems are an important instrument for governing such diseases, transmitting information vertically between Member State authorities and European agencies, horizontally between different Member State authorities, and cross-sectorally between authorities from different sectors. The information systems must be interoperable to manage information effectively. One of the critical issues in the chapter is the need for EU competencies to establish binding rules on case definitions and formats for national information systems. This limitation hampers the harmonization and standardization of data, making it difficult to compare and analyse public health information across Member States. However, the EU does have shared competence in public health safety, which allows it to establish binding rules for case definitions and formats in reporting adverse drug reactions to EudraVigilance. The chapter notes that the Regulations for building a European Health Union do not specifically address the issue of information management and interoperability. Consequently, amending the Treaties is deemed necessary to provide the EU with the competence and tools needed to enhance information management in the field of public health.

Chapter 6 then turns to the examples of borders and immigration. In 2013, the European Commission proposed the Smart Borders Package that aims to provide for a 'modern, effective and efficient management' of the EU's external borders. With the objective to curb irregular migration and overstays and to strengthen internal security, the Smart Borders Package comprises both the establishment of novel tools, such as the Entry/Exit System (EES) and the European Travel Information and Authorisation System (ETIAS), as well as corresponding modifications to the existing EU border framework, such as the Schengen Border Code. The Smart Borders Package is accompanied by the European Interoperability Framework (EIF) that does not only establishes technical interoperability of all relevant information systems but also introduces novel tools such as the Multi-Identity Detector (MID), which will allow for the detection of multiple identities to improve identity checks and fight identity fraud, Article 25(1) EIF Regulations. The aforementioned initiatives mark a trend towards the large-scale collection and processing of vast amounts of personal data for the purpose of performing automated risk assessment in an interoperable environment. Such risk assessments are especially foreseen under ETIAS and under the EIF Framework with the MID. The Passenger Name Record (PNR) Directive allows for similar data-driven risk assessments. The legal framework provides multiple Member State and Union authorities in the areas of both border control and law enforcement with access rights to the various relevant information systems and creates a situation in which various authorities can influence single decisions. At the same time, there are doubts about sufficient human involvement in decisions that are supported by data-driven risk assessments. This is particularly dangerous where the risk assessments are not accurate or the quality of the underlying data is uncertain. These considerations raise concerns, especially regarding the legitimacy of decision-making processes, individual rights and access to legal remedies, and efficient and independent supervision. Data quality is a major concern in the field of borders and immigration due to its direct impact on assessment accuracy and fairness. The chapter emphasizes the necessity for more clarity and safeguards in legal frameworks for individually reviewing automated risk assessments. Authorities responsible for decision-making should provide clear guidelines for manual assessment and offer training to decision-makers. Transparency in risk assessment criteria and data is crucial for understanding the decision grounds. Language barriers, rectification rights, and system complexity were additional concerns hindering supervision and individual rights exercise. Using non-transparent machine learning models raised legitimacy and legal remedy issues, emphasizing the importance of transparency. Fundamental rights, including data protection, data retention, purpose limitation, the right to good administration, and non-discrimination are central criteria of legality. Safeguarding these rights is essential in developing automated risk assessment systems at smart borders. The chapter underscores the need for interdisciplinary dialogue, regular checks, impact assessments, and accountability mechanisms to protect rights and ensure compliance. These measures are essential for addressing concerns related to automated risk assessments and promoting a fair and transparent decision-making process at smart borders.

Chapter 7 moves on to discuss, from a comparative law point of view, the judicial review of the use of ADM. Prominent instances of ADM practices before courts, such as fraud detection, teacher placement, credit scoring, and dismissing workers, offer valuable insights into how judges interpret these practices. The chapter identifies the socio-technical quality of ADM practices and argues how this quality might be used for meaningful human participation in decision-making processes and a possible human-centric provision of the relevant EU legal instruments. It explores the role of judicial interpretation in identifying critical elements of ADM within decision-making procedures and in defining the conditions of involvement of humans in such decision-making processes and examines four judicial cases which surfaced in public and private contexts in the Netherlands, Italy, and Germany. The case studies lead to a discussion of various facets of judicial interpretation regarding ADM practices. These include discussions of epistemic knowledge, socio-technical and legal dimensions of expertise, and methodological questions addressing the specialist knowledge contained in the programming of systems used for decision-making with far-reaching consequences. These dynamics prove the pivotal role of judicial interpretation in comprehending the technical aspects of automation and ensuring meaningful human participation in decision-making processes.

A very different policy area is addressed in Chapter 8, which focuses on the potential arguments for regulating online targeted political advertising in a field in which AI-based ADM systems will be central in pursuing the public policy objective of ensuring fair and free elections. Advertising is a central element of creating political majorities and influencing open democracy and the rule of law thus depends on functioning public dialogue. The chapter looks at four main areas of legal regulation: regulation which focuses on the protection of personal data under the General Data Protection Regulation (GDPR); regulation which focuses on economic digital spaces under the DSA; regulation which focuses on the freedom of expression and information under the Charter of Fundamental Rights (CFR) and the European Convention on Human Rights; and regulation which looks at political advertising per se under the proposed Political Advertising Regulation. It then considers whether, because of the fractured perspectives and approaches, there is a risk that framing the issue of automated political advertising through so many different lenses could distort the issue, creating inappropriate or unnecessarily confusing regulation. Finally, the chapter pulls together the various elements and considers several key lessons for EU laws which may touch upon automated political advertising, whether incidentally as part of other regulatory areas or as dedicated legislation directed to the topic. Online targeted political advertising can be subjected to various regulations, each presenting the phenomenon from different angles as stated above. It then questions whether the multiplicity of perspectives and approaches in these regulations might lead to the risk of distorting the issue of automated political advertising, potentially resulting in inappropriate or overly complex regulation. Finally, it discusses that while there are many reasons why one might argue for the regulation of online targeted political advertising, if the regulation of political advertising is to be successful, we need to have a clear vision of what the problems are and how we actually define a successful regulation of those problems. Where a subject matter is governed by one law, this may not cause any particular problems, even if it does leave space for us to agree or disagree with the law's approach. However, online targeted political advertising can fall under the scope of many different regulations, each of which take a different approach to, or perspective of, the problem.

Chapter 9 focuses on two key aspects. First, it delves into the connection between 'explainability' and related terms like 'interpretability' and 'transparency'. The discussion centres around why explainability is often utilized alongside these terms or overlaps them, underlining the notion that the versatility of this concept is justified by its inherent multidimensional nature. Secondly, the chapter explores the practical implementation of explainability in the context of ADM within the EU Administration. It does so by referencing the legal framework currently governing the requirements for explainability in automated systems used by EU bodies. The chapter provided insight into some of the significant obligations and rights that EU bodies must address when employing ADM systems. Additionally, it discusses the necessity for EU bodies to employ various eXplainable artificial intelligence (XAI) methods to address diverse explanatory aspects, acknowledging that there is no one-size-fits-all approach for every scenario. This chapter thus explores the interplay between the technical explainability of AI systems, also known as XAI, and its lawfulness from the point of view of the EU administrative law. This interplay has only been tackled by a few studies thus far and deserves more effort and analysis. Moreover, while these few works mainly consider the idea of local and global explainability, a more detailed and comprehensive account of the many explainability techniques and their lawfulness is mostly missing, probably due to the growing number of XAI methodologies. In this chapter the authors show what the main techniques of XAI are so far and what degree of lawfulness they can provide. The extraordinary importance of these considerations on streamlining the legal and computer science understanding of transparency and explainability is emphasized. Legal predeterminations of what counts as a sufficient explanation is crucial for the development of future AI-driven ADM systems. Key factors of this work are explainability, interpretability, and transparency. Important lessons arising from the study of computer science work in the area is that re-engineering ADM by computer-assisted models such as partial dependency plots and others allows one to reanalyse a decision, changing the input variable and measuring how output differs. Interpretability becomes relevant in the automated translation of these output values into natural language couched in terms of legal review. This would then allow the establishment of the real-life relevance of various factors. It does, however, not completely solve the problem of understanding which information was taken into account in the first place and the issue of transparency. It then links transparency to the notion of tagging data points entering into the system so that their effects can be measured. The chapter concludes that in terms of reasoning obligations, concepts of explainability of ADM systems will require 'employing different XAI (explainable AI) methods in order to tackle different explanatory angles, given that there is no perfect-for-any-scenario approach'.[2]

Chapter 10 then critically discusses the evolution of the European Interoperability Policy into a comprehensive framework for integration in the EU. It highlights programmes like the Interchange of Data between Administrations (IDA), the Interoperable Delivery of European eGovernment Services to Public

[2] Chapter 9 of the present book.

Administrations, Business and Citizens (IDABC), interoperability solutions for European public administrations (ISA) and ISA[2] that improved interoperability over the last decades. The Tallinn Declaration in 2017 introduced the principle of 'interoperability by default', outlining national and EU actions. Member States committed to improving solution reuse, open standards adoption, and public sector ICT accessibility. EU institutions committed to implementing the EIF and integrating digital considerations into policy. The chapter notes that the policy marked the shift from a national initiative to a top EU priority, aiming to achieve seamless interoperability across borders and all sectors. The Interoperable Europe Act Regulation Proposal further advanced interoperability to meet 2030 Digital Targets and reduce time and costs for citizens and businesses. It outlines legal foundations, evaluations, and measures for interoperability, promoting cross-border collaboration. The Proposal and the comprehensive framework are crucial for efficient EU interoperability, fostering collaboration and effective public service delivery across borders. The critical role of interoperability in AI-based data collections becomes clear from this approach but leaves open questions as to the possibility of ensuring data quality as a critical element of good decision-making.

C. Towards a concept of governing of automated decision-making in EU public law

The impact of ADM, often with the help of AI empowered technology, on EU public law is a topic which is relatively new in terms of real-life impact. Therefore, at this relatively early stage of technology adoption, it is all the more important to formulate EU public law's requirements on the use of automation technology and the effects on governance structures and regulatory regimes in EU law and policy. For GDPR purposes, the definition of fully automated decision-making has been clarified by the CJEU in *Schufa*,[3] where it was held that automated establishment of information (such as a probability value of individual credit worthiness) on which a third party such as a bank 'strongly' relies in its final decision-making is to be qualified as an automated decision. Therefore, a fully automated individual decision can contain a human component, if there is either little likelihood or little probability that the human, who is confronted with such an automated decision, will follow the proposal.[4] The regulatory approaches necessary for ADM systems, the digitalized governance of the single market, and the influence of targeted political advertising on democratic processes are each examples of such considerations

[3] Case C-634/21 *Schufa* ECLI:EU:C:2023:957, para 50.

[4] See for further discussion Diana-Urania Galetta and Herwig CH Hofmann, 'Evolving AI-based Automation—Continuing Relevance of Good Administration' (2023) 48 European Law Review 617–35.

relevant for the questions of ensuring legality and legitimacy of public powers in a digitalizing world. The use cases examined in the various chapters of this book further showed the great potential that AI can have for improving certain administrative functions, increasing their quality and effectiveness and not just reducing their cost. For some tasks it is already unimaginable *not* to use AI. This is the case for machine translation of texts, in which the Commission is investing large amounts of resources, as confirmed by several interviewees in the establishment of the case studies. Other examples showed how AI makes it possible to strengthen the control of agricultural subsidies and EU borders significantly as well as to speed up the food risk assessment process and to facilitate the consistency of decisions on the registration of trademarks.

Looking for an overarching framework, it appears that basic concepts of public law allow for many answers to the evolving challenges from new technologies. Many concepts of good administration of how to address situations with a fundamental right impact as well as those concerning access and transparency have been historically addressed in public law. It is important to revisit concepts of accountability by strengthening transparency, of reason-giving obligations, of clarity about the source of information, its treatment, and its impact on the final decision-making. It is important also to address matters of transparency and participation in rule-making. Many of these concepts are prime candidates for ensuring legality and quality of decision-making and it appears that alongside future principles concerning delegation of powers, they can be applied equally to human-only decision-making, to mixed human and automated decision-making, and to purely automated procedures with human judicial review that may occur in the future. This finding, visible throughout the chapters of this book, is a stark reminder of the necessity to review the wave of new EU legislative acts in the field of data and information, enacted following the European Strategy for Data of February 2020,[5] as to their applicability to public law and the interaction of their concepts with principles of public law. These EU regulations address the use of data and information by public administrations—a prime example of which is Regulation 1725/2018 on the protection of personal data by EU institutions, agencies, bodies, and offices—and also many of the matters relating to data availability for data-driven public administration. The European Commission's draft Interoperable Europe Act of November 2022 is a regulation which seeks to link data sources across Europe for use in public decision-making but is, at the same time, remarkably silent in discussing means to ensure data quality in such exchanges.[6] Other examples include

[5] There the European Commission introduced a concept for numerous data-related draft regulations to regulate the use of data and data services but also to foster data sharing across economic, government, cultural, and scientific sectors in areas such as health, mobility, and agriculture to create various European data spaces.

[6] See eg European Commission Proposal for a Regulation of the EP and the Council laying down measures for a high level of public sector interoperability across the Union (Interoperable Europe Act) of 18 November 2022, COM (2022) 720 final 2022/0379 (COD).

the Data Act and the Data Governance Act which come against the backdrop of the growing use of AI tools by the EU Administration itself as well as by Member States in implementing EU policies.[7]

I. Legality and legal basis

Regulatory limitations of individual freedoms are recognized in EU law as being protected in the context of the right to an effective remedy (Article 47 CFR)[8] in terms of a 'protection against arbitrary or disproportionate intervention by public authorities in the sphere of the private activities of any natural or legal person'.[9] Limitations of such freedom can arise at all three elements of ADM systems—the data and information collections, the interface of transfer of data to an administration undertaking the regulatory action and the ADM system-based processing of information and taking decisions. Requirements for the legal basis for ADM are accordingly high, when ADM systems are used as elements of regulatory decision-making. Therefore under Article 52(1) CFR, a legal basis will be necessary for the deployment of procedures with an ADM component. That will have to ensure that the overall procedure, including the ADM system (including the human input into the decision-making procedure in various of its phases) complies with principles of good administration. These are protected as general principles of EU law, largely in terms of defence rights, but are also more generally enumerated in Article 41 of the CFR including the right to fair and impartial decision-making, compliance with the duty of care (full and impartial assessment of all relevant facts), and encompassing the right to a hearing, access to one's file, and a reasoned decision. This package makes for a comprehensive set of criteria for the legality of ADM systems. Generally, they are essential procedural requirements, violations of which may lead to the annulment of acts. Of the essence for the rule of law is further the possibility of submitting public acts to an effective judicial review.[10]

Another aspect is that the value of General Principles of EU law and, more specifically, the value of principles of good administration lies in bridging the potential disconnect between ADM and the EU's public law legal framework arises from

[7] AI-supported automated decision-making systems, the analysis in this book showed, is used both by the authorities that have their own decision-making powers (such as eg EUIPO, EFSA—as regards the issuing of scientific opinions) and those that provide information systems to the Member States for the corresponding decisions to be taken (DG-Agri/ESA, eu-LISA).

[8] Case C-682/15 *Berlioz Investment Fund SA* ECLI:EU:C:2017:373, para 51; Case C-121/04 P *Minoan Lines v Commission* EU:C:2005:695, para 30; Case C-94/00, *Roquette Frères* ECLI:EU:C:2002:603, para 27; Joined Cases 46/87 and 227/88 *Hoechst v Commission* ECLI:U:C:1989:337, para 19.

[9] Case C-682/15 *Berlioz Investment Fund SA* ECLI:EU:C:2017:373, para 51.

[10] Amongst many see Case C-64/16 *Associação Sindical dos Juízes Portugueses* ECLI:EU:C:2018:117, paras 31, 40, and 41; Case C-216/18 *PPU Minister for Justice and Equality* (Deficiencies in the system of justice) ECLI:EU:C:2018:586, paras 63–67.

the fact that computer software is not a 'legal act' and thus not 'law' in the sense of Article 52(1) of the CFR. Hence, the question whether software governs reality or whether legal systems can impose their value choices over the technical realities. For this, it must be clear what the standards are to which ADM systems must comply. In terms of upholding the rule of law, next to notions of legality the procedural principles of good administration and rights to an effective and independent judicial remedy are relevant. The inclusion of decision-making with the help of ADM technology raises the level of complexities to be addressed in administrative law: the features of human–machine interfaces, access to and processing of data from multi-level data bases, integration of ADM into composite procedures, and the underlying complexities of AI programming undertaking this level of digitalization of decision-making all contribute to growing complexity. Design choices in law and technology need to be made to ensure that there is no disconnect between, on one hand, legal principles designed to ensure accountability and, on the other, the possibilities and restrictions of ADM technology and the real-life design of the procedures employed in the digitalization of government functions in the EU. Normative steering must be possible and as such is a requirement of the principles of democratic steering in a system under the rule of law. If this is the case, the use of ADM can make use of the increase in the decision-making speed and quality of data analysis made possible by technological advances. But technical approaches must be designed in a way to allow for accountability whilst the promises of using automation in decision-making can be enjoyed in the public sphere. Normative steering is a necessity to ensure accountability of ADM used in public policies.

Review then also requires distinguishing between, on the one hand, the generally applicable software—the quasi-normative element of decision-making—and, on the other hand, that a human reviewer has some form of profound conceptual understanding of the ADM system's individual decision concerning the concrete circumstances of a specific factual situation to independently of the ADM system. Therefore, distinguishing between conditions governing, on the one hand, the quasi rule-making character of ADM systems from, on the other, individual decisions made with the help of ADM technology is central to understanding reviewability. The first, the systemic element, requires considerations akin to those applied to administrative rule-making, whereas the application of ADM technology in individual procedures requires analysis from the consideration of legality of individual acts. The latter are generally 'quasi- or semi-automated decision-making'.[11]

[11] Council of Europe, 'Algorithms and Human Rights: Study on the Human Rights Dimensions of Automated Data Processing Techniques and Possible Regulatory Implications' (The Committee of Experts on Internet Intermediaries (MSI-NET) 2018) 7. Simona Demková, 'The Decisional Value of Information in European Semi-Automated Decision Making' (2021) Review of European Administrative Law 9.

II. Information, data, and training data

A regulatory framework which is clear and concise is all the more relevant since, as Chapter 3 showed, EU Administration has only very limited capacity to develop its own AI systems. As was outlined there, authorities generally rely on public procurement and non-commercial external partners to develop the necessary software. Whether access to training data of AI-based systems will be sufficiently relevant for assessing the quality of ADM-based procedures might become less relevant in a future of support of public activities using generative AI models based on large language models than it was previously with more purpose-specific programming. Access rights for public supervisory authorities to training data of very large online platforms or search engines (Article 31, 57 DSA)[12] indicate that the legislator would be able to develop an access and accountability framework also concerning training data for AI tools used for administrative decision-making. But in the case of large language models the training data is so vast and covers entire parts of data available on the Interne, that knowledge of the training data itself will not be sufficient as a control mechanism. By contrast, this book has shown that it will be vital to ensure that transparency about specific information is taken into account in an individual decision-making process: this transparency is crucial both for administrative forms of control and supervision as well as for the individuals who are affected by the decision. Ensuring such transparency however has important effects on the programming of ADM software and thus must be formulated as a normative requirement.

The EU-specific composite approach to data collections and the interoperability paradigm however also raise challenges concerning the quality and accuracy of data input into decision-making, which has, in turn, effects on accountability in ADM procedures based on such data.[13] This aspect is unfortunately not sufficiently considered in the literature and the discussion on ADM in (EU) public law. In view of this being possibly one of the most crucial aspects of the successful use of ADM and, at the same time, a topic of high concern for the exercise of individual rights, the use of ADM arguably requires supervision of the quality of data input.[14]

[12] Regulation (EU) 2022/2065 on a Single Market For Digital Services (Digital Services Act), OJ 2022 L 277/1, see especially recital 64.

[13] For example arts 17, 18 European Data Protection Regulation (EDPR) requires that data must be correct and up to date. This requires access to data, and its possible rectification are key in this context.

[14] See eg European Agency for the Operational Management of Large Scale IT Systems in the Area of Freedom, Security and Justice, *Data Quality and Interoperability: Addressing the Capability Gaps through Standardisation: Eu-LISA 12th Industry Roundtable, 3–5 November 2020, Tallinn (Online Event)* (Publications Office of the EU 2020) <https://data.europa.eu/doi/10.2857/497949> accessed 29 March 2023; European Union Agency for Fundamental Rights, *Data Quality and Artificial Intelligence—Mitigating Bias and Error to Protect Fundamental Rights* (Publications Office of the EU 2019) <https://fra.europa.eu/en/publication/2019/data-quality-and-artificial-intelligence-mitigating-bias-and-error-protect> accessed 29 March 2023. See also the EU efforts in standardizing the data quality requirements, for instance, in the context of biometric data collection and storing in EU area of freedom, security and

The latter concern regarding quality control is also of particular relevance due to the links between public and private data collections used as the basis for ADM in some policy areas.

III. The duty of care, good administration, and defence rights

Requirements for ADM procedures arise from the EU's specific notions of the duty of care, generally understood to be a component of good administration. Thereunder the reasoning of a measure[15] must provide for information about compliance with the elements summarized under the 'duty of care'. Any rationale for an act must demonstrate that the decision was taken on the basis of 'the most complete "factually accurate, reliable and consistent" information possible'.[16] The duty to reason requires documentation of a decision-maker to have reflected on all matters which may be subject to later judicial review.[17] Linked with the concept of the duty of care, proper reasoning will require documentation and reporting of the information-sourcing and information-processing activities.[18] Compliance with the duty of care is thus information-related in that a decision-maker must show how a specific decision was made and with which information, in terms of ADM systems requiring the traceability of information involved in the reasoning.

justice (AFSJ) systems. Commission Implementing Decision (EU) 2020/2165 of 9 December 2020 on laying down rules for the application of Regulation (EU) 2018/1861 of the European Parliament and of the Council as regards the minimum data quality standards and technical specifications for entering photographs and dactyloscopic data in the Schengen Information System (SIS) in the field of border checks and return, OJ L431/61, Brussels, 21.12.2020 and Commission Implementing Decision (EU) 2021/31 of 13 January 2021 on laying down rules for the application of Regulation (EU) 2018/1862 as regards the minimum data quality standards and technical specifications for entering photographs and dactyloscopic data in the [SIS] in the field of police cooperation and judicial cooperation in criminal matters, OJ L15/1, Brussels, 18.1.2021.

[15] See eg judgment of 5 November 2014, Case C-166/13 *Mukarubega v Seine-Saint-Denis* ECLI:EU:C:2014:2336 paras 43–49; of 8 May 2014 Case C-604/12 *H. N.* ECLI:EU:C:2014:302, para 49; and of 20 December 2017, Case C-521/15 *Spain v Council* ECLI:EU:C:2017:982, para 89.

[16] Herwig CH Hofmann, 'The Duty of Care in EU Public Law—A Principle Between Discretion and Proportionality' (2020) 13 Review of European Administrative Law 87, 100. Citing the judgment of 22 November 2007, Case C-525/04 *P Spain v Lenzing* ECLI:EU:C:2007:698, para 57. In this judgment, the Court reiterated that 'not only must the Community judicature establish whether the evidence relied on is factually accurate, reliable and consistent but also whether that evidence contains all the information which must be taken into account in order to assess a complex situation and whether it is capable of substantiating the conclusions drawn from it'. With further references to the relevant case law. See section D.I of this chapter for the conceptualization of the reasoning requirements arising from the principle of duty of care.

[17] The right to a reasoned decision is a right guaranteed under the right to good administration, also explicitly recognized in art 41(1)b) CFR, as well as under the right to an effective judicial remedy, as also recognized in art 47(1) CFR.

[18] European Union Agency for Fundamental Rights and Council of Europe, *Handbook on European Data Protection Law* (Publications Office of the European Union 2018) <http://fra.europa.eu/en/publication/2016/handbook-european-law-relating-access-justice> accessed 29 March 2023.

Such compliance is a particular mode of the requirement of transparency through reason-giving in public decision-making.[19] The recording of operations within a system and the source and the type of data used to general informational input into decision-making are factors contributing to the possibility of enabling reasoning and transparency. Information technology developments for securing information in the form of 'tamper-evident record that provides non-repudiable [sic] evidence of all nodes' action'[20] are becoming increasingly relevant to enhance the traceability of data across its sources. In fact, in the case of ADM, the reasoning must arguably be more complete as to the information taken into account and processed, as well as how the information has influenced the outcome of a decision than in a 'traditional' decision-making process since probability used by AI systems is not the same type of reasoning as a human causality-driven approach would entail.

This does not exclude that in individual cases reason-giving might also require explanations concerning the system-level functioning and logic of programs used in ADM.[21] But, importantly, it does not require these kinds of explanations since the system level might only indicate the outcome in programming, which is purpose-built and to a certain degree static with respect to the outcome, but with more advanced systems, including generative AI models, understanding systems logic will not reveal any valuable indicators as to how a specific proposal for a decision was developed. Therefore increasingly, in our view, to 'enable third parties to probe and review the behaviour of the algorithm' should be on the basis of explanatory models, as explained in Chapter 10 of this book. The fact that ADM systems, according to our suggestions, should be subject to *ex-ante* impact assessments and *ex-post* regular evaluation to their functioning sets the framework as to when and how they should be accompanied by a 'datasheet' that records the choices and manipulations of training data, where relevant to the system, and the 'composition, collection process, recommended uses'.[22]

Where an AI system relies on specific databases using personal data, one instance of anticipatory control is the requirement of conducting a Data Protection Impact Assessment (DPIA) under the GDPR.[23] Such an impact assessment will

[19] Ida Koivisto, *The Anatomy of Transparency: The Concept and its Multifarious Implications*, EUI MWP Working Papers 2016/09.

[20] Aziz Z Huq, 'Constitutional Rights in the Machine Learning State' (2020) SSRN.Com/abstract=3613282, 49; Deven R Desai and Joshua A Kroll, 'Trust but Verify: A Guide to Algorithms and the Law' (2017) 31 Harvard Journal of Law and Technology 1, 10–11. One currently increasingly widespread approach is based on distributed ledger technology, often known as 'blockchain'.

[21] Garry Coglianese and David Lehr, 'Regulating by Robot: Administrative Decision Making in the Machine-Learning Era' (2017) 105 The Georgetown Law Journal 1147–223, 1207, state that reason giving will require to also 'disclose algorithmic specifications, including the objective function being optimised, the method used for that optimisation and the algorithm's input variables'.

[22] Huq (n 20) 48.

[23] Additionally, this is necessary for systems under art 27 of Directive (EU) 2016/680 on the prevention, investigation, detection or prosecution of criminal offences, (2016) OJ L119/89. Under both arts

include questions of the definition of the human–machine interface in semi-automated decision-making and will be necessary in the context of all ADM systems which have a potential impact on decision-making.

The social impacts of the development of ADM technology are potentially considerable and thus merit an approach that makes AI impact assessments much broader than those required for data protection purposes only. Accordingly, the idea of the 'algorithmic IAs' as something different to DPIAs only, for instance, including human rights assessment in general or assessment of wider procedural issues, is highly relevant.[24]

The AI Act is less demanding concerning transparency requirements.[25] Only Article 11(1) of the Commission's draft AI Act foresees an obligation for high-risk AI systems to maintain technical documentation 'in such a way to demonstrate that the high-risk AI system complies with the requirements of the law and to allow supervisory authorities to verify such compliance'. Some demands of traceability of data movements and data processing by ADM, which had been made in legal literature,[26] have found their way into Article 12 of the Commission's draft AI Act, albeit only for high-risk AI systems requiring record-keeping facilities, to log and track operations sufficient to 'ensure a level of traceability of the AI system's functioning throughout its lifecycle'—allowing for regular reviews.[27]

IV. Oversight and effective remedies

Often in mixed semi-automated decision-making systems, as is the vast majority of current ADM systems, the automated element of decision-making serves as

35(7)a) GDPR and 39(7)a) EDPR, a 'systematic description of the envisaged processing operations and the purposes of the processing' is necessary.

[24] See, especially, the Model Rules on Impact Assessment of Algorithmic Decision-Making Systems Used by Public Administration, *Report of the European Law Institute* (European Law Institute, 2022) <https://www.europeanlawinstitute.eu/projects-publications/completed-projects-old/ai-and-public-administration/> accessed 1 July 2023; see especially art 6.

[25] Art 52 of the European Commission, Proposal for a Regulation of the EP and the Council laying down harmonised rules on Artificial Intelligence (Artificial Intelligence Act) of 21 April 2021, COM(2021) 206 final, 2021/0106 (COD) requires no specific type of transparency for AI systems that are not deemed to be high risk other than notifications to natural persons that they are interacting with an AI system, unless such is obvious (art 52(1)), and that they might be exposed to their data 'being processed by an emotion recognition system' (art 52(2)) or that their images have been artificially recreated or manipulated (art 52(3)) unless this is done for public security or other prevailing public interests. ibid.

[26] See eg Herwig CH Hofmann and Morgane Tidghi, 'Rights and Remedies in Implementation of EU Policies by Multi-Jurisdictional Networks' (2014) 20(1) European Public Law 147–64, discussing notions of tagging of information.

[27] Art 12(2) and the logging capabilities must provide at least 'recording of the period of each use of the system ... the reference database against which input data has been checked by the system; the input data for which the search has led to a match' as well as 'the identification of the natural persons involved in the verification of the results'.

input into a composite human–machine procedure. Review of the ADM element in decision-making thus requires a working interface between ADM systems and human review based on transparent information about the automated element of a final decision. In this sense, the EU's AI Act also foresees that 'high-risk' AI systems must provide appropriate 'human–machine interface tools' so they can be subject to human oversight by natural persons ensured through appropriate technical installations.[28] The individuals to whom human oversight is assigned must be enabled to 'fully understand the capacities and limitations of the high-risk AI system and be able to duly monitor its operation so that signs of anomalies, dysfunctions and unexpected performance can be detected as soon as possible'.[29] Next to the right to oppose ADM in matters concerning the processing of personal data, there is also a more general discussion about a right to human review. Given that the analysis of complex data collections by computer systems necessarily involves 'some margin of error',[30] any positive result obtained following the automated processing of information must be subject to the possibility of an individual re-examination by non-automated means 'before an individual measure adversely affecting the persons concerned' may be adopted.[31] This is not just a question of ensuring judicial review; it is also a question of the more general requirement to be able to re-construct the decision-making provisions and possible errors arising in the conduct of ADM.

The reflections made above emphasize the continued relevance of public law in the face of technological advances. The call to avoid black-box software and enhance visibility in decision-making processes underscores the intersection between law and technology. The envisioned solutions involve a comprehensive rethink of information management, emphasizing transparency, citizen orientation, and the rule of law. The trends in EU law towards integration through databases and shared administration with ADM highlight the evolving landscape that necessitates ongoing control and clarity in data and information management. Overall, the multifaceted challenges of introducing ADM into public procedures in the scope of EU law underscore the necessity for a comprehensive legal framework. However, this does not need to be invented entirely from scratch. Well-established principles of EU public law, if correctly applied to the challenges to the quantitative and qualitative effects that automation of information management entails, can serve to enhance accountability of semi-automated decision-making as well as fully automated decisions. As in all EU composite procedures—whether these

[28] Art 14(1) of the Proposal for a Regulation of the EP and the Council laying down harmonised rules on Artificial Intelligence (Artificial Intelligence Act) (n 25).

[29] ibid. They must also be trained to resist possible 'automation bias' whatever that may consist of, see art 14(4)(b) ibid.

[30] Case C-511-520/18 *La Quadrature du Net* ECLI:EU:C:2020:791, para 182 referring specifically to the analysis of traffic and location data.

[31] ibid.

integrate various actors from different levels or whether they integrate human and automated elements of decision-making—there is however the need for an organizational structure clearly identifying functional and procedural responsibilities. This is not only necessary in order to facilitate relevant factors such as for example inter-administrative data sharing through digital information systems but also in order to ensure procedural responsibilities such as conducting hearings, collecting other relevant information and taking finally binding decisions. Aspects which need further clarification and for which current EU public law principles offer no or only insufficient answers include considerations on ensuring data quality safeguards, data transparency, and adherence to interoperability standards. These aspects underscore the significance of adapting existing legal principles to the challenges of ADM. Safeguards for human intervention in flawed decision-making and the inclusion of procedural rights in composite procedures emerge as essential elements in the pursuit of accountability.

Index

For the benefit of digital users, indexed terms that span two pages (e.g., 52–53) may, on occasion, appear on only one of those pages.

Tables and figures are indicated by an italic *t and f* following the page number.